POLITICOTAINMENT

Toby Miller
General Editor

Vol. 13

PETER LANG
New York • Washington, D.C./Baltimore • Bern
Frankfurt am Main • Berlin • Brussels • Vienna • Oxford

POLITICOTAINMENT

Television's Take on the Real

Edited by Kristina Riegert

PETER LANG
New York • Washington, D.C./Baltimore • Bern
Frankfurt am Main • Berlin • Brussels • Vienna • Oxford

Library of Congress Cataloging-in-Publication Data

Politicotainment: television's take on the real / edited by Kristina Riegert.
p. cm. — (Popular culture and everyday life; vol. 13)
Includes bibliographical references.
1. Television and politics—United States.
2. Realism on television. I. Riegert, Kristina.
PN1992.6.P63   791.45'6580973—dc22   2006022467
ISBN 978-0-8204-8114-2
ISSN 1529-2428

Bibliographic information published by **Die Deutsche Bibliothek**.
Die Deutsche Bibliothek lists this publication in the "Deutsche
Nationalbibliografie"; detailed bibliographic data is available
on the Internet at http://dnb.ddb.de/.

Cover image supplied by WENN. Printed by permission.

The paper in this book meets the guidelines for permanence and durability
of the Committee on Production Guidelines for Book Longevity
of the Council of Library Resources.

© 2007 Peter Lang Publishing, Inc., New York
29 Broadway, 18th floor, New York, NY 10006
www.peterlang.com

Printed in the United States of America

Table of Contents

Acknowledgments

This book came into being thanks to the tireless encouragement and enthusiasm of Professor Toby Miller and his wonderful gift for bringing people together. Each author has written extensively on related subjects but it was thanks to Toby's ability to keep up on developments in media and popular culture that we could bring these people together in this book. Christoffer Bäckström and Stig Arne Nohrstedt of the Swedish National Defence College have been enthusiastic supporters of a research concept which was not immediately relevant to them. Damon Zucca has also been a source of encouragement and understanding, always prepared to give his time and advice. I am also grateful to the authors for their interest and enthusiasm for this project as a whole—the investigation of the political in entertainment programming. Last, but not least, we acknowledge and thank the Södertörn Publication Committee for its generous contribution.

Stockholm

September 2006

CHAPTER ONE

Introduction

KRISTINA RIEGERT

I n the summer of 2005, Steven Bochco's thirteen-part series *Over There* was announced. This new drama series about the current Iraq War marks the first time television drama has grappled with an American war in real time—that is, while that war is still being fought. *New York Times* critic Alessandra Stanley (2005) wrote that it is a "very violent distillation of the latest news reports and old war movies and television shows." By this she meant that fiction "has a way of showing time and putting a frame on a shifting, fragmented reality," whereas the suffering and slaughter of real war often goes unnoticed: a victim of constant repetition and the thirty-second sound bites of television news. Not unexpectedly, many found the program "a show business atrocity" despite the message of "hate the war, love the troops," which was easily overshadowed by the artistic representation and the technological finesse of the battle scenes. While some may be surprised at the timing of this program and the comparison with real-life politics, we are not.

The term "politicotainment" denotes the ways in which politics and political life are interpreted, negotiated, and represented by the entertainment industry, in particular by drama series and reality-based television programming. Politicotainment should not be confused with infotainment, defined by Brian McNair as "journalism in which entertainment values take precedence over information content, presented at an intellectual level low enough to appeal to the mass audiences which comprise the major media markets" (McNair 2000, 4). Infotainment evokes familiar complaints about political journalism's increasing preoccupation with sexual, moral, or financial deviance; about the abundance of pundits and their commentary; or about "the substance of political debate gradually being replaced by the superficial, entertainment-led spectacle of adversarial game-playing" (6).

Political communication scholars have long complained about the way the news media dramatizes, simplifies, and personalizes the political. That lament has become more high pitched in the 1990s with the proliferation of talk shows and "soft news" magazine programs touting human-interest stories, crime, scandal, and celebrities. However, we should not content ourselves with statements about the negative effects of infotainment, or the derisive effects of popular culture on political issues and television's blending of fact and fiction. If we have evidence that citizens make few distinctions between fictional and non-fictional television when processing information and formulating opinions, and that they reference a great variety of television-related personalities rather than politicians when discussing political issues (Jones 2005; Delli Carpini and Williams 1996), then we need to start thinking about these issues in different ways. Corner and Pels (2003) take useful steps in this direction by dealing with the changes in the political process that benefit lifestyle or consumer politics (and vice versa), the factors contributing to the rise of celebrity politicians and public relations, and the underlying structural causes of these shifts in media-political relations.

For their part, feminist, media, and cultural studies scholars have long concerned themselves with power and ideology in mediated cultural products. For them, popular culture, the private sphere, and the everyday have long been political—and those who insist on defining the political according to television's own division into factual and entertainment media are misguided (Hartley 1996; Miller, in press; Street 2001; Delli Carpini and Williams 1996). However, even this division is fast disappearing in today's television landscape, where the current trend is to use institutional branches of government as the settings for drama series (*JAG*, *24*, *Commander in Chief*, *The Agency*, or *D.H.S.–the Series*[1]). These provide "unprecedented" opportunities for interaction between government agencies and entertainment television as the former aids the latter in their attempts at "realism," but they should also force us to re-examine our assumptions about the boundaries of the political in the media (Jones 2005, 7).

Our approach is in line with this in that it explicitly addresses political subject matter in both old and new genres of television entertainment: in reality television, late-night comedy talk shows, in Brazilian *telenovelas*, and in political and historical drama series. As many would be quick to point out, politicotainment, or the political as subject matter in the service of entertainment, is nothing new. From Aeschylus's *Agamemnon* to William Shakespeare's *Richard III* to August Strindberg's *Erik XIV*, politics is and always has been the stuff of drama. However, we live in mediated societies where the very nature of "publicness" and of social interaction differs from that of previous epochs. As John B. Thompson (1995; 2000) has pointed out, since politics now takes place largely in and through the media space, communication is no longer necessarily anchored in a shared place and time. In the extended time/space of the mediated public sphere, to be visible is to exist, and at an ever-increasing pace. Indeed, it is this heightened visibility that political actors attempt to manage and control. Second, since much of our experience of "publicness" is no longer linked to face-to-face encounters, a new kind of intimacy is fueled through the media, blurring the boundaries between public and private life.

We do not intend to recount the scholarly and popular debates on the implications of the blurring of the boundaries between the public and private sphere or the effects of media commercialization on the public sphere. Suffice it to point out that despite the deep-seated anxieties about politics as spectacle and about the ways the media stereotypes, simplifies, and dramatizes political life, our starting point is that popular culture can be a forum for political activity, just as politics often borrows the language and formats of popular culture (Street 1997; 2001). This is because the latter, and in this case specifically entertainment television, articulates and directs emotions. Its use of images and symbols focuses experience and expresses ideas, and in this way, entertainment television can become a source of political thought and action (van Zoonen 2005).

Politicotainment:
Why Here, Why Now?

The chapters that follow deal with the ways in which the political is represented or negotiated by entertainment formats in what John Corner once called television's "greatly expanded popular images of the real." They should be read within the context of the structural changes taking place within three interrelated areas: (1) the political economy of television, which privileges cheap, non-scripted reality and live production; (2) the promotional machinery that markets various types of consumption, personalities, or political policies, whether these be celebrities or politicians; (3) the changes taking place within traditional news journalism, the decline in audiences for mainstream news, and the ascent of "multi-media jobs" and consultancy in related fields. While these structural changes cannot be treated in detail here, a brief comment on each will serve as a background to the chapters that follow.

Few will have missed the noticeable shift in prime-time television in many Western countries in the late 1990s from situation comedy, drama series, and current affairs programs to reality-based, light-entertainment programming.

The trend toward the ever-expanding "authentic moment" and the "entertaining real" has generated much attention in the popular and academic press. The roots of reality television can be found in the changing political economy of television, springing from union problems, financial downsizing, and government deregulation. These changes have prompted television's search for

> the possibility of new production and financing models, including the purchasing and selling of formats rather than completed programs, the expansion of merchandising techniques, an increased emphasis on audience interactivity, and the insertion of commercial messages within programs. (Murray and Ouellette 2004, 7)

While reality television may be denigrated as "cheap" or "trash" television, its ability to engage viewers to test their notions of what is authentic, what is ordinary, what is public and private, what constitutes participation and citizenship, are worth investigating further. Reality television distinguishes itself from fictional television by its claim to authenticity (real people, not actors) and in the unscripted format, which produces a sense that "anything" can happen. According to John Corner (2002), reality television is related to the observational documentary through the "handheld camera" and lack of narration, which imply "direct access to the experience of the observed subject." However, it differs significantly in that it establishes a playful reflexivity, an awareness of its own constructedness, of how people perform in a naturalistic setting, which appeals to savvy audiences less interested in "truth" than in truth's constructedness. The question is not only how our conceptions of what is "entertainment" change when the "real" becomes entertaining, but—even more pressing—how our notions of what is "real" change when the "real" must also be entertaining.

As political culture continually adapts to media logic (a logic that itself is shifting), we need to analyze those television programs that tap into people's motivations for political engagement, and their emotional needs and fantasies (Corner and Pels 2003). As Ian Scott (2001, 65) notes, to a population cultivated by the entertainment industry's images, iconography, rhetoric, and symbols of politics, the boundary between political life and fictionalized portrayal of politics is blurred. Films of the later 1990s, such as *Primary Colors* and *Bulworth*, are more like "the simulacra of real campaigns, an extension of reality fictionalised for an alternative form of presentation" than the realism in fiction. The packaging of policy, of image, of trustworthiness, of character, are common to both worlds, so it is not surprising that speechwriters and political consultants double as screenwriters for films about politics and vice versa.

In *Entertaining the Citizen*, Liesbet van Zoonen argues, "As stories, therefore, politics, political journalism, and political fiction are hard to distinguish since they are intertextually connected through the same basic frames" (2005,

109). She calls these narrative frames the quest, bureaucracy, conspiracy, and soap, although most stories are mixtures of the different frames. While each of these frames invites different audience understandings of politics, van Zoonen concludes they were signs that watching popular films and television series stimulated people to describe, reflect, and fantasize about politics—thereby providing tools, if not the motivation, for citizenship.

Mediatized Politics: The Cult of Personality

Nowhere is the intertwining of the political and entertainment worlds more clearly articulated than in the increasing presence of politicians in entertainment programming, on the one hand, and in the utilization of celebrity for political purposes, on the other. While the most choice examples of the latter can be found in the United States (Ronald Reagan, Jesse Ventura, Arnold Schwarzenegger, Sonny Bono), examples can be drawn from India,[2] the Philippines (where former President Joseph Estrada was a famous film actor), or the United Kingdom (just think of best-selling author Lord Jeffrey Archer). Even in less commercialized television landscapes like that of Sweden, where party politics plays a greater role than individual politicians, we see an increase in political involvement in live television events, on talk shows, morning television, and comedy shows. The phenomenon is clearly broader than that of the U.S. media and political system, although this should be established through more systematic cross-national comparisons looking at the conditions favoring different interactions between economic, political, and cultural spheres.

The mobility of celebrity illustrates not only the changing nature of democratic politics and its relationship to the media system but also articulates critical aspects of the media industry itself. The promise of instant celebrity that accompanies reality television formats plays on the wishes or desires of "ordinary people." This promise of authenticity is also mirrored in late-night comedy's use of celebrities (Politically Incorrect or The Daily Show) to talk about politics. According to Jones (2005, 172-175), fans enjoy seeing celebrities from other genres "playing themselves," as it were, comparing them to their performances in other venues. Above all, when celebrities give opinions about political issues, they are considered representative of the "average," nominally informed viewer. Jones invokes David Marshall's notion of the celebrity as a "public proxy" to the extent that as traditional party politics and institutions are seen to lose touch with what "real people" are talking about, celebrities fill this void, since they formulate their opinions from the same sources as audience members do, thereby making it easy for audiences to identify with the celebrity.

It should come as no surprise that the systems and techniques used to produce media celebrities differ little from those used to promote political personae (Turner 2004; Corner 2003; Street 2003). Indeed, the reality television programs discussed in the chapters to follow, *American Candidate* and *Vote for Me*, demonstrate that even the process of turning an "average Joe" into a politician—the image-making, the coaching, the control of appearances, the styling, and the staging of that person—are made into themes for public consumption. Whether the proliferation of spin doctors, public relations, and media management in Western democracies constitutes a threat to democracy, or is just a sign of the new "promotional culture," continues to be debated.

Graeme Turner is disturbed by the "celebrification" of politics (i.e., "the incorporation of the techniques of celebrity management into organized politics"), since the purpose of public relations is to control and manage the interests of the powerful in order to protect them rather than those of the public (2004, 135). This despite what he calls the "demotic turn," which describes the way the media (television, print, the Internet) represent, celebrate, and market a greater diversity of ordinary people and everyday life to an ever-increasing extent. This may be considered by some as the media opening up possibilities for minorities, for ordinary people, to see and be seen in greater numbers of media outlets than ever before. That there should be a shift in power from the producer to the consumer (as argued by John Hartley, in this volume) as new types of technologies spring up to service do-it-yourself consumer citizens, however, presupposes that the multiplication of outlets does not reproduce the concentration of ownership and symbolic power that presently exists in the media landscape. Finally, the very definition of celebrity remains a hierarchical category, Turner says, no matter how many new instant celebrities appear in reality television shows. He argues, therefore, that the promise of diversity and greater participation does not necessarily entail the fulfillment of the democratic potential of such a paradigm shift in television production.

Journalism in Transition

With regard to the changes within traditional journalism and the mainstream media's loss of readership/viewership, opinion polls have for the past decade documented a steady decline in public perception of journalistic credibility, at least in the United States and Northern Europe. Note that this credibility gap predates the attacks of September 11 and that they apply to other advanced capitalist countries as well.[3] Journalists are also aware of this; for example, a majority of U.S. journalists see lack of credibility as the most important issue facing the news media today.[4] They identify the blurring of the boundaries between commentary and news coverage, and between entertainment and information, as the root of the problem, with half saying that sloppy reporting, factual errors, and sensationalism contribute to this loss of trust. Television journalists, especially, say that the reasons for this are news executives' pressure to make a profit and other financial concerns.[5] The economic conditions for television journalism have led to constant cost-cutting and reduced staff in an age when the amount of time news organizations are expected to be on air has increased with the competition for news in "real time." The technologically driven demands of being on air all the time have increased the already prevalent tendency of television journalism to prioritize performance over analysis, and meticulousness about form over attention to content.

These changes are of course in large part the structural results of digital convergence and of deregulation, which has allowed for the increased concentration of media companies into the hands of a few multinational conglomerates that control large chunks of the new multichannel television environment. For national television, the increased competition from niche channels fragments the viewing audience, putting pressure on the traditional public-service channels, but not providing a greater diversity of content.

Göran Bolin (in this volume) provides an interesting twist on these structural changes. While accepting the increased commercialization of the media per se, an argument usually invoked to account for the decline in the quality of "objective" journalism, he says that the last few decades have witnessed the increased autonomy of journalism from the political sphere, as well as increasing its influence over other cultural forms in television production. In other words, the new light entertainment formats (talk shows, live television specials) are colonized by the techniques and aesthetics of journalism rather than the other way around. As television organizations diminish in size and prioritize financial constraints, a more flexible multi-tasking workforce is necessary, one in which the boundaries between previously separate divisions start to blur.

These structural changes to the media industry and television in particular leave traditional journalism with a diminished ability to penetrate and analyze special interests (see Jones, in this volume). This comes at a time when governments, business leaders, and special interests employ an unprecedented army of media consultants whose job is to break through the information "white noise" in order to promote the visibility of their clients. John Street (2001, 149) notes that as the news hole gets larger, more opportunities are opened up for public relations and media consultants to fill that hole with "their" news. Indeed, as job opportunities in traditional news diminish, journalists make the leap from journalism to public relations or become media consultants for political parties and governments where their knowledge and skills are greatly appreciated. This leap is also less of an occupational barrier when the boundaries between "hard" and "soft" news becomes blurred, and human-interest factors play a greater role in news programs. Another development with a bearing on the proliferation of entertainment venues for politics is the appearance of new information actors. The convergence of print and broadcasting with digital media, together with the availability of cheap digital technology, means that virtually anyone can document spectacular events as they happen and distribute them via the Internet. The blogosphere, new social movements, expert networks, even late-night comedy performers: these new information actors increase the media's scope and reach, but they also challenge traditional journalism's hegemony when it comes to covering and interpreting the news.

The Book

As discussed above, chapters 2 and 3 of this book delineate broader shifts in the production and formats of television, which account for the increase in political "reality" in entertainment television, and the concomitant emphasis on entertainment forms in factual television. In chapter 2, John Hartley suggests that we are witnessing a paradigm shift in modern societies from a political culture based on representation to one based on direct consumer participation. The media came to be an interlocutor between the governing and the governed, and a range of agents such as pollsters, media monitors, publicists, and marketing firms grew up to advise political and economic elites on how to maximize and manage audiences. Cultural content is sold based on ratings, but these are industry driven and reduce people to statistics, therefore missing much consumer activity and desire. New technologies allow for real numbers to be accessed and for consumers to produce their own content, so as we move into the era of digital interactive communication, the old ways of representing that audience will be replaced by direct "plebiscitary" industries. Hartley argues that production companies, agencies, and service providers that incorporate consumer practices in content production can be called plebiscitary industries, insofar as the act of voting or direct audience participation markets the product, provides much of the creative content, and, on a broader level, legitimizes the ideology of capitalism as the way to provide a range of consumer choices.

For Hartley, politics and entertainment have always been deeply intertwined, but this has been ignored since the modernist paradigm denigrated the easily manipulated (feminine) consumer from the politically active (masculine) citizen, rather than recognizing that the consumer and the citizen share the same body. Interactivity and audience participation are more than improvements in consumer sampling techniques; they constitute evidence that power has shifted from the producer to creative consumers who participate in the making of the product itself. It is among these survey, marketing, broadcasting, broadband, and telecommunications organizations that the new innovators develop the "new plebiscitary possibilities": "data-mining," electronic polling, multinational participant television, etc. Therefore, reality television shows from *Big Brother* to the runaway Chinese success, *The Mongolian Cow Sour Yoghurt Super Girl*, can be seen as experiences in choice and participation, i.e., in democracy, insofar as audiences are "doing something together" rather than being told what they have done. Technology now enables citizenship to merge with consumption, resulting in a new value web where producers and consumers become innovative "co-creators" in everything from user-led mobile applications to citizen journalism, says Hartley. We are moving from closed expert systems to open participation networks in which consumers will drive innovation and human connectedness, thereby transforming political culture.

As noted previously, Göran Bolin takes issue with the notion that quality journalism and serious current affairs programs have been marginalized by commercial entertainment and reality television. Rather, it may be more accurate to argue that it is the field of journalism that is colonizing live television entertainment, at least if we look at morning television, talk shows, game shows, or charity drives. Live television, whether for entertainment or factual purposes, shares a narrational and aesthetic structure derived from journalism in the sense that it claims to show "reality" as it happens.

Bolin goes on to apply Bourdieu's field theory to television production, saying that two shifts of power have occurred over the last decade in cultural production in Sweden and Europe generally. While it is true that the economic field has gained at the expense of the political field in relation to cultural production (of which journalism is one specific form), journalism, on the other hand, has become increasingly autonomous and has widened its influence in relation to both these fields of power. Often hosted by journalists, game shows and morning talk shows, as well as other light entertainment formats, are attractive to politicians, since they give them more exposure than sound-bite news, and because hard questions are seldom posed in these situations. However, this can also be interpreted as an enhancement of opportunities for journalists, who then have access to politicians in a variety of settings ranging from more formal interviews to more relaxed entertainment settings. In the case of election-night coverage and light factual programming, the production format of interviewing and stand-ups is a journalistic format where politicians must accommodate television's production values. The streamlining of television production and the textual sameness between factual and light entertainment and live television reflects journalism's increased power in the field of mass cultural production, which makes television production "obedient to the structure and demands of the journalistic field," writes Bolin.

Practicing Voting with Reality Television?

The shift in power from the producer to the consumer can be exemplified by the so-called reality television genres, where political life and democracy are enacted in participatory multimedia formats. Many are those who saw in the popularity of the reality television boom, with its interactivity, its use of "ordinary people," and its raw "authenticity," a parallel with democratization. Television producers in a number of Anglo-Saxon countries have attempted to utilize reality television formats and the attendant technologies (such as SMS messaging) as ways to get people—especially young people—interested in the political process. Chapters 4 and 5 consist of analyses of the U.S. experiment in reality television democracy and its British counterpart, *Vote for Me*. The chapters interrogate the promise of democracy implicit in these types of reality shows, assessing the motives, content, and the impact of these experiments on "real" politics. They investigate the claims of empowerment and access provided by interactivity and find that the format plays a decisive role in the outcome, and that the programs' emphasis on image-making, spin-doctoring, and politicking may serve to reinforce rather than alleviate the alienation of the viewer from the political system.

Mark Andrejevic investigates interactive entertainment as an example of "the relation between politics and entertainment in an era of digital de-differentiation—one in which interactivity promises (or threatens) to rearrange the boundaries between leisure and labor, advertising and content, as well as politics and consumption." The debate about *American Candidate* demonstrates both a "savvy skepticism" about the artifice of the political process and a "naïve belief in the virtues of behind-the-scenes access." Both of these traits have also contributed to the popularity of television drama series about politics, where behind-the-scenes access is linked to an emotional identification with the characters in the program (see Collins and Riegert, in this volume). Andrejevic describes how the interactive television program offloads labor onto the audiences, who produce not only part of the content of the show, but also help to market the show—to themselves. This labor is represented as educational, exciting, and desirable, and offers instant celebrity on a hitherto unattainable medium. However, *American Candidate* focused on media consultants or spin doctors teaching the candidates to market their images (clothes and hairstyle) and work the polls (hone their message to focus groups) rather than on working with the details of the policies they advocated. Andrejevic asks whether reality television's apparent access to endlessly deepening behind-the-scenes "realities" purporting to expose the artifice of politics really enhances the possibilities for democracy. Does this knowledge of fallible politicians, image-marketing, styling, focus-group manipulation, or secret deals really encourage people to participate in the real political system? If real politics is inauthentic and image-oriented, how will its reality television version revitalize civic engagement? In the "post-deferential age" we are offered a show that demonstrates the lack of authenticity in politics as the ultimate guarantee of authenticity. Andrejevic argues that we need to do more than point to the reality television format's potential for political participation. He is also critical of the notion that personal values, intuition, and judgments of character are viable alternatives to political deliberation. In an era of savvy skepticism—and here he cites Zizek—people may very well see through the rhetoric of "freedom and democracy," but they may not care what is done in their name so long as they "trust" their leaders.

Valentina Cardo and John Street describe a similar rationale in the British series *Vote for Me*. The show was marketed as a means of addressing democracy's crisis in Britain, that is, as a way to encourage real voter participation in a system that has alienated "the people." People have lost trust in politicians who are only out for themselves, the program intoned, but it promised to bring politics to "the people's level" by re-establishing a connection with what people "really" think about the issues. A panel of judges (former journalists and a television show presenter) whittled down the number to seven candidates, who got to demonstrate their "talent for politics" or get voted off by viewers. It was only after the audience had been shown the initial selection process and was introduced to the logic of the show that they were allowed to vote—and of this they were reminded an average of four times an hour.

The network's attachment to the program idea, the legal issues surrounding it, the frequency of episodes, and the "mandate" of the winning candidate differed from that of the *American Candidate*. Another key difference was the role played by the judges, who appeared to be independent commentators "helping" the audience decide from "left," "right," and "center" of the political spectrum. Like its U.S. counterpart, however, its message was that political success depended more on image and visibility (good relations with the media) than on substance. In both programs, the winner already had a following at the beginning of the program, but the authors argue that the format and the message of the program implicitly validated the winning candidate's views rather than interrogated them.

Late-Night Comedy, Telenovelas, and Celebrity

From reality television shows we move into the relatively new genre of late-night political comedy. Jeffrey P. Jones debunks the myth, which appears to be bordering on a moral panic in the United States, that a majority of young people are using late-night comedy as their main source of news. Jones asks what is it that people "learn" about political events from a "fake" news show, such as *The Daily Show with Jon Stewart*, compared to news items on the same subject on CNN. Is it possible that the sarcastic imitation of journalistic style, the parodying of politicians' speeches and campaign promises functioned better as a critical examination of the U.S. presidential campaign in 2004 than "objective" reporting did? *The Daily Show* consists of a news segment and a talk-show interview with a celebrity or a politician. In his close reading of a typical news report from CNN and a mock news report on the same event by *The Daily Show* late in the U.S. presidential campaign (October 2004), Jones attempts to find out just what kind of information audiences glean from these two sources.

News coverage rarely offers evidence of outright lies or contradictory statements but usually tries to find an expert or quote someone who will point this out. Comedy, in contrast, can do this without finding someone else. *The Daily Show*, like reality television, points out the artifice of political campaigning—the "man behind the curtain," as the famous phrase from *The Wizard of Oz* goes. It does so by keeping score of the events of the day: unfair or untrue attacks by political opponents or how repetition is invoked as propaganda. Jones points out that the news media tend to ignore politicians appearing on "soft" talk shows, because politicians are not asked questions about their stances on issues. However, *The Daily Show* highlights these appearances for what they say about these politicians' character and image management.

As previously pointed out, mainstream journalism in the United States has been experiencing fragmenting audiences due to the availability of alternative news sources on the Internet and to economic downsizing, not to mention various scandals involving journalistic ethics. As Andrejevic describes it, the public is aware of the mutually constituting institutions of the media and politics, that they are looking behind the façade to another façade which competes with a third, and whatever your stance, there is always someone around the corner ready to call it "an ideology." Maybe, Jones speculates, the media-savvy public realizes that CNN is no more "real" than *The Daily Show* is "fake." The post-deferential public, as Andrejevic calls it, may prefer to use political satire as a means of finding common-sense truths behind the artifice and spectacle of the powerful than continue to access existing journalistic forms.

A main feature of television's presentation of politics as entertainment is the cult of personality and celebrity. Whereas reality television cultivates instant celebrity, chapters 6 and 7 investigate the mobility and marketability of celebrities and other commodities from the entertainment world into the world of politics, and vice versa. Thaïs Machado-Borges analyzes one of Brazil's most popular television genres, the *novela*, popularly called the *telenovela*, which attracts daily audiences of over 40 million viewers. Akin to soap operas but with considerably more symbolic status, these programs often conform to real-life seasons and topics, raising controversial issues such as political and economic corruption, AIDS, same-sex marriage, child abuse as well as class and race issues. The telenovela actors are celebrities; they are used to promote certain politicians and social causes, as well as a range of urban lifestyle commodities through product placement (so-called merchandizing). Telenovelas are written very close to the time of broadcast, so upon negative audience feedback the writers, well-known *auteurs* in their own right, often adjust the plot or introduce new characters. This creates an intimate relationship between the telenovela in question and its audience.

Machado-Borges writes that fiction has been a shield for the writers of telenovelas to broach, comment, and critique politics in Brazil, a country with a tradition of oppressive political regimes. In contrast to the new wave of political drama series in the United States, telenovelas depict institutional politics as either corrupt or incompetent, and far from the everyday lives of people. Plots and characters are often lightly disguised versions of Brazilian political events and different settings form the backdrops for themes of social justice. The real political significance of the telenovela lies in its emphasis on traditionally feminine issues such as personal transformation, social mobility, and domestic violence, interwoven with class issues, sexual issues, race issues, or drug abuse. In order to market its social responsibility, the Globo network will often launch a campaign for social or health issues parallel to the plot developments of a given telenovela, even marketing itself as helping to "recover Brazilian citizenship." Does this "social merchandising treat its viewers as citizens in the same way that the product placement treats them as consumers?," asks Machado-Borges. The answer is dubious, for while the telenovelas reinforce a divide between institutional politics as a male-dominated, corrupt world, the social merchandising (the commodification of social engagement) is accomplished through the emotional engagement of strong female characters. One could see this as a focus on individual agency rather than collective action, defining these issues away from traditional politics. On the other hand, they could be seen as gradually redefining politics itself to include aspects of everyday life such as work, health, sexuality, and education through the configuration of the citizen-consumer.

Sue Collins asks how it is possible to combine celebrity, which sustains and is sustained by audiences within a hegemonic system for popular cultural production, and an activist agenda for radical issues without alienating the very audiences that support the celebrity-as-commodity. Commonly understood, celebrity is both the democratization and the commodification of fame, since its value is measured by the ability to gather audiences and circulate meaning. But celebrity meaning is fluid and can be diminished by scandal, overexposure, or by being associated with the "wrong" context—this is why agents and different promotional activities manage celebrity value. As John Street (2003) says, celebrities wanting to move into politics must take into account corporate sponsors, the conventions of the genre, and the constraints of the social movements they support, and they must create a political being that invokes credibility for their causes while not alienating those they seek to influence. For these reasons, the most common form of celebrity activism is what Collins calls "soft" activism, that is, calling attention to and raising money for social causes rather than challenging political issues, which could destabilize structures of power.

Celebrities who engage in counter-hegemonic activism that puts their careers at risk deal with this contradiction, in part, through generating meanings that are consonant in their on- and off-screen personas. Actor Martin Sheen is an example of a prominent antiwar activist (among other issues) who has managed to shield his star image from political attacks and thus create a new relationship with his audience, one in which the distinction between his authenticity as an actor/citizen and that of the character he is playing is collapsed. This is due not only to how he handles his activism privately, but also to the role he is famous for, President Jed Bartlet in *The West Wing* political drama series. The series's claims to the real and its ties with contemporary politics facilitates this "traversing of authenticities" in three ways, Collins says: first, through its *mise en scène* as a backstage region, where audiences are privy to the business of politics behind closed doors; second, through the continuity of the plotlines, the recurring debates, and the relationships among the characters which facilitate intimacy with the characters and reveals the "authentic" Bartlet to audiences; third, because Sheen himself chooses roles that do not conflict excessively with his private beliefs. In these ways, Sheen authenticates his activism and reproduces his celebrity capital.

Dramatizing the Political

The final section of the book contains chapters analyzing the ideology, the characters, and the plotlines of drama series about contemporary politics or historical figures. Key aspects of these chapters are not only how the media representations relate to the current political climate, the relationship between history, nation, and memory, but also the ways in which television drama can be situated in the context of the wave of reality in television, to real politics and political issues.

The drama series *The West Wing* is interesting, since the marketing of the program, the news discourse about it, and its fandom all take as a starting point *The West Wing*'s relationship to "real life" events and how things "really are" or "should be" at the White House. Kristina Riegert argues that *The West Wing*'s televisual form and political content should be situated in the context of the emotional need to reconnect with authenticity as demonstrated by the proliferation of reality-based programming. *The West Wing* represents a wish fulfillment for the need to reconnect to the political sphere and to the way political leaders should behave. However, its relationship to the "real" is more dubious than this; a textual analysis reveals that the political issues raised on the program can be seen in terms of a dualism, where staunchly held progressive political ideals are tempered by the need for pragmatism and compromise, depicted as the only realistic alternative, sending the message that these ideals are noble but ultimately "unrealistic." *The West Wing*'s relationship to the "real" regarding foreign policy is even less benign: here universalist and particularist arguments coalesce to support the superiority of U.S. values above others in a clearly Orientalist stance (denigrating the Arab world), while at the same time giving the United States the right to place itself above the international community and take the law into its own hands.

Another television genre that often deals with biographical dramatizations of real-life political or historical figures is the miniseries, or what Rune Ottosen calls the docudrama. Produced in the style of "realist theater," the docudrama claims to provide a fairly accurate view of the actors and the events it portrays. Ottosen argues that it is precisely in this regard—in relation to historical events and for ethical reasons relating to dramatizing the lives of real people—that *The Reagans* series is deeply problematic. Furthermore, when taking into account the political economy of media conglomerates, the relationship between Hollywood and the Pentagon, as well as the contemporary political climate, it would have been surprising if the media conglomerate Viacom (responsible for the series) really had taken a critical look at the former U.S. president, he says.

In line with scholarship on dramatizations of historical events, *The Reagans* displayed the following characteristics: (1) history is depicted in light of the current political climate; (2) history is distorted for the sake of entertainment and spectacle; and (3) systemic social problems are seldom fairly presented, and the dominant cultural understanding is reinforced. Ottosen's analysis demonstrates that with regard to political and historical issues, the series concentrates on shifting responsibility for mistakes away from the president himself and framing historical fact according to a mainstream Republican agenda. For example, the Iran-Contra scandal is framed as Oliver North's personal responsibility and not part of the wider U.S. foreign policy involving the president or his advisors. Second, while Ronald Reagan is an early example of an actor using his celebrity status to market himself as a politician, the series offers only limited insight into Ronald Reagan's extensive use of public relations, something which has since become a hallmark of American presidential campaigning. Ottosen is most critical when it comes to how the series avoids the militarization of American society and the draining of its resources through the unrealizable SDI or so-called Star Wars program, crediting Ronald Reagan with ending the Cold War. The series writes this important epoch in history through the eyes of Ronald Reagan, only idiosyncratically presenting any opposition to his policies. The only critical views are Reagan's non-response to the AIDS crisis and the "excessive" influence of Nancy Reagan on him, neither of which damage the image of Ronald Reagan as the "winner of the Cold War." Rather, the glorification of the arms race and the U.S. military interventions of the period feed into the mainstream discourse of the military-industrial complex touted by much Hollywood-produced entertainment that are little more than propaganda.

Rikke Schubart analyzes the use of factual footage in war films, especially Steven Spielberg's *Saving Private Ryan* (1998) and the television series *Band of Brothers* (2001), and the relationship between the war genre, nation, and history. She calls the use of factual footage or texts in war drama "historical pieces," since they draw attention to themselves as different from the fictional representation, while at the same time anchoring the fictional to what audiences will recognize as an historical reality. Schubart argues that historical pieces have become common enough to constitute a new development within the "postmodern" war drama in the post-1989 period and may constitute an attempt to repair what Jean Baudrillard has called the "retreat of history."

There are several different ways historical pieces are used in the war film: to create "filmic realism," to affirm a link between real history and fiction, to document that something took "place as narrated by fiction," to repair history, and as memory, i.e., using eyewitnesses to insert the past into the present. Eyewitnesses are linked to notions of truth and justice, and therefore we could see this as a bridge between the past and the present in the service of "truth." Eyewitnesses are structuring principles in both *Saving Private Ryan* and *Band of Brothers,* and the life stories of the soldiers are used to invoke the grander narratives (and collective memory) of sacrifice, valor, and victory.

Schubert finds it significant that historical pieces are rarely employed in Vietnam War films, critical or otherwise. The themes in these are about the loss of innocence, of purpose, and of value, because the wound was too fresh for a return to history to find meaning. Within the context of television's use of docudramas and reality television, the use of historical pieces in the postmodern war drama is an attempt to find a meaningful life-story to insert into our collective memory—an effort to document, recollect, and repair history through "traces" of the real. It should be noted that when Schubert talks about the rewriting of history, she has another relationship to truth than implied by Rune Ottosen. In her account, when it comes to history, truth is not the opposite of a lie, as black is to white, but rather a certain selection of "traces" gathered to reconstruct a version of reality. Fiction is neither true nor false, but a selection of elements gathered to tell a collective memory.

This collection of essays attempts to link television's claims of authenticity, and of "reality," with the medium's dominance as a means of understanding political culture. The authors address important trends in television (new genres such as reality television, politics in comedy talk shows) as well as the relationship of popular culture to political processes (celebrity and political content in entertainment formats). Although they vary in their assessments of these developments, the authors share the notion that television's entertainment formats are important sources of political culture and inform political processes. More than ever before, political performance, interactivity, and engagement generated by real political issues, whether dramatized or not, are converging in today's television tableau.

Notes

[1] D.H.S.: Department of Homeland Security.

[2] "The Tamil film industry has a long intertwining link with creating future politicians. The first non congress Chief minister C.N. Annadurai and the current opposition leader M. Karunanidhi wrote cine scripts. Long time Tamil Nadu Chief Minister M. G. Ramachandran (MGR) was a well known actor in Kollywood. The current chief minister J. Jayalalithaa was also a popular actress. Moreover many in the field are currently in houses of parliament or assembly." http://en.wikipedia.org/wiki/Kollywood. Accessed 21 February 2006.

[3] So this is not an example of what appears to be a common opinion in the United States these days. As George Clooney recently put it in an interview, "No, that is what newspapers and reporters are for. Unfortunately, over the last three years, until the Katrina incident, news took a pass on actually asking the tough questions and cinema took up a some of that slack." Interview with Gunnar Rehlin, *Kulturnyheterna*, SVT, 14 February 2006.

[4] Journalism.org., "The State of the News Media 2005." Annual Report on American Journalism, 2005. http://www.stateofthenewsmedia.org/2005/narrative_overview_publicattitudes.asp?cat=7&media=1. Accessed 15 February 2006. Pew Center for the People and the Press, "Striking the Balance, Audience Interests, Business Pressures and Journalists' Values' 30 March 1999. Sektion I–V. Available at people-press.org/reports/display.php3?ReportID=67. Accessed 20 November 2003. Or Per Jansson, "Förtroendet för dagspress minskar," *Journalisten.se*. 16 June 2003. http://www.journalisten.se/a.asp?article_id=5488. 22 November 2003.

[5] Pew Center for the People and the Press, "Striking the Balance, Audience Interests, Business Pressures and Journalists' Values," 30 March 1999. Sektion I, p. 1. http://people-presp.org/reports/display.php3?ReportID=67. 20 November 2003.

References

Corner, John. 2002. "Performing the Real: Documentary Diversions." *Television and New Media* 3(3): 255–269.

———. 2003. "Mediated Persona and Political Culture." In *Media and the Restyling of Politics: Consumerism, Celebrity and Cynicism*, edited by John Corner and Dick Pels. London: Sage.

———, and Pels, Dick. 2003. "Introduction: The Re-Styling of Politics." In *Media and the Restyling of Politics: Consumerism, Celebrity and Cynicism*, edited by John Corner and Dick Pels. London: Sage.

Delli Carpini, Michael X., and Williams, Bruce. 1996. "Constructing Political Opinion: The Uses of Fiction and Nonfictional Television in Conversations about the Environment." In *The Psychology of Political Communication*, edited by A. Crigler. Ann Arbor: University of Michigan Press.

Hartley, John. 1996. *Popular Reality: Journalism, Modernity, Popular Culture*. London: Arnold.

Jones, Jeffrey P. 2005. *Entertaining Politics: New Political Television and Civic Culture*. Lanham, MD: Rowman & Littlefield.

McNair, Brian. 2000. *Journalism and Democracy: An Evaluation of the Political Public Sphere*. London and New York: Routledge.

Miller, Toby (in press). *Cultural Citizenship*. Philadelphia: Temple University Press.

Murray, Susan, and Ouellette, Laurie. 2004. "Introduction." In *Reality Television: Remaking Television Culture*, edited by Susan Murray and Laurie Ouellette. New York: New York University Press.

Scott, Ian. 2001. *American Politics in Hollywood Film*. Edinburgh: Edinburgh University Press.

Stanley, Alessandra. 2005. "A Real-Time War Drama." *International Herald Tribune*, Television/Media/Movies, 29 July.

Street, John. 1997. *Politics and Popular Culture*. London: Polity Press.

——. 2001. *Mass Media, Politics and Democracy*. Basingstoke: Palgrave.

——. 2003. "The Celebrity Politician: Political Style and Popular Culture." In *Media and the Restyling of Politics: Consumerism, Celebrity and Cynicism*, edited by John Corner and Dick Pels. London: Sage.

Thompson, John B. 1995. *The Media and Modernity: A Social Theory of the Media*. Cambridge: Polity Press.

——. 2000. *Political Scandal: Power and Visibility in the Media Age*. Cambridge: Polity Press.

Turner, Graeme. 2004. *Understanding Celebrity*. London: Sage.

Zoonen, Liesbet van. 2005. *Entertaining the Citizen: When Politics and Popular Culture Converge*. Lanham, MD: Rowman & Littlefield.

CHAPTER TWO

"Reality" and the Plebiscite

JOHN HARTLEY

"Politicotainment"

T he very form of Kristina Riegert's neologism says something about
how the realms of politics and entertainment have crash-merged. The
term itself is not a pretty sight, perhaps because it describes an
unlikely amalgam: two opposing worlds whose "heterogeneous ideas are yoked
by violence together," as Dr. Johnson would have put it.[1] The resulting idea is
counter-intuitive, since it seems to betray the essence of both the originating
terms. Surely entertainment is characterized by escapism, while politics ought
not to be confused with private pleasure consumption. So says traditional
political science, at any rate.

At the root of democratic politics is the vote. In the spirit of "politicotainment," this chapter shows how the vote is faring in entertainment formats,
especially "reality" television, where it seems to be thriving, as if someone had
pressed the refresh button on one of the oldest technologies of democracy.[2]
The chapter opens (part I) by arguing that "politicotainment" is as old as
democracy itself. What is new, it is argued (part II), is a shift from "modern"
democratic processes to a new paradigm based not on representation but on
direct participation, a shift led from consumer rather than from political
culture. It goes on (part III) to identify a new form of intermediary that has
grown up in the interface between consumers and popular media, which I call
the "plebiscitary industries." These may be defined as those agencies, production companies, and technical service-providers whose business it is to com-
mercialize the popular vote by turning it into an entertainment format. They
have evolved from existing ratings, polling, marketing, and production
agencies, which themselves grew out of an earlier "representative" rather than
"direct" model of mediation. But the "plebiscitary industries" are not the same
as "pollsters" in just the same way that the "creative industries" differ from the

"cultural industries"—they belong to a new paradigm of business practice that values consumers for what they *do* rather than for how they can be made to *behave*. During the modern era of "mass" communication, the preferences of consumers and audiences were "represented" in media only indirectly, notably via ratings. Now it is possible for individuals to express their views and votes directly, and the evidence suggests that they're having a ball while doing so. The plebiscitary industries have caught the digital wave and are using new interactive technologies and software for what Stephen Coleman calls "conversational democracy" (Coleman 2005). Part of its appeal is the straightforward fun to be had from making public, by voting, the personal act of choice.

The chapter goes on (part IV) to sample some "reality" television formats that use the plebiscite to a lesser and a greater extent, drawn particularly from talent shows in fashion and music. These plebiscitary *formats* may be distinguished from plebiscitary *industries* in the same way that *Big Brother* can be distinguished from Endemol (which makes it), the aggregators who collect the votes, and the various television networks that screen the show. Plebiscitary formats have proven very popular internationally in recent years. For the industry they are a live experiment in different ways to incorporate voting into existing light entertainment. The plebiscitary format is sometimes "about" politics (*American Candidate*) but more often the formal world of politics is the last thing on its mind (*Idol, Big Brother*). However, the "politico-" and the "-tainment" ends of the "reality" spectrum are both expressions of something new—a widespread popular desire for participation in a direct open network rather than control by closed expert systems. In fact, plebiscitary formats in "reality" television may be seen as *transitional forms* through which the plebiscitary industries are conducting R&D to see how far they can maintain the scale of modern "behavioral" or "mass" communication while accommodating new demand for personal choice and direct participation in large-scale communicative interaction. In some of these formats "democratic" progress is minimal—viewers do little more than vote (and the votes are rigged). But even among these early and hesitant experiments, the "medium is the message"—the "plebiscitary format" *is* an experience of democracy; the demos is *doing* something together, not just being told what to do or how it has behaved. Thus the chapter concludes (part V) with comments on the pressure that is now being exerted on "representative" models of both media and politics to reform, in order to make space for the desire for direct, active participation by consumers in the very human process of choosing their own representations. This process has not yet reached maturity, but in the meantime the plebiscitary industries (not formal politics) are the place to look for both technical and imaginative progress.

Part I: Politics and Entertainment

Crash-Merging Politics and Media—The Story of Modernity?

The plebiscitary industries and plebiscitary "reality" formats, taken together, are acting as a catalyst for the mutual modification of politics (democratic deliberation, policy decisions, national identity, security) and entertainment (engagement/affect, narrative, personal identity, conflict). The admixture of power and pleasure, decision-making and celebrity, reason and "affect," democratic deliberation and individual identity, citizenship and consumption, war and drama, has long been the center of attention in cultural and media studies, especially those emanating from an interest in popular culture and the everyday life and audiencehood of ordinary people. But political science has been much slower to accept that mediated entertainment is at the center of the political process. Political scientists are generally trained in the formal operations of the democratic process and government, such as deliberative debate, lobbyism, political parties and elections, government agencies and NGOs, policy formation and participation, and also public opinion (seen as a science of measurement). The nearest they get to mediated popular culture is "the news media," on the model or ideal type of political coverage in newspapers of record. While political scientists are well aware that the media are a crucial component of politics, it is to CNN, Fox, and the electronic or latterly Internet-based *news* media that they turn to see what's going on. This is natural enough, but it ignores two crucial truths about the media: first, that news is a small and declining component of the overall media mix (some media like cinema have learned to do without it altogether); and second, that what attracts and holds popular media audiences is not news, never mind politics. In short, political science has a skewed image of the media. From that blinkered perspective, most of what people do with and like about their television usage is invisible. And so the antics of "reality" television formats must seem very foreign, a continuation of what has long been seen as a contamination of the political process by demagogic mass spectacle or populist manipulation by corporate interests. But the political process has never been pure (as media theorists have long been arguing). Indeed, it must be mediated, using the rhetorical arts and media technologies of its time. Politics depends on the arts of persuasion and on the power of emotion; these need to be communicated to vast cross-demographic publics in real time.

Meanwhile, using the same means of communication, the world of "escapist" entertainment is often able to use dramatic conflict and narrative, character and action, not least via celebrity-personifications, to get very close indeed to fundamental human, social, cultural (and political) dilemmas in ways that may capture and fire up the popular imagination for straightforwardly political purposes. Think back to popular drama from Greek tragedy to Shakespeare or popular literature from Dickens to Orwell; children's fantasy from *The Wizard of Oz* to *Lord of the Rings*; or on television how a single show like *Cathy Come Home* (U.K.) in the 1960s might directly change government policy; or how a movie like *Apocalypse Now* (U.S.) summed up a war for a generation; or how black music from the blues onward expressed minority experience and carried new political consciousness across the world; or how the counterculture learned its politics and ethics from songs by Bob Dylan; or how Band Aid and its successors Live Aid and Live8 conjoined pop music and global foreign policy. (See also Spigel and Curtin 1997; Curtin 1995; Torres 2003.)

So there's nothing new in the basic idea of "politicotainment." In fact, the confusion of politics and entertainment can be traced back to any originating moment of any contemporary polity that you care to name, including the great modernizing political "revolutions" of the United States in 1776 and France in 1789. The same applies to Russia in 1917 and China in 1949, not to mention Italy in 1922 and Germany in 1933—whose totalitarian visions of mass politics as emotion-laden entertainment and spectacle served as a dreadful warning of just how potent the mixture could be in unscrupulous hands.

Despite the warnings of Frankfurt School critics against the aestheticization of politics, of Hannah Arendt against populist demagoguery, or even Susan Sontag against "fascinating fascism," there is no type of popular political participation, ancient or modern, that is not also mediated, spectacular, irrational, and emotion-laden. Democratic polities, as well as totalitarian ones, are served by "politicotainment" both routinely in the daily news round and at crucial times of heightened political risk such as elections, wars, scandals, and economic downturns. Semiotic as well as social leadership has always been needed to capture the popular imagination, alongside or even in advance of reasoned argument. Democracy was fanned and disseminated by popular journalism as well as by political activism. Since Camille Desmoulins, Tom Paine, Joseph Pulitzer, *Life*, *Picture Post*, James Cameron, Ed Murrow,[3] good journalism has always prioritized a clear story, dramatic conflict, and latterly compelling visuals as the means by which it must address the information- and enlightenment-seeking citizen. Michael Schudson (1999; see also Schudson 1998) has pointed out that when the idea of the rational "informed citizen" took over in the United States in the 1880s from the previous model of political participation based on spectacular partisanship, actual voting numbers dropped. People had to be brought back to the ballot box by showbiz razzmatazz and campaigning chutzpah.

But the use of entertainment techniques to reach the popular voter was not a corruption of previously pure political communication. It was constitutionally required by the very form of modern representative democracy. Political modernity is inaugurated in any country when the source of sovereignty shifts from the monarch (think Charles I, Louis XVI, Nicholas II, or Cixi Dowager Empress of China) as the personification of divine authority, and thus in a real sense the "author" of his or her people, to "the people" (think Jefferson, Adams, and Paine).

In this shift, "the people" remained a *representation*—there are no *direct* democracies working at the industrial scale of mass societies.[4] Instead, "the people" themselves were "textualized" via a series of mechanisms both directly political (e.g., foundational "representation of the people" acts) and mediated, i.e., "the press" as both representative and representation of the public ("the fourth estate"). The further that suffrage was extended—eventually to become more or less universal—the more a democratic polity needed a universal medium of communication that linked active political representatives and economic leaders with the formally sovereign voters, and vice versa. The only mechanisms to come anywhere near this ideal were the pulpit and the press; and in an era of secular, scientific empiricism, where truth was held to reside in objective facts rather than revealed faith, and where in any case competition among religious sects meant that there was never a time when just one sect could prevail over all the others, the fact-hungry press quickly attained universal supremacy as the intermediary between "the people" and their representatives in politics, government, and business.

Nevertheless, sovereign citizens were not directly involved in the arts of business and government, and the daily run of news events was often of little intrinsic interest to the general population. It was therefore necessary for the press to find reliable techniques for getting lay people to attend to them and to follow issues that bored or repelled them. The trick of getting uncommitted nonprofessionals to read things they don't want to know about should not be underestimated, but success in achieving it is a precondition for media power. It must always come first. As Lord Beaverbrook pointed out to the Royal Commission on the Press in the 1940s, there was no point in owning a newspaper, even if one's intention was to use it for proprietorial propaganda, as was the case with his *Daily Express*, unless it was in a "thoroughly good financial position;" as he said, "in order to make the propaganda effective the paper had to be successful" (Royal Commission 1948, para. 8660). Such success was at least partly in the hands of the readers themselves, who did not put up with everything that was thrown at them, no matter how powerful and manipulative the "regime" of ownership and control. It became imperative to know what sovereign citizens *liked*, what they thought, and how they would act. Three great questions of commercial democracies needed answers, every day anew:

- *Will they vote* (for me)?
- *Will they buy* (this product or message)?
- *Will they riot* (against what)?

A range of intermediate agencies developed, including pollsters, circulation auditors and media monitors, publicists and marketing firms, whose purpose was to gauge public opinion and advise both commercial and political clients on how (and whether) their campaigns were "playing in Peoria." From political propaganda to celebrity endorsement, they were on hand to monitor and manage the risky interface between popular entertainment and public affairs. As can be gauged by the wealth and influence of the sector and the prominence of its successful practitioners, these intermediaries remain at the heart of the democratic process. They produce the polls, ratings, circulation figures, charts—and now the direct votes—that take the daily temperature of the demos: what's hot, and what's not.

Consumption and Citizenship

"Politicotainment"—entertaining mediations of politics and business—is in fact only the sharp end of a much wider phenomenon that pervades popular media in the modern era. In a 1999 book I coined the comparable term "democratainment." It refers to a wider range of content on broadcast television than the purely political. Indeed, it suggests that commercial media as a whole, especially routine television entertainment formats like drama and comedy, perform a public function, representing—and *teaching*—aspects of contemporary citizenship to vast cross-demographic populations (Hartley 1999, chs. 12 and 14).

If "democratainment" can be found in sitcoms, then public participation in the democratic process is not confined to television "election specials" with entertaining pedagogic devices like Bob McKenzie's 1955 "swingometer."[5] It extends through to the deep bedrock of television entertainment, linking the top of society with the bottom, right down to children's shows that teach citizenly values. My example was Nickelodeon's *Clarissa Explains It All*, but the whole point about that show is that there's nothing special about it: check out *Daria* or *The Simpsons* in the animated format, or *Dead Like Me* and *What I Like About You* in live comedy-drama. Commercial entertainment *in general* explores, explains, and exploits public and civic values; in a sense all of popular broadcast television is "democratainment."

Perhaps the reason that political science remained skeptical about the civic attributes of television entertainment was that the latter was seen as "mere consumption." Modernist politics was never very comfortable with "the consumer" as opposed to "the citizen"—perversely hanging on to the idea that the consumer was an *effect* of commercial or political manipulation while the citizen was a *cause* of the political process, despite the fact that consumers and citizens were sited within the same corporeal persons. Throughout the modern period, that contradiction was masked by gendering it. Citizens were imagined as activist (read masculine), rational individuals participating in the democratic process, guided by the press and political parties, while consumers were feminized as housewives at home who read "lifestyle" magazines for purposeless private pleasure, which nevertheless guided their choices in the supermarket. Out of the blokey mateship of citizenship were forged such heroic attributes as national identity and the public sphere, with "civil society" represented by news media that militantly mythologized their own status as watchdogs of the democratic process. This was the ground cultivated by political science. The private and feminized world of consumption was seen as *behavior*, not *action*. It was barely recognized as part of the political process at all. Instead it was seen as the effect of manipulation by marketing; of "government" by private enterprise, not public institutions. But it was here in this unworthy place that media studies pitched its analytical tent.

Small wonder that there's little interdisciplinary traffic between political science and media studies, although the idea has grown that public communication requires engagement and "affect" as well as information and evidence, as participation in the formal mechanism of politics has dropped, especially in the United States.

Part II: A Paradigm Shift

Shifting Along the Value Chain

In other publications (e.g., Hartley 2004), I've taken the idea of the "value chain" in its simplest business sense (i.e., the links from producer/originator, via commodity/distribution, to the consumer/user) and argued that the concept applies to cultural and symbolic "values" as well as economic ones. The "cultural" value chain links author/producer, via text, to audience or reader. I've argued further that over time the *source* of value (or what is taken to be the "source" of *meaning*) has been located on different links of the chain, shifting down a link over three distinct historical periods—pre-modern,

modern, and contemporary:

- from *author* [producer]—modeled on the medieval Christian God as "author" of all meanings, which gave rise to intentionalist interpretations of the source of meaning more generally, as in "what Shakespeare really meant;"
- via *text* [commodity/distribution]—modeled on modern (i.e., post-Francis Bacon) scientific observation of the properties of objects in themselves, which in the cultural domain means texts. Meanings arise directly from observation of empirical or documentary evidence including physical properties of objects;
- to *reader* or *audience* [consumer]—nowadays, widely shared cultural meanings are tested by investigating how many consumers choose a particular meaning.

In other words, the shift down the value chain in both economic and symbolic values is *epochal*, so that one can speak of *pre-modern*, *modern*, and *contemporary* (or *global*) epochs, in which a specific link in the value chain is dominant, resulting in something like a "paradigm" for each epoch. Further, I argue that the current period (the last and the next half-century) is witnessing an epochal shift from the modern to a new global paradigm, across many different but homologous domains.

One manifestation of such a shift is the pervasive sense of crisis (positively in a desire for innovation and opportunity; negatively in fear of destructive change) associated with the modernist paradigm as a whole. This extends into every nook and cranny of modern life, including the very terms of trade upon which entire industrial-cultural sectors are founded, among them both the entertainment media and representative politics. Therefore, I take current disquiet about audience measurement and new initiatives in "direct representation" of personal choices as symptoms of more than mere technological improvements in consumer sampling techniques. I suggest that they're part of the evidence of a new paradigm beginning to take shape.

Consumers as Cause, Not Effect

The dynamic and innovative branch of the creative industries is the digital content sector (see Hartley 2005). It depends for success not only on *production* (which in this sector comprises ideas or intellectual property rather than manufacturing—the data not the disk) and the *commodity* ("content" in various formats), but also on creative *consumers*.

In industrialized manufacturing industries of the modern era, the locus of power and profitability lay in control over the production end of the value chain: the Fordist assembly line, where consumers could "have any color they liked so long as it was black." In the modern cultural industries, power came from control over distribution, with newspapers, cinema, and broadcasting leading the way. But since the "information society" took hold in advanced economies in the 1990s, and with the rise of the creative industries, the locus of both economic power and social impact has increasingly shifted decisively along the value chain—to the consumer.

Consumers have not merely been "active" as the spenders whose collective dollar drives economic growth. They have also taken on a new role as drivers of innovation and makers of content in the information, creative, and media sectors. The value "chain" is no longer linear; it's more like a value "web," because consumers and producers are *co-creators*.

So at last changes in the economic sphere have forced a wider reconceptualization of the very idea of the consumer, such that even among skeptics the mixture of citizenship and consumption can now be seen as having positive aspects and not solely a disaster for democracy.[6] The changes include all manner of consumer-driven innovations in the creative industries, especially in digital (as opposed to analogue) media content. For examples, think of: consumer-created content from "tribute films" (amateur remakes of *Star Wars*) and fansites to zines and blogs; the input of players into the development or evolution of games (like *The Sims*); the entire open source movement (Linux); the creative commons; "ProAms" in services (Leadbeater and Miller 2004); music-sharing and podcasting; "citizen journalism"; digital storytelling; the Wikipedia; flickr and deviantART (photo and picture archives and networks); genealogy websites (etc.); YouTube, jumpcut.com and BitTorrent; massive multiplayer games (like worldofwarcraft.com, which has five million paying users worldwide); and user-led mobile applications.

In an open innovation network everything connects: consumers become producers, and producers become consumers. In December 2005, gimlet-eyed bloggers reported the modest beginnings of a personal blog by the inventor of the world wide web, (Sir) Tim Berners-Lee, who quietly launched "timbl's blog" with "So I have a blog"—provoking several hundred delighted messages from around the blogosphere before he turned off the comments. In short, Sir Tim wanted to remain a member of the community he'd created in 1989. He was looking for "discourse through communal authorship.... So I am going to try this blog thing using blog tools."[7]

These changes have transformed the "model" of the consumer from *behavior* to *action*. Of course "action" isn't the same as "activism," but this isn't an "either/or" game. It's a change in the generative model of "the consumer" from one where "she" (like a 1950s-style housewife) was behaviorally manipulated by experts, to one where consumers (like Sir Tim Berners-Lee as blogger) do things for themselves and for their own purposes. With a change in the enabling model, whole new industries can arise that understand and respond to that. Simultaneously, knowledge-creation has changed, too. Charles Leadbeater, among others, has noted that the "model" of innovation itself has shifted from one where control over an expert system was thought to be vital to one where participation in an open network is seen as the key to success (Leadbeater and Miller 2004). The difference between a *closed expert system* and an *open participation network* is also the difference between modern representations of consumer preference (knowledge produced exclusively by experts) and new "DIY" participation in open networks by producer/consumers themselves, increasingly expressing their preferences directly. In this scenario, consumer "action" may not be "activism" in the sense of modernist militancy, but it is the driver of innovation based on human connectedness and therefore also of social change.

Part III: Plebiscitary Industries—A New Paradigm Shift?

Modern Expertise: Reducing Culture to Numbers

The *experts* advising the cultural industries have long learned how to convert consumer preferences into measurable scale via television ratings (there are also ratings agencies for non-broadcast media like outdoor advertising), audited circulation figures (for newspapers and magazines), or sales (of theatrical and cinema admissions, recorded music charts, software, and games). Popularity being the key to advertising dollars, sophisticated mechanisms have evolved that measure the number of eyeballs in front of which a given bit of content may have passed, down to the minute or less.

Some of these techniques of measurement have become established as general currency among competing distributors and network providers. In countries where consumer choice is well established as a market principle, it is important to establish a yardstick by which to measure success; otherwise companies have no agreed mark against which to compete with each other. This is especially the case in the creative industries, such as broadcasting and publishing, where consumer choice is essentially arbitrary. The "use value" of cultural commodities is novelty, so the economic value of a given title or product can change from bomb to blockbuster (and vice versa), sometimes overnight. "Modern" consumers drive innovation indirectly but essentially unpredictably, simply by changing their minds about what they like (Caves 2000, 202). Agreed measurement techniques reduce unpredictability and therefore assist creative producers and distributors in managing risk.

In countries or periods where agencies dedicated to the neutral measurement of consumer choice do not exist or are poorly developed (historically in the West; currently in China) or are not agreed among competitors, the consumer market may be corrupted by false circulation claims, by confusion, or by the intervention of non-market values such as official approval for products that consumers don't actually like (and vice versa). So these agencies are vital in leveling the playing field for a "free market" to perform fairly.

But it does need to be emphasized that this is exactly what they are for. The expert agencies that measure consumer preferences in modernity work for industry, not for consumers directly. They cluster around the media of distribution, not the audience. In short, the modern cultural industries have managed to turn consumer choice into a representation for their own purposes—a textual form upon which interested parties can agree in order to compete with each other.

Representative Ratings: From Surveys to Servers

Given that audiences don't directly purchase a good deal of cultural content such as television programs, "the bottom line" is not sales but *ratings*—the textual form taken by consumers in the creative and cultural sphere. In order to be able to claim accuracy, ratings agencies must turn culture into numbers. Individuals fill in diaries of their media use, or they answer survey questions, or they express preferences in test screenings, or they talk in focus groups. These are all "textual" activities which, by the use of complex—not to say arcane—methods (the more "sophisticated" the better, because the *method* is the agency's intellectual property, or IP), are turned into ratings. Technological developments such as the PeopleMeter seek to reduce culture to numbers even further and to make the role of the consumer yet more passive, but as soon as digital media took off, the PeopleMeter was found to be inadequate even by its inventor, TNS (Taylor Nelson Sofres n.d.). Its numbers "missed" much of the consumers' desirable culture and activity, like Internet use.

Ratings agencies must persuade interested parties from governments to television networks that their numbers "count." They must have the power to command those whose very livelihoods, share-price, and companies depend on them. Such power has been achieved by borrowing scientific methods to reduce the built-in ambivalence of culture and textuality as much as possible by representing them numerically. The widespread trust that is placed in quantitative methods is itself a symptom of the modern scientific paradigm. But it only goes so far, because while the *method* must be quantitative, the actual *numbers* need to be kept within practical and affordable limits. So quantity meets its opposite in the concept of the "generalizable sample." Such samples are surprisingly small—Neilsen television ratings are based on the viewing practices of around 5,000 households in the United States (that's one per 60,000 of the United States' 300 million people; or one in 22,000 of the United States' 110 million television households), and around only 1,000 elsewhere.

During the modern era of representative democracy, such methods may have appeared democratic; certainly they aroused no widespread opposition, even though a constant, low-level warfare continued among rival ratings systems and technologies and between broadcasters and those among their audiences who didn't feel themselves to be represented (including, perhaps, many academics and intellectuals). They worked because they were useful to high-investment players in government and business and were accepted by broadcasters and advertisers whose profits and costs rose and fell with the numbers.

Among consumers themselves, ratings can only work when everyone accepts the logic of the regime of "representative democracy." We must all be able to say: "This show is crap but I can see why it is on TV if xxx million people like it (even though I don't know anyone who does)." Or in the immortal words of Australia's Federal Communications Minister Senator Bob Collins (Labor), during the 1992 run-up to the launch of pay television in Australia: "If people want to pay to watch crud, that is what will be broadcast to them. I'm not going to put myself in a position of telling them they cannot have crud if crud is what they want.... If pay TV doesn't provide consumers with what they want, it will go broke" (*Green Left Weekly* 1992). Such acceptance requires quite a few acts of faith, including the restriction of what is meant by "consumers" to "people in this country and timeslot," and a willingness to be governed by the "will of the national majority" in matters of taste.

As the epoch of modern representative media segues into the era of direct digital participation, both of these preconditions are now fatally undermined. New digital platforms and what Mark Pesce calls "hyperdistribution" (e.g., BitTorrent) (Pesce 2005; see also BitTorrent Inc. n.d.) mean that television content is increasingly available beyond the confines of broadcasting and beyond the domestic market, and so consumers may avoid (other people's) "crud" altogether. This opens television up to new business plans not based on "mass" communication to passive consumers but on niche marketing and customization for consumers who aren't just active but activist.

Even where such action is minimal, such as clicking a computer mouse, it can be traced. Agencies can convert the "clickstream" of myriad users into what they call "robust data"—making the mechanical act of choice into a "plebiscite." Combine what is already known about consumer choice at the "representative" or expert level—via *surveys*—with what can now be known directly—via *servers*—and you have the conditions of existence for the plebiscitary industries.

Most of the organizations in the plebiscitary industries are also active in some other capacity. (Commercializing voting is not all that they do.) They are forming on the site of the same agencies they are in the processes of supplanting, popping up *ad hoc* as technological opportunity or entrepreneurial instincts allow. They combine all three "new economy" levels of infrastructure, connectivity, and content. They range across the fields of telecommunications, broadcasting, and broadband. They use the skills—the dark arts, some might say—of marketing, publicity, surveying, and opinion polling, as well as those of production and broadcasting, applied to the global market in entertainment media. It is from among these existing "representative" agencies that Internet-savvy "early adopters" have developed new plebiscitary possibilities using digital platforms. So the new plebiscitary industries are forming around technical and professional innovators who can exploit globally connected networks, massive computational power, and software wizardry. Their products and services range from data-mining and mobile aggregating to electronic polling, multinational participant television to pop charts. While most of these skills and professions were honed in the "analogue" era of representative politics and mass entertainment, the plebiscitary industries extend them to the Internet, mobile platforms, and e-democracy.

Behind all this apparently random activity and opportunism, something more patterned can be discerned. The contemporary era is dedicated to the proposition that sovereignty is evenly distributed among a population. (That's what the universal franchise and even "the free market" is meant to express.) No longer can an expert determine on "our" behalf what is good, right, beautiful, or true. Those decisions belong to the populace. It follows that truth itself can only assume its traditional power to command once it has been sampled, bundled, scaled up, processed, and re-presented in the form of a plebiscite.

If it is the case that a paradigm shift is under way that sources sovereignty, meaning, and even truth to myriad consumers rather than to god-like author-producers or to modernist scientific-age experts, then it is imperative to develop reliable measures to find out what they mean. The number of people involved means that you can't collect individual choices one by one, so you have to bundle them up. It's a specialist job, and it is only now becoming a practical possibility with computational power measured by the petabyte (en.wikipedia.org/wiki/Petabyte).

Reality television, with voting as entertainment, is a symptom of the shift to the plebiscite as the preferred methodology of our era for revealing what anything might mean. So are the endlessly proliferating charts telling us what is best and worst in a given category. These judgments are not based on the godlike taste of a judge or the intrinsic qualities of an object as revealed by scientific or professional expertise, but on the vote of the punters.

Part IV: Plebiscitary Formats—"Reality" Television

Reality Television—A Matter of Talent, Mostly

America's/Australia's Next Top Model
Not all "reality" television formats are plebiscitary (yet). A good example of one that is not is *America's Next Top Model*, created, produced, and hosted by Tyra Banks. An Australian re-version of the show also exists; it went into its second season in early 2006. The "reality" aspect is that the contestants must perform various modeling-related tasks throughout the series, where they—and viewers—are introduced to the real world of fashion shows and photography.

Tyra Banks enjoyed a successful career as a top international model, which lent credibility to the format, but fashion values were not in fact ascendant on *ANTM*. Despite the "top model" tagline, it was not primarily looking for a contestant who would win acceptance in the international fashion world. The appeal of the show rested heavily on its qualities as "good television." Compare the *real* "next top model" during the same period (2003–5): Australian teenager Gemma Ward. She was discovered at age 15 in the audience for the Perth heats of *Search for a Supermodel* in 2002. She was persuaded to enter the competition but went no further than her hometown heats, where she was one of twenty finalists. She didn't make it to the national finals or on to Ford Models' *Supermodel of the World* international competition. However, a photograph of her ended up on a desk at IMG in New York. Described by the scout who spotted her in Perth as "surreal, beautiful, very European, wide-set eyes, angelic, not a skerrick of make-up," there has never been a contestant like her on *America's Next Top Model*.[8] Instead, contestants of non-standard height or build (compared with the look favored by "directional designers') were over-represented among finalists, as were women of color, either because Tyra wanted to make a point about their aptitude and beauty, or because such contestants were thought to represent aspirations among the target audience demographic, or both.

America's Next Top Model is perhaps a late example of "reality" television as a closed expert system. The role of the audience is merely to like it or lump it, take it or leave it. Each week the young woman chosen for elimination, and also the eventual winner, were selected by an expert panel in a process not shown to viewers, although it seemed to have been heavily influenced by Tyra herself. Neither the viewer nor the fashion world played a direct part in deciding the outcome. Not surprisingly, then, finalists and winners across the first five "cycles" of the show (to date) tended to emerge from "reality" (or "soapie") values—authentic self-expression, overcoming adversity, personal growth during the series, eye candy, coping with tests and with the competitive dynamics and dramas of the group. Human values and personal conflict were foregrounded, as was the dominance of Tyra Banks herself, who was simultaneously the contestants' role-model, soul-sister, and executioner. And the eventual winners gravitated toward U.S.-based television careers, not toward international fashion, where Gemma Ward (among innumerable Eastern European and Brazilian teenagers) reigned supreme.

Plebiscitary Television

Plebiscitary television shows are those that find a way to make voting and viewers' choices a part of the show, influencing the outcome of stories or events in the plot. The plebiscite has shifted from industry tool to creative content and has become a prominent feature of the entertainment package itself, notably (although not only) in "reality" formats, from *Big Brother* to *Mongolian Cow Sour Yoghurt Super Voice Girl.*[9]

Plebiscitary television was kick-started by the wide availability of mobile phones and the cheap cost of SMS messaging. Previously "representative" voting (by panels) had played its part in variety entertainment, for instance in *Juke Box Jury* (BBC, 1959–67) and *Thank Your Lucky Stars* (ITV, 1961–66). The former used celebrity panelists to vote a song a hit or a miss. The latter went a step further by introducing representatives of the target demographic, in the shape of guest teenagers who rated recent singles on a scale of one to five. Most famous was Midlands schoolgirl Janice Nicholls, "a 16 year old Black Country lass" who "became a star overnight when she uttered the immortal words 'Oi'll give it foive.' She remained on the panel for three years and the phrase became part of British colloquial language...."[10]

While most such shows have long since disappeared, the *Eurovision Song Contest* has carried on for fifty years since 1955. One of its principal attractions is the vote, where a panel from each participating country (which have grown in number from ten to thirty-nine) awards points to the others.[11] This practice is prey to nationalist sentiment among other biases; for instance, Cyprus was notorious for always awarding maximum points to Greece and the minimum to Turkey (who both returned the favor). The Benelux, Nordic, and Eastern European countries were suspected of voting *en bloc*, too. Germany nearly always lost, despite being Europe's largest country. (It only won once, in 1982.) And some progressive countries (like Sweden) criticized the "backward" musical tastes of "New European" countries across the Baltic Sea. Under the Eurovision kitsch, there always simmered political (or rather national) rivalries. The voting system was constantly modified to minimize them.

Thus, Eurovision adopted interactive and audience-participation technologies as they became available. In 1998, as soon as it was technically feasible (though not all participant countries had the infrastructure for it), "televoting" was introduced as a complement to panel voting.[12] That year, though not necessarily as a result, the contest was won by Israeli transsexual diva Dana International. The contest was streamed over the Internet from 2000, and by 2004 "centralized televoting" was installed, resulting in over 5 million votes being cast during ten-minute live windows in the semifinal and final.[13] The plebiscite had become the pleasure.

Talent Shows as Presidential Election Campaigns

American/Australian/Pop Idol
Talent contests such as the *Eurovision Song Contest* are a hybrid between the true plebiscite and previous "representative" or "expert systems" formats, because they combine viewer voting with judging panels. The latter can occasionally override the popular vote, just as the Electoral College sometimes does in U.S. presidential elections. (It happened in the Australian version of *Dancing with the Stars*. The event sparked controversy, as reported in *The Age*, 16 February 2005.)

The *Idol* family of shows marks a definite shift away from traditional musical talent shows like *Pot of Gold*, *New Faces*, and *Young Talent Time* (and ANTM, too). Comments by professional judges about the aesthetic, commercial, and talent aspects of contestants' performances are designed to guide viewer choice: like all others, this is a "guided democracy" where "leadership" plays a strong role. Expert advice is still seen as necessary, not least perhaps because the successful contestant wins a recording contract, so attention needs to be paid to commercial realities. However, the relative autonomy of the viewing experience (human values) from the commercial imperative (musical appeal) is demonstrated by the fact that several *Idol* losers have gone on to more successful recording careers than their season's winners.

Effectively, each *Idol* series *is* a twelve- or thirteen-week election campaign. The rhythm of the campaign follows that of an American presidential election.

Early rounds parallel the open primaries where devoted fans (like registered party members) whittle down the candidates to two. These finalists contest the ultimate prize via a large-scale, national election in the final episode. If all goes well, the finale will attract a much larger audience than the "primaries," and all "citizens of media" within this population are able to vote (putting aside questions of literacy and access that plague all elections), whether they are "party members" (loyal viewers) or not.

The perception that the winner of *Idol* is the contestant with the most votes is integral to the *Idol* format. Plebiscitary service providers have sprung up to conduct the vote and keep it clean. A company called Telescope Inc. managed the mechanics of the SMS-voting for *American Idol* on behalf of FremantleMedia (producer) and Fox (broadcaster).[14]

As in presidential elections, hanging chads notwithstanding,[15] the process itself is subjected to close scrutiny (Higgins and Seibel 2004). Indeed, viewers grew cynical about the legitimacy of *Idol*'s voting process:

▪ Fans were concerned about phone-line congestion. Though in the 2003 season phone companies recorded 100 million+ calls, Fox recorded 24 million votes (ibid.).
▪ Auto-dialers potentially skewed the vote by enabling some viewers to find an open line to vote through, while simultaneously contributing to line congestion (ibid.; Seibel 2004).
▪ There was evidence that AT&T digital text-message votes had a greater chance of getting through than land-line phone votes (Seibel 2004).

The latter issue seemed to indicate phone company opportunism, because phone lines were tariff-free while SMS voting was charged at ten cents a message.[16] Deborah Starr Seibel (2004) argued that the phone-line problems reduced the democratic nature of *Idol*. The winner was chosen only by those who could get through, not all those who wanted to vote. Fan discontent was registered in discussions online and in complaints to the FCC and Fox:

> The FCC has received more than a thousand complaints (69 e-mails sent to the FCC directly, 1,140 sent to Fox and copied to the FCC) about legitimate *Idol* voting. Most of them are from last season and center on the inability of Aiken fans to get through. The agency doesn't make public whether it is considering a formal investigation. But the trigger for such an investigation, according to the FCC's Rosemary Kimball, would be clear evidence of the show's intentionally "fixing" the numbers. (Ibid.)

The *Idol* format "enacts" the process of democratic choice by following the rhythms of real election campaigns, but it also introduces a new character into broadcast entertainment—"the vote." This is like the old anarchist slogan: "it doesn't matter who you vote for, the government gets in." In this case it doesn't matter which contestant you vote for, or even what motivates your choice. What matters is that the show cannot come to a conclusion without a vote, and the viewer "at home" (or on the mobile) is complicit in that vote even if they don't exercise it. Viewers become "actors" on one side of the screen, while contestants (as viewers' proxies) are "actors" on the other. The vote itself is a force—like a Fairy Godmother or *deus ex machina*. Without it the wish fulfillment elements (which are largely the point of the show) can't be fulfilled. *Idol*'s format insists that the fame and celebrity enjoyed by winners belongs to the consumer, because it is the *act* of the scaled-up viewer that produces both plot development and narrative closure.

More Votes Than the President

Mongolian Cow Sour Yogurt Super Girl
The *Mongolian Cow Sour Yogurt Super Girl Contest*, produced by Hunan Satellite television in South Central Hunan Province for its Entertainment Channel, was an open singing contest.[17] The 2005 version was one of the most viewed programs in the history of Chinese television—the *International Herald Tribune* (27 November 2005) reported more than 400 million people tuned in for the finals in August. *The Times* reported that the figure exceeded the estimated 400 million who watched the *Chinese New Year Festival Gala* on CCTV but pointed out that no official figures were available (Macartney 2005, 25). But *The Times* did show how much *Super Voice Girl* outstripped Western audiences:

- Australia: 3.3 million watched *Australian Idol* (2003 final)
- United Kingdom: *Pop Idol* topped 12 million (2003 final)
- United States: Nearly 48 million watched *American Idol* (2004 final)
- India: *Indian Idol* hit 48 million.

The plebiscitary element of the show was unprecedented in China. Over 8 million votes (or "messages of support"—the term "vote" was avoided) were cast by mobile phone for the three finalists (Marquand 2005). These participatory statistics were widely reported, as were the economic implications of the show. Danwei, for instance, carried a commentary by Li Yu (2005), translated from the Chinese *Legal Mirror*:

> *Supergirl* is a money game. Income from mobile phone SMS topped 30 million yuan (US$3.7 million); naming rights took 1.4 million Yuan (US$173,000); the seven commercial spots during the finals pushed 20 million (US$2.47 million); and printing pictures of "supergirls" on T-shirts, accessories, toys and other items had immense potential—production ended up somewhere north of several million Yuan. Experts

have calculated that the *Supergirl* brand by itself is worth at least 100 million Yuan (US$12.3 million). When a *Super Voice Girl* can bring in this sort of cash, how can we not submit?

One of the things that appealed to viewers about *Super Voice Girl* was that anyone (except boys) could go on the show, regardless of talent, looks, or aptitude. The initial number of hopeful contestants topped 150,000. Many were ordinary girls without singing skills who just wanted their "fifteen minutes of fame" on television. The whole thing *felt* democratic to participants and viewers alike.

The eventual winner, Li Yuchun,[18] was a surprising alternative to the beauty-school types who are generally endorsed as pop singers in China (Marquand 2005; Yardley 2005, 4.3). Said the *Economist*: "*Super Girl*...appealed mainly because of its racy format...and the pleasure that many take from watching amateur singers embarrass themselves. Rebellious young women apparently identified with the self-confident and boyish-looking winner, Li Yuchun" (*Economist* 2005). *Time Asia* commented:

> The Li Yuchun phenomenon, however, goes far beyond her voice, which even the most ardent fans admit is pretty weak: her vocal range drifts between Cher territory and that place your little brother's voice went the summer before seventh grade. As a dancer, she's not much better.... What Li did possess was attitude, originality and a proud androgyny that defied Chinese norms.... For an audience reared on the bubble-gum, lip-gloss standards of Chinese girl pop, Li's disregard for the rule book produced an unfamiliar knee-weakening. Her fans wept openly and frantically shrieked when Li took the stage. (Jakes 2005)

The Age also commented on the winner's appearance in emancipationist terms, reporting that Li's "transgender appeal" suggested to some Chinese observers that her win "signalled that men could no longer dictate how women should dress and look. Li Yinhe, China's best-known researcher on gender issues, likened her appeal to that of Boy George or Michael Jackson" (McDonald 2005).

The degree to which the show resonated with people seems to have unsettled the government's propaganda leaders. Fans crowded shopping centers holding posters of their favorite contestant in an attempt to rouse votes. Unruly fans caused security guards to be called into one shopping center. *The Economist* (9 October 2005) reports some songs were raunchy, although by the time of the finals, song choice had bowed to official sensibilities: "They included folk songs, communist favorites and Western numbers such as *The Color of My Love* by Celine Dion, and Ricky Martin's *Maria*. Gone were the raunchier songs of previous rounds." And apparently its appeal was not confined to the masses. *The Christian Science Monitor* reported:

Even older Chinese have been caught up in the show. One high-ranking minister who was hosting a lengthy business reception scheduled to last until 9 P.M. was suddenly missing at 8 P.M on Friday night. Sources close to the minister noted that *Super Girl* started at 8:30 P.M. (Marquand 2005)

As soon as the popular success of the series became apparent, speculation surfaced that future series would be cancelled. Officials criticized the show for being too "worldly," for being vulgar, boorish, "and lacking social responsibility" (Macartney 2005, 25). CCTV, the main state-run television network, was particularly critical. "Technically, CCTV officials can shut down *Super Girl*, since they hold a monopoly position on broadcast decisions." But a rat was smelled:

Many ordinary Chinese say that it won't be worldliness that prompts any shutdown, but the fact that CCTV's advertising revenue on Friday night was lower than that of its modest Hunan competitor. A pilot of an official version of *Super Girl* produced by CCTV reportedly failed. (Marquand 2005)

Western media such as *The New York Times* noted that "Unlike China's leader, Hu Jintao, Ms. Li was popularly elected" (Yardley 2005), celebrating the program as a democratic incursion into China. As *Time Asia* put it: "Like *American Idol*, but unlike China itself, *Super Girl's Voice* is run democratically." *The Economist* reported as "frank" a front-page headline in *Beijing Today* that read: "Is *Super Girl* a Force for Democracy?" An article circulating on official websites in China suggested the contest had caused Chinese intellectuals to "fantasise about arrangements for democratic elections and notice the awakening of democratic consciousness among the younger generation" (*Economist* 2005). Australian papers labeled the program "cultural democracy":

The country's media experts have been transfixed as much by the program's formula as by the outcome. Some labelled the show "vulgar" and called for more classical shows of culture on TV, but the well known critic Zhu Dake said the show had "blazed a trail for cultural democracy." It showed the public breaking loose from the "elitist aesthetics" strangling China's entertainment industry, he told the *China Daily*. (McDonald and AFP 2005: 8)[19]

But in Danwei, Li Yu (2005) remained skeptical about its democratic potential:

Some people have said that Chinese people have poured their enthusiasm for voting into Super Voice Girl. Commentaries with titles like The Civic Awareness in the Supergirl Selection Process, Super Voice Girl and Civil Society, Super Voice Girl and the Construction of a Democratic System, and Rays of Idealism in the Super Voice Girl Selection Process have poured forth. Super Voice Girl has become "the dawn of civic society." But can Super Voice Girl really carry such a large burden?

The *China Daily* pondered: "How come an imitation of a democratic system ends up selecting the singer who has the least ability to carry a tune?" (Macartney 2005; Yardley 2005; *Economist* 2005). *The Economist* had a ready reply: "That, of course, is democracy."

Reality President

American Candidate

Eventually the worlds of plebiscitary "reality" entertainment and formal politics had to collide, and they did with *American Candidate*. This show was initially developed by FX from an original plan to make a documentary that followed a young candidate who hoped to run for president in 2012 (Franklin 2004). In the reality version it became a political *American Idol*, where viewers were to choose a candidate who would then enter the upcoming presidential election. The plan was for a candidate to be chosen and then left on his own to run for office with his own cash. That idea was dumped (*New York Times* 2005). The concept was picked up by Showtime, which ran it as a fake presidential election (Franklin 2004).[20]

The format became "a simulated presidential campaign on national television," debating a range of issues and offering the winner US$200,000 and "the chance to address the nation on TV" (Boykin 2004, 54). The program featured a series of primary-style events after which candidates chose the weakest among them for elimination. The outcome was eventually opened up to viewing voters. A Christian lobby group got behind the eventual winner (as in recent political elections).

The Advocate describes the program as "part civics lesson, part *Survivor*" and offers "props" to the program for "reserving spots in the cast for an openly gay man and a lesbian" (Graham 2004). *The Advocate* also explores some of the intersections between the program and formal politics in the United States:

> Showtime has placed its bets on *American Candidate* because the American electorate is extremely polarized and attentive to anything political at the moment—even if it is a fictional reality show. Gephardt and Boykin both say they probably wouldn't run for the real presidency because candidates are placed in fishbowls and every detail of their lives are picked apart. However, the 2004 Bush-Kerry race is never far from their minds. Like most politically active gay men and lesbians, they are pained by the attempts by George W. Bush and the Republican Party to gaybait voters. Meanwhile, they are not pleased that Democratic presidential nominee John Kerry does not support marriage rights for same-sex couples.

Says Chrissy Gephardt, lesbian presidential candidate interviewed in *The Advocate* article, the program makes politics interesting by adding a *Survivor* edge to it.

> They put an entertainment factor in it—sort of like a *Survivor*-type elimination process, and it combines entertainment and politics. If it was just politics, it would be CNN or C-SPAN. They've made it interesting with character development, which makes for a good story. We're more than just candidates; they do a bio on us and talk about who we are as people. The audience becomes engaged by our life stories.

American Candidate was not exactly run "democratically," however. *People* magazine criticized the campaign model in the program:

> The winner receives $200,000 and what host Montel Williams vaguely calls "a chance to address the nation." Too bad viewers don't get to vote till the series' last two weeks. Up to that point, each episode includes some sort of campaign challenge (a straw poll here, a focus group there), and the two competitors who perform least impressively must face off in an "elimination debate." The loser is determined by a vote of the other candidates. Sad to say, that makes *American Candidate* less democratic than *American Idol*. (*People* 2004)

In the world of "reality" television, of course, as in politics itself, "democratic" doesn't mean "attractive," just as formal democratic processes like the vote don't necessarily result in freedom for all voters. However, it is clear that the same urge that drives political activists to make the democratic process as transparent and open as possible also motivates the plebiscitary format on television. It's an urge to move away from representative and toward direct democracy. Yet to be faced are the problems associated with getting what you wanted, including a democratic process that produces "unworthy" winners like singers who can't sing or candidates with reprehensible views.

Mirror, Mirror on the Wall, Which Is the Purest Plebiscite of Them All?

Big Brother

Big Brother, now legendary in television terms, remains the purest of the "reality" television plebiscites, because viewers vote for (or rather against) contestants on the basis of what Martin Luther King Jr., called "the content of their characters." Musical or other talents, no matter how dubious, are not the criteria for survival or success. In short, *Big Brother* is a polity.

Claims of "political disengagement" are frequently made by political scientists in the language of crisis, and it is usually said to be the voters, particularly younger citizens, who are disengaged from politics. People are blamed for failing in their civic obligation to engage with the democratic process. But Stephen Coleman (2003) suggests that an alternative perspective on the question of political disengagement would put the boot on the other foot. Political elites and agencies have moved away from the citizen, who is nevertheless still the root of democracy. In this scenario it would be very unwise to assume that "the demos" is disengaged from democracy. Instead, the formal apparatus of politics and government has disengaged from it.

Coleman identified declines in voting rates, in participation in broader political activities such as joining political parties, and in watching news and reading newspapers (particularly political commentary). He also found that people's trust in politicians, to represent the public interest ahead of party, fell. Most respondents, but particularly those under thirty, showed low faith in the efficacy of government, particularly in its legal or formal capacities or activities (Coleman 2003).

While these figures seem to suggest a drift away from politics, they may in fact indicate that people want to participate, but there's limited access to a democratic machine that responds to their desires. One indicator that people are willing to vote (and even pay for the privilege) is, of course, plebiscitary television. The numbers who "vote early and vote often" for *Big Brother* do not suggest disengagement but rather that *Big Brother* provides them with an activity and a mechanism that inspires them to participate in elections.

Does it follow that those who do vote in "reality" television shows are interested only in mundane or trivial things? No; Coleman's study suggests that young people are interested in mainstream political issues but not participating in mainstream political processes. Their participation in *Big Brother* votes is driven by a different mode of engagement. Coleman suggests that those who vote in *Big Brother* employ a form of emotional intelligence to assess candidates. Four general features were admired:

- honesty
- the ability to get on in the world
- cleverness
- people who are witty and amusing

Honesty emerged as a predictive quality, especially when it related to perceived authenticity: those who were seen as honest were generally considered to possess an authenticity, and they were usually not voted out. The qualities of politicians were compared against the same scale. The same hierarchy applied to them. Again, consistency of values was not as important as honesty.

Voting in *Big Brother* measures contestants' achievement on an emotional scale rather than by assessing natural talents, as in programs such as *Idol* or

Dancing with the Stars, where the relative merits of an individual performance can be judged against others. However, one of the attractions of *Dancing with the Stars* is to follow the embarrassments and improvements of those who—like many of the audience at home—can't dance very well. Thus, good dancers are often eliminated before celebrities who can't dance but are "up for it" when it comes to trying. In other words, emotional attachment, authenticity, and honesty pay off even in talent-based plebiscites.

The failure of a German re-version of *Big Brother* suggests that the plebiscitary aspect is itself a key element in the entertainment. German broadcaster RTL 2 announced plans to produce *Big Brother: The Village*—a version that conceivably might never end (Koehl 2004; McGuinness 2005). It was touted as an open-ended reality soap opera. The set-up involved the construction of an entire village, segregated into class regions, featuring living quarters and workplaces. Participants were to live in the town "indefinitely." Launched in March 2005, the program was cancelled in November because of low ratings. This echoes the failure of the Fox program *Forever Eden* in May 2004, which had similarly been touted as a conceivably never-ending reality soap opera (Fienberg 2004).[21] While *Big Brother: The Village* offered a "€1 million" prize (*BBC News* 2005), the idea that the program was an ongoing soap opera rather than an electoral race that would come to a compelling conclusion may be seen as a contributing factor in its demise. Indeed, the thrill of voting has been claimed as part of the appeal of successful shows. Discussing the short window of opportunity *American Idol* voters have to cast their vote, Fox Networks Group President Tony Vinciquerra argued that the window "increases the excitement for the show" by offering participation in "the most democratic way—it's first come, first served" (Higgins and Seibel 2004).

"So What if He Wore a Leotard?"

Celebrity Big Brother
Politics and reality television were literally "con-fused" when a British Member of Parliament entered the *Big Brother* house for the fourth series of *Celebrity Big Brother* in January 2006. George Galloway, MP for Bethnal Green and Bow in London, already had a colorful reputation as a politician, having been a Labour MP in his native Scotland. He was expelled from the Labour Party in 2003 for his opposition to the Iraq War, but won the London seat in 2005 for "Respect" (an alliance based on the Socialist Workers' Party), defeating high-profile Blairite MP Oona King (one of the United Kingdom's few black MPs) by eight hundred votes. Galloway was a long-term supporter of the Palestinian cause and had a strong track record as a firebrand speaker "on the anti-

imperialist left," supporting Pakistani claims in Kashmir and taking an interest in Libya and the Arab-Israeli conflict. His notoriety became global when he was accused of benefiting from the U.N. oil-for-food program in Iraq and appeared in front of a U.S. Senate committee in 2005 to deny the corruption allegations. Video of him meeting Saddam Hussein and his son Uday also circulated around the world.

Meanwhile, Galloway's performance as a voting parliamentarian was minimal. As Respect MP since 2005, he had the lowest possible voting record, being placed 634th out of 645 MPs. The eleven with lower voting records than himself were five Sinn Fein members (who don't take their seats), the Speaker and his two deputies (who are ineligible to vote), two members who had died, and the Prime Minister.[22] During *Celebrity Big Brother*, his sequestration in the BB house meant that he missed at least one vote in the House of Commons that directly concerned his own constituency.

It is clear from his views, his career, and his voting record that George Galloway had little respect for traditional politics. He claimed that his sojourn in the BB house was an attempt to reach young people who were otherwise disengaged from politics, to speak up for Palestinian people, and to raise funds for a Palestinian charity. But it was not George Galloway the politician and philanthropist whom viewers saw on *Celebrity Big Brother*; it was Galloway the narcissist and egoist. As with any other version of *Big Brother*, it was not his views or his intentions that interested viewers; it was his conduct and interaction with the housemates, which the newspapers agreed was "gripping and appalling in equal measure." His housemates variously described him as a "manipulative bully"; "two-faced"; "unworthy of respect"; "a wicked, wicked, wicked man"; and "as democratic as a Nazi" (Kelbie, 2006: 3).

Galloway's antics included various fancy-dress charades, provoking not only astonished reactions among viewers but also apoplectic articles in the following day's newspapers. He dressed up as Dracula and Elvis, did an impression of a cat lapping pretend milk from actress Rula Lenska's hand, and donned a scarlet leotard to complete a task set by Big Brother: Galloway and transvestite singer Pete Burns (of the 1980s band Dead or Alive) were told to express "the emotions of bewilderment when a small puppy won't come to you" through the medium of robotic dance (see picture).

Soon after this, real voting took over, and Galloway was evicted. *The Sun* was gleeful, even vengeful: "Is this most hated man in Britain?" it asked (26 January 2006) and sought to answer its own question in the affirmative:

Galloway...was last night booted out of the house to a chorus of jeers as:

Young viewers he had hoped to attract by his participation in the show railed against him.

A Radio 1 poll about his antics showed 92.5 listeners despised him.

Hordes of his constituents in Bethnal Green and Bow, East London, said they regret-ted backing him....

More than 25,000 *Sun* readers have now signed our petition calling for Galloway to be suspended from the Commons (*Sun*, 2006: 4–5).

George Galloway MP and housemate Pete Burns express "emotions of bewilderment" on *Celebrity Big Brother* (U.K.), January 2006. Picture supplied by WENN; used with permission.

Here were subsidiary plebiscites in the press and on radio to supplement the reality plebiscite on *Celebrity Big Brother* that had all-too-evidently been taken more seriously than Galloway's own parliamentary vote or his constituency voters.

Was this a gain for democracy? Writing in *The Observer*, Nick Cohen lam-basted the "liberals who think it's worse to appear on a TV show than in the court of a fascist tyrant" (15 January 2006, 11). Tim Gardam, former director of television at Channel Four, wrote in the *Evening Standard*: "Big Brother is the great leveller; and Celebrity Big Brother has shown once again its true democratic virtues; one might argue that it is one of the most effective current affairs programs on television" (19 January 2006, 39). As former head of current affairs for the BBC and controller of news for Channel Five, Gardam was in a position to judge. He wrote:

> In its first series, more people voted for the housemates than had just voted in the Scottish, Welsh and London mayoral elections combined. In 2002, class war broke out as the house was segregated into rich and poor. Last year, as the housemates divided along ethnic lines, it laid bare the incipient racism that lies not too far from the surface of modern Britain. And now it has succeeded where the Labour Government, the U.S. Congress and the Daily Telegraph have all failed. It has allowed George Galloway to destroy himself. (*Evening Standard*, 19 January 2006, 39)

Galloway felt it necessary to "conduct a highly orchestrated media offensive" to restore his standing with his constituents. *The Independent* reported that "despite an avalanche of negative publicity and polls suggesting plummeting popularity in his constituency, the Bangladeshi community of Whitechapel appeared fairly unperturbed by the politician's three-week stint on *Celebrity Big Brother*" (27 January 2006, 5). Even so, when asked "if he was glad he had done the show, Galloway replied: 'Well not after I've seen those press cuttings'" (*Independent*, 26 January 2006, 3).

The power of the plebiscite was felt among the parliamentary and pundit classes, but its real achievement in this series of *Celebrity Big Brother* had nothing to do with George Galloway. The eventual winner was not a celebrity at all but a "once unknown Essex girl" named Chantelle Houghton, who had been planted in the house by Big Brother to con the housemates that she was a celebrity, too. In this she succeeded, so she was allowed to stay. At the end she outpolled all the "real" celebrities and naturally became one herself the instant she emerged from the house. *The Guardian* commented: "Though nobody in the crowd dared say it, they knew they were taking part in a new peak for reality television. When storylines emerge like Chantelle's everyone must see why the master dramatists...number among Big Brother's more vocal fans" (*Guardian*, 28 January 2006, front page).

Reality television had reduced dramatists to fans; the plebiscite had made a celebrity where there was not one before. Soon a Chantelle look-alike (a copy of the fake who won anyway) was on the prowl (www.thisishertfordshire.co.uk/display.var.687334.0.0.php). Channel Four basked in ratings glory:

> The fourth series of *Celebrity Big Brother* proved to be a ratings success, with Friday's

show attracting 7.5 million viewers, not to mention enormous media coverage. Sharon Powers, executive producer of the show, said: "This series has had everything—moments of jaw-dropping amazement, moments where you wanted to scream at the television, moments of high drama and utter hilarity."

(www.thisishertfordshire.co.uk/news/borehamwood/display.var.683353.0.big_brother _mania_strikes.php)

Part V: The Plebiscite Goes Industrial

That Obscure Object of Choice

Across the world, various pay-television operators have included a plebiscitary button on the remote control. Shows like *Sky News* run instant polls every day on some topical issue, and the results become part of the show they're watching. The pleasure of the vote is now a business plan in its own right. Opinion.com.au (Australia) offers people a place to vote on pretty much anything: "Did you see the Jude Law penis photos before they were censored?," and "What is ur opinion of brazillian ppl? [sic]—for which the two voting options are: "never met one" and "their ok" [sic]. The purpose of the site seems to be merely to vote.[23] Other voting sites are more traditional in their political focus, for instance, Vote.com (U.S.). Meanwhile, online petition sites like Petitiononline.com encourage petitions on politics and government, entertainment and media, environment, religion, and technology and business. The most active sites include those petitioning to bring back loved but cancelled television shows, like *Arrested Development* and *Dead Like Me*.

There is a new format of television reality show based on the plebiscite, where viewers can choose the "greatest" person or "favorite" object in a category. The BBC seems to be a lead player in this game. In 2002 they ran a series of television documentaries on the *Top Ten Great Britons*, a list that was itself derived from a top hundred nominations by 30,000 people. Each episode of the series was introduced by a celebrity "champion" of the nominee. Viewers were then invited to vote on "the greatest" of them all:

The Top Ten Great Britons (and their champions) were:

Nominee	Votes	Percentage	Champion
Winston Churchill	456,498	(28.1%)	Mo Mowlam
Isambard Kingdom Brunel	398,526	(24.6%)	Jeremy Clarkson

Diana, Princess of Wales	225,584	(13.9%)	Rosie Boycott
Charles Darwin	112,496	(6.9%)	Andrew Marr
William Shakespeare	109,919	(6.8%)	Fiona Shaw
Isaac Newton	84,628	(5.2%)	Tristram Hunt
Queen Elizabeth I	71,928	(4.4%)	Michael Portillo
John Lennon	68,445	(4.2%)	Alan Davies
Horatio Nelson	49,171	(3%)	Lucy Moore
Oliver Cromwell	45,053	(2.8%)	Richard Holmes [24]

The format has proven to be both portable and versatile. The Discovery Channel shortlisted the twenty-five greatest Americans. No surprises there, but an online poll conducted for BBC television's *What the World Thinks of America* (June 2003) received over 37,000 votes—nearly half of them for Homer Simpson. The BBC felt constrained to warn viewers: "Results are indicative and may not reflect public opinion."[25]

Who is the Greatest American?

Homer Simpson	47.17%
Abraham Lincoln	9.67%
Martin Luther King, Jr.	8.54%
Mr. T	7.83%
Thomas Jefferson	5.68%
George Washington	5.12%
Bob Dylan	4.71%
Benjamin Franklin	4.10%
Franklin D. Roosevelt	3.65%
Bill Clinton	3.53%

37,102 Votes Cast

The BBC also ran an egghead version of the idea, receiving 34,000 votes in a radio poll to discover the "Greatest Philosopher." The winner was Karl

Marx with 28 percent of the vote, followed by Hume, Wittgenstein, Nietzsche, Plato, Kant, Aquinas, Socrates, Aristotle, and Popper—five Germans, three Greeks, an Italian, and an economist (no one from outside Europe; no women). Elsewhere, you could vote for the best PM of India, or find out who was "elected" as the greatest Czech of all time (Charles IV).[26] In 2004, the CBC received 1.2 million votes for the greatest Canadian (someone named Tommy Douglas).

In April 2003, the BBC featured *The Big Read*. ABC (Australia) ran a television special along the same lines in December 2004 called *My Favourite Book*, featuring a National Top 100 (and 10) and a Kids' Top 10. While the same book, JRR Tolkien's *Lord of the Rings*, topped the BBC and both adult and children's ABC lists, there was criticism of the ABC show in *The Age* and at Crikey.com. The criticisms demonstrated common responses to the plebiscite, commenting on the scrupulousness of the method, the size and composition of the "electorate," and the height of its collective brow.[27]

But the BBC, at least, is not to be put off. It is a plebiscitary serial offender. Without even mentioning sport, you can vote for:

- the best opening and closing sequences from a cult show
- your favorite sitcom
- your favorite Top Screen Scientist
- best *Blackadder* episode
- the hottest burning issue on *EastEnders*[28]

All of this activity suggests that voting is something of a craze. The idea that there might be such a thing as purposeless voting, or voting for pleasure, does not go down well in political science, where it is generally seen as a sort of work, or at least a duty, rather than play. However, the plebiscitary industries have discovered that people like to vote and are providing them with plenty of opportunities to do so. Scorning that as pointless is perhaps to miss the point. It is doubtful whether people really expect instrumental outcomes, for instance, to a petition to bring back a favorite show, but that doesn't stop tens of thousands of them from going online and voting—often leaving detailed comments about why they're doing it. So, just as people use magazines, television, and even the news itself as an accompaniment to the rhythms of everyday life, they're also using the plebiscite to put on public record what they think about this and that. It's quite possible that as time goes on, the craze will decline, although places with the most people—China and India—seem the least jaded in this respect.

In the meantime, it is important not to dismiss voting for pleasure as inconsequential—or worse—without first trying to identify why such activities are popular. An example of counterintuitive meanings in this regard might help. Nobody in their right mind would label go-karting or paintball battles as "democratic practices." However, a recent report from Iran showed how young people in that country are using these pastimes precisely to get away from its heavily regulated "public sphere." Go-karting is popular, for instance, because it allows the sexes to mix, and this is seen as "defiance of the religious men who run the country" (Woodruff 2006). Bearing this in mind, beware critical complaints that people doing what they like doesn't amount to democracy. At best it's merely demotic, they say (see Turner 2006); at worst it's a simulacrum that authoritarian regimes seek to install in place of the real thing (Victor 2005). Despite such criticism, it is still a good idea to ask what it is that people like to do, just in case they're on to something. It's politics, Jim; but not as we know it.

Toward Direct "DIY" Participation in "Reality"

The *human appeal* of voting in the digital age has been developed first not by political but by marketing and media specialists. They have both popularized and monetized it through various plebiscitary formats in "reality" television and elsewhere for their own commercial purposes, by the use of interactive media that can instantly convert individual choice into measurable scale. So the "plebiscitary industries" have stolen a march on many more directly political uses of the same technologies, which tend to be supply-driven, top-down, earnest, and unpopular.

However, commentators from the political side of the fence have begun to take notice and are seeking to import the human element back into the democratic process itself. Popular politics has something to learn from popular media. E-democracy advocates seek new ways to engage citizens and gauge public opinion via interactive media (Coleman 2003). The relationship between the plebiscitary industries and the democratic process is now the subject of intense interest on both sides of the political/entertainment divide.

The democratic credentials of content distribution based on a mere *representation* of the audience (no matter how scientifically achieved) may now be questioned and even rejected. Jason Mittell, stung by the cancellation of his favorite show, writes:

> Ratings are seen by many in the industry as the site of viewer democracy, as people vote with their eyeballs what shows they want to watch and what they avoid. But Nielsen ratings are less like voting than like exit polling (and if exit polls were the measure of democracy, hello President Kerry!)—people cannot choose to participate in Nielsen ratings, and Nielsen only measures a miniscule fragment of the television viewing population. Unless you're in one of the 5,000 households who comprise the bulk of

Nielsen's sample, your viewing habits (along with 99.995% of all other viewers!) simply do not register within the media economy—hardly a participatory democracy. (Mittell 2005)

Mittell's vision of the future is to invoke the idea of the *passionate* consumer rather than the numerous (but passive) ones, suggesting that advertisers will want to reach opinion leaders and early adopters in the field of content (including educators such as himself), just as they do in technology. The endpoint is for consumers to become the producers not only of content but also of programming:

The basic structure of the commercial television industry using ratings as central currency is in crisis in the wake of new technologies and an active participatory youth audience that refuses to watch television solely on networks' own terms. A sizable, motivated, and demographically desirable audience...awaits the advertisers and distributors who are willing to buck the centrality of ratings as determinant of television's hits and misses. Can the industry change the terrain of broadcasting by asking not "who's watching what?" but "how are people watching?"... By only investing in the traditional currency of ratings, networks ignore the multitude of ways that viewers are already actively engaging with their programs, and forego the option for people to actually participate in the selection of television programming that they want to see. (Ibid.)

Jonathan Gray (2005) commented on this issue:

I find it amazing and sad, too, that while the networks, cable channels, and cable and satellite companies constantly try to convince us that what they offer is democracy in action (the logic being that the choice of what to watch is the choice over human destiny), there is so little consumer outrage about the crudeness of this supposed democracy's voting system.

This is where the plebiscite comes into its own. It can be both a response by traditional broadcasters to the challenge of consumer activism and passionate choice, and a potential way forward for the reform of "consumer democracy" in the creative industries. Do you like the idea? Vote now!

Notes

[1]See en.wikipedia.org/wiki/Metaphysical_poetry; also enjoyment.independent.co.uk/ music/features/article221903.ece for a recent discovery that shows how the metaphysical poet John Donne may in fact have been a popular songwriter—"yoking by violence together" the long-assumed opposition between intellectual high-end poetry and popular music with a wide (and female) fan base—an early example of politicotainment, perhaps.

[2] I would like to acknowledge the assistance of Dr. Joshua Green in the preparation of this paper and to thank him and Jean Burgess for the conversations in which we developed some of the ideas. (Would that we had written them down at the time.)

[3] Any list would be indiscriminate because it represents a pervasive quality among journalists and editors rather than a scarce category.

[4] In his *Politics*, Aristotle (7.4) confined the size of a state governed by direct democracy to "the largest number which suffices for the purposes of life, and can be taken in at a single view." Some representative democracies do retain elements of direct democracy—two prominent contemporary examples being the state of California and the Confederation of Switzerland, both of which use plebiscites to decide specific issues of policy on a regular basis. Many other countries use referenda as well as general elections. But the overwhelming majority of nation states are governed representatively; plebiscites are the exception.

[5] See en.wikipedia.org/wiki/Swingometer; the swingometer is still in use in U.K. elections (by Peter Snow). Originally a piece of cardboard with an arrow attached, it has been digitally jazzed up by the BBC.

[6] Toby Miller, who in most of these matters is a critical skeptic, has coined the term "citsumer" for the amalgam of citizen and consumer (Miller et al. 2001, 178–181).

[7] Timbl's blog is at dig.csail.mit.edu/breadcrumbs/blog/4.

[8] See Valerie Lawson's write-up in *The Age* (Melbourne), 30 October 2004: www.theage.com.au/ articles/2004/10/29/1098992287790.html?from=storyrhs; and www.imdb.com/ title/tt0266186/ for the IMDb entry on *Search for a Supermodel*.

[9] *Big Brother* is plebiscitary in most of its national formats, the one exception being the U.S. version, where housemates themselves vote to evict housemates. In all other versions, housemates nominate each other for eviction, but viewers vote them out.

[10] See: www.nostalgiacentral.com/tv/variety/thankyourluckystars.htm; see also members.lycos.co.uk/foive/ (Janice's own website); www.retrosellers.com/features26.htm(interview); and www.nostalgiacentral.com/tv/variety/jukeboxjury.htm.

[11] See: www.eurovision.tv/english/611.htm.

[12] See: www.digame.de/ (in German)—the service provider for Eurovision televoting; and see www.redwoodtech.com/applications/televoting.asp.

For how to vote see www.eurovision.tv/english/2035.htm.
Televotes cast for the 2004 Eurovision Song Contest by country:

Andorra	3,003
Albania	812
Austria	284,902
Bosnia & Herzegovina	95,062
Belgium	76,123
Belarus	16,204
Cyprus	117,751
Germany	1,061,049
Denmark	136,769
Estonia	34,615
Spain	39,005
Finland	45,952
France	54,495
United Kingdom	415,558
Greece	192,564
Croatia	40,220
Ireland	36,998
Israel	14,297
Iceland	46,310
Lithuania	19,627
Latvia	40,453
Monaco	110
FYR Macedonia	47,599
Malta	12,392
Netherlands	158,559
Norway	81,278
Poland	72,295
Portugal	8,597
Romania	11,698
Russia	96,955
Serbia & Montenegro	20,909
Slovenia	61,844
Switzerland	503,627
Sweden	294,828

Turkey	121,008
Ukraine	4,323
Total countries	36
Total calls	4,267,791

Source: www.eurovision.tv/english/1182.html.

[14] See www.telescope.tv/americanIdol2.html for details.

[15] See, for instance, archives.cnn.com/2000/ALLPOLITICS/stories/11/16/recount.chads/.

[16] See www.telescope.tv/americanIdol2.html.

[17] See www.chinadaily.com.cn/english/doc/2005-08/12/content_468543.htm; see also www.danwei.org/archives/002149.html and www.danwei.org/archives/002157.html for Danwei's take on the show. Danwei is produced in Hong Kong and hosted in the United States. See also www.danwei.org/archives/002322.html (unexpected product spin-off); and www.hollywoodchina.motime.com/post/491066 (a spoof item applying Super Voice Girl type SMS voting to Sino-Taiwanese situation). A good roundup of commentary from many sources on "Super Girls and Democracy" can be found at zonaeuropa.com/20050829_1.htm.

[18] One of Li Yuchun's prizes was to be invited to London to join Lord Mayor Ken Livingstone to celebrate Chinese New Year and "the largest celebration of Chinese culture" in London by lighting giant red lanterns over Oxford Street and performing to a "large crowd" of shoppers (*People's Daily*: english.people.com.cn/200601/27/eng20060127_238672.html).

[19] McDonald reports figures for estimated number of viewers and the number of contestants that conflict with other reports. (They're significantly lower.)

[20] See also American Candidate at *Reality Blurred*, www.realityblurred.com/realitytv/archives/american_candidate/.

[21] See also Forever Eden at *Reality Blurred*, www.realityblurred.com/realitytv/archives/forever_eden/.

[22] See: en.wikipedia.org/wiki/George_Galloway.

[23] See also Hot or Not, www.hotornot.com/ and Australian site Hottest On TV: www.hottestontv.com.au/.

[24] See: www.bbc.co.uk/history/programmes/greatbritons.shtml.

[25] See: dsc.discovery.com/convergence/greatestamerican/greatestamerican.html; news.bbc.co.uk/1/hi/programmes/wtwta/2997144.stm.

[26] See www.cbc.ca/greatest/; www.bbc.co.uk/radio4/history/inourtime/greatest_philosopher_vote_result.shtml; sify.com/itihaas/top10.php?cid=13385804; www.radio.cz/en/article/67495.

[27] See www.telescope.tv/americanIdol2.html for details.

[28] See www.bbc.co.uk/cult/classic/titles/best/vote.shtml?configfile=vote/best/votecontrol.xml; www.bbc.co.uk/sitcom/winner.shtml; www.bbc.co.uk/cult/scientists/beakerhoneydew.shtml; www.bbc.co.uk/comedy/blackadder/vote/; www.bbc.co.uk/eastenders/haveyoursay/vote/vote_hub.shtml.

References

The Age (Melbourne). 2005. "Dancing Controversy." 17 March. www.theage.com.au/news/TV--Radio/Dancing-controversy/2005/03/16/1110913657005.html (accessed 19 December 2005).

Aristotle. 350 B.C.E. *Politics.* Internet Classics Archive, Web Atomics. classics.mit.edu/Aristotle/politics.7.seven.html.

Barboza, David. 2005. "Hunan Television Cancels the Bland to Bring the Offbeat to China." *International Herald Tribune,* 27 November.

BBC News. 2005. "German Big Brother to End Early." 30 November. news.bbc.co.uk/1/hi/entertainment/4484726.stm (accessed 28 December 2005).

Berners-Lee, Timothy. n.d. *timbl's blog.* dig.csail.mit.edu/breadcrumbs/blog/4 (accessed 22 December 2005).

BitTorrent Inc. n.d. "What Is BitTorrent?" BitTorrent website—FAQ. www.bittorrent.com/introduction.html (accessed 19 December 2005).

Boykin, Keith. 2004. "I'm Not a Presidential Candidate...." *The Crisis* 111(5): 54.

Caves, Richard. 2000. *Creative Industries: Contracts Between Art and Commerce.* Cambridge, MA: Harvard University Press.

Coleman, Stephen. 2003. *A Tale of Two Houses: The House of Commons, the Big Brother House and the People at Home,* London: The Hansard Society.

——. 2005. *Direct Representation: Towards a Conversation Democracy.* London: Institute for Public Policy Research (ippr exchange). Available online at www.ippr.org.uk/ecomm/files/Stephen_Coleman_Pamphlet.pdf.

Curtin, Michael. 1995. *Redeeming the Wasteland: Television Documentary and Cold War Politics.* New York: Rutgers University Press.

Economist. 2005. "Democracy Idol." 9 October. 376(8443): 42.

Fienberg, D. 2004. "No Closure for Truncated FOX Shows." *ZAP2IT,* 20 May. tv.zap2it.com/tveditorial/tve_main/1,1002,271|88327|1|,00.html (accessed 28 December 2005).

Franklin, Nancy. 2004. "See How They Run; On Television." *The New Yorker,* August, p. 100.

Graham, Chad. 2004. "The Other Presidential Race." *The Advocate* (921): 49–50.

Gray, Jonathan. 2005. "Why ACNielsens Aren't Invited to My Birthday Party." Comment in response to Mittell (2005). jot.communication.utexas.edu/flow/?jot=view&id=1354. (accessed 20 July 2006).

Green Left Weekly. 1992. "Money for Crud." July, 1(61). www.greenleft.org.au/back/1992/61/61p5can.htm (accessed 22 December 2005).

Hartley, John. 1999. *Uses of Television.* London and New York: Routledge.

——. 2004. "The 'Value Chain of Meaning' and the New Economy." *International Journal of Cultural Studies* 7(1): 129–141.

——, ed. 2005. *Creative Industries.* Oxford: Blackwell.

Higgins, John M., and Seibel, Deborah Starr. 2004. "American Idol vs. Speed Dialers."

Broadcasting & Cable, 24 May, p. 1.

Jakes, Susan. 2005. "Li Yuchun: Loved for Being Herself." *Time Asia*, 2 October. www.time.com/time/asia/2005/heroes/li_yuchun.html (accessed 20 December 2005).

Kelbie, Paul. 2006. "The Voters Decide: Galloway is Evicted from 'Big Brother' to Face Public Ridicule." *The Independent* (London), 26 January: p. 3.

Koehl, Christian. 2004. "'Big' Plan Has No End; In Latest Skein, Residents Filmed in Studio 'Hood." *Daily Variety*, 18–19 October. www.variety.com/article/VR1117912141?categoryid=18&cs=1.

Lawson, Valerie. 2004. "The Very Model of Super." *The Age* (Melbourne), 30 October, sec. A2, p. 3.

Leadbeater, Charles, and Miller, Paul. 2004. *The ProAm Revolution*. London: Demos.

Li, Yu. 2005. "What Is 'Supergirl?'" *Legal Mirror* (China), 8 August. bj.ynet.com/view.jsp?oid=6200618 (accessed 19 December 2005). Translated at Danwei: www.danwei.org/archives/002157.html.

Macartney, Jane. 2005. "TV Talent Contest 'Too Democratic' for China's Censors." *Times* (London), 29 August, p. 25.

Marquand, Robert. 2005. "In China, It's Mongolian Cow Yogurt Super Girl." *Christian Science Monitor*, 29 August, p. 1.

Martinsen, Joel. 2005. "The Meaning(lessness) of 'Super Voice Girl.'" *Danwei*, 29 August. www.danwei.org/archives/002157.html (accessed 28 December 2005).

McDonald, Hamish. 2005. "Pop Culture Grabs Limelight." *The Age*, 29 August, p. 9.

——, and Agence France-Presse (last paragraph only). 2005. "Pop Singers Give New Range to Cultural Democracy." *The Sydney Morning Herald*, 29 August, p. 8.

McGuinness, Damien. 2005. "German Big Brother to Run and Run." *BBC News*, 7 March. news.bbc.co.uk/1/hi/entertainment/tv_and_radio/4318943.stm (accessed 20 December 2005).

Miller, Toby; Govil, Nitin; McMurria, John; and Maxwell, Richard. 2001. *Global Hollywood*. 1st ed. London: British Film Institute.

Mittell, Jason. 2005. "An Arresting Development." *Flow* 3(8). http://www.flowtv.org (accessed 20 July 2006).

New York Times. 2005. "FX Drops Plans for a Candidate Show." 3 May.

People. 2004. "American Candidate." August, p. 40.

Pesce, Mark. 2005. "Piracy Is Good? Hyperdistribution and the New Laws of Television." *Mindjack*, 13 May. www.mindjack.com/feature/piracy051305.html (accessed 19 December 2005).

Royal Commission on the Press. 1948. *Minutes of Evidence, 26th Day*. London: HMSO.

Schudson, Michael. 1998. "Changing Concepts of Democracy." In *Democracy and Digital Media Conference*. Cambridge, MA: MIT. web.mit.edu/m-i-t/articles/schudson.html (accessed 28 December 2005).

——. 1999. *The Good Citizen: A History of American Civic Life*. Cambridge, MA: Harvard University Press.

Seibel, Deborah Starr. 2004. "American Idol Outrage: Your Vote Doesn't Count." *Broadcasting & Cable*, 17 May, p. 1.

Spigel, Lynn, and Curtin, Michael, eds. 1997. The Revolution Wasn't Televised: Sixties Television and Social Conflict. New York: Routledge.

Sun. 2006. "BB Says Good Riddance To Britain's Most Hated Man." *The Sun*, 26 January, pp. 4-5.

Taylor, Nelson Sofres. n.d. "Television at the Tipping Point." The Shape of Things to Come. TNS Corporate Website. www.tns-global.com/ corporate/Rooms/DisplayPages/ LayoutInitial?Container=com.webridge.entity.Entity[OID[46727FE6F335574EACECBAF 0255573A4 (accessed 22 December 2005).

Torres, Sasha. 2003. Black, White, and in Color: Television and Black Civil Rights. Princeton: Princeton University Press.

Turner, Graeme. 2006. "The Mass Production of Celebrity: 'Celetoids,' Reality Television and the 'Demotic Turn.'" International Journal of Cultural Studies 9(2): 153-65.

Victor, S. 2005. "Democracy Comes to China! (Well, Actually just for Mongolian Cow Yogurt Super Girl)." *The Apostate Windbag*, 12 October. http://apostatewindbag.blogspot.com/ 2005/10/democracy-comes-to-china-well-actually.html (accessed 6 January 2006).

Woodruff, Bob. 2006. "Go-karts, Paintball Appeal to Young Iranians: Country's Youth Stand in Contradiction to Hardline Government." ABC (USA) *World News Tonight*, 3 January. http://abcnews.go.com/WNT/story?id=1467301&CMP=OTC-RSSFeeds0312 (accessed 6 January 2006).

Yardley, Jim. 2005. "The Chinese Get the Vote, if only for 'Super Girl.'" *New York Times*, 4 September, p. 4.3

The Politics of Cultural Production: The Journalistic Field, Television, and Politics

GÖRAN BOLIN

T he dominant view of the transformation of the European television system over the last couple of decades seems to be that there has been a clear and steady shift toward commercialization, trivialization, and fragmentation of content and, following from that, a fragmentation of the viewership into niche audiences. The general take on the causal chain of development has been similar: because of the commercial financing of television production, broadcasting companies tend to regard viewers as customers rather than citizens (cf. Syvertsen 2004). Consequently, the argument goes, these broadcasters will target the lowest common denominator of audience demand, and this desperate search for audience attention (Ang 1991) will inevitably result in an increase in entertainment and light factual programming in order to reach audiences to sell to advertisers.

When the European public-service monopolies encountered commercial competitors on the television market, they adapted to the situation either through competition with the commercial companies over audiences and broadcasting rights (to sports events, for example), or through the creation of distinctive corporate images accompanied by a concentration on programming not provided by their competitors. Irrespective of the strategy taken in this competitive situation, the evaluation of its results by television critics and scholars has most often been negative: the television landscape as a whole has become increasingly dominated by entertainment, reality shows, and docu-soaps. Axiomatic to this evaluation of the development of television is that this is bad, and that it has been detrimental to public knowledge (Brants 1998; cf. Corner 1991).

The increase in entertainment and reality television programming is often seen as having evolved at the cost of neglect on the part of the television producers of high-quality journalism. Serious journalism, political debates, current affairs programs, and other fora where politicians as well as citizens and journalists can discuss matters of common interest are today seen as yielding to entertainment settings, or as having to adjust to rules set by the commercial media who, according to Pierre Bourdieu (1996/1998), increasingly demand "fast thinkers" who can fill space on talk shows and comment on most every topic, and the production of "omnibus" television—television programming that does not shock anyone, is not controversial, does not annoy, and is supposedly of universal interest. An additional cost of this programming is that people who rely solely on television as their source of information are deprived of access to the means to act as enlightened citizens.

The empirical facts behind this historical description are hard to deny. The fact that there has been an enormous increase in the amount of available television programs and channels to choose from, and the subsequent fragmentation of the audience into niche audiences, is well established and has been demonstrated by numerous empirical studies (e.g., Reimer 1994). That current affairs programs and interviews and debates with and among politicians and political commentators (most often journalists, sometimes political scientists) have been increasingly fragmented and reduced to soundbite journalism is also empirically well established (e.g., by Esaiasson and Håkansson [2002] in Sweden).

Admittedly, there are those who have tried to re-evaluate this development and point to the possibility that entertainment might strengthen the basis for an active, critical citizenry, or at least might engage citizens in public discourse. Liesbet van Zoonen (2005) has, for example, argued for the rejuvenation of citizenship and the possible increase in political knowledge of the democratic process in light of the growth of popular culture in general and television in particular. She argues that fiction series such as *The West Wing* and the increasing adjustment of politics to narrative forms laid out by the popular media actually can function in an inclusive way for audiences, turning them into responsible citizens. These arguments are based in opposition to the so-called "public knowledge project," which has been labeled by John Corner (1991, 268) "the popular culture project," and which stresses "the implications for social consciousness of the media as a source of entertainment, and is thereby connected with the social problematics of 'taste' and of pleasure."

It is not my task here to argue against the historical description of the development of European television. Neither shall I side with any of the parties in the normative public knowledge-popular culture debate outlined schematically above. What I wish to do, however, is to present an alternative view of the causal argument and make a case against the perception that commercial entertainment and reality television programming have marginalized journalism and political debate. I will propose that it is in fact the other way around and suggest that it is the growing autonomy of the field of journalism that has led to the fact that the journalistic institution has colonized entertainment and incorporated televised popular entertainment in particular, as well as parts of other popular culture, into journalism, rather than as a sphere outside of and in competition with it. I will do this against the background of the situation in Sweden, since this is the media sphere where I can claim expertise. I believe, however, that this is a general tendency in journalism and entertainment that can also be extended beyond the boundaries of Sweden and thus is valid for many other countries in the Western world. There will naturally be variations in details, and perhaps Sweden is extreme in this respect (although I suspect not). To the extent that I can find evidence in accounts from other parts of the world, I will try to point it out.

In order to support my argument about the growing dominance of journalism over entertainment, I will proceed as follows. In the first section I will introduce my analytical model and at the same time describe the historical context for the examples that follow. These examples concern live television programs: entertainment shows, morning television, and factual programs such as election-night programming. It must be stressed that my interest is in those programs that play on liveness and on producing a reality effect by broadcasting "things as they happen"—those programs that are at the crossroads between fact and entertainment. The liveness component of these programs is one of the important qualities for the construction of reality as a genre (if that concept could be used), or the "constructed unmediation" of events in programs, as Misha Kavka calls the specific technique of documentation, and which arguably is a narrational practice derived from journalism aiming to produce in the viewer a sense of "seemingly *direct* transmission" (Kavka 2005, 94, italics in original). The first two of my examples are entertainment programs. Although my third example—election nights—is probably not thought of as entertainment, I will try to show that these specific programs are in fact narrationally structured in the same way as entertainment programs. I will try to show that because of the circumstances of production, this in fact makes them approximate to one another when it comes to program form.

Admittedly, there is a fair amount of academic attention (e.g., Holmes and Jermyn 2004; Andrejevic 2003) given to reality shows that broadcast "unscripted, on-stage footage of crime and emergency services" (Hill 2005, 8), as well as to other programs in which people act together in an unscripted way in specific settings, such as *Big Brother*, *Paradise Hotel*, etc. And there is an equal amount of attention given to the phenomenon in the general culture debate (Biltereyst 2004). These are, however, not the kinds of programs that I will focus on in this chapter. I will rather take on a discussion of live television productions. The reason for choosing to analyze live television is, as I will try to show, that this is the sphere of production in which narrative and aesthetic components from news and other factual programming most obviously blend with features from entertainment and fiction. What I will concentrate on in those programs are those occasions when politicians appear in less politically formal ways in live entertainment talk shows or game shows. My point is that the presence of politicians on those occasions has implications for real-life politics (and in that capacity *is* real-life politics). And although this phenomenon is not new to the same extent as "docusoaps" are, it is possible to observe an increased presence of politicians in entertainment or "light" factual programming.

In the second section I will give an account of the rise and establishment of the journalistic field. I will argue that the phenomenon of politicians in entertainment settings could be seen as connected to a wider and more general shift in the power relations in Western society, among the sphere of politics, economy, and the media, over the last couple of decades. As has been argued by, for example, Jan Ekecrantz and Tom Olsson (1994) in a study of twentieth-century Swedish journalism, there has been an obvious shift in the status of what they call the "journalistic institution" in society, where, to an increasing extent, journalism has become engaged in producing discourses that are active in "the construction of societal models, within which both the present and the future are defined" (Ekecrantz 1997, 410).

Against the background of these shifts in power relations between media, politics, economy (and the academy), I will, in the third section, discuss some empirical examples from both entertainment and factual live television production, where politicians appear. I will then end with some remarks on the relationship between journalism and entertainment.

Changes in the Power Structures of European Television Production

The power structures that are characteristic of television production are naturally closely related to the way in which television production is organized. The most fundamental difference in this respect is between the systems of public-service and commercial television. In contrast to the United States and other parts of the world, Europe did not adopt a commercial system for broadcasting, either for radio or television, when the broadcast media were introduced. (For an account, see Brants and De Bens 2000, 8ff.). With the re-regulation of European television from the mid-1980s and onward, commercial competitors gradually came to challenge the public-service broadcasters. This has led to the present situation, where there are both strong public-service companies (although obviously not as strong as previously) *and* strong commercial broadcasters.

The fundamental difference between the systems of production could, with the inspiration of a model from Pierre Bourdieu (1996), be described as a relation between different fields of power in society.[1] Analytically, it is naturally possible to divide society into many different kinds of power fields, or spheres, at different levels. For the purposes of this chapter, it is sufficient to take four such major fields into account: the economic, political, cultural, and academic power fields. Characteristic of each of these is the fact that they are relatively autonomous in relation to one another. This is because the value at their core differs: for the economic field, for example, money is the most important value, while cultural prestige is more important within the field of cultural production. The relations between the fields of power are schematically illustrated in Figure 1.

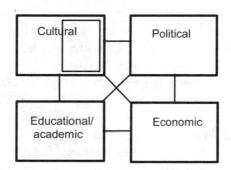

Figure 1. Outline of the relations between the fields of power.

The autonomy of a field is always relative: no field exists in isolation. Hence, all fields in the above figure are connected to one another. High autonomy rather indicates the strength of the value at the center of the field, and also how it is recognized as a value in other fields.[2] A symbolic capital, or value, produced within a field of advanced autonomy is recognized by all other fields of power in society. Money and wealth, the consecrated value form within the sphere of the economy, is of course legitimate within other fields: it is recognized as a value and can be used or converted in other fields. Academic prestige is also widely recognized and lends the holder of high academic credentials certain respect in the economic field as well (although it will not be as strong as it is within the field where it is produced, that is, within the academy). Likewise, political authority is recognized in other fields, and politicians can therefore count on being respected in other contexts than the parliament and other institutions in the field of political power. This also means that the value can be converted into a value that is effective in another field. To take a recent example, one could point to the event where Swedish Prime Minister Göran Persson received an honorary doctorate from Örebro University on the grounds that he had promoted the former college to a university. Thus, he could benefit from his position in the field of political power and also be recognized within the academic field by receiving a sign of respect and legitimacy therein (the title of "Doctor").

This example, however, also points to another characteristic of the relations between the fields of power, and it is a clear sign of the relative status of their autonomy. Not surprisingly, there was a debate after this elevation of the prime minister to doctor's status. One explanation of the critique leveled at both Örebro University and the prime minister is that the conferring of the degree too obviously revealed the mechanisms of conversion of capital between spheres (the exchange of one form of capital into another). Another explanation of a related phenomenon—that the prime minister actually was accused of bribery—is that it too obviously revealed the dependency of the academic field on the field of political power. All fields strive toward autonomy, and to admit to being dependent on another field for the consecration of value becomes a sign of weakness for a field. In this respect, the event revealed the weakened status of the field of knowledge production within the academy, which could explain the intense debate.

Now, if we leave the relations between the fields of politics and the academy and engage exclusively in the field of cultural production, we can start by describing this field as the one in which cultural objects, artifacts, and values are produced, among which are television programs. The field of cultural production is structured along two axes: at the north pole of the field—if the cartographical analogy can be accepted—we can find production that is considered legitimate. (Illegitimate culture can be found at the south pole.) To the west we find production aimed at a restricted market; in its most extreme form this means production for other producers. This is the part of the field where art is produced for its own sake (l'art pour l'art). To the east we find cultural production aimed at a large-scale market (mass production). The most prestigious cultural production, then, can be found in the north-west corner of the field. These are the consecrated and recognized artists of their age, those who may have started from a lower (but still westerly) position as an avant-garde who have challenged the canon but now have risen to respectable status. It is characteristic of these artists that they seldom acquire widespread recognition during their lifetimes, when they are found within the subfield of restricted production, but rather may become popular in posterity (and popular not only among other artists, but also among the general public).

To the east we find mass-produced culture (journalism, popular literature, music, film) spread over a range of different media technologies, of which television is the focus of this chapter. This is represented by the smaller square within the field of cultural production. However, there are obvious differences between television productions of various kinds. It seems, for example, hard to compare an episode of *Expedition: Robinson* (the Swedish version of *Survivor*, broadcast from 1997 onward) with one episode of *The Singing Detective* (1986). These two series will be assessed and valued differently by television critics, academics, politicians, cultural debaters, etc. If discussed academically, for instance, *The Singing Detective* will provoke a focus on the text as a "work" and a piece of art, or on the author according to auteur theory (e.g., Creeber 1998; Cook 1995/1998), while *Expedition: Robinson* is unlikely to be recognized for its director, but rather for its status as indicative of trends in society or as a popular phenomenon (what it does to those who watch it). Although both are produced for a large-scale market, they have different degrees of legitimacy in the field of cultural production.

As with all other fields in society, the field of cultural production is not altogether autonomous, and this is especially so for the sub-field of large-scale production. This is the sub-field in which success is measured in economic terms, in contrast to the sub-field of restricted production, where success is measured by recognized artistic quality—a value that stands in *opposition* to the economy (cf. Bourdieu 1993). This means that the capital accumulated within the sphere of restricted production is more autonomous within the field than the economically dependent symbolic capital that is produced within the sub-field of large-scale production. This is illustrated by the closer proximity of the sub-field of large-scale cultural production to the field of the economy in Figure 1.

Now, I have not chosen my television examples randomly—I wish them to exemplify a complication connected to television production in the model under discussion. Television deviates from other kinds of large-scale production (popular novels, records, film, computer games) because not all television production, however large-scale in kind, aims at producing economic value. This is because there are two basic kinds of television production—commercial and public-service—of which only commercial television production aims at producing economic surplus value. And, as expected, public-service television usually is on the winning end when it comes to artistic and journalistic quality and legitimacy if judged by the prizes and awards given (at least in Europe), that is, if judged by the consecrating institutions within the field. It is therefore not surprising that the BBC, the producing and distributing organization behind *The Singing Detective*, is part of the artistic success behind the series. This is in fact congruent with the theory. However, if we consider the fact that one of the forerunners of the docusoap explosion in Sweden was *Expedition: Robinson* (the Swedish version of *Survivor*), produced and broadcast by the public-service organization Swedish Television (SVT), this seems to fit more loosely into the field model. The explanation for this is, however, public service's reliance on political rather than economic capital, since the economic conditions for the production of the show are not set by the market but by political decisions (license fees). Thus we can conclude that large-scale television production is only semi-autonomous if considered as a sub-field within the field of cultural production. Where commercial production is mostly reliant on the economic field of power, public-service production is reliant on the political field of power (their production being regulated by license agreements with the state). And as such, it seems as though the combination of political values with cultural production is more effective when seen from the perspective of accumulation of symbolic capital within a field of production, than when seen from the perspective of the combination of economic values and culture. This is the case as long as the political values are not accompanied by censorship or direct state control. (Propaganda is hardly ever prestigious as art, although there are examples from the early Soviet Union in the works of certain filmmakers, painters, and poets.)

If the above argument can be agreed upon, and I have tried to lay out some evidence for this in greater detail elsewhere (Bolin 2004), it can then be generally concluded that there have been two kinds of change in the power relations involved in television production over the last couple of decades. On the one hand, there are changes external to television production, affecting it from the outside. These are the changes in dominance between the political and the economic power field. On the other hand, other kinds of changes have occurred within the field of television production, or, to be more precise, within the field of journalism. These are the changes dealt with in the next section.

From the Political Reign over Journalism...

One of the fundamental difficulties with Pierre Bourdieu's *Sur la télévision* (1996/1998) is its reception. Many of the critics of this short pamphlet have regarded it as a conservative evaluation of television as a destructive force in society, comparing it with traditional conservative critique (for examples, see Marlière 1998, Neveu 2005). In a way, this is to miss the point of the pamphlet entirely, and perhaps it is the book's title that has misguided its readers. If there is a weakness in Bourdieu's analysis, it is not so much its concentration on the ways in which economic power influences the field of cultural production, but on its relative neglect of the influences by the field of politics.

The most important conclusion drawn from his analysis is not so much that television has had an effect on the other fields of power, but rather that the autonomy of the journalistic field and its power to influence all other fields is increasing. This analysis is, however, not very detailed in Bourdieu's account, and it is necessary to elaborate on this theme a bit in order to understand how the field of journalism came into being and how it has become increasingly autonomous. Bourdieu can hardly be considered an expert on journalism as an empiricist, but if we adopt the model inspired by him and relate it to empirical work on the history of journalism, it is possible to grasp the emerging field and its growth over the last century.

The argument is, then, that the field of journalism has grown increasingly autonomous over the last couple of decades—in Sweden as well as in the Western world generally. In their analysis of the emerging Swedish journalistic institution, Jan Ekecrantz and Tom Olsson (1994) give an account of how journalistic reporting has changed from being information that took the form of telegrams sent to the newspapers and relayed to readers, to the active journalism that chooses which events to cover and which are not worth covering. This last form of journalism is, in the words of Ekecrantz and Olsson, "editing" society, that is, constructing society according to a systematic approach developed alongside the growing power of the journalistic "institution." As an institution, it is an organized practice with its own internal rules and norms, which are also naturalized and thus not reflected upon in the everyday doings of citizens or journalists (cf. Douglas 1987). In Sweden this occurred after the Second World War, although it occurred earlier in, for example, the United States and other nations (Hallin 2005, 229ff.). One component in the process of the growing power of journalism is the introduction of the journalistic interview. As Michael Schudson (1994) has shown, the interview started to appear at the end of the nineteenth century in the United

States. In Sweden it took somewhat longer for the interview to be introduced and established as a journalistic method. In the early days of journalism, newspapers were composed of incoming telegrams and announcements, by which followed that the journalists were tied to their desks and the editorial office. With the introduction of the interview, journalists started to work outside of the office, entering into the surrounding society and actively seeking out news. A consequence of this was that journalists increasingly gained control over the reality they set out to describe. One aspect of this was that journalists now played an active role in the selection of people to interview.

With the practice of interviewing also came the questioning of political and commercial authority, which led the way to the gradual move toward autonomy in relation to the state and market systems (Schudson 1994). Journalistic praxis in Sweden changed dramatically over the years, for example, in the ways journalists approached politicians. From the quite humble and devout approach of the early 1900s of addressing politicians by title or surname, the approach shifted at the end of the twentieth century toward being more offensive, with a more critical and questioning attitude toward those in power (cf. Ekecrantz 1997; Esaiasson and Håkansson 2002, 113ff.).

The relationship between journalists and politicians is indicative of this shift in power between the two spheres in society. From being the ones to relay political statements in early journalistic praxis, journalists have become constructors of political information. Alongside the growing control over content by journalists, a field of journalistic production has been established and is gradually becoming more and more autonomous. As with all autonomous fields, the journalistic field has managed to naturalize itself, to play down its own power status and the logic by which it operates. The ideology of objectivity that is central for journalism has also been the focus of several research accounts (e.g., Schudson 1978), and journalism's insistence on being in the service of its readers (or listeners, viewers), disguises the fact that what is published is an effect of the conditions within the field as such. And over the course of the 1900s, all other fields have to an increasing extent become affected by, and sometimes dependent on, the journalistic field of power (cf. Ekecrantz and Olsson 1994, 83).

A condition that has been held forth as specific to the Swedish journalistic field is the fact that newspapers from the start were heavily dependent on the political field of power, in the sense that many papers were run by, closely related to, or heavily dependent on political parties. As Jan Ekecrantz (2005, 99) has argued, the "autonomy of journalism vis-à-vis other institutions in society, including the political system, has grown successively over the last century. In relative terms the early dependence on the political *party* turned into a dependence on the *state*, later replaced by the *market*."

However, one must not confuse the fact that fields to a certain degree are dependent on economic capital with a lack of autonomy when it comes to value aggregation within the field, as, for example, Michael Schudson (2005, especially p. 219) does.[3] It is important to realize that all kinds of field autonomy are *relative*–the condition of having totally autonomous fields for economy, politics, culture, etc., would mean that society was altogether fragmented in non-communicating spheres isolated from one another. The growing importance of commercial financing and technological advancement when it comes to processes of production does not necessarily affect the internal value generation within the field. There are in fact strong indications that the forms of journalistic reporting reveal an "astounding lack of change in the media's representational strategies over the past 75 years" (Ekecrantz 2004, 44), although it is quite obvious that the conditions for engaging in those practices have changed dramatically. The ways of reporting seem to follow similar formal structures over the years, which indicates a high degree of autonomy when it comes to the production practices (although the content of reporting naturally can be affected). The growing autonomy of the field of journalism is, then, clearly connected to its institutionalization over the last hundred years, where the journalistic institution has developed consecrating instances such as prizes, formalized educations (in Sweden since the 1960s), ethical guidelines, etc.

A paradox concerning the doxa of journalism is its anti-academic ideology: although journalism training today has been integrated into the academy, there is a strong anti-academic tradition among both teachers and students of journalism. And, in fact, this is quite natural if seen from a perspective of a field of growing autonomy: it needs to be autonomous from the field of academic knowledge production in order not to become subsumed under it. In a similar way, the hostility that can be observed from the academy toward the journalists can be explained by the threat from the journalistic field of devaluing the capital within the field of the academy (cf. Bourdieu 1984/1990, 112).

This is why the journalistic ideal of objectivity is so important, as it prevents the journalistic value from being absorbed by other values. When journalists argue for the importance of describing events in society irrespective of their consequences, this is a sign of autonomy–this kind of reporting is only true to its own doxic belief in the value of objective journalism. The value produced within the field is news. And just as art is supposed to stand outside of moral, political, cognitive judgment in order to be discriminating within the field of cultural production, news as a pure value would stand at the center of the journalistic field. Each value at the center of a field needs to be "pure" and independent of all other values in that sense.

Having described the status of the journalistic field's growing autonomy and its relation to the economic and the political fields of power, leading— among other things—to possible interventions by journalism in these two fields of power, I will in the next section concentrate on showing how this applies to television entertainment and fictional programming in the early twenty-first century.

...to the Reign of Journalism over Politics and Entertainment

It might be good to keep in mind in the course of the following argument that although I will primarily discuss politics and politicians appearing in entertainment program genres, most appearances by politicians in television are in news programs, current affairs programming, etc. These are also the program genres most obviously dominated by journalists. This is true for the present as well as historically. It could be argued, however, that there has been an increase in the number of times in which politicians appear in light factual programming and in entertainment (more seldom in fiction). In this section, I will, on the one hand, try to trace this phenomenon back in history, and on the other, give examples from different kinds of programming. These examples will include politicians appearing on entertainment shows, politicians appearing in light factual television, and the growing influence of entertainment television on factual programming, with a focus on those light factual programs where politicians are involved (election-night coverage). I will primarily give examples from Swedish television. However, there is good reason to believe that Sweden is similar to the rest of the Western world in this respect, although there might be time lags in various areas.

Entertaining Politicians

So, if we are to go back in history to see when politicians started to engage (or started to become engaged) in television entertainment, we might go back to 1962, when Swedish Prime Minister Tage Erlander appeared as a guest on the legendary Saturday-night entertainment show *Hylands Hörna* (Sjögren 1997, 243). *Hylands Hörna* [Hyland's Corner] was hosted by Lennart Hyland, who had a long career to his credit as a sports journalist in the local press and, starting in 1945, as a radio reporter at Swedish Radio (Dahlén 1999, 220ff.).

Although his main interest seemed to have been sports, Hyland, as well as other journalists of his time, were all-round reporters, covering various kinds of news events. All through his career, which lasted well into the 1980s, Hyland upheld the task of being both a sports journalist and an entertainment talk-show host. In fact, as early as 1958, during the very first years of Swedish Television, the network sent Hyland on a journey to the United States to study television talk shows. This journey naturally had consequences for his style of running television shows throughout his career, not least in the quite visible influence of Jack Paar (Sjögren 1997, 242ff.).

When the prime minister appeared on the show in 1962, he accommodated himself to the entertainment setting by telling a joke. This has since affected expectations about how politicians should behave in television talk shows and in other light entertainment. The expected behavior has been to adapt to the entertainment format of the occasion, which makes it possible for politicians to appear in a less formal and serious manner—or even prescribes such behavior—partaking in games and quizzes, being interviewed about private life or early careers, giving personal anecdotes from political life, etc.

A variant of the above is when politicians are engaged to fulfill some kind of function in the show, such as assisting the host by giving prizes, etc. The broadcasting of a charity event is the typical occasion for such an appearance, where politicians sometimes are given the role of adding sincerity to the event and legitimizing it before presumptive donors. Lars Leijonborg, the leader of the Liberal Party in Sweden, once appeared on a TV4 charity show in 2003 to raise funds to reduce breast cancer rates, where he accompanied Swedish pop singer Lena Philipson on the piano.

When the politician acts in the capacity of an assistant to the program host, his role is much more formal than when he is being interviewed on a talk or game show. However, the appearance of the politician as assistant at times also focuses on his or her emotional engagement in the objective of the fundraising, and thus at times features actual visits to disaster areas. In this capacity, the politician has become a celebrity on a par with sports figures or actors, who also are often engaged for such charity events (sometimes displaying their commitment to the specific problem at hand). However, although the politician on those occasions has a function in the narrative of the show, he or she is also usually interviewed, if only briefly, by the host.

A Swedish entertainment show that has had politicians as guests on several occasions is the weekend entertainment game show *Bingolotto*, which has been broadcast on the "hybrid" channel TV4 since 1991, first on Saturday evenings and currently on Sundays.[4] The program was originally put together for local television in Gothenburg in order to raise money to support local sports clubs but soon became broadcast nationally. This was accomplished through the selling of bingo/lottery tickets. One third of ticket sales then went back to the sports clubs, which has meant that the sports movement in Sweden received around 1 billion SEK annually on average during the running of the program. Since the program has been beneficial for the maintenance of the economic standards of the sports movement in general, and youth sports in particular, the program has invited ministers on several occasions to take part in the game and to assist in the distribution of prizes. (For a fuller account, see Bolin 2002.)

Having Swedish Prime Minister Göran Persson appear on *Bingolotto* in 2001 for the tenth anniversary of the program's existence on national television, where he praised the program and the lottery for its support of national sports, is naturally a sign of high political legitimization, something of which the broadcaster obviously takes advantage (cf. Bolin 2002, 195; 2004, 283). And this has not been the only occasion where ministers have appeared: in the first program in the fall of 2005, Swedish Minister of Finance Bosse Ringholm appeared. On both occasions the ministers were asked about their personal engagement in sports and sports associations.

A special kind of interview setting for light factual or "infotainment" where politicians are often found is on the morning television shows—broadcast in the time slot between 5:30 and 9:30 A.M., and which "generally have the format of a magazine, and a basic structure of regularly repeated and updated news broadcasts" (Wieten 2000, 177). In between the news broadcasts there are interviews with experts in the studio: politicians, journalists, artists, researchers, etc. The hosts of morning television shows most often have a background in news journalism, and usually one of the hosts acts as news anchor at the news breaks, shifting position to the news desk. After the break for news, he or she returns to the sofa. (Lately this has changed, as the burden of shifting roles has become a problem for the journalists.) The characteristic pieces of furniture are the combination of the news desk and sofa surrounded by easy chairs, indicating the intimate relation between news formats and the morning television shows. For example, Swedish TV4 uses the same studio for morning television and ordinary news, the studio being permanently organized to suit both programs.

In Europe, breakfast television is quite recent and appeared only in the 1980s with the establishment of large-scale commercial television (Wieten 2000, 178ff.). Peter Dahlgren (1995, 56) explains the growing interest on the part of politicians in the fact that morning television "can be understood in part as a response to the shrinking sound bites they are allotted on the news programs." As a reaction to this, they would prefer morning television, since those shows provide politicians with "lots of public exposure, but also a setting in which they are hardly ever challenged with any difficult questions."[5] Some politicians have taken advantage of this more than others. Carl Bildt, former prime minister in the Conservative government from 1991 to 1994, was, for example, a frequent guest on the morning talk shows of both SVT and TV4—possibly a strategy to return to the unquestioned authority politicians had in relation to journalists in the beginning of the 1900s, when the field of journalism was less autonomous.

So, to sum up, we can see that within new formats of live entertainment shows, such as *Bingolotto* or charity events, politicians appear quite often. And although the phenomenon of politicians in entertainment settings is far from new, the number of such programs in which politicians appear has increased radically, providing new arenas for political action. These arenas are also qualitatively different from the traditional current affairs magazine settings, or news interviews. The hosts of the entertainment shows are often journalists or have a journalistic background. This is even more true when it comes to light factual entertainment such as breakfast television. Thus, we can see that there are quite a few journalists involved in what is usually labeled entertainment, and they bring with them journalistic practices such as the interview format, although here they are of a more subservient nature. But what can we say about programs traditionally thought of as factual, such as election-night coverage?

Entertaining Elections

Television's impact on opinion formation before upcoming elections has often been pointed out, both in Sweden as well as internationally (see, e.g., Esaiasson and Håkansson [2002] for a Swedish perspective, and several examples in Bennett and Entman [2001] for international, or at least Anglo-American, accounts). As argued above, however, it is not so much television as a technical medium that has been of importance, but rather the combination of the medium and the changed status of the journalistic field. One milestone in the relation between politicians and television journalists can be dated to the mid-1960s, when interviews with politicians before the upcoming elections were increasingly made by journalists (rather than being a debate between politicians). This fact is often pointed to in accounts of political communication and has been described as a revolution (e.g., Esaiasson and Håkansson 2002, 95ff.; Djerf-Pierre and Weibull 2001, 264ff.).

This is also the point in history when the composition of the staff at Swedish Radio changed. Originally, Swedish Radio staff were recruited from the academy, and they held doctorate or licentiate degrees. (The latter is a Swedish academic exam at a level between the Masters and Ph.D. levels.) Around the 1950s this changed, and the staff recruited to television and radio were primarily journalists with newspaper backgrounds. Furthermore, if we look at how executives were recruited, we can see that they were to an increasing extent recruited internally (Engblom 1998). All this was a classic development for a field moving toward autonomy, something that can be verified by other accounts of the history of Swedish radio and television, although not analyzed from a field perspective (e.g., Thurén 1997, 105).

This changed yet again with the introduction of interviewers from entertainment and light factual programs. This was first observed before the Swedish national elections in 1998. Most controversial in the cultural and public discourse was the action taken by TV4, which engaged the host of its entertainment show *Bingolotto* (together with a former union leader and a public relations consultant) to interview party leaders before the election. This is most often claimed to be in line with the trend to let the interviewers represent the voters, but it has also been explained by the fact that the medium of television privileges lighter entertainment, structured by the pace of "between-commercials-television" before lengthy arguments and analysis.

However, it is possible to see this not as a shift from journalists to celebrities and entertainers taking command over politics. It can, in line with my argument above, be seen as a diversification of the role of the journalists and also an expansion of the field of journalism, since the form of these programs is structured in line with the journalistic format. We can note that several things happened in the 1960s. First, journalists took command over the debates before elections, setting the conditions for the subsequent relationship between journalists and politicians, where the journalist became the active, interviewing component, and the politician the responsive interviewee who reacted to the questions posed by the journalist. Second, at about the same time, politicians started to appear in less formal settings where their roles as politicians and private individuals became blurred. These were also settings dictated by the media—and journalists. (Recall the background of Lennart Hyland.) And the predominant form of discursive interaction was the interview.

It is also important to stress that this development cannot be explained by the "commercialization thesis," since the change appeared long before the advent of commercial television in Sweden. Admittedly, Hyland (and other journalists) had been on trips to the United States to study commercial television programming, and it could of course be argued that the influences from commercial television set their mark on the Swedish, non-commercial, public-service television. But this is then a cultural influence, rather than an economic influence, and the changes cannot be attributed to the system of commercial funding as such. So, rather than with explanations in terms of political economy, which would hold that ownership and principles of funding would be decisive for the type of television programming privileged, this would have to be explained in terms of the growth of the journalistic field invading the field of entertainment television. This explanation does not contradict the fact that U.S. journalism has had an important cultural impact on Swedish television programming. It should rather be seen as strengthening the field thesis: since U.S. journalism was more autonomous, Swedish and other European journalists looked toward it for inspiration.

If we take a television genre such as election-night coverage, we can see how forms from entertainment as well as factual programs blend and create a structural sameness of entertainment and light factual television texts. Election-night programs are broadcast on the eve of an election day and consist of live coverage that follows the tallying of votes. During election nights there are political commentators (most often journalists and political scientists), politicians, ordinary voters, etc., in the studio, following the vote count and commenting on developments and the possible outcome of the election. There are also reports from the party headquarters where election workers and party officials are gathered to follow the proceedings. Election nights most often cover national elections but can also concern referenda such as whether a country should enter the European Monetary Union, as was the case in Sweden in September 2003. Although focused on national elections, and thereby being of concern primarily to national audiences, election nights seem to be structured in the same way in many countries, at least if judged from examples from the United Kingdom (Marriott 2000).

Since the re-regulation of the European television market, there have been at least two election-night broadcasts for each election in Sweden, one by Swedish Television (SVT) and one by the hybrid channel TV4. Both broadcasts have been narratively structured in a similar way, and TV4, as the newcomer to the field, has tried to "steal" viewers from SVT—at least the commercially valuable segment of the population.

Indicative of the shifting relations between journalists and politicians is that in the pre-election interviews with party leaders before the 2002 election, SVT had assigned two interviewers, one (male) political reporter and one (female) talk-show host with a background in journalism. Most often election nights work with two hosts, preferably one of each sex, who are assigned different but also typically gendered roles within the program. During the election nights, both commercial TV4 and public-service SVT gave the male host the function of delivering statistics and statistical commentary together with the political scientist,[6] addressing political questions of a factual kind, and relaying comments from the party headquarters—all from a typical news-desk setting. The female journalist interviews guests, celebrities, experts, and former politicians, often in more relaxed settings and often focusing on "softer" questions: "Nils Lundgren [of a newly founded political alternative party], is a former Social Democrat, and relatively known. How does that feel, Inger Segelström [also Social Democrat]?," asks SVT's female host, typically playing on the emotional side of the insinuated "betrayal" of the party line.[7]

There are features of the shows other than the hosting by male-female couples that are indicative of the approximation of form and content between live entertainment and factual television programs (the use of the same kinds of camera positions and movements, the similar use of steady-cams and cranes, lighting, etc.). It is also the case that there is no clear division of labor between the two macro genres when it comes to program production: producers, editors, set designers, etc., can and often do work with both kinds of genres, and they bring in production practices from one genre to the other, resulting in a common jargon for discussing character of programs, for example. In describing an election night, one project leader once stated that "an election is a four year long marathon—and we are broadcasting the finish."[8]

That (political) journalists use sports jargon when describing elections is not a new phenomenon but can be traced at least as far back as the 1950s. Shanto Iyengar, for example, describes the "effects of 'horse race' reporting" in terms of news stories "which have become a staple of campaign coverage, detail the candidates' electoral prospects—their poll standings, delegate counts, fund-raising efforts, and related campaign indicators—rather than the candidates' policy positions or personal characteristics" (Iyengar 1991, 134ff.). The sports jargon among the producers in my specific example can, however, also be ascribed to the fact that quite a few persons in the production staff, both at TV4 and SVT, have a background in producing sports television. New technologies have also made it possible to follow the development of the account for votes in detail minute by minute, which further aligns the narrative with the sports broadcast—or the entertainment contest. The way in which the votes are accounted for does not differ substantially from the way in which the national votes are presented in the Eurovision Song Contest (cf. Hartley in this volume, and Ericson 2002).

Conclusions

The above argument can be summed up in two major points explaining the increasing similarity, if not identity, of the textual forms of fact and entertainment. First, the approximation can be explained as an outcome of the increased streamlining of television production. The gradual professionalization of production means that producers adopt similar solutions to how they narrate in live productions. Since there is always a moment of unpredictability in live production, standardized practices reduce uncertainty in the production process. This fact accounts for the approximation between program *forms*.

Second, the shift in the relations between the economic and political power fields in society, as well as the growing autonomy of the journalistic field of production, has had a deep impact on television production, not only within the news and documentary genres but perhaps foremost within entertainment. It is therefore more accurate to say that journalism has expanded, diversified, and subsumed entertainment, than to claim the opposite. The above-described forms of reality and live television entertainment result from the growing autonomy of the journalistic field. This has spread to genres within television other than news in the process of autonomization of mass media production as a sub-field of the field of cultural production. This development is triggered by the growing autonomy of journalism as a specific part of the sub-field of mass cultural production and has led to the fact that other kinds of genre productions have become obedient to the structure and demands of the journalistic field.

It may be that Sweden is unusual when it comes to the development of the journalistic field in the way described above (although I doubt it). My descriptions have included some specific examples of increasing journalistic dominance over or influence in the field of entertainment. There are naturally other examples that can be referred to: the appointment of legendary news anchor Bengt Magnusson as the host for the Swedish version of *Who Wants To Be a Millionaire?* (incidentally the same Magnusson who used to be the male host for TV4's elections nights), to take another example from television. Indeed, it would be possible to extend the argument to other media forms, where journalists claim authority within spheres of cultural production not traditionally associated with journalists: the popular accounts of history by journalist Herman Lindqvist; the hugely popular fiction novels by journalists Jan Guillou and Liza Marklund, etc.; not to mention the area of "spin doctoring," largely created by journalists (cf. Turner 2004, 131ff.).

The fact that the proliferation of live television productions aiming for a "constructed unmediation" of events, of which political communication is one type, and reality genres generally, seems to be similar in many nations naturally triggers the thought that the journalistic practices that influence the form and structure of these programs are transnational, and that the field of cultural production in different parts of the world with minor variations are subjected to the same field logic. The rise and expansion of such formats, then, is not an example of the decline of journalism. It is the colonization of entertainment by journalism, and the strategy by which the journalistic field is naturalizing itself.

Notes

[1] Bourdieu theorizes this as one comprehensive power field in *The State Nobility* (1996), where the power field consists of the dominating positions *across* fields (that is, the power field consists of the sum of all the most elevated positions within each of the cultural, political, economic, etc., fields). All fields, however, are constructions made by the researcher in order to explain certain specific features of social reality. Fields, then, have specific functions in the analysis. For my purposes it is more productive to see the fields as power fields or fields of production, as this keeps the dynamic between the dominating and dominated positions in the field active.

[2] Consequently, a field of weak autonomy has a symbolic capital, or value, that is weak in the sense that it is hard to convert into other values, is not acknowledged within other fields, and does not provide its bearer (the individual agent) with any significant degree of distinctive power.

[3] This can most probably be ascribed to Schudson's mistaking the autonomy of the field with the autonomy of the individual journalist. It does not follow from the fact that a field has strong autonomy that the individual agents within it can act in any way they wish. On the contrary, it can be argued that fields characterized by strong autonomy circumscribe individual action more than fields with weak autonomy, since the institutions for judging and rewarding action are more powerful in the case of the former.

[4] A hybrid channel is commercially financed but has obligations similar to public-service companies through concessions in the channel's agreement with the state authorities. They thus occupy a position between public-service and commercial broadcasting (cf. Syvertsen 1996).

[5] Indeed, these occasions also involve risks on the part of the politician, as the expectations of sincerity in performance are higher for politicians in informal settings (Corner 2003, 79).

[6] Incidentally, both SVT and TV4 have hired political scientists from the same Political Science Department at Gothenburg University. It is also indicative that the older of the two (male) professors represents SVT, while the younger serves TV4. They have the same functions of commentators of the statistics and of giving historical substance and explanation for the figures presented.

[7] Election night for Swedish representatives to the European Parliament, 13 June 2004 (SVT1 + SVT2).

[8] Mikael Hake, project leader for election night, TV4, personal communication, 6 September 2002.

References

Andrejevic, Mark. 2003. *Reality TV: The Work of Being Watched.* Lanham, MD: Rowman & Littlefield.

Ang, Ien. 1991. *Desperately Seeking the Audience.* London: Routledge.

Bennett, Lance, and Entman, Robert M., eds. 2001. *Mediated Politics. Communication in the Future of Democracy.* Cambridge: Cambridge University Press.

Biltereyst, Daniel. 2004. "Reality TV, Troublesome Pictures and Panics: Reappraising the Public

Controversy Around Reality TV in Europe." In *Understanding Reality Television*, edited by Sue Holmes and Deborah Jermyn, pp. 91-110. London and New York: Routledge.

Bolin, Göran. 2002. "In the Market for Symbolic Commodities. Swedish Lottery Game Show 'Bingolotto' and the Marketing of Social and Cultural Values." *Nordicom Review* 23(1-2): 177-204.

——. 2004. "The Value of Being Public Service. The Shifting of Power Relations in Swedish Television Production." *Media, Culture & Society* 26(2): 277-287.

Bourdieu, Pierre. 1984/1990. *Homo Academicus*. Cambridge: Polity.

——. 1993. *The Field of Cultural Production. Essays on Art and Literature*. Cambridge: Polity.

——. 1996. *The State Nobility. Elite Schools in the Field of Power*. Cambridge: Polity.

——. 1996/1998. *Om televisionen*. Stockholm/Stehag: Brutus Östlings Bokförlag Symposion.

Brants, Kees. 1998. "Who's Afraid of Infotainment?" *European Journal of Communication* 13(3): 315-335.

——, and De Bens, Els. 2000. "The Status of TV Broadcasting in Europe." In *Television Across Europe*, edited by Jan Wieten, Graham Murdock, and Peter Dahlgren, pp. 7-22. London: Sage.

Cook, John. 1995/1998. *Dennis Potter: A Life on Screen*. Manchester and New York: Manchester University Press.

Corner, John. 1991. "Meaning, Genre and Context: The Problematics of 'Public Knowledge' in the New Audience Studies." In *Mass Media and Society*, edited by James Curran and Michael Gurevitch, pp. 267-284. London: Edward Arnold.

——. 2003. "Mediated Persona and Political Culture." In *Media and the Restyling of Politics*, edited by John Corner and Dick Pels, pp. 67-84. London: Sage.

Creeber, Glen. 1998. *Dennis Potter—Between Two Worlds: A Critical Reassessment*. Basingstoke: Macmillan.

Dahlén, Peter. 1999. *Från Vasaloppet till Sportextra. Radiosportens etablering och förgrening 1925- 1995*. Stockholm: Stiftelsen Etermedierna i Sverige.

Dahlgren, Peter. 1995. *Television and the Public Sphere. Citizenship, Democracy and the Media*. London: Sage.

Djerf-Pierre, Monika, and Weibull, Lennart. 2002. *Spegla, granska, tolka. Aktualitetsjournalistik i svensk radio och TV under 1900-talet*. Stockholm: Prisma.

Douglas, Mary. 1987. *How Institutions Think*. London and New York: Routledge.

Ekecrantz, Jan. 1997. "Journalism's 'Discursive Events' and Sociopolitical Change in Sweden 1925-1987." *Media, Culture & Society* 19(3): 393-412.

——. 2004. "In Other Worlds. Mainstream Imagery of Eastern Neighbors." In *News of the Other. Tracing Identity in Scandinavian Constructions of the Eastern Baltic Sea Region*, edited by Kristina Riegert, pp. 43-70. Göteborg: Nordicom.

——. 2005. "News Paradigms, Political Power and Cultural Contexts in 20th Century Sweden." In *Diffusion of the News Paradigm 1850-2000*, edited by Svennik Høyer and Horst Pöttker, pp. 93-104. Göteborg: Nordicom.

——, and Olsson, Tom. 1994. *Det redigerade samhället. Om journalistikens, beskrivningsmaktens och det informerade förnuftets historia*. Stockholm: Carlssons.

Engblom, Lars-Åke. 1998. *Radio- och TV-folket. Rekryteringen av programmedarbetare till radion och televisionen i Sverige 1925–1995*. Stockholm: Stiftelsen Etermedierna i Sverige.

Ericson, Staffan, ed. 2002. *Hello Europe! Tallinn Calling! Eurovision Song Contest 2002 som mediehändelse*. Mediestudier vid Södertörns högskola 2002:3. Huddinge: MKV.

Esaiasson, Peter, and Håkansson, Nicklas. 2002. *Besked ikväll! Valprogrammen i svensk radio och TV*. Stockholm: Stiftelsen Etermedierna i Sverige.

Hallin, Daniel. 2005. "Field Theory, Differentiation Theory, and Comparative Media Research." In *Bourdieu and the Journalistic Field*, edited by Rodney Benson and Erik Neveu, pp. 224–243. Cambridge: Polity.

Hill, Annette. 2005. *Reality TV. Audiences and Popular Factual Television*. London and New York: Routledge.

Holmes, Su, and Jermyn, Deborah, eds. 2004. *Understanding Reality Television*. London and New York: Routledge.

Iyengar, Shanto. 1991. *Is Anyone Responsible? How Television Frames Political Issues*. Chicago: University of Chicago Press.

Kavka, Misha. 2005. "Love 'n the Real: or, How I Learned to Love Reality TV." In *Spectacle of the Real: From Hollywood to Reality TV and Beyond*, edited by Geoff King, pp. 93–103. Bristol: Intellect Books.

Marlière, Philippe. 1998. "The Rules of the Journalistic Field. Pierre Bourdieu's Contribution to the Sociology of the Media." *European Journal of Communication* 13(2): 219–234.

Marriott, Stephanie. 2000. "Election Night." *Media, Culture & Society* 22: 131–148.

Neveu, Erik. 2005. "Bourdieu, the Frankfurt School, and Cultural Studies: On Some Misunderstandings." In *Bourdieu and the Journalistic Field*, edited by Rodney Benson and Erik Neveu, pp. 195–213. Cambridge: Polity.

Reimer, Bo. 1994. *The Most Common of Practices. On Mass Media Use in Late Modernity*. Stockholm: Almqvist & Wiksell International.

Schudson, Michael. 1978. *Discovering the News. A Social History of American Newspapers*. New York: Basic Books.

——. 1994. "Question Authority: A History of the News Interview in American Journalism, 1860s-1930s." *Media, Culture & Society* 16: 565–587.

——. 2005. "Autonomy from What?" In *Bourdieu and the Journalistic Field*, edited by Rodney Benson and Erik Neveu, pp. 214–223. Cambridge: Polity.

Sjögren, Olle. 1997. *Den goda underhållningen. Nöjesgenrer och artister i Sveriges radio och TV 1945–1995*. Stockholm: Stiftelsen Etermedierna i Sverige.

Syvertsen, Trine. 1996. "TV2 i Norge 1992-1995. Strategi och programpolitikk i en moderne hybridkanal." In *Nordisk forskning om public service. Radio och TV i allmänhetens tjänst*, edited by Olof Hultén, Henrik Søndergaard, and Ulla Carlsson, pp. 61–78. Göteborg: Nordicom.

——. 2004. "Citizens, Audiences, Customers and Players: A Conceptual Discussion of the Relationship Between Broadcasters and their Publics." *European Journal of Cultural Studies* 7(3): 363–380.

Thurén, Torsten. 1997. *Medier i blåsväder. Den svenska radion och televisionen som samhällsbevarare och samhällskritiker*. Stockholm: Stiftelsen Etermedierna i Sverige.

Turner, Graeme. 2004. *Understanding Celebrity*. London: Sage.

Wieten, Jan. 2000. "Breakfast Television: Infotainers at Daybreak." In *Television Across Europe*, edited by Jan Wieten, Graham Murdock, and Peter Dahlgren, pp. 175–197. London: Sage.

Zoonen, Liesbet. van 2005. *Entertaining the Citizen. When Politics and Popular Culture Converge.* Oxford: Rowman & Littlefield.

CHAPTER FOUR

Faking Democracy:
Reality Television Politics on
American Candidate

MARK ANDREJEVIC

T he television section of *USA Today* greeted the fifteenth anniversary edition of MTV's long-time reality series *The Real World* by applauding its move to Philadelphia, a city famous for the signing of the Declaration of Independence and as the home of the Liberty Bell: "What better place to celebrate the 15th season of MTV's revolutionary reality show *The Real World* but in the cradle of American democracy?" (Wloszczyna 2004). This reception by "America's newspaper" reflected the common-sense association of reality television with democratization that came to characterize the genre in its post-*Survivor* boom period.

Those who made the attempt to move beyond describing reality television in terms of audience voyeurism on one hand and exhibitionism on the other noted the genre's kinship with the enhanced interactivity fostered by the Internet era. As a researcher for *American Demographics* put it, summarizing the results of an audience survey, "The popularity of this format with youth also has a lot to do with their growing up in a democratized society, where the Internet, Web cams and other technologies give the average Joe the ability to personalize his entertainment" (Gardyn 2001, 39). The ready assimilation of personalized entertainment to political democratization via interactive media is a recurring theme in the celebratory neo-libertarian musings of writers like Virginia Postrel (who equates the "variety revolution" with consumer empowerment) and in the glib enthusiasm of the promoters of what Dan Schiller (1999) has called "digital capitalism." At its crudest, the democratic promise of mass customization conflates participation in marketing to ourselves with power sharing.

Folding reality television into the mix has led some critics and pundits to discern in the genre's persistent and global popularity evidence of a universal yearning for participatory democracy. Regardless of whether reality television caters to a universal drive for democratization, it apparently caters to a desire on the part of the pundits to perceive it as the people's genre—thereby toeing the publicity line drafted by producers. The chairman of the company that brought the popular reality show *Big Brother* to the United Kingdom, Peter Bazalgette, received widespread news coverage for his claim that reality television might serve as model for boosting public interest in the political process—suggesting that the British House of Commons would benefit from secret voting and regular online votes "to make Parliament more interactive" (Hinsliff 2003). Following the ratings and voter-turnout success of *Big Brother*, Bazalgette was appointed in 2003 to the Conservative Party's Commission for Democracy in order to, as one rather disparaging news account put it, "see if he can get people to vote for politicians as eagerly as they vote for TV trash" (Hanks 2002).

The next step, given Hollywood's passion for literalizing its metaphors, was perhaps inevitable: if reality television is the people's medium—a model for the democratization of entertainment—why not take it as a model for making democracy itself more entertaining and thus, presumably, engaging? In 2004 and 2005, three political reality shows were introduced—one each in Australia, Great Britain, and the United States—that featured a political competition, voting, and the selection of a winning candidate by viewers. In each case, the premise of the show was that the winner could draw on prize money and public exposure to mount a political campaign, although the U.S. version eventually switched the timing of the show to make it impossible for the winner to meet the ballot deadline.

In each case, the stated objective of the producers was to jump-start political engagement by drawing on the popularity of reality television. As political documentarian R.J. Cutler, the producer of the U.S. show *American Candidate*, put it, the show "has a very high civic objective in mind, which is to get people engaged in the process" (Goodale 2004, 11). The end result turned out to be less than inspiring: *American Candidate* failed to generate more than a half-hearted buzz and fared poorly in the ratings. The candidates fielded by both versions of *Vote for Me* did run for office but made hardly a dent in the election returns, with the British candidate finishing not only far behind the winner but also behind a candidate who called himself Lord Toby Jugg of the Monster Raving Looneys (Freeman 2004). Given the results, it would be hard to make the case for the significance, in its own right, of a show like *American Candidate*, despite the fact that it was for the most part an intelligent, well-constructed, and even engaging series.

The notion that interactive entertainment might serve as an emergent model for information-age democracy, however, provides some suggestive, perhaps fresh, angles of approach to the question of the relation between politics and entertainment in an era of digital de-differentiation—one in which interactivity promises (or threatens) to rearrange the boundaries between leisure and labor, advertising and content, as well as politics and consumption. The announcement of *American Candidate* generated more media commentary than the show itself, leading to a set of reactions that, taken together, trace the horizon in which a savvy skepticism toward the artifice of contemporary politics combines with a naïve faith in the virtues of "behind-the-scenes" access. Drawing on press accounts as well as interviews with participants and producers, the remainder of this chapter relates the elusive promise of democracy via interactivity to a critique of contemporary politics that emerges in the responses to *American Candidate* by pundits and politicians. In the end, the chapter rejects the reality television model of democracy, suggesting that the self-conscious reflexivity of the genre—its insistence on behind-the-scenes access as a guarantee of authenticity—goes too far in the direction of savvy debunkery and concedes the equation of politics with pure spin. A fascination with the more "authentic" reality behind the political façade can run the danger of undermining the efficacy and usefulness of the façade itself. The result is a paradoxical combination of generalized skepticism ("behind their fancy words, they're all liars, just out for themselves") that defaults to an apparently "unsavvy" faith in gut instinct ("but I can see into this one's heart"). After outlining a critique of reality-television democracy, this chapter closes with a consideration of how the savvy reflexivity modeled by reality television manifests itself in contemporary U.S. politics.

Tele-revolution?

The revolution will not be brought to you by Xerox
In four parts without commercial interruptions...
The revolution will not make you look five pounds
thinner, because the revolution will not be televised.

—Gil Scot-Heron

The revolution will be televised.

—American Candidate Website

Before exploring the relationship between reality television and the logic of the digitally enhanced, interactive, mass-customized economy, it's worth parsing the elements of the genre that allow the promise of democratization to emerge as what Chad Raphael (1997) describes as its "master trope." The two most obvious elements are, of course, the fact that the genre symbolically throws open the gates of celebrity to (selected members of) the masses, and that some formats incorporate viewer participation via voting and feedback. The promise of access goes hand in hand with that of shared control: by turning their shows over to the unscripted antics of selected audience members, producers claim they are relinquishing some of their accumulated control over media content. The symbolic transfer of control is made more explicit in shows that incorporate audience voting. The trappings of democracy, such as they are, underline the role played by viewers in guiding the course of a television show, thereby (ostensibly) making it their own. As Julie Chen, the host of the U.S. version of *Big Brother*, put it during her address to the audience during the finale of the first season, "Your participation made this a truly interactive show. You changed the lives of ten people." The promise of shared control embedded in this "we-all-did-it-together" finale illustrates the deployment of interactivity as a strategy for capitalizing on the viewer's productivity by getting them to perform the work of marketing to themselves, a strategy perhaps best illustrated by another successful interactive show, *American Idol*.

The promise of democratization is reinforced by reality television's association with the buzzword of the digital revolution: interactivity. Against the background of the emerging information economy, reality television isn't simply an isolated trend; it might be described as *the* programming genre of the interactive era. It deploys the same promise: flexible, inexpensive production based in part on the contribution of consumer labor. As will become evident in the discussion of *American Candidate*, producers rely on cast members not just as a cheap source of content, but to promote the show. Reality television offloads production duties onto selected members of the audience at a time when producers need to fill a growing programming schedule even as the advertising pie is increasingly subdivided. To the extent that these duties can be portrayed as glamorous or desirable—even educational—their cost can be held down.

Thus, the buildup of the culture of celebrity over the course of the twentieth century has a specific payoff for producers in the twenty-first. The construction of a privileged, rarefied sphere from which the masses are excluded allows access to the realm of celebrity to serve as a form of compensation in itself. The reward is based in large part on what Nick Couldry (2000) describes as the common-sense understanding "that the media world is somehow better, more intense than 'ordinary life' and that media people are somehow 'special'" (45). Just the promise of being on television can be used to recruit inexpensive labor from the audience ranks—often for little or no additional payment.

Blame or credit for this source of cheap labor doesn't belong solely to society's worship of celebrity culture. It is of a piece with the marketing of interactivity as participation in the digital era. The hallmark of cyber-celebratory rhetoric is the equation of feedback with empowerment. As Celia Pearce, author of *The Interactive Book*, puts it, "No matter which way you look at it, interactivity is inherently subversive" (1997, 244), presumably because its very premise is "one of intellectual, creative and social empowerment"(1997, 183). It is not hard to find a chorus of such claims in both the popular and academic literature on new media—claims that reinforce some of the more celebratory versions of audience activism that equate participation with empowerment. Henry Jenkins (2001), for example, has concluded that "on the whole, cyberspace will do more to foster true democracy than the old media did"—a bold claim indeed, considering the role played by the rise of print culture in the politics of the Enlightenment and subsequent democratic revolutions (see, for example, Habermas 1991; Eisenstein 1968; Carey 1995).

It is in this celebratory climate of the interactive "revolution" that the democratic promise of reality television takes root. Surely the trappings of democracy are crucial, as is the promise to throw open the doors to celebrity/political culture, but these are further reinforced and vindicated by broader claims regarding the subversive and empowering character of interactivity. If television can be blamed for degrading the political process, interactive television might be able to heal the wounds it has inflicted on the body politic. When producer R.J. Cutler announced his plans for *American Candidate*, which underwent several permutations before airing, he described it in one press account as an end run around the barriers of access to the political process. The goal, he said, was to open up political participation "to those who don't have access to the process" (Cook 2004). At the same time, the show would, according to Cutler, tap into the inherent drama of the political process, drawing in viewers and voters. The outcome—along with the response by politicians and pundits to Cutler's experiment—are the topics of the following section.

Mr. Murdoch Goes to Washington

The attempt to merge reality television and politics went through several incarnations before appearing in perhaps its least ambitious and most stripped-down version. Early on, producer R.J. Cutler announced plans to work with premium cable channel HBO to cultivate a candidate with presidential ambitions for the 2012 presidential race—enough lead time to skirt media regulations regarding promotions for political candidates, but perhaps too much for the attention span of the typical production deal. Subsequent changes shortened the time horizon and reformulated the show as a "people's choice" contest to select a viable candidate for the 2004 U.S. presidential election. The fact that the show had been picked up by Rupert Murdoch's FX cable channel prompted semi-serious speculation about the political ambitions of his network's handpicked candidate. In the end, FX pulled out of the project, and it appeared in its final iteration on the smaller network Showtime as a mock presidential election. The candidates were "real" people chosen from an applicant pool open to the general public, but the timing of the show was changed to run alongside the real campaign rather than in preparation for it. Candidates would compete not for a chance to run for president, but for the title of "American Candidate" and free air time to make a political speech—after the real nomination process had been completed but before the actual election.

The version of the show that garnered the most media publicity was the one that was never produced: the version that would have selected an "outsider," people's-choice candidate for president. It's fair to say that publicity surrounding this version of the show is responsible for the pre-production buzz that went into promoting the final, albeit substantially changed version. Generating preliminary audience interest meant pitching the show as a stepping-stone to the presidency, and Cutler emphasized at the time that "we will be making available to every American who is qualified, the opportunity to run for president" (de Moraes 2002). The idea was provocative enough to generate a flurry of speculation and pontification, either applauding the show as a latter-day experiment in Jacksonian democracy, or critiquing it for further trivializing the political process. Culture critic Roger Ebert (2002) speculated that the candidate who stood to lose the most from a reality television campaign launched by Murdoch's right-leaning media empire was George W. Bush. Calling the show "dangerous mischief," Ebert predicted that "Rupert Murdoch, who owns FX and quickly ascertains which way the wind is blowing, will bring it down with a thunderous oath, probably later this week."

FX did indeed back away from the project, citing costs and logistics, and mooting the question of whether Murdoch's connections in the world of conservative politics were concerned about the prospect of a reality television challenger to the president. The show was picked up by Showtime, a premium cable channel with a limited subscriber base of 13 million homes (only a fraction of the 85 million homes reached by FX) and fewer concerns about politics-shy advertisers. The network's entertainment director described Showtime as a good home for the series because "it doesn't have to worry about the wrath of advertisers uncomfortable with politics" (Keveney 2004). The move helped relegate the show to political irrelevance: not only would the timing make it impossible for the winner to enter the political campaign, but its placement on a niche network meant ratings were likely to be scant (the debut episode garnered only 128,000 viewers, and ratings declined to an average of fewer than 80,000 thereafter). The real campaign at the time had heated up to the point that a contrived campaign for fake candidates seemed stale fare, and Showtime, perhaps smelling failure, did little in the way of promoting it.

Details of the Show

The producers relied heavily on strategies for "offloading" promotional labor onto the would-be candidates by providing them with Web sites to gather on-line endorsements from members of the public, sending press releases to hometown newspapers and urging them to get the word out. The "campaign" element of American Candidate proved to be at least as much an advertising strategy for the show as for political candidates—a fact that was surely one of the selling points when the show was pitched. In the end, the online support had little to do with the casting process, according to producer R.J. Cutler, who said that "the decisions as to who gets on the show are made by producers of the show—by me—and by Showtime working together.... The online support is a way of building a community of people in common with American Candidate and support a forum for ideas outside the two-party process" (Smith 2004).

The ten cast members were clearly selected not only for the variety of rela-tively mainstream political perspectives they represented (with the possible exception of a radio-host conspiracy theorist and a pro-gun, pro-legal-marijuana libertarian), but for demonstrated political talent. As Cutler put it, "What we wanted were people who combined their vision for the country with their passion for that vision and talent to communicate it and lead with it" (Stewart 2004). The roster included the daughter of former Democratic presidential hopeful Dick Gephardt, as well as a black gay activist who served in the Clinton White House, a PETA (People for the Ethical Treatment of Animals) activist whose claim to fame was streaking in front of the Queen of England, and a Utah Libertarian whose challenge to the Brady Gun Bill prevailed before the Supreme Court, making him a hero to gun-rights activists.

For each week's show, the cast members engaged in a competition—sometimes to get the most votes from citizens in a particular locale and sometimes to gain the approval of a focus group. The two who scored lowest on the challenge then engaged in a debate followed by another vote in which the remaining candidates would decide who would be kicked off the show. The result was that early on, the least successful candidates in each location got the most debating time. The last two "evictions" from the show were decided upon not by the cast members, but by call-in and text message votes from television viewers. Early on, a born-again Christian history teacher, Park Gillespie, emerged as the most articulate and charismatic of the conservative candidates, and he coasted through most of the later episodes thanks in large part to the fact that the progressive candidates split the liberal vote during challenges.

Despite the overtly contrived nature of the competition, in which discussions of real politics were carefully qualified by the recurring reminder that candidates were "running" not for president but for the title of "American Candidate," the show paralleled aspects of the real campaign. The candidates with the more eccentric political platforms—including abolishing the IRS and exposing the government's alleged cover-up of Gulf War Syndrome– were eliminated early on. The first to go was Chrissy Gephardt, the openly gay daughter of Rep. Dick Gephardt (who dropped out of the real presidential race early on after a poor showing in Iowa). In perhaps the closest parallel to the real election, the conservative evangelical Christian candidate won the grand prize—a surprising outcome considering that Showtime, which aired a gay-themed show called *The L-Word* and a biography of Ronald Reagan that was fiercely criticized by conservatives, is not a popular network with the Christian right.

Gillespie's success was due in large part to the support of two conservative Christian organizations, the Home School Legal Defense Association and Focus on the Family, which used their organization to spread word of his candidacy to members, urging them to call in and vote regardless of whether they watched the show. The Focus on the Family's e-mail told members that "only one vote per phone will be counted, so if you believe in Gillespie's message and witness, you can copy this note and e-mail it to your friends and family so that they can vote, too" (Kirkpatrick 2004). The home school group alone circulated its message to more than 80,000 people—the average number of viewers for the show during its final episodes (Kirkpatrick 2004). According to press accounts, the organizations' goal was to provide a public forum to someone espousing their viewpoint. As the grand-prize winner, Gillespie received twenty minutes of uninterrupted airtime to address the American people, an opportunity that he used to endorse President Bush's candidacy, the war in Iraq, and the conservative attack on gay marriage and abortion.

Gillespie's formulaic—albeit articulate—campaigning was typical of the show, which, in keeping with Cutler's documentary work, focused more on behind-the-scenes strategizing and personal relationships than on political substance. Whereas most of the candidates could have used research assistants and economists to help sort out the details of the policies they advocated (ranging from national health care to abolishing the income tax), what they got were political consultants and pollsters focused on marketing and image rather than policy. The result was a rather uncontroversial "behind-the-scenes" look at the process of political grooming.

Perhaps in imitation of "real" politics (a theme taken up in more detail in the following section), the focus was on selling a message rather than developing a workable policy—appearance, not substance. B-list beltway celebrities who consulted with the candidates (including Howard Dean's campaign manager Joe Trippi, Republican pollster Frank Luntz, and former Republican National Committee Chairman Rich Bond) took a stance of professional neutrality—and instrumentalism. Their clear mission was to take *any* political agenda and sell it more effectively, as highlighted by the fact that conservative consultants were paired with progressive candidates and vice versa.

The result was an emphasis on the details of presentation and style: self-described "black, Italian, Puerto-Rican" candidate Malia Lazu was told to take out her tongue piercing, and animal-rights activist Bruce Friedrich was advised to change his image by wearing leather belts and shoes. Over the course of the show, viewers watched the candidates hone their delivery and presentation, tailor their messages to focus groups, and alter their wardrobes and hairstyles. By the time of the final debate, USC professor Martin Kaplan asked the obvious question: "One of the ideas behind the *American Candidate* is that fresh faces, new voices, real people would enter and be recognized by the political system. You've been Joe Trippied, and Ed Rollinsed and Donna Braziled and Dan Schnured and Fred Luntzed, and focus grouped. You've been taught how to dress and how to talk, you've both had makeovers.... What makes you different now at the end of this process than every other candidate that we're sick and tired of?" It certainly wasn't the political rhetoric, which by the end of the series was distilled down to a conservative candidate reflexively reprising the GOP party line ("If we don't fight the terrorists in Baghdad we will surely have to deal with them in Boston") and a liberal candidate who, while more overtly critical of Bush's policies than John Kerry, had little more to say than that the war was a bad idea and universal health care and more jobs would be good ones.

Thanks to the selection process, several of the candidates who appeared to be more informed about the issues and more willing to move beyond sound-bite platitudes had been eliminated, and the final debate sounded remarkably familiar to anyone who had been following the real campaign. What the show had demonstrated was not so much that television could be used to inject diversity into political discourse as that it could be used to transform selected members of the audience into a familiar media product—to mold diversity into business as usual. Taken one step further, *American Candidate* showcased the power of the media machine to manufacture credible candidates out of the raw material provided by members of the audience. The message was more about the talent of the consultants and the power of the public-relations machine than the raw political ability of the candidates. As in the case of reality television in general, the narrative was in large part about the power of the media itself to turn "nobodies" into celebrities—or, by the same token, potentially viable political candidates. The show suggested that the image machine could mold just about anyone who could rub a couple of thoughts together into a serviceable candidate. Indeed, the show's winner came across as a more sincere and articulate—and slightly less hypocritical—version of the real candidates. After his work on the series, political consultant Ed Rollins, former campaign manager for actor-turned-president Ronald Reagan, noted in a telling flash of candor, "I could take any one of these people and could make it [sic] into serious Congressional and, in a couple of cases, into serious gubernatorial candidates. They were more articulate or more sure of their positions than the vast majority of candidates that I've worked with" (Lee 2004).

Reality Television and Savvy Audiences

One of the reality television lessons of *American Candidate* was that the desire for access to "behind-the-scenes" reality can be addressed by exposing the reality of artifice: by staging the scene of the spectacle. A common misconception on the part of pundits regarding the promise of reality television is that viewers are duped into the false belief that they are being provided access to behind-the-scenes *reality*. In fact, a common response to reality shows by viewers—and fans—is the obvious observation that they are not *really* real (Andrejevic 2004). Hence the name reality *television*—with the emphasis on the second word. It is this acknowledged level of contrivance—and the way it caters to a reflexively savvy audience that creates one more link between reality television and the spectacle of contemporary politics.

Perhaps one explanation for the enduring lifespan of reality television, in addition to the fact that it provides cheap, plentiful programming, is that it endlessly defers delivery on the qualified promise of access to reality. This deferral operates in two complementary registers. The first mobilizes an infinitely receding horizon of reality: behind every reality show is the *real* reality that eludes it—perhaps to be captured in a "making-of..." or "behind-the-scenes-of..." sequel. MTV's *The Real World* has exploited this logic, offering debriefing shows wherein, for example, cast members describe what the camera left out: who was having an affair with one of the producers, what one cast member told another that never appeared on camera, and so on. The spiral can be continued indefinitely.

The second register of deferral, by contrast, encompasses this infinite recess by offering up the spectacle of artifice as the ultimate "behind-the-scenes" reality. Conceding the reality of contrivance amounts to the admission that "reality" as such has become completely colonized by artifice in the type of postmodern collapse envisioned by Jean Baudrillard's (1983) account of the simulacrum. By the same token, politics is reduced to pure spin; public deliberation to public relations, collective practice to a political marketplace. This collapse—albeit incoherent, as suggested in the following sections—highlights the failure of reality television as a model for democratic practice. Or, to put it slightly differently, it is the deadlock of the savvy response highlighted by reality television that sheds light on the impasse of *real* contemporary democratic politics. This impasse is the subject of the following sections, which consider the relationship between two aspects of the critical response to *American Candidate*: the assertion that perhaps reality television can provide "real" democracy, and the observation that politics is becoming more and more like reality television.

Upstaging Politics

The secret of the democratic appeal of reality television—an appeal that politics should tap into, according to the authors of a British report comparing reality television to parliamentary politics—is the promise of authenticity: "If the audience could see everything in an edited version at the end of the day, just as they can on *Big Brother*, they would love it.... The cameras just show the staged version, the bit that doesn't interest most of us. Real politics is about how ideas and people interact. Staged politics—the public part—is just about the presentation of the image" (Coleman 2003, 42). The message of the report, "A Tale of Two Houses," is that a "reality-television" approach to politics would show us how the process really works: the back-scratching and - stabbing, the intrigue and drama: the "whole story" (Coleman 2003, 43). The author of these words appeals to a spirit of savvy debunkery—a challenge to the staged and supposedly alienating officiousness of the political process:

> Politicians would love you to believe that their House is very different from the Big Brother house—that theirs is a place of rational deliberation, conducted for the good of the nation.... In reality, the two houses are very much alike: in the House of Commons, there is just as much sexual tension, conspiracy, betrayal, drunkenness, ambition, loutish behavior, secrecy, cheating.... The real difference is that in the Big Brother house, it's there for everyone to see. In the House of Commons, they hide it as best they can. (Coleman 2003, 41)

The author's assertion is that this strategy of concealment is alienating and undemocratic because it treats viewers (the category to which the public has been assimilated) as dupes—as if they are dim enough to believe that politicians are somehow different from, and better than, the rest of us. Reality television, on the contrary, caters to a non-duped audience that sees through such self-serving claptrap. In what the authors of "A Tale of Two Houses" describe as a "post-deferential age," reality television is the great leveler that promises we can all be politicians, not by aspiring to some higher state of civic responsibility, but by understanding that politicians are just like us, complete with foibles, failings, and frailties.

Indeed, the notion of politics as an avocation irreducible to both the banality and pleasures of the marketplace pursuit of individual self-interest becomes an object of critique in the era of the savvy citizen. As Coleman (2003) puts it:

> Political parties began life as secular versions of evangelical crusades and the engaged were often expected to remove themselves from many of the everyday affairs of society in order to make the world a better place. In the present post-ideological and post-deferential age, people are both too critically minded and culturally volatile to make such intense and rigid commitments. (38)

The appeal to political authenticity via "behind-the-scenes" access is, of course, an invitation to the journey of infinite deferral outlined above. As in the case of an *American Candidate*—or reality television in general—once the cameras highlight the background scenes and scenery, the latter become part of the spectacle itself. The process is already well underway: politicians want to show us carefully crafted images of their family lives in order to share the sets of personal values and daily life experiences that add authenticity to the political spectacle. Staying true to the spirit of reality television, Coleman (2003) speaks approvingly of this model of democratization via authentication: "some democratic theorists [who remain nameless—but apparently have much in common with Coleman] would argue that the emphasis upon values, behavior and informal discourses contributes to the democratization of political life—as opposed to the institutionalization of democracy" (32).

The result—as anticipated by reality television—would be the staging of authenticity, or, at the very least, a savvy skepticism that encountered such authenticity as one more spectacle. *Real* authenticity, as it were, continues to elude the camera, which always leaves something beyond its frame. The whole picture escapes us. But that formulation is a bit too simple, for it ignores the obverse of the infinite regress of the real, the savvy concession that it's all just one more contrivance. If that is the case, then, of course, the real no longer recedes indefinitely. It becomes indistinguishable from the performance. The directly given appearance becomes indistinguishable from the behind-the-scenes reality. And yet, even the ability to discern the reality of contrivance paradoxically conserves the distinction it ostensibly obliterates.

Bearing this formulation in mind, consider once more the example of *American Candidate*, and in particular the way in which the possibility of a "reality television candidate" was greeted by politicians and pundits—its savvy reception among those whose jobs revolve around the political. The response to announcement of the F/X version of the show was predictably divided between those who welcomed the implicit critique offered by the show and those who accused it of making a mockery of the political process. Typical of the latter group was *Variety* television critic Brian Lowry, who accused the show of "trivializing politics by transferring the trappings of 'Survivor' and network dating shows into a new attention-grabbing milieu" (Lowry 2004). Trivialization was the buzzword of the show's critics, a group that included media sociologist Todd Gitlin, who accused the show of capitalizing "in a cynical way on the degradation that has become normal in politics, in which roughly half the population is sitting it out in any given year.... The worst damage this show does is to contribute to the already widespread belief that politics is a trivial pursuit" (Shesgreen 2002). Among the groups most resistant to the show's premise, according to Joshua J. Scott, program director for the University of Virginia's Center for Politics (and a member of the show's advisory board), were activists across the political spectrum: "They said 'There's a real election going on: Why do you want us to do this with fake candidates?'" (Scott 2005). The Center for Politics came on board only after the producers had backed away from the project of grooming a real candidate—a prospect that would have raised some concerns at the center over the attempt to substitute celebrity for political credentials: "Any kind of candidate that's using celebrity is grounds for criticism in terms of electoral politics; just because they have fame or money does that make them the right person to run for office?" (Scott 2005).

The obvious rejoinder—taken up by those more favorably disposed toward the show—was that money and celebrity have already established such a firm foothold in the political process that indignant admonitions about saving politics from their influence remain at best quaint and outdated, at worst hypocritical. As a columnist for the *Chicago Tribune* put it, "Anybody who immediately dismisses the idea of the 'American Candidate' show hasn't checked into what the presidential election system has become" (Warren 2004). The problem is not, in other words, that reality television is a poor substitute for politics, but that politics has already become all but indistinguishable from it. As the *Tribune* columnist put it,

> In the age of television and short attention spans, the real process of choosing a president is every bit as slick, calculated, commercial, and creepy as the show.... Those of us who have slogged through the frigid New Hampshire comedy of "the nation's first presidential primary," the quaint cornfield drama of the Iowa caucuses or the aw-shucks charm of the gunny sack races of the summer state fair circuit know there's got to be a better way to choose a president. (Warren 2004)

Many of those who embraced the show's premise suggested that in an era when politics had become such a self-consciously staged and scripted spectacle, only a fake campaign could revitalize real politics. In a *New York Times* opinion piece, Georgetown professor Michael Kazin wrote that the show represented the continuation of "a noble political tradition. Since the early 19th century, Americans have found ways to pressure the major parties or to circumvent them entirely. Their efforts often brought new groups of voters to the polls and always invigorated the civic debate" (Kazin 2002).

At worst, such observations suggested, the process would merely replicate what politics had already become: a high-budget, high-stakes reality show. As if to drive the point home, the real 2004 campaign easily broke records for fund-raising and advertising expenditures, contributing handsomely to media coffers. The Alliance for Better Campaigns reported that media spending during the campaign doubled compared to the previous election, with television expenditures topping half a billion dollars.

In an era in which reality television had become the pop-culture dominant, comparisons to *Survivor* and similar formats were easy to come by. Complementing the references to reality television as politics were those to politics as reality television—an easy equation to make in the era of the California recall election, which featured, in addition to action star Arnold

Schwarzenegger, a roster of semi-celebrities that included porn star Mary Carey and former child star Gary Coleman. By the time the political conventions for the 2004 campaign got underway, the *Washington Post* noted that

> We Americans watch this contest—who's the most authentic?—the way we watch reality TV shows. After all, the Democratic contest so far even looks like reality TV, with its shaky, hand-held cameras, internecine squabbles, quickly evolving plot and, most importantly, a ridiculous premise: that one performer can somehow be more authentic than the others in a scripted setting. The truth is that there has never been anything authentic about authenticity in politics. (Signer 2004)

The political consultants—those whose expertise lies in stage-managing the spectacle—took easily to the reality television comparison. Democratic consultant Joe Trippi, who worked on *American Candidate*, observed that "politics is more like a reality show than most of the gimmicks that people build other reality shows on" (Lee 2004). Liberal political observer John Powers (2004) argued prior to the 2004 election that the Bush Administration, with its contrived sense of reality, its competitive streak, its obliteration of the distinction between image and reality, and its winner-take-all mentality captured the spirit of the reality television era.

The advocates of political resuscitation via reality television found themselves calling for spectacular politics to pull itself up by its own bootstraps: if real politics is staged—if the promise of authentic democracy remains largely cosmetic—why not *stage* the image of a truly democratic process? This is the question that lies at the heart of Cutler's project, and it's the one around which the various responses to the show revolve. The discussion so far has assembled several pieces of a possible answer that, in the following section, I attempt to organize into an argument highlighting some of the shortcomings of reality television populism. The answer I propose—that reality television politics undermines itself by conceding the skepticism it ostensibly addresses— is admittedly a provisional and polemic one. My goal is not to suggest that the impasse of the current moment is definitive, nor to rule out the progressive potential of popular culture. Rather it is to suggest some arguments that I think need to be addressed by those who would make a simple equation between the forms of engagement and participation fostered (exploited?) by reality television and the revitalization of civic engagement. The fact that this ready equation has found such a firm foothold in the popular discourse on the interactive character of new media suggests that it is unlikely to be rethought on the basis of mere facts, including the qualified failure of the recent round of political reality-television experiments. Such rethinking requires more than the repeated assertion of the potential for resistance and the power of participation; it requires some engagement with the circumstances that have so far negated or reconfigured this potential and power. The following critique is offered not in the spirit of pointy-headed pessimism, but as an attempt to highlight challenges that must be met and addressed rather than glossed over by any attempt to resuscitate political engagement via popular culture or otherwise.

Politics in an Era of Savvy Reflexivity

It is telling that seemingly the most disingenuous response to *American Candidate* was the indignant claim that television shouldn't trivialize politics by reducing it to entertainment and marketing. From the perspective of the author of "A Tale of Two Houses," which compares the *Big Brother* house with the House of Commons, such a response evinces the arrogance and elitism of a viewer group described as political junkies (as opposed to reality television fans, with whom there is little overlap): those who maintain an ostensibly anachronistic hierarchical distinction between politics and popular culture. One of the defining characteristics of the "post-deferential age" the author invokes is that the public has seen through the attempt to conceal the fate of politics: its capture by special interests, its reduction to sound-bite marketing and mediated manipulation. Perhaps it has always been so, to a greater or lesser extent, even if it might not always have been *seen* to be so. The post-deferential perspective debunks the promise that it might be otherwise. It is this pervasive and knowing cynicism toward the political that serves both as a condition of possibility for a show like *American Candidate* (if politics is already staged, why not stage the political?) and renders it a dead end. It forecloses in advance the possibility that the politics of spectacle could pull itself up to the level of what Coleman (2003) calls "authenticity" via its own bootstraps. To do so would be to create an inauthentic show, one that didn't show how politics *really* works. This is the paradox of a reflexive savviness: by conceding the character of politics as contrivance, it debunks in advance any attempt to portray an authentic politics. Or to put it somewhat differently, it suggests that an authentic portrayal would necessarily concede its own lack of authenticity. It is, on this account, no coincidence that *American Candidate* focused on the behind-the-scenes staging of the spectacle: the focus-group testing and political-guru consulting—the crafting of an image, the jostling for position, and the infighting. Nor, as I will suggest a bit later in the discussion, is it a coincidence that the articulate Bush surrogate—speaking in the blankly manipulative sound-bites of the Rove-Cheney propaganda apparatus—prevailed. The authenticity of the show's final result—strictly according to the terms of its premise—was measured by the accuracy of its depiction of *inauthentic* politics (or its implicit critique of the claim to authenticity).

The impasse at work here is described by the culture critic Slavoj Zizek (1999) in terms of what he calls, borrowing from Claude Lévi-Straus, the "decline of symbolic efficiency" (323). The efficacy of the "symbolic order"—of the shared system of representations according to which we organize our world—relies on an acceptance of the non-identical and contradictory character of the symbol itself: the fact that, for example, it is irreducible to the reality it designates (and vice versa). To illustrate the role that symbolic efficacy plays in opening up a space of possibility beyond the seemingly irrevocably given character of directly experienced reality, Zizek invokes the Groucho Marx question, "Who do you believe, your eyes or my words?" (1999, 323). It is not, of course, an uncommon experience to trust the evidence of the symbolic ("your words") over our direct experience ("my eyes"), as when, for example, we concede that the earth orbits the sun. Symbolic efficacy has, Zizek suggests, an important role to play at the level of social and political institutions in which

> ...the symbolic mask-mandate matters more than the direct reality of the individual who wears this mask and/or assumes this mandate. This function involves the structure of fetishistic disavowal: "I know very well that things are the way I see them [that this person is a corrupt weakling], but none the less I treat him with respect, since he wears the insignia of a judge, so that when he speaks it is the Law itself which speaks through him." (1999, 323)

Post-deferential authenticity, reality-television-style, short circuits this logic by brushing aside the symbolic mandate and getting directly at the "corrupt weakling" behind the black robe. It is, as Zizek suggests, the space of the symbolic (along with its productive contradictions) that is foreclosed by the cynicism of the "non-duped."

Put in slightly different terms, a generalized savviness collapses contradictions: there can no longer be a discrepancy between a portrayal and that which it ostensibly portrays. In more concrete terms this logic appears in contemporary political discourse as a kind of postmodern nominalism: if the United States, for example, pursues its imperialistic ambitions in the name of fostering democracy, its supporters stretch the definition of democracy to include whatever imperialism deems necessary. If the United States did it, it was by definition in the name of democracy and freedom. By the same token, from a different perspective, its critics may then dismiss democracy itself as nothing more than (or entirely reducible to) a ruse for imperialism. There is a frustrating flatness to what passes for the symbolic in a savvy, post-deferential context in which reality is preemptively subsumed to spin and artifice with a knowing, ironic wink. Paradoxically, it finds itself unable to pull away from the brute facticity of the given. This flatness is another way of describing the logic of reality television outlined earlier: offering up the reality of artifice as the final truth of reality itself in order to elide the contradictions of representation.

The handicap faced by a show like *American Candidate* is not merely the savvy challenge to symbolic efficacy, but the fact that it concedes this challenge in advance. As a genre that offers up the collapse of image and reality as the ultimate guarantee of its authenticity, reality television can do little to open up the gap between symbolic mandate and "real person" foreclosed in a "post-deferential" age. A more concrete way of putting this is to try to imagine a version of the show that would focus not on the behind-the-scenes staging of the spectacle, but upon, let's say, the substance of political debates: a show that filled the vacuum of sound-bite culture with detailed, concrete discussion and deliberation of the key policy issues facing contemporary citizens. Could such a show come across as anything but phony and contrived in a post-deferential era? Wouldn't the attempt come across as elitist and self-serving artifice, amounting to the most insulting form of manipulation in a culture that prides itself on savvy skepticism: an attempt to treat citizens as "dupes"?

In his afterword to "A Tale of Two Houses," Stephan Shakespeare (Coleman 2003) concedes as much when he observes that the very attempt to present political decisions as the result of research, debate, and careful consideration is what alienates viewers, because, as he puts it, we all know that politics is pursued "as much for the joy of control as for the benefit of the nation"—as much through petty infighting and self-interest as for the common good, "and the difference between what we know and what the politicians try to present is the source of disaffection among the audience" (42). Presaging *American Candidate*, he suggests that the reality television solution is to expose reality in its entirety: "Could TV provide a format that increases involvement in the political process? I believe it could if TV could show the whole reality of politics" (Coleman 2003, 44). Once more, however, we are provided with an infinitely receding horizon of authenticity: any representation will necessarily fall short of the "whole reality"—leaving the process of representation, if it is to avoid the charge of dissembling, to foreground the reality of artifice. Shakespeare would have it slightly differently: that there is room for an understanding of human foibles—of the petty personal motives of the corrupt coward behind the judge's robe—alongside a sense of "reassurance that there is nothing suspect about the way a decision is reached" (Coleman 2003, 43).

But once the symbolic mandate is debunked, what might serve as the basis for such reassurance? The answer lies in the obverse (and inseparable correlate) of savvy skepticism: a revitalized faith in instinctive direct access to the true character of the political performer (enter the politics of "character" and "personal values"). One of the more famous examples of this intuitive capability was provided by George W. Bush during his highly publicized first meeting with Russian leader Vladimir Putin. Shortly after the meeting, Bush, famous both for his creative awkwardness with words and his evident mistrust of them, noted that he had been able to bypass speech and cut straight to the essence of his interlocutor: "I looked the man in the eye; I found him to be very straightforward and trustworthy.... I was able to get a sense of his soul" (Hillman 2001). Coleman (2003) describes this kind of communication as an experience that is "sensed" rather than "rationally apprehended" and describes it as a crucial element of the communication experience that is devalued by elitist political discourse. He suggests (somewhat condescendingly) that voter disaffection is a symptom of the failure of politicians to indulge in this more vernacular, intuitive form of interaction (a form of interaction that might presumably be facilitated by reality television). Zizek (1999), by contrast, suggests that a default to the criterion of intuitive access to personal authenticity (coupled with the debunking of anything that might count for political authenticity) is a symptom of the demobilizing decline of symbolic efficacy.

A turn away from reality television politics to political reality might help adjudicate between these accounts. The authors of "A Tale of Two Houses" suggest that total access, reality-television-style, is the missing ingredient of authenticity; paradoxically, citizens might be less inclined to cynical mistrust of politicians if only the politicians would stop *pretending* that they are so unimpeachably trustworthy. A little glimpse of behind-the-scenes chicanery—openly revealed to the cameras—might somehow bolster public confidence in their representatives, because it would connote authenticity (honesty about being dishonest?) rather than the ostensibly dishonest posture required by the symbolic mandate: the pretense of transcending personal interest and moral foibles. Political debate might, on this account, be revitalized, and trust in political discourse reinstated thanks to pervasive public disclosure. There are, of course, no guarantees in these reflexively savvy times, and Shakespeare concedes that "if we no longer live in an age of deference, and we don't trust any party to deliver a real difference in our lives...it would become an act of self-assertion not to vote" (Coleman 2003, 44).

It is this form of engagement—non-participation as a form of "self-assertion"—that seems the most likely outcome of reality television politics. If, as Joshua Meyrowitz (1985) has argued, the close-up, humanizing access to public figures ushered in by the television era contributed, at least in part, to their (post-deferential) demystification, the contributors to "A Tale of Two Houses" advocate pushing the process to its limit in order to resuscitate, albeit in a new form, what was lost. Such an argument might in practice help explain why, for example, U.S. President Bill Clinton's job approval rating increased after the highly detailed and publicized account of his affair with a White House intern. The Republican-backed investigation of his personal life seemed to backfire, resulting in the resignation of archconservative Clinton foe Newt Gingrich as Speaker of the House and a rare mid-term election gain of congressional seats by the party controlling the White House. Perhaps the president's public apology—his admission of his personal failings (and subsequent detailed description of them on national television)—connoted "authenticity," if not exemplary personal values. Alternatively, it's not hard to see the public reaction as a backlash against a hypocritical, costly, and partisan investigation of the president's *personal* life: not a call for more exposure—or for the displacement of the collective interest by an investigation of personal behavior—but for a turn away from the attempt to manipulate the "character issue."

The upshot of an appeal to authenticity in the form of "personal values" is a table-turning gesture that owes much to a popularized postmodern dismantling of symbolic efficacy by consigning old-fashioned political deliberation to the realm of ideology (a manipulative pretense of a transcendent commitment to a collective good). Such a critique is presented, in a right-wing parody of Foucault (and an echo of the ostensibly anti-elitist politics of "direct intuition"), as emancipatory and democratizing—an anti-elitist populism that concedes the reduction of political commitments to the ruses of power. However, the tools of debunkery that once challenged the so-called truths of established power turn out to be even more effective when coupled with that power. There is a certain leverage to be gained by those in power through the adoption of a facile form of relativism in which all critiques can be portrayed as purely perspectival. As political commentator Josh Marshall put it in his description of Bush's "postmodern" presidency, "revisionist ideologues seek to expose 'the facts' as nothing more than the spin of experts blinded by their own unacknowledged biases" (2003).

The indeterminacy and malleability of deliberative discourse is a hallmark of the Bush Administration, whose strategy has not been to seek deliberative consensus so much as to disrupt it by throwing up a tangle of discourses that contradict one another and thereby demonstrate the futility of informed deliberation itself—better just to go with one's instinct, intuition, and soul-reading sonar. This strategy is crafted for an era of information glut, one in which citizens are overwhelmed by competing stories that circulate online and in cable news commentaries multiplying over the course of the news cycle. As demonstrated repeatedly by, for example, the ongoing debate over Bush's Vietnam-era record, the buildup to the Iraq war, the administration's handling of the war, and so on, more information can amount to less. The proliferation of stories results in a tangle of contradictions and inconsistencies that indict the process itself: clearly some of the stories are wrong, but which ones, and how best to judge? Perhaps direct intuition can cut through the Gordian knot. A *New York Times* op-ed writer lamented the process as leading to what he described as the death of persuasion: in the face of the metastasis of cable news commentary, Internet speculation, and political spin, the author wonders whether it's "possible in America today to convince anyone of anything he doesn't already believe" (Miller 2005). In a now-famous account of a discussion with an unnamed Bush aide, reporter Ron Suskind (2004) summarized the administration's dismissive attitude toward the process of research and deliberation—and those (symbolic) institutions that remain in thrall to outdated, Enlightenment concepts of reality:

> The aide said that guys like me were "in what we call the reality-based community," which he defined as people who "believe that solutions emerge from your judicious study of discernible reality.... That's not the way the world really works anymore.... We're an empire now, and when we act, we create our own reality. And while you're studying that reality—judiciously, as you will—we'll act again, creating other new realities, which you can study too, and that's how things will sort out." (44)

If, in a savvy culture, everyone knows that so-called knowledge is a ruse of power, such an approach threatens to cede the contest to those in charge. Political deliberation is relegated to the status of debunked authenticity—as smokescreen—which is how it has been deployed by the Bush Administration and, of course, by the dissolution of reality figured in reality television. The result is that even Bush's supporters needn't believe the rhetoric—like him, they are in on the secret that it's purely strategic.

Shortly after Bush's re-election, the *New York Times*, apparently still firmly ensconced in the reality-based community, noted that polling results represented an "apparently conflicting" portrait of voter attitudes: support for Bush coupled with disbelief in his campaign promises (Nagourney and Elder 2005). The majority of respondents indicated that they didn't expect Bush to "make progress in improving education, the economy, lowering taxes, or reducing the threat of terrorism" (1). Almost 80 percent, including a majority of those who voted for his re-election, said it wouldn't be possible for the president to fulfill his campaign promises of overhauling Social Security, cutting taxes, and paying for the Iraq war without running up the budget deficit" (1).

It is hard to avoid the conclusion that the populace has, in a sense, adopted what the authors of "A Tale of Two Houses" describe as a post-deferential attitude toward both the political process and itself as well. Although the authors don't make the timeline clear, it seems safe to assume that in the World War II era, deference still reigned: not only were leaders sheltered from the close scrutiny of the coming era of television, but they retained a symbolic mandate not yet fully debunked. Through this mandate the populace was perhaps able to retain a certain faith in the principles to which it ostensibly adhered—to really believe, for example, in the notion that U.S. foreign intervention took place in the name of freedom and democracy (despite plenty of evidence to the contrary). In the era of savvy skepticism, the rhetoric remains the same, but its function has shifted slightly: the populace is in on the shared secret of the functioning of ideology. The post-deferential subject has acquired a savvy distance toward ideology, whose functioning can thus be exposed without—and this is the crucial point—ceasing to function. The difference is that contradiction no longer manifests itself at the level of the symbolic but is displaced into the split between a canny and knowing sense of reflexive distance and the direct access of imaginary identification, neither of which has purchase on the other.

The missing ingredient in this formulation is its relation to the short-circuit of direct identification: "we" may see through the ideology, but we imagine that we identify intuitively with the actions they seek to justify—so much so in fact that we can dismiss the ideology as such and continue to identify with the actions. Much has been made, for example, of the fact that Americans seemed woefully uninformed about the (lack of) connections between Saddam Hussein and the 9/11 attacks, with the implicit assumption that the populace was, at least in part, duped into a war it might otherwise have opposed. By contrast, Zizek's (1989) analysis suggests the possibility that a large part of the populace understood the administration propaganda as such (not that they knew the facts—rather that they knew they didn't need or care to know them), but nonetheless directly identified with the desire to target a hostile tinhorn dictator (WMDs or not) to secure control over a troublesome oil-rich region, and to defy the will of what it perceived to be a hostile world with designs upon the United States's rapidly eroding economic and geopolitical prowess.

It would be nice to believe that the American public was duped into re-electing George W. Bush—not least because it would support one of the commonly repeated truisms about international opinion that, for the most part, citizens of other countries have a lower opinion of U.S. political leadership than of the U.S. public. But Zizek's (1989) formulation pushes in a different direction: the fact that the public sees through the administration's campaign promises (knowing them to be misleading and unattainable) is not evidence of mistrust in Bush and his agenda, but of this gut-level identification. It understands and supports the need to dissimulate the "by-any-means-necessary" final stand of U.S. global hegemony—even to itself. The reflexive undermining of representation performed by reality television offers not an alternative to, but the logical extension of this process, which is why the winner of *American Candidate* was perhaps more accurate than he realized when he announced in his victory address that the principles that brought him victory "are most fully embodied in the real presidential election by George W. Bush."

References

Andrejevic, Mark. 2004. *Reality TV: The Work of Being Watched.* Lanham, MD: Rowman & Littlefield.

Baudrillard, J. 1983. *Simulations.* New York: Semiotext(e).

Carey, J. 1995. "The Press, Public Opinion, and Public Discourse." In *Public Opinion and the Communication of Consent,* edited by T.L. Glasser and C. T. Salmon, pp. 373–402. New York: Guilford.

Coleman, Stephen. 2003. "A Tale of Two Houses: The House of Commons, The Big Brother House." *The Hansard Society.* http://www.clubepublic.org/eve/030708/Hansardb_b.pdf (accessed 24 July 2005).

Cook, John. 2004. "Another Political Campaign Launches—This One on Cable." *Chicago Tribune,* 1 August, p. C9.

Couldry, Nick. 2000. *The Place of Media Power: Pilgrims and Witnesses of the Media Age.* New York: Routledge.

de Moraes, Lisa. 2002. "Political 'Reality': Viewers to Pick 2004 Candidate." *The New York Times,* 21 September, p. C1.

Ebert, Roger. 2002. "Murdoch Is Playing with Democracy." *Chicago Sun Times,* 23 September, p. 39.

Eisenstein, E. 1968. "Some Conjectures about the Impact of Printing on Western Society and Thought." *Journal of Modern History* 40(1), pp. 1-56.

Freeman, Simon. 2004. "Election Night: How It Unfolded." *The Times* (London), 6 May, p. 1.

Gardyn, Rebecca. 2001. "The Tribe Has Spoken." *American Demographics,* September, pp. 34–40.

Goodale, Gloria. 2004. "As Nation Gets More Political, So Does TV." *Christian Science Monitor,* 9 August, p. 11.

Habermas, J. 1991. *The Structural Transformation of the Public Sphere.* Cambridge, MA: MIT Press.

Hanks, Robert. 2002. "Last Night: Reality TV Has Yet Another Winner But Who Loses?" *The Independent,* 14 December, p. 9.

Hillman, G.R. 2001. "Bush, Putin Swap Praise after Meeting." *The Seattle Times,* 17 June, p. A2.

Hinsliff, Gaby 2003. "Is Big Brother Key to Winning Next Election?" *The Observer,* 1 June, p. 15.

Jenkins, Henry. 2001. "Challenging the Consensus." *Boston Review,* Summer, available online at: http://www.bostonreview.net/BR26.3/jenkins.html.

Kazin, Michael. 2002. "Reality TV Meets Politics." *The New York Times,* 28 September, p. 17.

Keveney, Bill. 2004. "Turned Off by 2 Presidential Choices? Try These 10." *USA Today,* 29 July, p. 7D.

Kirkpatrick, David. 2004. "Fake Presidency, at Least, Captured by a Conservative." *The New York Times,* 12 October, p. E3.

Lee, Jennifer. 2004. "I am a Political Consultant, and I Play One on TV." *The New York Times,* 8 August, Sec. 2, p. 29.

Lowry, Brian. 2004. "American Candidate." *Variety,* 30 July. http://www.variety.com/review/VE1117924504?categoryid=32&cs=1 (accessed 28 July 2005).

Marshall, Joshua 2003. "The Post-Modern President." *Washington Monthly*, September (accessed 30 August 2005 at: http://www.washingtonmonthly.com/features/2003/0309.marshall.html).

Merrin, William. 2005. *Baudrillard and the Media: A Critical Introduction*. London: Blackwell. Page proofs supplied by the author.

Meyrowitz, Joshua. 1985. *No Sense of Place: The Impact of Electronic Media on Social Behavior*. New York: Oxford University Press.

Miller, Matt. 2005. "Is Persuasion Dead?" *The New York* Times, 4 July, p. 15.

Nagourney, Adam, and Elder, Janet 2005. "Public Voicing Doubts on Iraq and the Economy, Poll Finds." *The New York Times*, 20 January, p. A1.

Pearce, Celia. 1997. *The Interactive Book: A Guide to the Interactive Revolution*. Indianapolis, IN: Macmillan Technical.

Powers, John. 2004. *Sore Winners (and the Rest of Us) in George Bush's America*. New York: Doubleday.

Raphael, Chad. 1997. "The Political Economy of Reali-TV." *Jump Cut* 41: 102–109.

Schiller, Dan. 1999. *Digital Capitalism*. Cambridge, MA: MIT Press.

Scott, Joshua J. 2005. Telephone interview with author, 26 August.

Shesgreen, Deirdre. 2002. "Viewers Will Pick 2004 'People's Candidate' on Reality TV Show." *St. Louis Post-Dispatch*, 30 September, p. 1.

Showtime Public Relations Release. 2004. "Showtime to Introduce *American Candidate*." 8 January.

Signer, Michael. 2004. "It's Showtime for This Eager Candidate. The Candidates Are What We Want Them To Be, After All." *The Washington Post*, 18 January, p. B01.

Smith, Matt. 2004. "Medea Benjamin for President." *San Francisco Weekly*, 2 June: http://www.sfweekly.com/issues/2004-06-02/smith.html.

Stewart, Rhonda. 2004. "It's Showtime for This Eager Candidate." *The Boston Globe*, 29 July, p. C1.

Sunstein, Cass. 2001. *Republic.Com*. Princeton: Princeton University Press.

Suskind, Ron. 2004. "Without a Doubt." *The New York Times Magazine*, 17 October, pp. 44–70.

Warren, Ellen. 2004. "Why Shouldn't a Reality TV Show Pick Our Next President?" *Chicago Tribune*, 2 October, p. 1.

Wloszczyna, Susan. 2004. "The Real World Grows Up." *USA Today*, 1 September, p. 1D.

Zizek, Slavoj. 1989. *The Sublime Object of Ideology*. London: Verso.

——. 1999. *The Ticklish Subject*. London: Verso.

CHAPTER FIVE

Vote for Me: Playing at Politics

VALENTINA CARDO AND JOHN STREET

Introduction

I n the run-up to the 2005 General Election, one of the United Kingdom's main television channels broadcast, over the course of a week, a program called *Vote for Me*. It was a political version of reality television shows such as *Big Brother*, *Pop Idol*, and *Fame Academy*. Contestants were required to play at being politicians, just as their equivalents in other shows played at being pop stars. The prize was the opportunity to stand in the General Election.

Vote for Me was not the first of its kind. In the United States, a cable company had launched *American Candidate* in the hope of finding, according to one television executive, "a Detroit plumber who tells it like it is." And in Argentina in 2002, there was *The People's Candidate*, the winner of which was to stand for Congress (van Zoonen 2005).

This chapter discusses the rise of such television shows, ones that deliberately blur the distinction between politics and entertainment, creating a new crossover genre. It briefly traces their rise, putting them into the broader context of shifts in the businesses of both politics and television. Its main concern, however, is with the arguments that are used to justify programs like *Vote for Me*. There are three such arguments in particular. The first is that these programs provide a "public service," enabling viewers to engage with democratic politics. The format of the program, it is implied, gives viewers access to politics. The second argument is that of populism. The suggestion is that by allowing viewers to participate directly in the selection of candidates, the program avoids the elitist and distorting effects of party involvement. And the third justifying argument is that in allowing citizen-viewers to engage in this way, the program helps to address the perceived "crisis" in democracy. The Argentinean experiment, for example, was presented as an attempt to re-engage people with politics; *Vote for Me* was justified as an attempt to "raise interest in democracy."

Behind these justifying arguments is a larger rationale. This is the belief that in order for politics to be "popularized," it has to engage with "entertainment." This assumption is made by broadcasters, but it is also made by others. When the United Kingdom's Electoral Commission, a government-funded body responsible for monitoring and promoting political participation, wanted to increase turnout in elections, it created a *Big Brother*-style road show to tour the nation's cities. In a similar vein, following the predicted low turnout in the 2002 English Local Election, the Electoral Commission praised programs like *Pop Idol* for having positioned the finalists as "party candidates," hence finding a "positive means of engaging youth and next generation voters" (Electoral Commission 2002). The same assumption appears to underlie the activities of political parties and politicians. When they want to enhance their image, they turn to celebrities (and those who create such people) to do so (West and Orman 2003).

This widespread assumption—that popularizing politics means making it "entertaining"—is, of course, also challenged and falls victim to the equally ubiquitous accusation of "dumbing down." The turn to entertainment has been criticized as frequently as it has been celebrated (Street 2004). In this chapter, we argue that in order to move beyond the impasse that is typically the product of such stand-offs, we need to look more closely at the processes that bring programs like *Vote for Me* into existence and at the actual format and content of the programs.

The Rationale for *Vote for Me*

Vote for Me was announced well ahead of the General Election: reports of its existence first appeared in April 2003 and then again the following year;[1] but it was not broadcast by Independent Television (ITV) until January 2005. The official publicity for the program made it clear that it was aimed at engaging reality television audiences—generally understood to be young and politically disengaged. ITV's head of current affairs, Steve Anderson, who commissioned *Vote for Me*, was reported as saying that "the program was intended to 'enrich' democracy: 'What we are trying to do is come up with a new political format, to get people engaged in politics'" (Wells 2004). Moreover, according to an ITV spokeswoman, "It is not Pop Idol. It has been put together by the controller of current affairs so it's not reality television. All politicians have been saying for a long time that we need to engage young people. They've thrown down the gauntlet to the media and broadcasters to engage people in the political process. This is a genuine attempt to find someone to stand in an election" (Burrell 2004).

From the very beginning, program-makers made it clear that the aim of *Vote for Me* was to "put things right,"[2] because "we don't seem to like politics very much...and we don't like politicians either"; or, as the official website put it, to find "the person who, according to TV viewers, has the right credentials to be a candidate for a seat in the House of Commons."[3]

The hope appeared to be that it would combine high viewing ratings with a socially and politically proactive content and, as such, it seemed to be the answer to program producers' and politicians' needs. However, a late-night schedule,[4] coupled with limited advance publicity[5] and misguided editorial decisions, especially over the choice of judges, produced a program that, judged by ratings alone, failed to realize the promises made for it. But even if the program was a failure, it was an interesting and potentially important one.

Vote for Me has to be understood in the context not only of an alleged (and possibly exaggerated) crisis of democracy in the United Kingdom (Parry et al. 1992; Pattie et al. 2004), but also of public-service broadcasting. While talk of the state of British politics formed the backdrop for *Vote for Me*, the impetus behind it also owed much to the politics of broadcasting. Following the deregulation of British broadcasting in the 1980s, the rationale for and organization of public-service broadcasting has been subject to increasing scrutiny. This has been partly a question about funding, but it has also been one about the extent of content regulation. ITV, in particular, funded by advertising but subject to public-service content and scheduling rules, has struggled to manage its conflicting imperatives. Ratings and advertisers have tended to win, as news and current affairs programs have been increasingly marginalized in the schedule and their content "tabloidized" (Franklin 2004). *Vote for Me* can be seen as a product of these same pressures—a serious subject, presented in an entertaining format and scheduled away from prime time. ITV's attempt to meet its different obligations, it might be said, force it to create programs like *Vote for Me*. As they wrestle with this difficulty, Ofcom, the newly created body with overall responsibility for communications in the United Kingdom, has itself published an extensive report on the current meaning of "public service broadcasting."[6] In it, they reflect upon the place of entertainment—and reality television—in public-service broadcasting. The temptation to dismiss *Vote for Me* as just a dumb piece of programming could be missing the point if such judgments were not made in the wider context of public-service broadcasting, and the particular place of ITV within it.

The Format of *Vote for Me*

The format adopted for *Vote for Me* recalls that of other successful reality television programs such as *Pop Idol*.[7] A panel of judges auditions the applicants and whittles down numbers before a small number of candidates can demonstrate their "talent" and be kept in or voted out by viewers. In the case of *Vote for Me*, the three judges initially examined the "manifestos" written by (according to the official website and the program's presenter) "hundreds of people."[8] The best sixty were invited to an audition in Birmingham, where they were asked to give a one-minute speech. Twenty-five people were selected for the next round. They had thirty minutes to lobby the judges. The fifteen chosen at this stage then had to defend their "manifesto" during cross-examination by the judges.

This process of selection, which resulted in a final line-up of seven candidates, occupied the first of the five shows that were broadcast. As with *Pop Idol* and its ilk, the audience saw the selection program (broadcast on Monday, 10 January 2005) as a docudrama of ambition and embarrassment, public success and failure. Political preferment was made to become a mixture of the traditional (at least in the United Kingdom) party candidate selection process, where aspiring candidates are interviewed by the local party, and of the theatrical audition (and its reality television variants). That this mixture was built into the format is reflected in the choice of judges. John Sergeant, ex-political editor of ITV news, was joined by Kelvin MacKenzie, ex-editor of the *Sun*, and Lorraine Kelly, a presenter of daytime television.

It was only after the audience had been shown the initial selection process and introduced to the logic of the show (on the Monday on which the first episode of *Vote for Me* was broadcast) that they were allowed to participate in it. From the second night onward, the audience was able to vote (as often as any individual wanted) for one of the finalists. It was only at this point that the audience appeared to take over the formal "democratic" reins of power. After this point, the public vote determined the fortunes of the candidates, until two were left on the fifth and final night. The winner of this head-to-head went on to stand in the General Election, standing against the leader of the Conservative Party, Michael Howard, in his Folkestone constituency. The *Vote for Me* candidate secured a derisory 153 (0.3 percent) votes. Mr. Howard received 26,161 (53.9 percent).

The Rhetoric of *Vote for Me*

Pervasive in the sequence of programs is a rhetoric that serves to justify what is happening in both political and dramatic terms. Much is made of the "crisis" of democracy and the way in which *Vote for Me* can address it. It is constantly asserted that "the people" dislike politics and politicians. The official website reports that "we live in an age when voter apathy is rife throughout the U.K. In the last General Election, only 59% of the U.K. population exercised their right to vote—the lowest turnout since 1918. *Vote for Me* is ITV's response."[9] The point is hammered home in the second program where "canvassing" is filmed in Liverpool in "the constituency with the lowest turnout in the U.K.,[10] where "they don't like politics and they don't like politicians." *Vote for Me* presents itself as the solution to this crisis: while in the first program the "fate" of the contestants is in the hands of the judges, after this their fortunes are determined by the "people." And in ascribing power to the "people," the program enables the audience to "make a difference."

The first part of the opening episode explains the set-up, giving the rationale for the program and introducing the candidates and the judges. The dominant message of this section is that democracy is in crisis, since "the people" are uninterested in, and therefore not engaged with, politics. The reason for such disengagement, the program suggests, is that politicians cannot be trusted. As the official website puts it, "people don't trust politicians anymore...but would the people trust 'the people' as politicians?"[11] This point is highlighted throughout the first episode of *Vote for Me*, where "ordinary people" are interviewed and always seem to share the same opinion: politicians are "notorious liars," "they can't be fully trusted." In a later episode (Thursday, 13 January 2005), one of the contestants is praised (ironically) for avoiding the judges' questions: "[Irfan] proved his political credentials by blindly ignoring the questions being tossed in his direction."[12]

Throughout the week, *Vote for Me* tended to treat "politics" as that which politicians do, and as such it was tarnished by the negative views of politicians conveyed by the vox pop interviews, the presentation of the program, and the judges. There was little attempt to suggest that politics existed in other forms and in other settings than those which defined the (conventional account of) Westminster system of liberal democracy. The dominant message was that "politics" was something that "we don't seem to like...very much"; precisely because of the dislike of politicians "we" share. The official website gave credence to this negative view. In reporting the grilling and the humiliation of the candidates, the site comments that "it's politics after all." The assumption is that politics is cruel, a "dirty business."[13] And it is notable that the program-makers include the remarks of embittered losers who are allowed to cast doubt on the fairness of the electoral system. One loser is heard to comment: "I don't know why I didn't get picked, but this is what politics is all about," and another adds: "that's politics: I've been there before; I stood for council and didn't make it." The impression given is that talents and policies are not important, because politics is about being "the best" of a group selected through an arbitrary process. This is confirmed by the program presenter: "this is the political equivalent of a slaughter house" and "in politics, when you lose, you leave empty handed and although our losing candidates are heading home, their political convictions are stronger than ever."

On the other hand, the program sought to convey the impression that, despite the disillusionment with politicians and the political process (narrowly defined), "we" did care about "issues." It was said, for example, that "despite being fed up with politicians, the people we met still cared about the issues." In other words, the program operated with a familiar populist argument that sought to distinguish the essential goodness (and good sense of) people from the system that misrepresented or misused them. "Politics" is a process, by this account, that systematically represents or translates popular views into action. *Vote for Me* legitimated itself by claiming to re-establish the connection between what people thought about the "issues"—what they "really felt"—and those charged with representing them.

This populist rhetoric took another guise when the program implicitly and explicitly contrasted modern democratic politics with its traditional form. The idea of a rosy democratic past, when politicians said what they really thought (and, the implication was, were not managed by spin doctors and the like[14]), was evoked. The final episode was presented as an opportunity for "good, old-fashioned debating,"[15] and the suggestion was that to be a good politician you had to be "a great speaker." The tasks that finalists were assigned (writing manifestos, giving speeches, meeting the press, debating, etc.) fitted a very traditional view of politics.[16]

At the same time, to recover this golden era of public speaking and public debate, it was necessary to bring a "breath of fresh air to Westminster" and to introduce "the next generation of politician."[17] On the opening night of the show, the presenter (Jonathan Maitland) stated: "for the first time you get to choose the type of politician that you want." Later one of the judges (Lorraine Kelly) comments: "people are sick to death of spin and I think they are sick to death of being treated like babies." When another judge (Kelvin MacKenzie) had his opinion challenged by a number of candidates and the other judges, he remarked, "there is an outbreak of democracy."

In short, the rhetoric of *Vote for Me* is a classically populist one in which the appeal is to an "authentic" people who can recover the old values in a new guise and who can avoid the corrupting influence of those currently in office. This populist rhetoric is voiced in different forms and by different means throughout the sequence of programs. It is one that the contestants also buy into. One of them states in her "manifesto": "People keep saying that we haven't got a voice. Well, now I feel like I have." The implication is that traditional political practices, such as voting, the welfare state, and different levels of representation do not offer what *Vote for Me* is instead able to provide its viewers: "a man or woman chosen by the people to represent the people...to boost voter interest and thus election turnout by giving you the opportunity to select a candidate who will be free to stand in any one of the 656 constituencies across the UK."[18]

Voting and *Vote for Me*

A key element in the format and rhetoric of *Vote for Me* is, of course, the voting. The program systematically equates the act of voting offered by the television show with that offered by the formal political system. The program claimed, for instance, that it would "boost voter interest" by showing that "voting is easy: you call one number." The language of reality television, the constant call to "vote now," is connected to the ballot box.[19] The instructions on how to vote were repeated an average of four times in each one-hour episode,[20] with the number superimposed on the screen throughout the duration of the program. During the second episode (which sees the start of public voting) and the fifth (final) show, the numbers were given more times than in any other episode, as if to rally the voters. What is more, there was a suggestion that viewers have "responsibility" or even a "duty" to vote. Here it is not clear whether it is the public-service ethos or the thought of all the money to be made from those calls that is driving the exhortation to vote,[21] although, of course, the appearance was that the viewers were taking part in a genuine political contest. The presenter reminded the audience both how and why they were voting for the finalists: "remember you are looking for someone who'll bring a breath of fresh air to/you would like to see in Westminster"; "you choose who's got what it takes to be an MP"; "you get to decide who should stand at the next general election." This sense of the "importance" of the vote was also conveyed by the official website which, in selling the program, noted that "at the end of each show you will have the chance to eliminate one prospective MP,"[22] and that you'll be able "to keep your favourite candidates in the running."[23] The program was not, it seems, talking about winners or losers in a television game show, but "prospective" Members of Parliament. And in setting up the voting in this way, the show was made to imitate more closely the political system in the sense that favorite candidates are selected, and to downplay the typical reality-show focus on the one who was voted *out* (which was still the logic of *Vote for Me*, if not its rhetoric).

At the same time, the competitive/game-show element remained. The presenter urged the audience to "keep voting; it is very close: there is only 1% between the bottom 3 candidates"; "just 10 minutes left"; "lines close in a couple of minutes"; "they need your vote to survive"; and "the one with the least votes has to go." The telephone lines were kept open all day and night, and not just for the duration of the program.

In stressing the importance of the people's power as represented by their vote, the presenter constantly reminded the judges (and the audience) that it was "not up to the judges...it's up to you" and that they "don't have a vote, the viewers do." The people, not the experts (or the parties), decide. The judges were just there to act as intermediaries, exposing the strengths and weaknesses of the candidates.

As the program constructed the act of voting and its significance, it also articulated the criteria of selection. This, too, seemed to bring together the worlds of populist politics and popular entertainment. On the one hand, the voters were presented as an undifferentiated mass, as the "nation." There was no sense of regional or any other kind of differentiation, as there was in the real election. "The people" were, it was suggested, all of "us," choosing candidates who reflected us in the most literal of senses: they echoed our views. On the other hand, the audience was also constructed as the judges in a *Pop Idol*-style show in which we compare the talents of the competitors. Notions of "talent" appeal to the values of show business at odds with the political criteria also set in motion. This ambiguity was reflected in the role played by the judges and the "expertise" that they embodied as mediators of politics (John Sergeant) or as mediators of the public persona of celebrities (Kelvin MacKenzie and Lorraine Kelly).

Forms of (Political) Knowledge and Expertise

As with other reality television shows such as *Pop Idol*, the presence of judges is fundamental: they represent the "experts," those responsible for the judging, guiding, and training of the candidates. The *Vote for Me* judges, in particular, were expected to select candidates only on the first night of the show. In the remaining episodes, they provide an opportunity and a frame for judgment but have no power to act on them. Nonetheless, their role is crucial to the way the program constructs an account of politics.

The judges were responsible for giving voice to the rhetoric of democratic "crisis" by confirming its existence in their interjections. They also mediated between the public and the candidates, and by appearing to be independent commentators fulfilled a public-service function. They were described as an "independent panel, free of party allegiance, [which] will judge the entrants and select the final shortlist of ten."[24] Their function was to guide the viewers toward making the "best" decision. This was to be achieved through both the appropriate training of the contestants and the sharing of the judges' expertise with the audience. This particular role of the judges distinguishes *Vote for Me* from Andrejevic's account of *American Candidate*: while the latter focuses on "testing," "consulting," and "crafting," its British equivalent concentrates much more on what the expertise of the judges can do for the audience (in order for them to make an informed voting decision) rather than the contestants, hence recalling the "post-deferential culture" to which Coleman (2003, 754) refers in "A Tale of Two Houses."

These worthy intentions, however, have to be compared to the actual choice of judges and the way they performed. The ambiguity between the show-business and political criteria, referred to above, resurfaces in the character and behavior of the judges. None of them has the experience of standing for political office. They are all journalists, only one of whom, John Sergeant, worked exclusively in political journalism. And while Sergeant was a senior reporter for ITN, his subsequent career involved presenting himself as a witty raconteur, slightly mocking of politicians and the political process. Kelvin MacKenzie, another of the judges, was editor of the *Sun* during the time it enthusiastically backed Mrs. Thatcher. Since then his main role has been as head of a talk-radio station, which has come closest in the United Kingdom to imitating the "shock jock" populism of U.S. talk radio. The third judge, Lorraine Kelly, established her name sitting on the sofa of daytime television interviewing a mixture of show-business celebrities and public figures.

From this brief portrait, it can be seen that the judges embodied a particular kind of "expertise," in which "talent" or "political representativeness" would take particular forms. They tended to give considerable attention to "image" and "appearance." The suggestion was that in order to be good politicians, the candidates needed to cultivate both their image and their relationship with the media. Through the judges, *Vote for Me* suggested that "visibility" was more important than content in ensuring political success.

The emphasis on visibility was reinforced by the "tasks" that the contestants were required to perform. Apart from the manifesto-writing, lobbying, and cross-examination that formed part of the initial selection process, the subsequent episodes placed greatest importance on each one's media persona. The finalists took part in a radio phone-in, met the press, and participated in a round-table debate similar to other television debate formats (e.g., the United Kingdom's *Question Time*).

Even when the candidates engaged in more traditional political activities like canvassing, the program-makers selected those incidents and exchanges that were "entertaining" and fitted pre-existing media stereotypes about the nature of politics. The eventual winner, Rodney Hilton-Potts, was shown being told that he is "living in coo-coo land," and the runner-up, Eileen O'Connor, was seen with voters. Such images reinforced the judges' message that appearance mattered more than policy, mostly by commenting on candidates' behavior and appearance rather than their policies and ideas. For instance, one of the judges (John Sergeant) introduced a finalist by saying that "his problem is an image problem and that is that he looks and sounds like so many politicians we already know." Lorraine Kelly wondered whether, in the case of one contestant, "it's gonna go against him the fact that he does look like a Swedish tennis player"; to which Kelvin MacKenzie replied, "well, a good hair cut and a brain transplant probably [would do]." In a similar vein, Kelly pointed out to one of the contestants, "you actually have some sensible ideas and I do think you came across very well and very likable," and "I think [Julie] could be a real media darling: she is really bright and she came over really well."

The language and judgments derived directly from the professional experience of the judges. This comes across clearly in their behavior and the advice they impart during the show. While Sergeant ("Britain's favorite political uncle," "the sage of British politics," "the wise Buddha of politics") adopted the persona of the political journalist, asking direct questions and insisting on precise answers, Kelly and MacKenzie adopted a tabloid-like approach, focused on the sensationalist human side of stories and characters. Furthermore, they were also constructed as representative of some notional ideological spectrum. MacKenzie was portrayed as right-wing ("to the right of your screen...well, to the right in fact, a man described as a legendary media monster"); a hard-liner ("a man who tells it like it is and thinks that MPs should too"; and "a man, who, contrary to popular belief, does believe in equal opportunities, which is why he offends everyone equally"). Kelly is made to embody stereotypical female characteristics ("inside the velvet glove lurks an iron fist"), which were often portrayed as naïve, excessively sentimental, and negative. For instance, MacKenzie's comments ranged from "I'm hostile to inclusion and equality: I like a hierarchy in life" and "if...some stupid young kid has gone out and drunk 16 or 18 pints...give them a good beating, throw them out and hope that they die!" Kelly, by contrast, showed sympathy for candidates who advocated world peace and have battled breast cancer. She uses the embodiment of populist "common sense" ("I'm very impressed...: she's got what many politicians don't have—she's got lots and lots of common sense").

Thus, while *Vote for Me* appeared to constitute some notional political balance (from the far right to the liberal-left center), this was done in a way that mixed traditional political positions with other stereotypes and codes. And the consequence of this was that the MacKenzie position developed a form of "authority." While MacKenzie's remarks were often rude and even racist, they frequently carried more weight than Kelly's, precisely because of this depiction of the latter as unable to make rational decisions. This was clearly exemplified when Kelly applauded a disabled candidate and Sergeant admonished her: "You are not meant to clap as a judge"; to which Kelly replied: "Oh, I'm sorry but I really liked him and not because he is in a wheelie."

The sense of political balance and public service was also encoded in the function of the presenter, Jonathan Maitland. He could be seen as an additional member of the "experts" team, although he was not directly involved in the judging of the finalists. He did, however, fill the gaps left by editorial choices;[25] for example, by explaining to the camera who the candidates were, what the "tasks relevant to political life"[26] consisted of, and—more important—insisting that all finalists benefit from the same amount of time and coverage.

But as well as acting as an impartial referee, he was also a commentator. After a particularly heated debate, Maitland observed, "That was fun!," and just before announcing a commercial break he stated: "Join us after the break when things get even more uncomfortable for our final five." This view of politics as entertaining when unpleasant and involving arguing and bickering was in line with the attempt to popularize politics in order to make it appealing to the public. Finally, Maitland's role was fundamental in reminding the audience when, why, and how to vote.

So while the program evoked a rhetoric of returning to traditional politics and "real" issues, the logic that its format and its judges adopted set up quite a different kind of politics. At one level, it gave legitimacy to a typically right-wing political populism. At another, it celebrated the politics of image. Indeed, the importance of image was contained in the rationale of the program. It was aimed at finding "not...a professional politician, just something a bit different."[27] Even the title of the program, *Vote for Me*, not *for My Policies*, indicated that the real focus was on the person rather than a set of policies. The expertise that the judges offered was that of media actors and operators. Despite the suggestion that the candidates were given political "training," the judges' "political knowledge" and therefore the way they "train" the candidates was inseparable from their background as media personalities.

The People versus Politicians

Vote for Me plays on the distinction between politicians and "real people": the difference between these two categories is based upon a political judgment that favors those characteristics typical of "ordinary" people over those associated with politicians. This distinction between "real people" and politicians is established in the opening sequence of the first episode, in which disenchanted voters speak of wanting "things" to be different. Lorraine Kelly asks a passer-by: "If you could be in charge, what would you change?," to which the reply is: "Oh, blimey, everything I think." The assumption is that politicians will not achieve this change: "They are all out to feather their own nests." No opportunity is given to politicians to counter these accusations. It is almost as if they are irrelevant. The program was organized around the idea that it is for "the people," about "the people." There is a single, brief shot of an embarrassed Tony Blair, who tries to explain the low election turnout; otherwise politicians exist solely through the words of "ordinary" people and the judges.

The only politicians who appeared at all in the programs were two independent MPs: Martin Bell, an ex-BBC reporter who served as an MP for one parliament, and Dr. Richard Taylor, a doctor who stood (and was elected twice) on a local platform. Neither Bell nor Taylor have any formal party political associations. They are "independent" of party and, by implication, the corrupting system it entails. They stand for the "real" politician. Taylor was shown saying: "MP stands for Magic Pass: you can go anywhere, you can talk to anybody, write to anybody and get an answer."

This sense of the politician as "privileged," and hence removed from the world of ordinary people, was overlaid with the rhetoric of their corruption. Kelvin MacKenzie commented at one point: "What would really make me laugh is that at the end of the five days they start telling whoppers. Then I'll say: 'right, you have become a politician. Congratulations.'" And, in a similar mode, John Sergeant commented on the eventual winner: "He has been convicted for fraud and despite that, or maybe precisely because of that, he now wants to get into politics."

The sense of difference between politicians and the people was reinforced by the "training," which treated politics as the art of manipulation. Sergeant explains canvassing: "Seek out agreement, have a quick conversation, make the voter think you are on their side and then go," and "The whole fight is on the margin, trying to persuade people. If you can't do that well, don't expect to be good at politics. And it is amazing how you can get people very quickly to agree with you on certain points, but you must be good at that."

So despite drawing a distinction between the politicians and the people, the skills which *Vote for Me* appeared to value were exactly those that are associated with the professionalized modern politician and the contemporary celebrity. The *Vote for Me* exercise was ultimately about "making an impression," about being someone's "favorite candidate," "the people's champion," "winning," being "the best," and, eventually, being "a star." When Maitland introduced Kelly to the audience, he described her as "someone who's tried just about everybody on her sofas: from pop stars to politicians and everyone in between."

The Final Few

And who made it through to the final of *Vote for Me*? Whatever might be said about the seven finalists, they were not a socially representative sample. There were four male and three female candidates, five of whom were in their forties and fifties.[28] One finalist was Asian (Irfan Hanif), and one was disabled (Kevin Donnellon). Although neither the website nor the presenter gave details, only one candidate represented herself as "working class" (Julie Michen). Much was made of Michen's social class, Donnellon's disability, and Hanif's occupation (doctor). Described like this, the contestants came to resemble the structure (if not the content) of the *Big Brother* household. Their stereotypical characteristics created pegs on which to hang the program's narrative, while allowing grounds for some sense of "representing ordinary people."

The program-makers' strategy was echoed in the pronouncements of the contestants. Michen, for instance, presented herself as "your working class single parent candidate; I live your life and I'll fight your fights." She was "the voice of the people and the woman you can trust." When asked about how she did in her first task, she explained: "It went exactly the way I'd done it in the kitchen to my two cats!" Here she confirmed her representative ordinariness in the mundane associations she drew. And the same message was embodied in her explicitly stated political views: "We should never have gone into Iraq, it was always about money and oil it was never about the people. There were other fights we could have fought if it was about the people"; and "One of the ways I would raise money is by getting rid of half the MPs we use in this country."

This account of herself was reinforced by the judges and connected to the populist rhetoric of the program. MacKenzie said of Michen:

> I thought she did fantastically well, considering she hasn't probably got a political bone in her body. We are looking for people who are going to become voices of people currently not enfranchised. Our viewers will understand what she said a lot more than they will understand some of the gobbledygook that are spoken out by Gordon Brown [Chancellor of the Exchequer] or Oliver Letwin [Conservative Shadow Minister] or the Lib[eral] Dem[ocrat] guy.

Sergeant described her as someone who was "proud of living in a council estate."[29] Michen's "ordinariness" was confirmed in these judgments, which endorsed her self-identification.

The second finalist worth looking at in detail is Kevin Donnellon, who suffers from the effects of thalidomide. He used his disability to create a populist campaign in which he linked together other groups: "It will benefit people on a low fixed income, which includes pensioners, disabled people and students." And when MacKenzie questioned Donnellon's presence on the program ("If he weren't disabled, would Kevin have made it here tonight? Are we in fact patronizing Kevin in this way?"), Donnellon replied: "I've got as much right to be here as anybody." And, like Michen, he rooted his right to speak for others in the fact that he spoke from experience (and, the implication was, experience cannot be challenged or denied). When MacKenzie asked him, "Why on earth do you want elected representatives to be disabled?," Donnellon replied: "I'm not saying that you can't intellectualize it because you are not a disabled person, but I've got that quality of experience, if you like. So, I know what I'm talking about."

Irfan Hanif experienced a fate similar to Donnellon's. He was presented by Maitland as believing "in the politics of compassion," and his policies concentrated on "the vulnerable, the weak, the infirm." Moreover, he pointed out to the audience that "all the issues that I've raised so far affect me and you and you and you and you...," and he accuses politicians of stealing and lying ("There is money going into government coffers. It's not their money," and "If everybody today pulls together and forces the government to show us how much they've really got. Show us the books: show us how much is going in, how much is going out").

What was revealing about the self-presentation of these contestants—and the program's mediation of them—was the struggle over the notions of "ordinariness" and the representative claims attaching to them. The contestants all negotiated a claim to be one of the people, while the judges questioned these claims. The program, in this sense, seemed to be pushing implicitly and explicitly an account of people as an undifferentiated mass, but with a very particular political perspective. It constructed a classical populism, which finds itself revealed in the reactionary politics of the winner.

And the Winner Is... Rodney Hylton-Potts

From the beginning of the program, both the judges and the editorial team seemed to take a keen interest in Rodney Hylton-Potts. He was one of the few finalists who appeared in the short film about selection procedures at the beginning, who had a large group of supporters in the audience, and who had drawn attention to himself because of, according to presenter Maitland, "a million pound fraud," for which he "spent over two years in prison."

The judges displayed their own curiosity in him. Sergeant said: "The guy is interesting: he is the guy who went to prison," and "That's a tricky one, I must say: he's engaging in so many ways, but in other ways he is impossible, isn't he?" Kelly commented that "I wouldn't trust him as far as I could throw him"; "You just scratch the surface and his seediness comes out." She confessed: "I must admit I was a bit reluctant to put him through because I find most of his views extreme and some of them actually repellent." MacKenzie, whose views are closest to those of Hylton-Potts, was more equivocal: "Somebody like Rodney's future should be decided by the viewers and should not necessarily be decided by us."

Meanwhile, Hylton-Potts exploited his criminal record to show that he had both repented his wrongdoing and had been strengthened by it (made more "human" and "ordinary"). He presented himself as having paid his debt to society: "I'm ashamed of what happened to me, I work as a legal consultant, doing work for clients, everyday; I fight for them." He, like the other contestants, insisted on his ordinariness. The "extraordinary" experience of prison, he said, had made him more "ordinary." At the same time, he presented himself in terms of his "strength," as someone who would fight for his "people": "I have taken drugs. So I've known wealth and poverty and highs and lows and it's made me a street fighter." His partner is shown saying: "I think Rodney would make a fantastic MP. Because of what he's been through he never gives in." This (mock) heroic populism was yoked to a populist formula that demands that the people be freed from the demands of government. When he was asked for an opinion on whether pubs should be open twenty-four hours a day, he replied: "I think the government are doing it to get more tax. [This is] not for a government to legislate; it's for people to behave themselves and parents to guide people."

In typically populist terms, he described himself as offering a "cabby manifesto":[30] "Just ask a cabby, don't trust me...; just ask a cabby...what they think about immigration.... On the way here today I said to the cabby as promised:

'What do ordinary people think' and they all said the same: 'no more immigration.'" In the same vein he announced: "If you elect me, I'll fight for the pound...; I'll have a complete ban on immigration... 'cause Britain is full...; we are closed for businesses...; you watch out." He continued, "Let's get our great country back...; our pensioners didn't fight two world wars to save this great country to have it swamped with immigrants and governed by faceless bankers in Brussels." He denied that his policies were racist,

> but this country...has had quite enough of these liberal ideas. It's about time somebody thought about our pensioners and the prospect of the Tories and the Labour Party fighting to bring Turkey into the EU with 65 million people with the right to live in this country and work here, is a joke, we've lost the plot; ...we have a very proud tradition in this country of helping overseas countries but a client of mine last week died because she couldn't afford to put money in her gas meter in London this year, so there has to be a balance: let's think of our own people as well.

Neither the facts nor the logic of his arguments was challenged. Instead, his manifesto was denounced by the "experts" on the program as racist (MacKenzie asked, "Are you a secret Nazi?," and Maitland commented: "He's a cross between Lord Brocket and Mussolini"). Despite this, the program still effectively endorsed his views. The very structure of the format and its rhetoric invited this kind of conclusion. The people were right, and so their winner must be right, too. But the winner was less a product of popular choice than of the organization of that choice by the show's structure and format. Hylton-Potts's claim was that "most people...secretly agree with me"; to which MacKenzie added, "Unfortunately I imagine quite a few ITV viewers will agree with Rodney." They did, and he won.

The rhetoric that refers to "ordinary people" as more representative of the population than politicians was skillfully employed by the *Vote for Me* winner, not only in the description and display of himself but also in the formulation of his policies. He set himself apart from the professional politician, even as he recognized shared instincts ("I have seen politicians, I want to be one: I want to be obnoxious, offensive and win"). He was constructed as a loyal man who had learned hard lessons and would not sell out or lie to the people ("No matter what you think of me, if I'm elected I'll be loyal").[31] He claimed, implausibly: "At least, like Nelson Mandela, I did my time before politics, unlike the Tory A-team like Aetkin and Archer, who did it the other way around." More in keeping with the rhetoric of the program, MacKenzie talks of Hylton-Potts's joining "the rest of the crooks in the House of Parliament." It seems that this rhetoric struck a chord with those who bothered to vote.

Conclusion

Although Hylton-Potts went on to secure a paltry number of votes in the real election, the case of *Vote for Me* remains an interesting and important example of the conjunction of politics and entertainment. He may have secured less support than the Monster Raving Loony Party[32] (despite the endorsement of the Pensioners Party[33] and the far right, racist BNP[34]), but he represented the culmination of a particular kind of popular cultural logic. It was apparent that ITV ended up feeling more embarrassed about than proud of its attempts to save democracy.[35] Not only did the company give minimal attention to the winner, it also refused to publish viewing and voting figures in an attempt to invalidate the result of a program. The point was that the program in its rhetoric, format, and selection of candidates and judges, created a voice and platform for a populism that chimed with the widely disseminated, if not accurate, view that democratic politics was in crisis and that the cause of it was parties and politicians themselves. *Vote for Me* does not offer any basis for generalizing about the relationship between popular entertainment and politics any more than does any other single instance or example. What it does show is that the relationship between entertainment and politics is constructed by the producers of that culture. Our argument is that the winner is not produced by a popular vote but rather by the organization of that vote through the framing of politics in the program.

Notes

[1] Hellen (2003); Burrell (2004). Also see Aaronvitch (2004).

[2] All quotations in this chapter, unless stated otherwise, are taken from the *Vote for Me* program, recorded from ITV on 10–15 January 2005.

[3] As reported in http://www.itv.com/page.asp?partid=2454.

[4] The program was broadcast at 11 o'clock every night from 10 to 15 January. However, it could be argued that such scheduling coincides with pubs' closing times and therefore it targeted a specific audience. Moreover, as reported by *The Guardian* (16 April 2004), the program commissioner, Steve Anderson, "was keen to play down the showbiz aspects of the program, stressing the show would be screened after the 10.30 pm news rather than in a peak-time slot."

[5] It was launched exclusively to broadsheets and not tabloids, which clearly indicates the desire to attract an audience that usually does not watch reality television and is already interested in politics (Political Junkies, in Coleman's words [2003]), rather than the young and disenfranchised.

[6] *Ofcom Review of Public Service Television Broadcasting* (2004).

[7] Broadcast on ITV1 in 2001 and again in 2003 (*Pop Idol 2*); created by FremantleMedia and produced by Thames Television.

[8] According to *The Independent* (8 January 2005), "ten thousand people expressed an initial interest and the best 60 were auditioned." *The Express* (8 January 2005) stated that "when the producers advertised the program about 1,500 people expressed an interest" and then confirms that 60 will appear on the first show. *The Mail on Sunday* (16 January 2005) said: "a panel of judges...whittled 200 contestants down to 15 finalists." *The Observer* (9 January 2005) and *The Daily Telegraph* (10 January 2005) confirmed that 60 would audition on the first show.

[9] As reported in http://www.itv.com/page.asp?partid=2454.

[10] As reported in http://www.itv.com/page.asp?partid=2879.

[11] As quoted in http://www.itv.com/page.asp?partid=2877.

[12] As quoted in http://www.itv.com/page.asp?partid=2883.

[13] More on this in http://www.itv.com/page.asp?partid=2879. Here, the usually affable Kelly accuses one of the contestants (Dominic Carman) of being "a grey man in a grey suit."

[14] This point signals one of the major differences between *Vote for Me* and *American Candidate*: while the former strongly opposes the alleged manipulations of spin doctors, the latter allowed participants to use "political consultants and pollsters" (see Andrejevic in this volume). This, according to Andrejevic, resulted in the focus being shifted from "policy" and "substance" to "message" and "appearance," but does not seem to be viewed by the American public as a form of distorting politics and the "truth."

[15] As reported in http://www.itv.com/page.asp?partid=2887.

[16] For a contrasting view, see Andrejevic in this volume.

[17] As quoted, for example, in http://www.itv.com/page.asp?partid=2454.

[18] As reported in http://www.itv.com/page.asp?partid=2454.

19 Although this is equally true for programs such as *Big Brother* and *Pop Idol*, there are only seven *Vote for Me* finalists, which means that, depending on the favorite, there is only a one-digit number to add at the end of the number given by the presenter.

20 Six times (Tuesday show), twice (Wednesday), three times (Thursday), five (Friday).

21 A similar tension is noted by Andrejevic elsewhere in this volume.

22 As reported in http://www.itv.com/page.asp?partid=2454.

23 The only two exceptions being the statements "vote for the opening skirmish" in the first episode and "the guillotine is poised" in the final show.

24 As reported in http://www.itv.com/page.asp?partid=2454.

25 Interestingly, Maitland adopts a similar role in his book *Vote for...Who?*, which aims at "telling it like it is" (2005, xi).

26 As reported in http://www.itv.com/page.asp?partid=2454.

27 Similarities with this are noted by Andrejevic elsewhere in this volume.

28 According to the official website and the presentation made in the program, one contestant was in his twenties, one was in her thirties, three were in their forties, and two were in their fifties.

29 Although when asked why she lives on a council estate (MacKenzie: "you are probably the most intelligent person I've ever met who's lived in a council house and I am puzzled as to why you haven't moved out"), she replied:, "because I haven't got any choice: I have no money. I work hard. I've got two children I've raised alone. You know: not all of us are born with money and have the means to make it."

30 For more details on this, also see the Get Britain Back Party website and "Vote for Me"–Vote for Rodney Hylton-Potts website, which, according to Hylton-Potts, "has had 650 hits of support for my policy" thanks to the program.

31 Interestingly, this is the time of the Hutton report and the issue of the war in Iraq.

32 Election results as reported on BBC News website, Result for Folkestone & Hythe; the difference in percentage between Get Britain Back Party and Monster Raving Loony Party was 0.1.

33 Endorsements to the Get Britain Back Party to be found in http://www.getbritainback.com/. No confirmation of such endorsement can be found on the Pensioners Party website (http://www.thepensionersparty.org/index.html).

34 See, for instance, Bean (9 February 2005),
   in http://www.bnp.org.uk/columnists/notebook2.php?jbId=9.

35 See, for example, Burrell (29 March 2004) in *The Independent*; Hinsliff (9 January 2005) in *The Observer*; Hellen (28 March 2004) in *The Sunday Times*.

References

Aaronvitch, D. 2004. "Political Pop Idol? It Doesn't Get My Vote." *The Guardian*, 30 March.

Andrejevic, M. 2006. "Faking Democracy: Reality TV Politics on American Candidate." In *Politicotainment: Television's Take on the Real*, edited by Kristina Riegert. New York: Peter Lang.

Bean, J. 2005. *"Vote For Me" Was "Vote BNP,"* 9 February. http://www.bnp.org.uk/columnists/notebook2.php?jbId=9 (accessed 22 May 2005).

Burrell, I. 2004. "Want To Be an MP? ITV Plans 'Pop Idol'-Style Show To Find Election Star." *The Independent*, 29 March.

Coleman, S. 2003. "A Tale of Two Houses: The House of Commons, the Big Brother House and the People at Home." *Parliamentary Affairs* 56 (4): 733–758.

"Election 2005—Results: Folkestone & Hythe." http://news.bbc.co.uk/1/shared/vote2005/html/256.stm (accessed 20 May 2005).

The Electoral Commission—Media Centre—Press Releases. 2002. *The Electoral Commission Embarks upon Final Drive to Rally Voters for Next Week's Local Elections*, 23 April. http://www.electoralcommission.gov.uk/media-centre/newsreleasecampaigns.cfm/news/89. (accessed 20 May 2005).

Franklin, B. 2004. *Packaging Politics—Political Communication in Britain's Media Democracy.* London: Arnold.

"The Get Britain Back Party with Rodney Hylton-Potts." http://www.getbritainback.com/ (accessed 20 May 2005).

Hellen, N. 2003. "Vote for Your Local MP in New Reality Show." *The Sunday Times*, 13 April.

——. 2004. "Reality Show MP May Try to Grab Blair's Seat." *The Sunday Times*, 28 March.

Hinsliff, G. 2005. "MPs Blast 'Tawdry' Politics Idol Show." *The Observer*, 9 January.

Maitland, J. 2005. *Vote for...Who?* London: Metro Publishing, Ltd.

Ofcom Review of Public Service Television Broadcasting. 2004. http://www.ofcom.org.uk/consultations/past/psb/psb/?a=87101 (accessed 4 November 2004).

Parry, G.; Moyser, G.; and Day, N. 1992. *Political Participation and Democracy in Britain.* Cambridge: Cambridge University Press.

Pattie, C.; Seyd, P.; and Whitely, P. 2004. *Citizenship in Britain—Values, Participation and Democracy.* Cambridge: Cambridge University Press.

The Pensioners Party. http://www.thepensionersparty.org/index.html (accessed 20 May 2005).

Street, J. 2004. "Celebrity Politicians: Popular Culture and Political Representation." *British Journal of Politics and International Relations* 6: 435–452.

Zoonen, L. van 2005. *Entertaining the Citizen—When Politics and Popular Culture Converge.* Oxford: Rowman & Littlefield.

Vote for Me—ITV.com. http://www.itv.com/page.asp?partid=2454 (accessed 20 January 2005).

"Vote for Me"—Vote Rodney Hylton-Potts. http://www.voterodders.org/ (accessed 1 February 2005).

Wells, M. 2004. "Pop Idol-Style Show Will Select Potential MPs: ITV Launches Vote for Me To Tackle Political Apathy." *The Guardian*, 16 April.

West, D.M., and Orman, J. 2003. *Celebrity Politics.* Upper Saddle River, NJ: Prentice-Hall.

CHAPTER SIX

"Fake" News versus "Real" News as Sources of Political Information: *The Daily Show* and Postmodern Political Reality

JEFFREY P. JONES

A recurrent claim about young Americans is that they get more of their news about politics and current events from late-night television comedians than they do from the news media. This claim began with a statistic that appeared in a 2000 survey of the electorate conducted by the Pew Research Center for the People and the Press, which reported that 47 percent of people under thirty years old were "informed at least occasionally" about the presidential campaign by late-night talk shows.[1] Though there are numerous methodological and interpretive problems raised by this simple yet ultimately flawed statistic, journalists and other critics have nevertheless transformed it into a myth about young people and their news-consumption habits. Regardless of its accuracy, it seemingly explains why young people have increasingly turned away from traditional outlets of political communication, namely newspapers and television news (Mindich 2005). It also addresses journalistic concerns that audiences are attracted more to entertainment than serious public-affairs reporting, and what's worse, that they may not even be able to distinguish between the two. It also seemingly verifies fears of public ignorance of the political process (Delli Carpini and Keeter 1996), youth disengagement from politics (Buckingham 2000), a declining reading culture (Scheuer 1999), couch potato kids, the entertainmentization of politics (West and Orman 2003), and the cynicism that supposedly grips our society (Hart 1994; Chaloupka 1999).

This chapter begins, then, by examining and questioning this myth. But as with many myths that circulate in society, the critic's ability to refute the accuracy of the myth is not likely to diminish its popularity or widespread circulation. Instead, it may be more effective to show why the basic premise of the myth itself is incorrect. That is, in this instance, the idea that late-night comedic television does not (or cannot) impart important news or information about public affairs and thus, by definition, only traffics in the trivial, inane, or absurd. In this chapter, therefore, I turn the myth on its head by asking: What if the myth is true and young people *are* "getting their news" from popular late-night comedy programs such as *The Daily Show with Jon Stewart?* What is it they might learn about politics or current events from this show, and how does that compare with what they might learn about politics were they to watch more respected sources of news such as CNN instead? To begin answering this question, I compare a news item "reported" by *The Daily Show*, a fake news show that parodies a "legitimate" television news broadcast, with the same story as covered by CNN. I follow the Pew Center's lead by examining news reports of the 2004 presidential election, yet from broadcasts much later in the campaign when the viewing public is typically more raptly attuned. I analyze the type of information that is offered in the two reports and how the resulting meanings or "truths" compare.

I argue that even though *The Daily Show* is a fake news show, its faux journalistic style allows the show's writers and host to question, dispel, and critique the manipulative language and symbolizations coming from the presidential campaign while simultaneously opening up deeper truths about politics than those offered by the "objective" reporting of mainstream journalism. By actually showing the high levels of spin and rhetoric produced by the candidates and their campaigns, then offering humorous retorts that cut to the heart of the matter, *The Daily Show* offers its viewers particular (and perhaps more useful) "information" about the campaign that is often missing from "real" journalist reports on the news networks, and hence informs its viewers in ways that mainstream journalism rarely does. Given the extraordinary level of outright distortions, lies, and spin that dominated both the Republican and Democratic campaigns in this election, this chapter concludes that perhaps the postmodern notion that the "fake" is more real than the "real" is not such an unsettling notion when it comes to citizens looking for truth in contemporary political communication on television. And, in turn, perhaps young citizens—if they do indeed get their information from political comedians on television—may not be as misinformed as the current myth suggests.

The Myth of Young People and Knowledge of Public Affairs

In February 2000, the Pew Research Center for the People and the Press reported that 47 percent of people under the age of thirty were "informed at least occasionally" about the campaign or candidates by late-night talk shows (13 percent regularly and 34 percent sometimes). The poll was conducted from 4 to 11 January 2000, before any party primaries had taken place. In January 2004, the Pew Center repeated this survey (conducted 19 December 2003 through 4 January 2004), this time asking respondents if they "learned something" from comedy shows. Twenty-one percent of people under the age of thirty reported learning something from programs such as *Saturday Night Live* and *The Daily Show* (roughly the same number who learned something from the Internet). As the Pew study notes, "For Americans under 30, these comedy shows are now mentioned almost as frequently as newspapers and evening network news programs as regular sources for election news." Furthermore, the report exclaims, "one out of every two young people (50%) say they at least sometimes learn about the campaign from comedy shows, nearly twice the rate among people age 30–49 (27%) and four times the rate among people 50 and older."[2]

Before taking these statistics at face value, however, we should examine both the questions and the resulting statistics more closely. Certainly political insiders, heavy news readers/watchers, and political junkies are attuned to news so early in the campaign, for no other reason than to be able to handicap the upcoming horse race. As for the rest of the polity, however, the electoral contests in the small yet important states of Iowa and New Hampshire certainly receive much less of their attention because the party nominee is generally a forgone conclusion by the time most Americans have the opportunity to vote in their state primary election. Hence, for a poll to attempt to measure political knowledge and information about an election so early in the campaign is specious.

What is worse, though, is the wording of the question itself: "informed at least occasionally." What does it mean to be "informed" about the campaign—knowledge of who is running for office, what their positions are on issues, who is ahead in the race, who has the biggest war chest, what gaffes have occurred to this point, the names of their wives, what type of underwear they prefer? At what level can most any type of nonfiction program—news reports, talk shows, documentaries, stand-up comedy, advertisements—provide *some* of this information? The question doesn't help us understand the underlying normative assumption of whether the respondent should know the differences between Al Gore's and Bill Bradley's positions on Social Security reform, or whether the respondent is simply expected to know their names and that they are running for office. Furthermore, the question asks "at least occasionally." Does that mean every day, once a week, or once a month, or does it suggest a regular and consistent pattern of consumption? Finally, what assumptions of intentionality are included here? Does the question seek to identify whether citizens brush up against news, or whether they intentionally turn to certain forms of programming for "information"? The survey results provide no answers to these questions. In short, the response to this question really only tells us two things—that comedians mine current affairs for humorous content, and that different programming types differ in their popularity among different demographic groups. It certainly does *not* measure whether the only or primary source of information about current affairs is obtained by watching late-night comedians on television.

Nevertheless, that hasn't prevented journalists from using the statistic to develop a full-blown myth about young people and their news consumption habits. For instance, CNN anchor Judy Woodruff began a question to *The Daily Show* host Jon Stewart by stating, "We hear more and more that your show and shows like your show are the places that young people *are getting their news*" (emphasis added).[3] Ted Koppel, the anchor for ABC's late-night news show *Nightline* (a program that directly competes with these entertainment shows), similarly assailed Stewart by noting to his viewers, "A lot of television viewers, more, quite frankly, than I'm comfortable with, *get their news* from the comedy channel on a program called 'The Daily Show'" (emphasis added).[4] And perhaps most egregiously, *Newsday* reporter Verne Gay wrote, "A recent study from the Pew Center found that 8 percent of respondents *learned most everything they knew* about a candidate from shows like The Daily Show and Saturday Night Live" (emphasis added; Gay 2004).

As these quotes suggest, reporters have taken great liberty in revising and expanding what the statistic actually reveals. Yet the results of a campaign knowledge test conducted on over 19,000 citizens in the summer and fall of 2004 by the University of Pennsylvania's National Annenberg Election Survey did little to temper the myth. The survey reported that "viewers of late-night comedy programs, especially The Daily Show with Jon Stewart on Comedy Central, are more likely to know the issue positions and backgrounds of presidential candidates than people who do not watch late-night comedy," noting that *Daily Show* viewers "have higher campaign knowledge than national news viewers and newspaper readers."[5] The survey concludes, "traditional journalists have been voicing increasing concern that if young people are receiving political information from late-night comedy shows like

The Daily Show, they may not be adequately informed on the issues of the day. This data suggests that these fears may be unsubstantiated." The survey also points out, however, that "these findings do not show that The Daily Show is itself responsible for the higher knowledge among its viewers."

In summary, journalists and other critics of entertainment television have propagated a myth based on dubious evidence that late-night comedy television programming is a central location for the delivery of news (and, by inference, misinformation and ignorance about politics) for young people, a myth that competing quantitative evidence suggests is incorrect. What neither of these surveys reveals, however, is an assessment of the *content* of these shows—whether they offer viewers anything of value or are relatively meaningless, whether the information provided is accurate and truthful or biased and incorrect, or even how this material compares with other sources of information on public affairs. There is no qualitative assessment, only the assumption that what appears in these formats is not equivalent to that which could be obtained from traditional sources of political information. What follows, then, is an attempt to examine these questions directly, looking at how *The Daily Show* "reports" news and information, and its comparative value in light of reporting available on a more culturally acceptable and respected news source, CNN.

News Reports by *The Daily Show* and CNN

Every weeknight (except Fridays), Comedy Central airs *The Daily Show*, a mock news program and hybrid talk show that parodies television news for the first half of the program, then segues into a more typical talk-show interview between host Jon Stewart and a guest. The first half—the news segment—mimics the anchor-centered style of television news reporting, where Stewart narrates the day's top stories accompanied by video evidence. The news segment also uses the news convention of the anchor interviewing reporters "on location," in this instance, with Stewart talking to his faux "senior correspondents," who pretend to be reporting live via satellite (in front of a background image of, say, Baghdad or the White House). The primary interest of my investigation is this "news" segment of the show.

I examined one week of the program during the late stages of the presidential campaign—4 to 7 October 2004—one week after the first presidential debate. I selected one program during this period as a representative text (Thursday, 7 October) for a close textual analysis. This limited selection allows for an in-depth analysis of the information and commentary provided, as well as a direct comparison with news reports from CNN. While the limited range of texts can be criticized as overly restricted, such a close reading of *The Daily Show* has not been conducted to date. Instead, existing studies have examined a broader range of texts from the program across numerous episodes and months of programming (see, for instance, Jones 2005a; and Baym 2005). Here, though, the intention is to make a direct comparison of two entire news reports on the same event. The selection of a single news report also limits the generalizability of my argument, yet the episode selected for scrutiny is not extraordinary. Rather, it is fairly representative, by my reading, of a typical *Daily Show* broadcast. Furthermore, the intentional circumscribing allows for the close reading of a text that cultural studies has proven to be of value. The episode selected illustrates the type of information provided in typical news reports by both *The Daily Show* and CNN, allowing us to compare not just the variety but also the quality of the reports and conclusions that can be drawn from them. The CNN reports come from three programs, all of which appeared on the same day as *The Daily Show* broadcast: *American Morning* (7 A.M.), *CNN Live Today* (10 A.M.), and *News from CNN* (12 P.M.).[6]

CNN began its 7 A.M. broadcast by reporting on Bush's campaign appearances the previous day, as well as the release of the CIA's Iraq Survey Group report investigating the existence of weapons of mass destruction in Iraq. In reporting Bush's campaign stop in Pennsylvania, CNN White House Correspondent Elaine Quijano pointed out that the president made no mention of a new report by the Iraq Survey Group, which found no evidence of stockpiles of weapons of mass destruction in Iraq when the United States invaded in 2003. Still, Mr. Bush is standing by his decision, insisting that after September 11 the country had to assess every potential threat in a new light.

> (Video clip of President Bush speaking in Wilkes-Barre, Pennsylvania): Our nation awakened to an even greater danger, the prospect that terrorists who killed thousands with hijacked airplanes would kill many more with weapons of mass murder. We had to take a hard look at every place where terrorists might get those weapons. One regime stood out, the dictatorship of Saddam Hussein.

During the 10 A.M. report, CNN decided not to continue airing the clip of Bush's speech, instead letting Quijano summarize the president's central point in the statement, as well as note the official White House "reading" of the report, attributed here to "administration officials."

But the president did not mention that new CIA report, which found no weapons of mass destruction in Iraq when the United States invaded in 2003. Instead Mr. Bush repeated his argument that taking Saddam Hussein out of power has made the world safer. Administration officials say they believe the report shows Saddam Hussein was a threat that the United States needed to take seriously. They also say they believe it shows that he had the intent and capability to develop weapons of mass destruction.

By 12 P.M., CNN was simply reporting the release of the report as this: "Bush also defended the war in Iraq, just as the CIA prepares to report that Saddam Hussein did not have weapons of mass destruction or the means to produce them before U.S. troops invaded Iraq."

Jon Stewart also began his broadcast by announcing the release of the CIA report and noting its conclusions:

> Everything we've been waiting for happened today. The official CIA report, the Dulfer Report, has come out, the one they've been working on for the past two years. It will be the definitive answer on the weapons of mass destruction programs in Iraq, and as it turns out, not so much. Apparently, there were no weapons of mass destruction in Iraq, and their capabilities have been degraded and they had pretty much stopped trying anything in '98. And both the president and vice president have come out today in response to the findings and said that they clearly justified the invasion of Iraq. Some people look at a glass as half full, while other people look at a glass and say that it's a dragon.

In this segment, Stewart provides roughly the same amount and type of information provided by CNN, but then goes out of his way to establish that despite clear and convincing evidence to the contrary, Bush and Cheney continue their act as either liars or highly delusional people; they see what they want to see. Here Stewart offers not just the facts, but also draws conclusions from those facts. Journalistic adherence to norms of objectivity generally prevents many reporters and anchors from looking across specific events to explicitly point out repeated patterns of deception or misjudgment by politicians and government officials (unless the reporting occurs in investigative or opinion-editorial pieces). *The Daily Show*, as a fake news program, is not limited by such professional constraints. Viewers are thus invited to focus on the most important aspect of this news event—that this is not just another investigation that proves the official reason for invading Iraq was misguided and wrong. Rather, the import is that the Bush Administration repeatedly refuses to admit its mistake.

CNN, on the other hand, simply repeats the administration's position, as is standard journalistic convention. Yet since numerous investigations have produced the same findings (which in the world of science and social science would amount to the establishment of "truth"), why should news media continue to repeat a position that has no basis in fact—just because the government continues to assert the position? Is that "newsworthy," and if not, what news value is being fulfilled? Daniel Boorstin contends that assertions such as this amount to "pseudo-events," a story created by politicians and journalists that has no intrinsic value as a news event *per se*, but is only deemed as such by journalists in the era of "objectivity" (Boorstin 1960). Stewart refuses to play along and, again, ignores the administration's "reading" or justifications because they have no basis in reality (as determined by the numerous other officials, institutions, and nations that have concluded the same thing).

Stewart then turns his attention to a Bush campaign stop the day before. "Let's begin tonight on the campaign trail," he says, while talking over a video clip of President Bush in Wilkes-Barre, Pennsylvania. Bush is standing in front of a backdrop/banner with the words "A Safer America, A Stronger Economy" adorned over both of his shoulders. "Yesterday, President Bush's advisors alerted the networks he would be making a major policy speech in Wilkes-Barre, Pennsylvania. The subject...[*the graphic highlights the slogan "A Safer America"*]—no, not that. [*The graphic highlights "A Stronger Economy."*] Uh, wrong again. [*The graphic then shows a crossed-out slogan, superimposing the hand-scrawled message, "Recover from unbelievably poor debate performance."*]. That's it! That was the subject. Yes, in the week of his, let's call it 'weak' showing against Senator John Kerry on Thursday, the president and his handlers snookered the cable news networks into giving him one hour of free full-on campaign stop pabulum."

CNN also covered this campaign stop in all three of its morning broadcasts. For both the 7 A.M. and 10 A.M. reports, Quijano simply referred to two campaign stops (one of which was in Pennsylvania), noting that Bush had "stepped up his attacks" and had come "out swinging hard" against his opponent, "blasting" Kerry and delivering a "blistering assault on Kerry's record." The reporter seeks to summarize the tone and substance of the president's speeches, while characterizing him as on the offensive—exactly what the campaign hopes will be reported. Only the 12 P.M. broadcast noted the campaign's intentions in changing the focus of the speech. Wolf Blitzer introduced the subject by referring to Bush's "attempt to try to reestablish some political momentum," while the correspondent reporting the event pointed out the change in plans: "Well, Wolf, as you know, initially this was a speech that was supposed to focus on medical liability reform. But after President Bush's widely viewed disappointing performance in the first presidential debate, there was a difference in strategy, a change in strategy from the campaign. They changed this to sharp attacks against Senator Kerry and his record on the war on terror, as well as the economy."

CNN's reporting of this event is characterized by three tendencies that political scientists argue are typical of news media's reporting in elections: (1) elections are treated as a sports contest between two combatants (typically horse racing or, in this instance, boxing); (2) the press focuses on the campaign's strategies more than the issues themselves; and (3) the press often parrots the message that political campaigns want them to report, circulating the rhetoric and slogans without intensive scrutiny or criticism (see, for instance, Patterson 1993). Stewart also points out the campaign's strategy of deflecting attention from Bush's weak showing in the presidential debates by going on the offensive, but insists on calling attention to the manipulative aspects of the event—both the campaign's misleading the press about making a major policy statement (when the presence of the banner itself clearly shows the forethought and planning for this attack speech) and the oral and visual rhetoric that the campaign wants the news media to report and show its viewers. Stewart doesn't accept the contention that the speech is about national security or the economy and focuses instead on the artifice of the event. It is an artifice that the news media help create and facilitate by uncritically continuing to air the Bush speech live, even though the speech does not include the policy material they initially agreed merited free air time as a newsworthy *presidential* statement (as opposed to that of a candidate for office). As Stewart has noted about his show in an earlier interview, "What we try to do is point out the artifice of things, that there's a guy behind the curtain pulling levers" (Hedgpeth 2000). Here he does just that.

Stewart then shows several clips from the Bush speech that CNN chose not to air in any of its three reports.

STEWART: [Bush] began by throwing out the first pander.

BUSH: It's great to be in Wilkes-Barre, Pennsylvania. It's such an honor to be back here. It's great to be in a part of the world where people work hard, they love their families....

STEWART: [*said out of the side of his mouth*] Yeah, not like New York—family hating jackasses; lazy family haters.

CNN does not show this clip because, given the news values of main-stream journalism, such statements by politicians are not newsworthy; they are typical of political speeches. For reporters assigned to follow the candidate's campaign, in fact, they have heard such statements countless times by this point in the campaign, said to different crowds in different places. For Stewart, however, the clip merits the viewers' attention because it shows that not only is the statement itself ridiculous, but that it is not beneath the president to pander to audiences. This is part of the overall point that Stewart attempts to make throughout the entire news segment—he continually asks the viewer to step outside the staged event to assess what information is available that might shed light on both presidential candidates' fundamental character as people and leaders.

Stewart continues covering the event by again showing another clip that CNN chose not to air:

STEWART: But then it was rival bashing time. Bush warmed up with a few insults aimed at the Democrats' number two man and his performance in Tuesday night's debate.

BUSH: America saw two very different visions of our country and two different hair-dos. I didn't pick my vice president for his hairdo. I picked him for his judgment, his experience....

STEWART: [*showing a picture of a bald Dick Cheney*] which, sadly, is as good as his hairdo.

If pandering isn't enough, Stewart shows that it is not beneath Bush to engage in *ad hominem* attacks. Again, CNN chose not to report this part of the president's speech, recognizing that attacks on one's opponents are simply part of electoral politics. Stewart, however, shows the clip not just to provide evidence of Bush's character and campaign style, but also to question the actual point that Bush is attempting to make so unproblematically—the quality of his administration's "judgment and experience" in the conduct of governmental affairs. Both CNN and *The Daily Show* have already provided evidence earlier in their broadcasts that the administration's "experience" of deciding to wage war, based on its "judgment" that there was trustworthy information to do so, was faulty. *The Daily Show*, however, is the only one to make the connection and point it out to viewers.

Like CNN, Stewart then focuses on the major policy statements within Bush's speech.

STEWART: Bush then moved onto his economic policy regarding Kerry.

BUSH: Now the Senator's proposing higher taxes on more than 900,000 small business owners. He says the tax increase is only for the rich. You've heard that kind of rhetoric before. The rich hire lawyers and accountants for a reason—to stick you with the tab.

STEWART: Let me get this straight. Don't tax the rich because they'll get out of it? So your policy is, tax the hard working people because they're dumb-asses and they'll never figure it out? So vote for me, goodnight?

Only during its 12 P.M. broadcast did CNN report this aspect of the president's speech, noting that Bush "also twisted Kerry's plan to roll back the cut taxes for those making more than $200,000, describing it as a tax increase for more than 900,000 small businesses." The CNN report is critical at this juncture by pointing out the Bush campaign's distortion of Kerry's proposal (that is, rolling back Bush's tax cuts does not amount to a proposed tax increase). CNN's focus is on the rhetorical sleight of hand. But that is the extent of their report. Stewart, however, returns the focus to the president's rhetoric by carrying the point to its logical conclusion. He illuminates the contradictory nature of the populist statement by questioning what it is exactly that Bush is trying to articulate, while also reminding viewers of where Bush really stands on taxes and how his policies actually belie the rhetoric employed here. It merits noting that news programs rarely offer direct and damning evidence of contradictory statements or duplicitous comments. The convention they typically rely on is to quote someone else who will point this out (Tuchman 1978). CNN did not even air the actual clip, relying instead on its reporter to summarize Bush's statement. One might argue that CNN has done Bush a favor by *not* airing a statement that is logically somewhat ridiculous and, instead, doing the hard work of actually deciphering for the viewing audience what the president means, thereby making him look more presidential in the process.[7]

The only clip of the president's speech that CNN showed in all three of its broadcasts occurred in the 7 A.M report—his statement concerning the supposed threat posed by "the dictatorship of Saddam Hussein" (quoted above). *The Daily Show* also reported this part of the speech, but with much more scrutiny to what Bush actually said. Stewart here engages in a rhetorical back-and-forth with the video clip of Bush's statement, attempting to come up with the right answer for which nation it is *exactly* that threatens America with weapons of mass destruction:

STEWART: Finally, the president brought the mood down a little, as only he can.

BUSH: After September 11, America had to assess every potential threat in a new light. We had to take a hard look at every place where terrorists might get those weapons and one regime stood out.

STEWART: Well, that's true. It would be Saudi Arabia. Fifteen of the nineteen terrorists were actually from there.

BUSH: ...the dictatorship of Saddam Hussein.

STEWART: No, no. I don't think that's it. Um. Oh. It was Iran—proven Al-Qaeda ties, building up the nukes program. I think it was them.

BUSH: [*repeating the tape of Bush*] ...the dictatorship of Saddam Hussein.

STEWART: No, no. I'm sure...[pause]...Pakistan. Top scientists sold nuclear secrets to...

BUSH: [*repeating the tape of Bush*] ...the dictatorship of Saddam Hussein.

STEWART: Could be Yemen. [*a graphic of a clock face with spinning hands is superimposed over a slightly faded image of Stewart, suggesting his thinking for quite some time of the possible countries, all the while Stewart thinks out loud*]. Oh.... Kazakhstan is actually a very dangerous.... Uzbekistan has always created problems in that region.... Turkey—very dangerous. Lebanon has some.... Qatar [*the graphic removes the clock face, and the camera focus on Stewart again becomes clear*].... Oh, oh, oh. North Korea. They have the bomb. Their leader is crazy. North Korea.

BUSH: [*repeating the tape of Bush*] ...the dictatorship of Saddam Hussein.

STEWART: [holding out his arms in front of him, like a robot, said in a slow monotone voice, with a staccato cadence]: The-dic-ta-tor-ship-of-Sad-dam-Hus-sein. Too-tired-to-fight-it. Must-learn. Re-pe-ti-tion.

Stewart scrutinizes the president's statement on its own terms—"in *every* place where terrorists might get those weapons": Saudi Arabia, Iran, Pakistan, North Korea, and so on. Then, through video repetition, Stewart highlights how the administration continues to repeat assertions over and over until the viewer is turned into an unthinking (or worn out) robot. In the speech itself, of course, Bush does not repeat the line. Yet Stewart recognizes that single speech events such as this do not constitute the reality that news media report and, in turn, help create. Instead, his use of manipulated video emphasizes the repeated pattern of administration efforts to establish something that is untrue, yet which citizens must work to resist because of its repeated assertion. As Stewart is quoted as saying, "We're out to stop that political trend of repeating things again and again until people are forced to believe them" (Armstrong 2003).

Stewart finishes the show's coverage of the Bush speech by returning one last time to a Bush pronouncement that was simply too good to pass up for its comedic value, yet also affirms the point about Bush's character that he has attempted to make throughout the telecast:

STEWART: But for all that, perhaps the most telling line of the speech came during Bush's seemingly innocuous segue into a story about his wife.

BUSH: You're not going to believe this. It's a true story, or kind of true.

STEWART: [*said with sheepish grin*] George W. Bush—I can tell I lie.

Again, CNN doesn't air this clip because there is no news value here—from their perspective, it is a meaningless aside unrelated to either campaign strategy or policy stances. For Stewart, however, it not only ties in nicely with the previous statement about Saddam Hussein and 9/11, but it also neatly demonstrates *exactly* what is at stake in the election of the president. Bush's proclivity to lie, in fact, was something the news media generally ignored in the election campaign, yet was an important criticism of Bush often addressed in numerous venues of popular culture during the campaign—most famously in Michael Moore's documentary film *Fahrenheit 9/11* (Jones 2005b).

Stewart concludes the news segment of the show by turning to an event not widely covered by the news media—both John Kerry and Bush soliciting votes by appearing on the afternoon therapy and relationship talk show, *Dr. Phil*. Here he attempts to highlight the deeper truths at work again, this time with the Democratic nominee:

> STEWART: But like Bush's speech, Kerry's *Dr. Phil* appearance had one moment that most clearly captured the essence of the candidate.
>
> DR. PHIL'S WIFE [*Video clip of the Dr. Phil Show, an interview with Senator Kerry conducted with the assistance of Dr. Phil's wife*]: Is one of your daughters more like you than the other?
>
> KERRY: Yes. No. That's...gosh...I'd like to...yes. But I guess...yes, the answer is yes.
>
> DR. PHIL'S WIFE: Which one do you think is more like you?
>
> KERRY: Well...um...I...that's why I hesitated, because I think in some ways my daughter Alexandra is more like me, but in other ways my daughter Vanessa is more like me.
>
> STEWART: [Burying his face into his hands, then moving his hands over his bowed head, gripping his hair, then the back of his neck. Stewart makes no comment, but simply looks at the camera with exasperation and dismay. The audience erupts in laughter.]

When presidential candidates first began appearing on such talk shows with regularity in 1992, the news media covered these appearances as newsworthy events. They did so, in particular, because of the unusual nature of the appearances, but also because the news media disliked the "softball" questions offered up by these "illegitimate" non-reporters (Debenport 1992). Because such appearances rarely feature the candidates' saying much about their position on issues (focusing more instead on personal matters), the news media now generally turn a blind eye to these "campaign stops," treating them as *de rigueur* in the hustle to reach disparate voter groups. *The Daily Show*, however, calls attention to the spectacle performance not just for its groveling and humiliating aspects, but rather to highlight how such performances might actually tell us something important about the candidates. In this instance, Kerry confirmed everything the Bush campaign had said about him: that Kerry is unwilling to be pinned down on anything (despite how insignificant the matter), yet paradoxically will say anything to get elected if he believes that is what the audience wants to hear. That truth comes to light very clearly for viewers when the matter is something as trivial as reflecting upon the relationship with one's daughter. Viewers may not be able to discern whether Kerry is a flip-flopper on foreign-policy issues (say, for instance, his various votes on the Iraq war), but they can certainly recognize mealy-mouthed remarks when it comes to interpersonal relationships.

The Daily Show, therefore, has constructed a narrative, weaving together campaign events to give the viewer insight into the candidates and who they might really be. This narrative is formulated from information derived from planned campaign events, yet woven together to tell a story that allows for evaluation of the candidates. Perhaps this is simply an entertainmentized version of a "news analysis" or "op-ed" journalism. But it is a particular brand of "reporting" that might illuminate for viewers the larger issues at stake beyond the isolated events that typically dominate news reporting.

In summary, then, *The Daily Show* has provided viewers information on several major political events that occurred the day before: the CIA report on weapons of mass destruction, Bush's campaign speech, and Kerry's appearance on a popular television program. The audience learns what the CIA report says, learns two of the main points in Bush's speech also reported by news outlets, and learns about Kerry's personal life. *The Daily Show* has not, therefore, short-changed viewers on information they would have seen by watching a "real" newscast.

Yet *The Daily Show's* audience also sees more material on these events than that provided by CNN, learning things that CNN didn't report. First, *The Daily Show* highlights political rhetoric itself, showing the false statements, *ad hominem* attacks, pandering, and populist appeals of candidate Bush, not seeing such language as a "given" in politics, but instead as a disturbing quality that exemplifies the character of the politician. Second, and perhaps more important, the program offers viewers information they have heard before, yet are reminded of here as a means of making sense of the events covered in the daily news report: there were no weapons of mass destruction; the administration's actions exemplify its use of bad judgment because it went after the wrong regime; its economic policies are the opposite of what they say they are. Continually, Stewart will not let the viewer lose sight of the greater truths at stake here. He is constantly keeping score, adding it all up, reminding the viewer of what this says about the candidates and the larger terms upon which they should be evaluated. In a single news report, the television news reporters rarely put things together in such a manner. And what the news media ignore may actually provide citizens with the type of meaningful information upon which they can base their electoral decisions. By Stewart's doing so in a typical news-reporting format, he demonstrates the failings of news media in informing viewers, drawing attention to how media serve as conduits for false information and image management, and how it would be easy for citizens to become the unthinking drones and robots that such unquestioned lies and manipulative imagery could lead them to become.

One might be tempted to criticize *The Daily Show* for selecting damning video clips that are taken out of context and then used to ridicule or embarrass politicians, all for a laugh. As we have seen, however, the clips used by Stewart are no more out of context than the single clip shown by CNN. Both Stewart and CNN actually highlight the context of the speech—the poor debate performance, as well as the release of the CIA report—yet it is *The Daily Show* that provides even more depth to the speech by showing viewers more of it (six clips compared to one by CNN). Just because CNN and other news organizations make claims of neutrality and objectivity doesn't mean they aren't being selective in what they report and how they report it. Furthermore, Stewart reports the same events and highlights the same "newsworthy" items as CNN, including reaching many of their same conclusions. As journalism critics have pointed out, not only have the length of sound bites drastically decreased over the last twenty years, they are increasingly disappearing altogether from television news reports (despite a very large news hole with twenty-four-hour cable channels). Instead, reporters are simply summarizing what candidates and government officials say, then interpreting those comments in a conversation with the news anchor. Yet as we have also seen, those interpretations offer the viewer little in the way of substantive critical assessments because of the norms and conventions of the profession.

In short, *The Daily Show* has matched CNN's coverage of this particular campaign event, even surpassing it by providing viewers additional information about the candidates beyond policy positions and campaign strategies and maneuvers. Of course, CNN provides a wealth of information about national and world affairs that a comedy program like *The Daily Show* can never cover. Nor would I suggest that citizens could be fully informed by watching a comedy show that provides little more than ten minutes of "reporting." Nevertheless, if we are to assess the quality of information about the presidential campaign provided by a fake news show versus a real one (as the Pew study normatively asserts), then the analysis here suggests that *The Daily Show* can provide quality information that citizens can use in making informed choices about electoral politics.

Fakeness, Reality, and the Postmodern Viewing Public

By most accounts, the institution of journalism is in a state of crisis in America (Hachten 2005; Kovach and Rosenstiel 2001). As discussed above, the myth that young people get their news from late-night comedians is partly a desire to explain why young people, in particular, are turning away from broadcast news or print journalism as primary sources of news and information (Mindich 2005). With declining readership and viewership, the institution is economically challenged by dwindling advertising revenues as well as increased costs of production (Roberts et al. 2001; Seelye 2005a). Recent scandals related to professional norms and ethics (from story fabrication by Jason Blair at *The New York Times* and Stephen Glass at *The New Republic* to poor fact-checking on President Bush's Air National Guard records by Dan Rather at *CBS News*) have contributed to a decline in trust with news media consumers (Johnson 2003; Hachten 2005, 102–112). Concurrently, with new media technologies such as blogs and search-engine portals, citizens are questioning the top-down, gatekeeper role of news media and, instead, increasingly desire a more active role in the determination and construction of what constitutes news and who gets to make it (Gillmor 2004; Seelye 2005b). Furthermore, the press's timidity in questioning and thwarting overt propaganda efforts by the Bush Administration (as both *The New York Times* and *Washington Post* offered *mea culpas* for their lack of serious reporting on assertions and evidence by the Bush Administration in the run-up to the Iraq war) also weakens the news media's claim to serving as effective and trustworthy watchdogs to power (Younge 2004; Seelye 2005c). Indeed, government propaganda combined with competition between news outlets that offer not just "competing views of the world, but different realities" (such as Fox News, *The New York Times*, and Al-Jazeera) leads to what Kristina Riegert calls the "struggle for credibility" with viewing audiences and voting publics (Riegert 2005).

Hence, what is also in crisis is the belief that news media provide a *realistic* picture of the world. The public is well aware that both television and politics are spectacle performances and, indeed, that the press and government are two mutually reinforcing and constituting institutions.[8] News media are *part of* the political spectacle (Edelman 1988), including journalists-cum-talk-show-pundits (who act more like lapdogs to power than watchdogs of it), cheerleading embedded reporters, and patriotic news anchors who wear their hearts on their sleeves. An increasingly media-savvy public realizes that news programs such as CNN are no more "real" than *The Daily Show* is "fake." Yet mainstream news media continue to believe their claims to truth—and the authenticity of those claims—because of their *authority* to make them in the first place. It is an authority they have asserted (and the public has granted) through their title, special status, institutional-based legitimacy, access to power, and the means of production and distribution. But as Foucault also reminds us, "'truth' is a type of discourse that societies accept and *make function as true*" (emphasis added; Foucault 1980, 132). And as postmodernists would have it, the "authentic" exists only in "the imaginings of those who yearn for it" (Webster 1995, 170). Were that to change, or should citizens come to believe that news is inauthentic, untrue, or just another form of constructed spectacle (that is, the credibility gap becomes a chasm), then they might yearn for other means of establishing truth and reality.

The institutional practice of journalism is a modernist means of constructing knowledge of public life that for many years has been widely accepted. Increasingly, though, this means of taking account of the world is being questioned, if not discredited.[9] In a useful summary of postmodernist thinking, Frank Webster argues that,

> the modernist enthusiasm for genres and styles [of which news is one] is rejected and mocked for its pretensions [by postmodernists]. From this it is but a short step to the postmodern penchant for parody, for tongue-in-cheek reactions to established styles, for a pastiche mode which delights in irony and happily mixes and matches in a 'bricolage' manner. (Webster 1995, 169–170)

And in steps *The Daily Show*, with a tendency for just such postmodern playfulness. But *The Daily Show* is "fake" only in that it refuses to make claims to authenticity (as demonstrated in the analysis above). But being fake does not mean that the information it imparts is untrue. Indeed, as with most social and political satire, its humor offers a means of reestablishing common-sense truths to counter the spectacle, ritual, pageantry, artifice, and verbosity that often cloak the powerful. The rationality of political satire is that it "reminds of common values," and "in its negative response to political excess, it serves to restore equilibrium to politics" (Schutz 1977, 327-28). Citizens know that public artifice exists, which is ultimately why the satire that points it out is funny—they just need someone skillful enough to articulate the critique. The type of fake-yet-real "reporting" performed by *The Daily Show* has led one commentator to claim that *The Daily Show* is "reinventing political journalism" (Baym 2005). Perhaps more to the point, the postmodern audience that comprises its viewership and has made it popular are themselves reinventing what it is they want from political communication.

Though scholars often attack the press for its supposed cynicism (for example, the way in which reporters point out the man behind the curtain), I contend that the press may not do this enough. Shelving journalistic conventions to get at important truths is less cynical than turning a blind eye to the manipulation by either contending that politics will always be this way or assuming that viewers *should* be informed enough or smart enough to connect all the dots themselves. A program like *The Daily Show* refuses to sit idly by while political lies and manipulative rhetoric go unchallenged (or, as Stewart says, "until it becomes true"). Unhindered by the self-imposed constraints placed on reporters by the profession (as well as the co-dependent relationship that exists between government and the press), *The Daily Show* uses a fake news platform to offer discussions of news events that are informative *and* critical, factual *and* interpretive, thorough *yet* succinct. Does that make it biased, unfair, or unbalanced? Not when the program sets its sights on the powerful. As Bryan Keefer, editor of Spinsanity.com, has argued, "the media need to understand that pointing out the truth isn't the same as taking sides."[10] This, of course, is what a fake news show is licensed to do, and why I contend that it provides such an important voice of political critique on the American political landscape (Jones 2005a).

In an opinion piece in the *Washington Post*, Keefer dares to speak for his generation, justifying its changing relationship to traditional news media and its search for better alternatives. He contends that

> we live in an era when PR pros have figured out how to bend the news cycle to their whims, and much of what's broadcast on the networks bears a striking resemblance to the commercials airing between segments. Like other twenty-somethings, I've been raised in an era when advertising invades every aspect of pop culture, and to me the information provided by mainstream news outlets too often feels like one more product, produced by politicians and publicists. (Keefer 2004)

If the myth of young citizens turning to comedians for news and information about politics ends up proving true, then as this analysis suggests, the fate of the republic doesn't seem in jeopardy if a comedy program like *The Daily Show* is a source for their knowledge of public affairs. As Keefer's comments suggest, at least when people watch a program that blatantly embraces its fakeness, they don't feel like they are being sold a bill of goods. Hence, the postmodern claim that the "fake" is more real than the "real" is perhaps not such an unsettling notion after all.

Notes

[1] http://people-press.org/reports/display.php3?ReportID=46.

[2] http://people-press.org/reports/display.php3?ReportID=200.

[3] "Jon Stewart," *Inside Politics*, CNN.com, 3 May 2002.

[4] Transcript of *Nightline*, ABC News, 28 July 2004 (accessed from Lexis-Nexis Academic Universe, 4 August 2004).

[5] http://www.naes04.org.

[6] Transcripts of CNN, 7 October 2004 (accessed from Lexis-Nexis Academic Universe, 28 March 2005). I analyze three morning broadcasts of CNN to get some idea of the different ways that a news network reports a story, as well as how these brief reports are modified as the morning progresses.

[7] As one news analyst has noted, "Network newscasts hold to standard conventions, and in so doing reduce Bush's sloppy, pause-saturated speech to a tightly constructed set of words that suggest clarity of thought and purpose." Such conventions, therefore, make the news media "susceptible to manipulation by the professional speech writers and media handlers who seed public information with pre-scripted soundbites and spin" (Baym 2005, 265).

[8] One only needs to look at popular narratives of either news media or the interactions of media and politics to see this recurrent theme. For examples, see films such as *Hero*, *Power*, *Broadcast News*, *A Face in the Crowd*, *Meet John Doe*, *The Candidate*, *Wag the Dog*, *Bulworth*, *Bob Roberts*, and *Dave*.

[9] Again, witness the movement toward blogging (and even the news media's embrace of it) as a manifestation of this questioning and reformulation. See, for instance, "'The State' (Columbia, S.C.) Launches Community Blog, Citizen Journalism Push," *Editor & Publisher*, 30 August 2005; and Saul Hansell, "The CBS Evening Blog," *New York Times*, 13 July 2005.

[10] One might be tempted to assert that this is exactly what competing "news" outlets like Fox News claim—that they are simply pointing out alternative truths. The crucial distinction between a program of political satire and a news organization like Fox that claims to be "fair and balanced," however, is their relationships to power. One is committed to critiquing power wherever it lies, while the other has proven its intentional commitment to supporting the powerful through highly orchestrated and sustained efforts by the media corporation's leadership (see Robert Greenwald's documentary *Outfoxed: Rupert Murdoch's War on Journalism*).

References

Armstrong, S. 2003. "I Can Scratch the Itch." *The Guardian*, 17 March , p. 8.

Baym, G. 2005. "The Daily Show: Discursive Integration and the Reinvention of Political Journalism." *Political Communication* 22: 259–276.

Boorstin, D. 1960. *The Image: A Guide to Pseudo Events in America*. New York: Atheneum.

Buckingham, D. 2000. *The Making of Citizens: Young People, News and Politics*. London:

Routledge.

Chaloupka, W. 1999. *Everybody Knows: Cynicism in America*. Minneapolis: University of Minnesota Press.

Debenport, E. 1992. "Candidates Try To Cut Media Filter." *St. Petersburg Times* (Florida), 11 June, p. 1A.

Delli Carpini, M.X., and Keeter, S. 1996. *What Americans Know About Politics and Why It Matters*. New Haven: Yale University Press.

Edelman, M. 1988. *Constructing the Political Spectacle*. Chicago: University of Chicago Press.

Foucault M. 1980. *Power/Knowledge: Selected Interviews and Other Writings, 1972–1977*. Brighton: Harvester Press.

Gay, V. 2004. "Not Necessarily the News: Meet the Players Who Will Influence Coverage of the 2004 Campaign." *Newsday*, 19 January, p. B6.

Gillmor, D. 2004. *We the people: Grassroots journalism, by the people, for the people*. Sebastopol, CA: O'Reilly.

Hachten, W.A. 2005. *The Troubles of Journalism*. 3rd ed. Mahwah, NJ: Lawrence Erlbaum Associates.

Hart, R.P. 1994. *Seducing America: How Television Charms the Modern Voter*. New York: Oxford University Press.

Hedgpeth, S. 2000. "Daily Show's Satiric Eye." *Plain Dealer* (Cleveland), 30 July, p. 6I.

Johnson, P. 2003. 'Trust of Media Keeps on Slipping." *USA Today*, 28 May.

Jones, J.P. 2005a. *Entertaining Politics: New Political Television and Civic Culture*. Lanham, MD: Rowman & Littlefield.

——. 2005b. "The Shadow Campaign in Popular Culture." In *The 2004 Presidential Campaign: A Communication Perspective* (pp. 195-216), edited by R Denton. Lanham, MD: Rowman & Littlefield.

Keefer, B. 2004. "You Call That News? I Don't." *Washington Post*, 12 September, p. B2.

Kovach, B., and Rosenstiel, T. 2001. *The Elements of Journalism: What Newspeople Should Know and the Public Should Expect*. New York: Crown.

Mindich, D.T.Z. 2005. *Tuned Out: Why Americans Under 40 Don't Follow the News*. New York: Oxford University Press.

Patterson, T.E. 1993. *Out of Order*. New York: Random House.

Rich, F. 2003. "Jon Stewart's Perfect Pitch." *New York Times*, 20 April, sec. 2, p. 1.

Riegert, K., with Johansson, A. 2005. "The Struggle for Credibility in the Iraq War." In *The Iraq War: European Perspectives on Politics, Strategy, and Operations*. London: Routledge.

Roberts, G.; Kunkle, T.; and Layton, C. 2001. *Leaving Readers Behind: The Age of Corporate Newspapering*. Fayetteville: University of Arkansas Press.

Scheuer, J. 1999. *The Sound Bite Society: Television and the American Mind*. New York: Four Walls Eight Windows.

Schutz, C. 1977. *Political Humor: From Aristophanes to Sam Ervin*. New York: Fairleigh Dickinson University Press.

Seelye, K.Q. 2005a. "At Newspapers, Some Clipping." *New York Times*, 10 October , p. C1.

——. 2005b. "Why Newspapers Are Betting on Audience Participation." *New York Times*, 4 July.

——. 2005c. "Survey on News Media Finds Wide Displeasure." *New York Times*, 27 June.

Tuchman, G. 1978. *Making News: A Study in the Construction of Reality*. New York: Free Press.

Webster, F. 1995. *Theories of the Information Society*. London: Routledge.

West, D.M., and Orman, J. 2003. *Celebrity Politics*. Upper Saddle River, NJ: Prentice-Hall.

Younge, G. 2004. "Washington Post Apologizes for Underplaying WMD Scepticism." *The Guardian*, 13 August, p. 2.

CHAPTER SEVEN

Brazilian Telenovelas, Fictionalized Politics, and the Merchandising of Social Issues

THAÏS MACHADO-BORGES

In the waiting room of a private hospital.

BARBARA [A middle-aged, white, upper-class woman]: I'm worried. It's been several hours since the doctor said we would be able to see the babies, and so far nothing has happened!

EUGÊNIO [A white millionaire in his early thirties. Barbara's adopted son and the ex-husband of Teodora, the mother of the babies]: Calm down, mother! I've understood that the babies are well. It was a complicated birth.

CAIO [A white, young publisher. Eugênio's best friend and Teodora's admirer]: I'm so nervous that it's almost as if I was the father of those children! I'm dying to see their little faces.

[...]

The doctor comes in.

EUGÊNIO: Doctor!

BARBARA: Is there any kind of problem, doctor?

DOCTOR: No, the babies are fine, thank God. But I want to talk to Teodora, because I want to know if there was any change in her request at the sperm bank. Do you know anything about it?

EUGÊNIO: No, Doctor. What is this all about?

CAIO: My God, these things never work!

DOCTOR: Would you follow me to the nursery?

The doctor points to two black babies.

BARBARA: I can't believe it!

EUGÊNIO: How?

CAIO: What now?

CLARICE [A white university teacher. Barbara's adopted daughter and Caio's girl-friend]: Does she know about it?

To be continued...

Historically, since the inauguration of the Republican regime in 1889 (only one year after the abolition of slavery), discrimination on the basis of race or color has been illegal in Brazil. However, a closer look at the Brazilian situation reveals an interesting dilemma: on the one hand, there are no polarized races but a complex taxonomy that classifies people according to their appearance rather than their genealogy (Nogueira 1985). The myth of racial democracy, i.e., the harmonious mixture of Africans, Amerindians, and Europeans, is still alive and works many times as a trademark of Brazilianness (DaMatta 1978; Freyre 1933; Fry 2000). On the other hand, recent statistics (IBGE 2003) show that white Brazilians are still far more educated and earn much more than the non-white population.[1] The average income of the non-white population, according to the 2001 census, was a little less than half that of the whites. So, in spite of a strong belief in the myth of racial democracy, non-whites remain poorer and less socially mobile than whites. It is also important to keep in mind that Brazil has one of the most unequal income distributions in the world. The richest 20 percent of the Brazilian population earns twenty-nine times as much as the poorest (World Bank 2001). Roughly 30 percent of Brazilians live in abject poverty, earning less than US$100 a month. Forty percent of the population makes less than US$300 a month (Reis 2000; Schneider 1996). In spite of the socio-economic disparities separating Brazilians, one common practice unites them all: television watching. It is against this background that the suspense and thrill involving the birth of two black babies by a white, upper-class mother becomes intelligible.

Brazil has one of the largest television audiences in the world. Eighty-eight percent of the households in the country have at least one television set—in sheer numbers, this means 40 million television households.[2] One of the most-broadcast—and most-watched—types of programs is the television *novela* (to which, in accordance with most English-language academic writing on this topic, I will generally refer with the term *telenovela*).

Telenovelas are broadcast throughout the country six days a week, in the afternoon and during prime time. They attract a daily audience of more than 40 million viewers. Individual telenovelas are able to catch and maintain the attention of a faithful audience during their duration of six to eight months. Unlike the U.S. or British soap operas that may last for many years, a Brazilian telenovela ends after 150 to 200 episodes and is immediately replaced by a new one. Telenovela plots can conform to real-life seasons and holidays. Often, these programs introduce fashions and products, approach polemical subjects, and comment upon (in a realistic or parodic way) contemporary social issues such as corruption, AIDS, undesired pregnancies, same-sex relationships, donation of organs, prostitution, and racism.

This chapter discusses the relationship between telenovelas and Brazilian politics. Are telenovelas a means of talking about politics in a country that for decades—and until relatively recently—lived under oppressive political regimes? And what is considered to be "political" within this context? Are telenovelas' representations of the "political" gendered? Do telenovelas contribute to the configuration of Brazilian citizens?

In order to address these questions, this chapter begins with a discussion of television's role within Brazilian society and looks at the place of telenovelas within Brazilian television.

Television, Telenovelas, and Brazilian Society

A first-time visitor to Brazil will certainly notice the importance of television in the country's daily life. Televisions are everywhere; in cities it is impossible to pass a street without seeing a shop, a bar, a restaurant, or an office with a television. Through communication satellites, reception dishes, and retransmitting ground stations, television reaches people even in the most remote villages of the country.

To understand the development of television in Brazil, one has to look at the political context of 1950, when television was introduced into the country. At that time, television sets were expensive commodities that had to be imported from other countries. Television was a medium available only to the few who formed society's elite. Mattos (1990) notes that a television set cost only slightly less than a new car. The spread and popularization of television started in the late 1950s, when television sets started being produced in Brazil, which made them cheaper and thus available to more people. This was also a period when industrialization, modernization, and regional development were keywords in the Kubitschek government (1956–1961). Brasília, the capital of Brazil, was under construction (the city was officially inaugurated in 1960), with an eye toward propelling the country forward to modernity. The idea behind the construction of the new capital city was that the whole country would then "catch up with the innovations of Brasília" (Holston 1989, 18). Introduced to the country during this march toward development, television—with its innovative technology—became itself a sign of modernity.

From its infancy, television was seen as a way to convey oral and visual information to all kinds of viewers, including a considerable number of illiterate persons. Its spread throughout the country was seen as an issue of great importance to the government. In 1962, the first Brazilian telecommunication code was promulgated. It entrusted to the state "the responsibility of installing and operating the telecommunication networks," and it confirmed "the private status of radio and television broadcasting" (Mattelart and Mattelart 1990, 20).

The military coup that overthrew President João Goulart on 31 March 1964 resulted in increased state intervention in the implementation and programming of television. As Mattos (1990) reports, the right to grant or refuse the permission to start a television network came to rest exclusively in the hands of the country's president. Political preferences inevitably played an important role in the concession of television rights.[3] In 1965, the network Globo (nowadays Brazil's largest television corporation and the fourth-largest television corporation in the world) was founded with the financial and technological support of the U.S. Time-Life organization. By 1967, however, measures were taken to hinder foreign participation in Brazilian communication. Globo's partnership with the Time-Life group was seen by the Brazilian government as going against national interests: communication was a national matter, and should not be subject to interference from foreign groups. So, in 1969, the Globo network was nationalized (see Ribeiro and Botelho 1979).

Television was also seen by the military government (as it was by previous governments) as a way to create a national identity, linking the remote regions near Brazil's borders to the rest of the country (Straubhaar 1982, 1984; Tufte 1993). In 1965, the Brazilian national communication company Embratel was created. Its motto was "Communication is Integration" (Mattelart and Mattelart 1990, 20).

The military government encouraged the expansion of private, commercial television networks and favored those networks whose programming would help in the preservation (and construction) of a national memory (Kehl 1979). A regime of strong state interference was combined with economic liberalism. Mattelart and Mattelart (1990) summarize this contradictory situation:

> [In order] to assure a minimum of consensus for a political project that was forced to resort to coercion and police control, state power had to call in the commercial machinery of mass culture, the product of a society in which opinion is a recognized actor in the public sphere, a mass culture linked to the idea of representative democracy and free access to the market economy of information, culture and entertainment. (31)

The private, commercial development of television was also supported by the military government because it helped to create a consumer economy. Television was a perfect medium for creating a domestic consumer market and attracting local and foreign capital: its ability to reach the whole nation made television a means to address Brazilians as potential consumers (Lopez 1995).

Profiling itself as a faithful ally of the state, the network Globo explicitly adopted the task of showing Brazil on television. In 1969, Globo's National news report (the *Jornal Nacional*) was broadcast for the first time simultaneously throughout the entire country. In 1970, the whole nation could watch Brazil win the soccer World Cup. National broadcasting opened the door for a series of programs about Brazil. Nowadays there are five main independent commercial networks in the country—Rede Globo, SBT (Sistema Brasileiro de Televisão), Rede TV!, Bandeirantes, and TV Record, and other (paid) channels (MTV, Canal 21, CNT, Gazeta, Rede Brasil, Rede Mulher, Rede Vida, Rede Senado). Globo, Latin America's largest television corporation, portrays itself as a network that cares for the quality (moral and aesthetic) of its programs. Media researcher Amelia Simpson (1993, 63) affirms that "of every ten television sets turned on [in Brazil], an average of six are tuned to Globo." The network's power in the Brazilian entertainment world has been compared to Metro-Goldwyn-Mayer's influence in the movie-making industry of the 1930s and 1940s. The network reaches almost the entire country.[4] Globo is known for (and advertises itself as having) an emphasis on quality, manifested on a visual level by a certain sumptuousness in the scenery and costumes of its actors, the professionalism of program hosts and news anchors, and by the use of innovative technology (Vink 1988, 44). Textually, Globo's "quality model" is manifested by a concern with the use (in program promotions, variety shows, and news broadcasting programs) of correct grammar and a predominantly southeastern accent, either from the states of Rio or São Paulo. Its innovative technology (*Veja* 1996; Vink 1988), combined with continuous marketing and audience research, has contributed to its leading position among television networks. Globo produces more than 60 percent of the programs it broadcasts.

Put in a broader, historical context, it can thus be said that television in Brazil was given a unifying function: first it integrated the nation culturally by spreading understanding of southeastern, middle-, and upper-class standards of life (such as eating habits, leisure activities, dressing, and decorating styles) to the rest of the country (Schelling 2004). The southeastern region (i.e., the economic center of the country) formed by the states of Rio de Janeiro, São Paulo, Minas Gerais, and Espírito Santo, became a model of progress, development, and urbanization.[5] Television not only contributed to the spread of middle- and upper-class values from the center to the periphery of Brazil, but its positive portrayal of the southeastern region and its cities might also have contributed to an increased rural migration and other demographic changes (Faria and Potter 1999). Television spreads representations of lifestyles, consumption practices, and consumer goods—as well as representations of the people who consume these goods—throughout the country.[6] As will be shown, the destiny of Teodora, a white, upper-class character from the telenovela *Salsa e Merengue* (broadcast by Globo, 1997) is an illustration of this. Desperately trying to conquer the man she loves, Teodora has herself artificially inseminated in Canada in order to deceive her ex-husband back into a relationship. Her plan is to argue that she conceived with him before their marriage broke down. Throughout her pregnancy Teodora dreams that she will have white babies with blue eyes who (because they came from a Canadian donor) would look like her former (but still beloved) husband. Teodora's initial plan fails, but she eventually manages to win back her ex-husband.

Back to Teodora's room at the hospital. Teodora's maid, a working-class white woman named Sexta-Feira [whose name means "Friday"] is also there:

CAIO: She is waking up.

TEODORA [An upper-class, white woman in her early thirties]: Where are my children? Barbara, are they beautiful?

BARBARA: They are beautiful! Caio, Eugênio, would you please say something?

CAIO: Eugênio knows how to say these things better than I do.

EUGÊNIO: Teodora, the babies are healthy and they are wonderful. But there is a small detail....

TEODORA: What detail? Tell me Eugênio! What happened to my children?...

EUGÊNIO: Teodora, when you were inseminated, did you choose the donor?

TEODORA: Yes, I did. I wanted certain physical traits. I wanted the donor to be a Canadian. I've always liked Canada. What happened, Eugênio? Why all this mystery?

BARBARA: There is no mystery. The donor might well be Canadian, but his physical traits are not.

TEODORA: What do you mean?

SEXTA-FEIRA: Let me explain: *Dona* Teodora, there might have been a mistake when they sent you "those things." I think they might have mixed the labels.

CAIO [to Sexta-Feira]: Stop it!

TEODORA: What are you saying Sexta-Feira? I don't understand!

SEXTA-FEIRA: What I'm saying *Dona* Teodora, is that the things that they've sent to you might be Canadian, but the donor was a black man (*um negão*). You've given birth to two wonderful mulattos, *Dona* Teodora.

TEODORA: Mulattos? What do you mean?

[...]

(Excerpts from dialogue in *Salsa e Merengue*, 1997, Globo)

And now...Telenovelas!!

These excerpts from the telenovela *Salsa e Merengue* are a typical example of the intrigues that make up a telenovela. Telenovelas have a serial form consisting of daily episodes, each of which has four or five segments punctuated by commercial breaks. Each segment ends with a "cliff-hanger"—a plotline that reaches its climax, and the problem is solved in the next segment or in the next episodes.

Globo is the main producer of telenovelas, broadcasting five a day. Telenovelas are generally broadcast at around six, seven, and eight o'clock in the evening, and people refer to them as the "six," "seven," and "eight o'clock *novelas*." The six o'clock telenovela is generally romantic and lighthearted. Its plots often center on periods in Brazil's history, such as life at the end of the nineteenth century or at the beginning of the twentieth century. The seven and eight o'clock telenovelas deal with a broader variety of subjects. They can either be humorous, or they can deal with controversial subjects. Broadcast after the evening news report, the eight o'clock telenovelas are the most popular and reach daily audiences of 40 million viewers.

Anthropologist Lila Abu-Lughod (1999, 94) suggests that melodrama-inspired television serials such as soap operas and telenovelas, due to their "focus on the emotionally laden interpersonal domestic world," have been associated with a women's world.[7] Indeed, as we shall see, Brazilian telenovelas place great emphasis on interpersonal relationships and emotions, and they focus heavily on strong female characters. In this sense, they are a "woman's genre," and, as Brazilian anthropologist Esther Hamburger (1999) has documented, they are produced with a female target audience in mind. Statistics show, however, that telenovelas are watched by both men and women. Within a four-year period (1990–1994), 27.2 percent of Brazilian men watched Globo's eight o'clock telenovela, as compared to 37.2 percent of Brazilian women. As to the relationship between telenovelas and class, during a four-year period (1990–1994), the majority of the audience belonged to lower- and lower-middle classes (approximately 35.3 percent), followed by the middle-class (approximately 33.8 percent), and the upper-middle and upper classes (approximately 27.5 percent). Telenovelas are watched mostly by people between the ages of 14 and 25 and by people older than age 40.[8]

Connecting fiction and reality, many telenovelas follow the real calendar: telenovela characters celebrate Carnival, Christmas, and New Year's on the same days as their audience. Telenovela characters wear the same fashions that can be seen in shops and magazines, and they speak about problems that are shared by the audience.[9] By establishing a parallel temporality, telenovelas incorporate, to a certain extent, a part of viewers' experiences into fiction at the same time that they allow viewers to incorporate telenovela themes into their lives. A dialogue between fiction and reality, viewers and telenovelas, is generated.

In terms of specific content, telenovelas deal with a great variety of subjects. They address issues of social positioning and power, social ascension, gender relationships, love, sexuality, and politics. The contents of telenovelas connect (often through seduction and love) different and clear-cut universes, thus promoting individual transformation and social mobility. The excerpts from the telenovela *Salsa e Merengue*, depicting the eventful life of the character Teodora, are a good illustration of individual transformation and change.

Still in the hospital room. Teodora is carrying both babies in her arms.

TEODORA: Oh, they are so beautiful! Look at their hands, Clarice. So wonderful!

SEXTA-FEIRA: There was just this tiny problem, wasn't it, *Dona* Teodora? The babies came with the wrong color.

TEODORA: Sexta, don't talk like this about my children!

CAIO: I wanted to say that they look like someone, but I really can't.

TEODORA: But they look like me! They are just like me. They have my traits: big mouth, vivid eyes...

(Excerpts from dialogue in *Salsa e Merengue*, 1997, Globo)

Telenovela Writers

Telenovela writers are famous. They are often better known than Brazilian authors who write fiction (Lopez 1995, 261). Until the beginning of the 1980s, a single writer was the only person responsible for the development of a telenovela plot. Today it is common to divide authorship into a series of separate tasks. Thus, a telenovela has a main writer who sketches the initial plot and sometimes helps to cast some of the main characters. This writer is assisted by researchers who report on particular professions, situations, or historical times that are going to be portrayed in the telenovela. The main writer will also be helped by one or two co-writers, who are either responsible for writing dialogue or for writing certain sequences of the telenovela (Ortiz et al. 1991; *Veja* 1996). However, even though the division of tasks within the telenovela industry has become quite elaborate, it is still the main writer who has the responsibility for the success or failure of a telenovela.

Telenovela plots are written approximately one month (fifteen to twenty episodes) in advance of their broadcast date, which is a way for the writer to cope with unexpected events such as the pregnancy of an actress or the illness or death of a leading actor. Writers modify the plot depending on the feedback they receive from the audience. When writing the telenovela *O Dono do Mundo* ("King of the World," 1991-92, Globo), the writer Gilberto Braga wished to portray class differences in a realistic way: poor people only got poorer, and the rich got richer. Braga wanted the telenovela to have no hero. The main character, Felipe Barreto, was a mean, successful, and rich character. The two leading female characters were portrayed as passive and superficial. The audience reacted against these portrayals, and the telenovela had disastrous ratings. In a 1991 interview with *TV Programa*, Braga explained some of the measures he took in order to improve viewership:

> I had to change the personality of some of the characters such as Vicente [a disillu-
> sioned old man who worked as a taxi driver]. His character was too sad for the
> telenovela. A new character was introduced, a good and idealistic young doctor.
> Felipe Barreto, the evil character, had to pay for his sins and lose all his money. I had
> to give more strength to the middle-class characters in the plot, in order to please the
> middle-class audience.

There is an intrinsic relationship between the telenovela writer and the audience. Some writers might change the plot to please the audience; others might give a leading role to a secondary character because of the public's reaction. Manoel Carlos, who also wrote *Baila Comigo* ("Dance with Me," 1981, Globo) explained in an interview the modifications he was obliged to make in the plot of that telenovela because of the unexpected popularity of a secondary character:

> Plínio was only a secondary type, destined to die in Episode 58. But when the telenovela started to be broadcast, everything changed. People started to talk about Plínio as a member of the family and so they saved his life. Many people wrote me letters saying they felt like Plínio's children and I did not want to assume the responsibility for a bunch of orphans. (Quoted in Vink 1988, 144)

Telenovela writers have different backgrounds and styles. While some of them were involved with theater and journalism before they moved into telenovela writing (during the military dictatorship many script writers, playwrights, and intellectuals found in telenovelas a medium to reach the masses and comment, metaphorically, on the country's situation: fictive small villages with clear-cut hierarchical structures and conflicts worked many times as reminders of actual structures and conflicts at a national level), others started as telenovela writers and then eventually moved toward other domains of dramatic expression. Top-ranked writers have managed to create a personal telenovela style and to specialize in certain telenovela types—urban, regional, romantic, socially engaged, humorous, fantastic, or historical.

Most writers have also publicly expressed an opinion about their profession and about their social role as creators of national dramas:

> As a *novela* writer, I try to give as much information as possible to the spectator, since this is a country of people who don't read. So I try, through my *novelas*, even if sometimes I have to sacrifice their aesthetic quality, to inform the masses. (Interview with Lauro César Muniz, in Ortiz et al. 1991, 162)

> We were doing anti-bourgeois theatre and had a bourgeois audience. What I do on television, according to the statistics, is seen even by bandits. This is what I call a popular audience. (Interview with Dias Gomes, in Ortiz et al. 1991, 163)

> I was irritated with that story of protest *novelas* [i.e., telenovelas that would, through their plots, approach the theme of social injustice]. I wanted to make a big joke, a *novelão* [a big telenovela] with all the obvious clichés from classic *feuilleton*. (Interview with Aguinaldo Silva, in Ortiz et al. 1991, 166)

> Telenovelas make the whole country discuss a particular subject. If we [as writers] manage to make people discuss relevant matters, then we might contribute to making Brazil a better place to live. (Interview with Gloria Perez, in Alencar 2002, 94)

While some writers argue that telenovelas are a cathartic force, others emphasize the entertaining, light-hearted, or romantic character of telenovelas. Still others say that telenovelas can be used as a means of informing people and a way to comment on Brazilian society.

Telenovela Stars

Telenovela actors and actresses play an important role in the media world and in Brazilian society. Film and media scholar Ana M. Lopez (1995, 258) suggests that for actors and actresses to "work in a telenovela today is often to have reached the apex of one's professional career." I would add that to work in a telenovela is also a way for an actor or actress to gain visibility in various media circuits. Telenovela actors and actresses have the strong support of various media, and they participate in publicity campaigns, promotions, interviews, advertisements, Carnival parades, information campaigns about health matters (breast cancer, prevention of tropical diseases, use of condoms, drug abuse), education, and even the privatization of national companies. Moreover, they are often invited to participate in political campaigns to show their support for a certain candidate or a certain political party. It is not unusual to see actresses and actors, sometimes together with famous musicians, by the side of a candidate or the head of a political party at an electoral campaign. The term *showmício*, a blend of the words *show* and *comício* (in English, campaign), has recently been used to indicate the kind of promotion organized by some political candidates or parties.[10] For instance, in 2002, the presidential campaign of Ciro Gomes, the candidate of the Popular Socialist Party (PPS), placed the candidate's wife, well-known telenovela actress Patricia Pillar, in a prominent role. Her popularity was seen as one reason for Ciro's surge in the polls in July 2002 (Htun 2002, 744).

Yet another example: in 2005, Brazil held a referendum in which people were supposed to vote for or against the prohibition of weapon sales to civilians. Several television actresses and actors participated, campaigning in favor of the prohibition. As it turned out, Brazilians voted against the prohibition of weapon sales. This example is interesting because it illustrates the visibility of telenovela stars in Brazil at the same time that it also shows that the impact of the celebrities on public opinion is strong, but certainly not unlimited (Globo Online 2005).

Through their visibility in different kinds of popular contexts and media, telenovela actors and actresses become familiar faces to the audience. Audiences know them not only as telenovela characters but also as public persons with certain opinions about social and political issues (see Collins, in this volume). Participation in public events functions as self-promotion, contributing to the increased visibility of these actors and actresses.[11] At the same time, the presence of telenovela stars at public events gives a touch of glamour to the occasion and attracts the attention of more people.

Telenovela$

Many television networks have organized telenovela industries so carefully that as soon as a telenovela is over—this generally happens on a Friday, with a repeat of the last episode on Saturday—there will be a new one to substitute for it the following Monday. So, even if different telenovelas come and go, the certainty that one telenovela will be followed by another, and the viewers' expectation of seeing very well-known actors' faces reincarnated in new fictional characters, makes this apparently fragmented rhythm of telenovelas into a cyclical one—a telenovela continuum.

In 1985, the average cost of an hour-long Globo telenovela episode was US$20,000–30,000. In 1992, however, Globo executives announced that an "ambitious" telenovela could cost as much as US$120,000 per episode (Lopez 1995, 259). These costs, as Lopez (1995) and Alencar (2002) observe, are easily covered by domestic advertising revenues. Besides repaying advertising revenues, Brazilian telenovelas have been exported to more than one hundred countries (Allen 1995, 13; Mazziotti 1993, 25). From the mid-1970s to the mid-1980s, Globo's annual profits on telenovela sales had risen to US$20 million (Allen 1995, 13).[12]

Advertisements are either placed in a commercial break within a telenovela or in the actual action of the telenovela. An article in *Folha de São Paulo* (*TV Folha* 1995) addressed the subject of product placement (or "merchandising," as it is called in Brazil) in telenovela plots. According to this article, there are many ways to promote a product within a telenovela. A more discreet alternative is to show a character holding or buying a certain product, filmed in close-up so that the product's brand name can be seen. Another alternative is to insert the product into a dialog taking place between characters.

According to the *TV Folha* article, companies that invest in product placement seem to find this kind of investment worthwhile, because it reaches viewers when they are paying attention to the telenovela, and it complicates the distinction between reality and fiction, encouraging people to acquire things that are shown within a fictive frame. Media scholars Armand and Michelle Mattelart (1990) suggest that the development of television and of a national telenovela industry go hand in hand with the development of an urban consumer society.

Telenovelas have also generated a variety of spin-off products: there are television and radio shows about telenovelas and their stars; there are gossip magazines (such as *Amiga, AnaMaria, Caras, Contigo!*, and *Tititi*);[13] there are fashion magazines reporting the latest telenovela fashions (such as *Moda Moldes* and *Manequim*); and, last but not least, there are the cassettes and CDs with national and international tunes that are played during a telenovela. Since 1971, the Globo network has been selling records with the same songs that are played during a telenovela. Due to the success of sales, the network expanded telenovela music to consist always of two CDs—one with national and the other with international tunes (Ortiz et al. 1991). Other networks have followed this idea and are now producing their own telenovela CDs. Of course, some of the CDs and songs are more popular and sell better than others, but there seems to be a steady market for these products in the country.

To summarize: Besides attracting millions of viewers, telenovelas also attract millions in advertising revenue. Telenovelas promote a range of commodities, desires, and representations, making them available for the television viewer. Events from everyday Brazilian life are exaggerated, visualized, and performed in beautiful landscapes by good-looking actors and actresses, with a soundtrack of Brazilian and international tunes and a guaranteed happy ending. Can we then say that telenovelas are like Balinese cockfights, in anthropologist Clifford Geertz's (1973) rendering? That is, is it possible to suggest that they teach their viewers something about Brazilian politics and society?

Telenovelas and the Fictionalization of Politics

Brazil has had a turbulent political history: authoritarian governments, military dictatorship, democratization, presidential impeachment, and, more recently, the scandalous allegations of corruption and bribes within the ruling Worker's Party (PT) have shaken Brazilians' and non-Brazilians' trust in institutional politics and politicians (BBC News 2005).

In a country that for decades—and until relatively recently—lived under oppressive political regimes, the fictiveness of telenovela plots has worked as a protective shield for telenovela writers who comment upon Brazilian society and talk about politics. Every telenovela has, when it is first presented, a disclaimer stating that any similarity between telenovela characters or plots and real persons or events is merely coincidental.[14] Thus officially separated from reality, telenovela plots are free to elaborate on everyday events, making them glossier and sassier. The inevitable comparison between the world of the telenovela and the real world works in this sense as a kind of meta-commentary on Brazil as it is, and as it could be.

In what follows, it is argued that telenovelas fictionalize, comment upon, and criticize political events. They create and reproduce preferred readings of Brazilian politics and define what is considered to be "political" in Brazil. Below are some examples illustrating the way politics is fictionalized and discussed in telenovelas.

In 1985, the telenovela *Roque Santeiro* ("Roque, the Saint-Maker," 1985–86, Globo) told the story of a small town whose life revolved around a local hero: Roque Santeiro, a young man who had supposedly died defending the city from dangerous bandits and was proclaimed a local saint. Decades later, Roque Santeiro returns: he was not a hero or a myth but a completely ordinary man. Roque's return shakes the local elite, who do not want to unveil the reality behind the myth to the population. Besides Roque, one of the main characters in this telenovela was Sinhozinho Malta—the most powerful and unscrupulous man in town. Eager to keep his political influence (and the financial benefits deriving therefrom) at any price, he eliminated anyone who would threaten his position. Dias Gomes, the writer of this telenovela, wrote two possible endings for the main intrigue: in the first one, Porcina, the leading female character, left the powerful and evil Sinhozinho Malta, to whom she was engaged, and chose the love of Roque, the charming anti-hero. In this version, Malta was punished for all the crimes he had committed during the course of the telenovela. In the other ending, Porcina prefers money and power instead of love and stays with Sinhozinho Malta. *Roque Santeiro* left the audience in suspense until the last episode. Both endings were recorded, but nobody knew which one would be broadcast. Finally, the second ending, in which Porcina hesitates but decides to stay with an unpunished Sinhozinho Malta, was broadcast. The writer justified his choice by pointing out that the romantic and happy ending, even though it would have pleased many of the telenovela's viewers, would not have been a faithful reflection of what really goes on in Brazilian society, where rich people take impunity for granted.

In 1989, the telenovela *O Salvador da Pátria* ("The Savior of the Nation," 1989, Globo), featured as one of the main characters a charismatic, uneducated rural worker, who became involved in politics. There was a striking likeness between this character and Luís Inácio Lula da Silva (Brazil's first viable left-wing presidential candidate, who came from a modest background and who, in the 2002 elections, became Brazil's president). Since democratic presidential elections were going to take place the same year as *O Salvador da Pátria* was broadcast (i.e., 1989), Lauro César Muniz, the author of this telenovela, was pressured by politicians and network producers to change the plot and the character in order not to influence the real presidential elections (*Veja*, 12 February 1997).

In December 1992, Brazil's then-president, Fernando Collor, was impeached by the congress and accused of corruption. In 1993, the telenovela *Fera Ferida* ("Wounded Beast," by Aguinaldo Silva, broadcast by Globo) portrayed the impeachment of the fictive mayor of the city of Asa Branca ("White Wings"—a clear allusion to the government and the capital city of Brasília, whose original master plan was the shape of an airplane).

In 1996, the telenovela *O Rei do Gado* ("The King of Cattle," 1996–97, Globo) discussed the viability of a national agrarian reform and the Landless Rural Workers Movement (in Portuguese, "Movimento dos Trabalhadores Rurais Sem-Terra," or MST). In the course of the telenovela, two senators from the Brazilian congress, Mr. Eduardo Suplicy and Mrs. Benedita da Silva, made a special guest appearance. Playing themselves, they attended the wake of the fictive senator Caxias and praised his political agenda, even as they offered their condolences to the senator's widow.

In *A Indomada* ("The Untamed Woman," 1997, Globo), the fictive small town of Greenville was ruled by an incompetent, egocentric mayor with crazy ambitions: searching to resurrect Greenville's connections with England, the mayor tried to implement left-hand traffic rules in the city, resulting in enormous chaos.

The relationship between media and politics has long been the subject of vivid debates as to what kinds of implications these media representations might have regarding the "kind of investment people should make in politics" and the "kind of expectation that they should have on politicians" (Abu-Lughod 2005; Corner and Pels 2003, 6). Here I identify three fundamental, overlapping ways of looking at the relationship between telenovelas and politics.

A Negative Representation of Institutional Politics

When touching upon "political" matters in their plots and representations, telenovelas are in fact depicting aspects of institutional politics, i.e., official laws, bureaucracies, political parties and politicians, and other forms of regulated power working at local, regional, and national levels.

With a few exceptions, telenovelas depict institutional politics and politicians (generally men) either as corrupt or incompetent.[15] Politicians who lack integrity, who thirst for power and money, and who spend tax money on monumental but useless reforms have been part of innumerable telenovela plots. Institutional politics is often represented in telenovelas as being a world apart from people's everyday lives and concerns. It is represented as being a world soiled by corruption, egocentrism, and lack of interest in social issues. Telenovelas' preferred representation of institutional politics and politicians is therefore a rather negative one. It is possible that this negative image reflects the history of Brazil's authoritarian political regimes, a time when civil society stood in direct opposition to a repressive state apparatus.[16] Unfortunately, actual corruption scandals involving politicians in high positions still keep on feeding fiction with reality. In this sense, telenovelas work as an instrument for commenting upon and criticizing Brazilian institutional politics and politicians, by representing it negatively, associating it with corruption and abuse of power, and dissociating it from average people.

Philosopher and media analyst Renato J. Ribeiro (2001) presents an interesting take on this subject: he suggests that the Brazilian media do not prioritize arenas where diverse political tendencies and ideologies would meet, debate, and confront one another. Lack of political consensus, Ribeiro maintains, is experienced in Brazil as being exclusively negative and unproductive. When set against this background, it becomes easier to understand the media's emphasis on the depiction of corruption: as a theme, corruption offers a clear-cut distinction between what is right and wrong. As such, it easily promotes a feeling of consensus among its consumers and viewers.

In my investigation into viewers' reception of telenovelas (see Machado-Borges 2003), I came to realize that most of my informants recognized and understood the parallels certain telenovelas drew between fictive and real-life politics and politicians. Several of my informants agreed with telenovelas' critical representation of corrupted politicians. At the time of my most extensive period of fieldwork in 1997, I could detect, among my informants, a major sense of disillusionment regarding institutional politics and a certain satisfaction in seeing this disillusionment represented in national fictive serials. However, when viewers were asked to mention what they most liked in a particular telenovela, politics and the representation of politicians were seldom named as their favorite topics. Instead, it was revenge, the turning of tables, and individual transformations that made the hearts of many telenovela viewers beat faster.

Telenovelas and the Alienation of Citizens

There is another way of looking at the relationship between Brazilian telenovelas and politics. As anthropologist Esther Hamburger (1999) points out, telenovela plots can shadow important political events in the country. On

29 December 1992, at the same time when then-president Fernando Collor was being formally impeached, an eight o'clock telenovela actress, Daniella Perez, was found murdered on the outskirts of Rio. The assassination of Daniella Perez by an actor (who played the part of her lover in the telenovela) and his pregnant wife received more attention and took more media space than the unique political event of the impeachment of Brazil's first democratically elected president in twenty-five years.

Another coincidental event had occurred four years before that: Chico Mendes, an environmental activist, was murdered at the same time that Odette Roitman, the popular villain in an ongoing telenovela, was murdered on the show. The fictional character's assassination, like the assassination of the actress Daniella Perez, diverted Brazilians' attention from important national political events.

Following this reasoning, telenovelas might be said to contribute to keeping viewers from participating in institutional politics. While field-working, I met several people who suggested that media producers and networks had no interest in giving priority to discussions of political matters. Some of them even suggested that Brazil was in fact ruled by the Globo network. The idea expressed by these people (most of them university students studying communications) was that powerful media networks not only made products to satisfy their audiences, but they also created needs, moods, preferences, and audiences for their products. The following excerpt illustrates this idea:

> Novelas tell people what to wear, what to buy, how to cut or wear one's hair, what to eat.... (Marcelo, 19, undergraduate student. Excerpt from a class essay on telenovelas)

Telenovelas were claimed to have a negative influence upon their viewers, since they promoted an escape from reality and diverted viewers' attention (through love stories, intrigues, fashion, and glamour) from urgent social and political issues. Media networks, according to this reasoning, create consumers, not citizens.

Is the Personal Political?

So far, the relationship between telenovelas and politics has been discussed from two different perspectives. On the one hand, it was argued that telenovelas reduce "politics" (in a broad sense) to institutional politics. Institutional politics, as has been shown, is generally portrayed (with very few exceptions) as being corrupt, hard to understand, and, for the members of the civil society, inaccessible. The depiction of institutional politics in Brazilian telenovelas can also be said to be highly gendered: institutional politics is portrayed as being part of a male-dominated and corrupt arena.

Telenovelas' emphasis on consumption, love, intrigue, and other kinds of personal matters (which are, by the way, traditionally considered to be feminine matters) has, on the other hand, been pointed to as a contributing factor in decreased political participation: telenovelas would, according to this reasoning, direct viewers toward consumption and direct their attention away from more important issues. These programs would thus have a negative impact on political practices.

A third possible way of seeing the relationship between telenovelas and Brazilian politics draws on the feminist movement of the 1970s and the questioning of the divide between political and personal matters. The emphasis in telenovelas on personal issues such as the home, relationships, families, women's oppression, and domestic violence can be understood within a broader social background. The idea is that personal matters—just like the destiny of white, upper-class Teodora and her black babies—are intrinsically related to relevant social issues that require political measures. As film and media studies scholar Charlotte Brunsdon (1995, 59) puts it, if "the personal is political...," then "the media construction and representation of personal life becomes fascinating and an urgent object of study."

Keeping in mind past and present political scandals that reinforce Brazilians' disillusionment with institutional politics (and telenovelas' representations of politics), it becomes interesting to investigate whether telenovelas present personal matters in a way that reveals a political element to them. Is the personal political when it comes to Brazilian telenovelas? Or is the mistrust with institutionalized politics so strong that one way to counteract and oppose official measures and procedures is to stand outside the frame of institutional politics?[17] Would telenovelas, by incorporating aspects of everyday life (work, family, health, sexuality, and education) into the public agenda, contribute to a broadening of the definition of politics and of concepts such as democracy and democratic participation (Alvarez 1990; Pitanguy 2002; Waisbord 2002)?

Let us take a look at the way in which some of these personal matters are discussed and fictionalized.

Teodora's home, later. She is sitting in the living room and talking to Caio:

TEODORA: Caio, I need to ask you a favor. I want you to buy me some books. I want to read Martin Luther King, Malcolm X and Nelson Mandela. I want the best of black literature!

CAIO: But why Teodora?

TEODORA: Because I need to prepare myself to raise these children! They will never be chic if they live in a world full of prejudices. I don't want my children to be afraid. I admit, I wasn't prepared for this caprice of destiny. But, if God wanted it that way, it's because He is telling me something. By the way, I want also a copy of the Afonso Arinos'[18] law.

CAIO: Come on! Are you crazy?

TEODORA: No Caio, I know the jungle we live in. My children will not pay for that. All my money will at least serve a good cause. Caio, I will sue anyone who makes a joke, or even insinuates anything…. I'm afraid, Caio. I think I'd better send my children to Europe, to Switzerland. I'm afraid of raising these children here in Brazil.

CAIO: Your children won't be happier living in a boarding school in Switzerland.

TEODORA: Really? I have my doubts….

(Excerpts from dialogue in *Salsa e Merengue*, 1997, Globo)

Fictionalizing Social Engagement—Individual Transformations and "Social Merchandising"

The content of telenovelas could be described as a sequence of euphoric articulations—unexpected, improbable, implausible interrelations that make characters go through personal transformations that often result in some kind of social mobility.

For example, Joventino, the youngest son of a rich cattle farmer, and the main character in *Pantanal* (1990, Manchete) was brought up in the city of São Paulo. His life takes an unexpected turn when he falls in love with Juma, a modest, brave, and independent young woman who lives all by herself in the wilderness of western Brazil. Dara—one of the main characters in *Explode Coração* ("Bursting Heart," 1995, Globo)—is an urban, middle-class gypsy who challenges the traditions of her people when she refuses to marry a gypsy man and opts instead for the love of a stranger she met through the Internet. In *O Rei do Gado* ("The King of Cattle," 1996, Globo) Luana, an active member of the MST, an organization that struggles for agricultural reform, falls in love with Bruno, a powerful landowner and "the King of Cattle." In *Salsa e Merengue* (1997, Globo), Jacinta, a black, working-class, live-in female servant, gets married to a blond German count.

As one can see from the examples above, seduction and love are often the driving force behind transformations and social mobility. Different spheres of activity are brought together by telenovela characters who seduce and love one another. A message that seems to run through all telenovela plots is that seduction and love slip through the social hierarchies of class, age, race, and sexuality.

Sexual desire, seduction, and love are intrinsic to plots of telenovelas. They work as a means of putting together and articulating separate universes, promoting transformations and social mobility. In telenovelas, the subjects who most consistently represent and embody transformation and movement across social hierarchies are women. These transformations are depicted as individual renegotiations of the self. As such, they do not imply major social changes. Teodora (in *Salsa e Merengue*, 1997, Globo), the arrogant, white, upper-class woman who, in her thirties, becomes the single mother of two black children, crystallizes all that. The character, as illustrated in the excerpts throughout this chapter, rethinks her own biases and attitudes, but she does not even imagine engaging herself in any kind of collective action against racism.

Most cases of social mobility depicted by telenovelas are achieved on an individual basis and usually result in some kind of change within the domestic sphere—a marriage, the recovering of custody of one's children, the building of a family. Besides emphasizing transformations and articulations between separate spheres of Brazilian society, telenovelas fictionalize social engagement in another way. As mentioned earlier in this chapter, product placement is called "merchandising" in Brazil. The insertion of social issues in the plots of telenovelas is, following the same terminology, called "social merchandising." Social merchandising is a term frequently used among media producers and even among media scholars (Alencar 2002; Schiavo 1998) to designate the discussion of polemical social issues in entertainment programs. As the term indicates, social issues, just like any other products, are inserted into telenovelas' plots. The procedure is similar to that used in telenovelas' merchandising, with the difference being that what is being "sold" is an issue of social character. This brings us back to the discussion about the relationship among telenovelas, consumerism, and the potential tension between market values and democratic participation: when it comes to telenovelas, is it possible to combine fiction, reality, consumerism, politics, and entertainment in one single program? If product placement in telenovelas treats viewers as consumers, does social merchandising address them as citizens?

Let us look at some examples that illustrate telenovelas' social merchandising.

The telenovela *Explode Coração* ("Bursting Heart," 1995, Globo), written by Glória Perez (who was also the mother of Daniella Perez, the actress murdered in 1992), launched a campaign in 1995 to help parents find their missing children. Real mothers were given roles in the plot to ask characters/viewers for help in their searching. And, indeed, many children were found (*Veja*, 29 January 1997).

Questions related to gender, sexuality, race, and class are an omnipresent feature of Brazilian telenovelas and a continual theme for academic and popular debates. The telenovela *Zazá* ("Zazá," 1997–98, Globo) approached the subject of AIDS and the exploitation of working children. *A Indomada* ("The Untamed Woman," 1997, Globo) discussed the subjects of prostitution, autism, and women's oppression. *Salsa e Merengue* ("Salsa and Merengue," 1997, Globo) depicted the love affair between two women and, as has been shown here, discussed racism through the story of the upper-class, white character Teodora and her newly born black children.

In 2001, one of the characters in *Laços de Família* ("Family Links," 2000–2001, Globo) found out that she was suffering from leukemia and that she would have to go through a bone marrow transplant in order to survive. The telenovela launched a national campaign to promote and encourage the donation of organs (*Veja* 2001). According to the records kept by the Brazilian Association of Voluntary Donors of Bone Marrow, the number of donors in November 2000 was approximately twenty persons a month. When the telenovela discussed leukemia and organ donation, this number increased to 900 donors a month—an increase of 4,500 percent (Alencar 2002). This same telenovela also discussed the stigmas of prostitution and sexual impotency suffered by other characters in the plot.

In 2001–2, the telenovela *O Clone* ("The Clone," Globo) interspersed the subjects of genetic engineering and drug abuse with complicated love intrigues. More recently, the telenovela *Mulheres Apaixonadas* ("Women in Love," 2004, Globo) discussed domestic violence and problems encountered by elderly people, and campaigned against civilians' use of firearms (*Folha OnLine*, 10 March 2004). The telenovela *America* (broadcast by Globo in 2005) approached subjects such as the situation of Brazilian immigrants in the United States, homosexuality, the life and everyday problems encountered by the blind, kleptomania, and the story of a boy who was sexually harassed by an adult he had met through the Internet.[19]

In 2004, the *Globo* network launched a campaign of self-promotion. It proclaimed itself to be a major actor in the process of "recovery of citizenship" (*Folha OnLine*, 21 March 2004). Twelve advertisements were produced and broadcast by the network. The protagonists in these advertisements were, among others, the president of the Chamber of Deputies, a senator from the Worker's Party (the PT, the party of Brazil's actual president, Luís Inácio Lula da Silva), the head of the state of São Paulo's cultural department, and the coordinator of a national center for children's rights in society. Their participation, according to the *Folha* article, were voluntary. The advertisements had the same basic structure. The screen was divided in two: on one side, a Globo program was shown; on the other side, the invited protagonist would iterate phrases such as "Globo is just like Brazil" (*Globo tem a cara do Brasil*) or "Globo's telenovelas have contributed largely to the recovery of citizenship" (*As novelas da Globo têm dado uma grande colaboração para a recuperação da cidadania*). All the advertisements ended with the voice-over of a famous telenovela actor, Tony Ramos, who—with only one exception—has always played the role of good characters, saying: "Our vocation is to believe in Brazil" (*Acreditar no Brasil é a nossa vocação*).

Through social merchandising, Globo presents itself as the producer of programs that contribute to the recovery of a sense of citizenship. "Our vocation is to believe in Brazil": the network presents itself as an independent actor that discusses and promotes certain social issues (managing even to engage politicians in them), at the same time that it uses these very social issues as a strong selling point—social merchandising in a nutshell.

Telenovelas combine fiction, reality, consumerism, politics, and entertainment in one single program. By addressing viewers as *citizens*, they manage to reach them as *consumers*. In times of national and global inequality, fictional politics and the representation of social issues become strong selling arguments. Are we about to watch the creation of citizen-consumers? What kinds of implications might this hybrid configuration, which blends values of consumerism and democratic participation, have on people? Do telenovelas promote or domesticate agency?

> *Teodora is in the living-room, talking to Lidia [an upper-middle class, white business woman].*
>
> TEODORA: My insemination didn't turn out the way I expected.
>
> LIDIA : What happened? Any problem with the babies?
>
> TEODORA: No, they are fine. The problem is the world out there. You see, the donor, the Canadian that I requested for the insemination...it turned out that he is black.
>
> LIDIA: Black? But you asked for a blond type, with blue eyes and physical traits that would remind you of Eugênio's! I remember that.
>
> TEODORA: Yes, I did. But there was a mistake, an exchange, I really don't know. A caprice of destiny. My children are mulattos. And according to Sexta-Feira, who is showing herself to be an expert on the subject, they will get darker.
>
> LIDIA: Oh, really?
>
> TEODORA: Wait a minute! You don't have to look sorry! They are simply wonderful, my dear! Beautiful! I'll tell you something, Lidia. I've found out that I was a warrior without a cause. I fought against windmills. Now, my darling, with my children, I'll

have a good cause to fight for!

(Excerpts from dialogue in *Salsa e Merengue*, 1997, Globo)

As the destiny and transformation of the character Teodora has illustrated, telenovelas are saturated with images and narratives of female characters who, in order to achieve love, happiness, and social mobility, allow themselves to undergo a series of self-transformations—transformations of their values, and often even of their bodies. These modifications guarantee a place in the world and, usually, in the hearts of the men around them. In doing this, these women forge links between divided social spheres and between different levels of social hierarchy. They circumvent social divisions without ever changing them. Individual mobility and transformation is achieved within an unaltered (and unthreatened) social system. As discussed previously, transformations are the motor of most telenovela plots: characters change from poor to rich, from unattractive women to seductresses, from prostitutes to respectable housewives, from elitist whites to politically aware mothers of black children. These transformations in attractiveness, knowledge, or status are usually experienced by women and connected to social mobility.

Telenovela plots foreground social hierarchies at the same time that they present strategies for circumventing, though not altering, these hierarchies. The innumerable examples of social mobility that are found in telenovela plots can be understood as strategies that allow one to work within the system. Anthropologist Purmina Mankekar (1999, 149) observes that Indian state-sponsored television serials do not depict strategies for mobilizing women as a collectivity. Instead, they advocate individual "upliftment." The same could be said about telenovelas. Their focus is on women's individual (not collective) agency and mobility. In this sense, one could say that telenovelas domesticate agency because they present mobility and change as individual experiences, not as collective, political changes.

On the other hand, it is important to remember that these not-so-threatening, domestic, individual cases of social mobility, transformation, and change are repeated, played out, and reiterated every day, several times a day, and broadcast on a massive scale to the whole nation. In this sense, agency is not domesticated. On the contrary, by being transposed from a domestic to a public arena, agency is emphasized, discussed, visualized, and even politicized.

Conclusion

This chapter has discussed several aspects of the relationship between telenovelas and politics. It has been argued that telenovelas re-style Brazilian politics. When touching upon "political" matters, telenovelas are in fact depicting aspects of institutional politics. Politics and politicians in telenovelas are generally portrayed in a negative way. Through fiction, telenovelas provide narratives that make sense of and represent institutional politics. By the same token, they create and reproduce preferred readings of Brazilian politics and of what is considered to be "political" in Brazil. In this sense, it is possible to say that telenovelas, through their representations, reinforce the divide between institutional politics and social issues represented through individual or personal experiences and matters.

There is also a latent gender aspect in these representations: telenovelas' emphasis on interpersonal relationships and emotions, and their focus on strong female characters, have been associated with a woman's world. The insertion of politics (i.e., male-dominated, institutionalized politics) might be a means for telenovela producers to flirt with a potential male audience.[20] Politics is generally represented in telenovelas as being male territory. On the other hand, when social issues are brought up in telenovelas, they are, in addition to being generally connected to the *individual* destinies of *female* characters, disconnected from the political sphere and presented as part of the telenovela's social merchandising. So, if on the one hand there is the association among men, (institutional) politics, corruption, and abuse, there is on the other hand an association among women, social issues, and individual agency. Marked as feminine and/or domestic and/or personal, social engagement is thus disconnected from (institutional) politics. (See Craske 1999 for an analysis of women's political participation in Latin America since the 1940s.)

Telenovelas downplay the political character of social issues by depicting them as being the result of individual and emotional engagement. At the same time, telenovelas commodify social engagement through their "social merchandising" campaigns. Social engagement becomes an instrument in the production of a favorable image of the Globo network.

The kind of social engagement that is portrayed in telenovelas promotes, at best, individual—not collective—action. However, these individual stories of change and transformation are broadcast daily, repeated and reiterated for millions of viewers all over Brazil. Between the lines, telenovela plots seem to be iterating the point that there are lots of things to be done to make Brazil a better place to live.

Telenovelas' foregrounding of social issues might, in this sense, be pointing toward a redefinition of the concept of politics itself. By incorporating practices of everyday life (work, family, health, sexuality, and education) into the public agenda, telenovela plots would, through social merchandising, be encouraging viewers to take stands on certain social issues. Emotional engagement would trigger a social engagement that is political, though not dependent on institutionalized and official politics.

For analytical purposes I outlined three major ways of approaching the relationship between telenovelas and politics. I now want to stress once more that these three perspectives should not be seen as distinct and isolated from one another. In reality, they are juxtaposed and interconnected. Their combination results, as we have seen, in amazing and bewildering kaleidoscopic patterns where politics is reduced to "institutional politics," where the divide between institutional politics and social matters is reinforced and maintained, where women occupy a central position, where personal matters are brought to a public arena, where social problems are discussed and the need for change is emphasized, and where individual agency is presented as the way to go about accomplishing transformations.

In a traditional telenovela style, this chapter ends with a cliffhanger. As one champions the possibility that viewers, if addressed as citizen-consumers, would use their skills to bring a "consumer mentality to their relations with the government, judging state services much like any other purchased goods, by the personal benefit that they derive from them" (Cohen 2001, 220),[21] one wonders whether the configuration of citizen-consumers, on the contrary, would imply that citizenship might be determined by one's status as a consumer: if one has the money to consume, if one can afford to watch Globo's telenovelas, then—and only then—one can be considered to be a citizen.

Notes

[1] According to the 1999 Brazilian census, the figures for color groups for the whole country were as follows: 54 percent white, 5.4 percent black, 40.1 percent brown, and 0.5 percent Asians and native Americans (in Sansone 2003).

[2] According to www.worldscreen.com/latinamerica.php (accessed 20 January 2006).

[3] This was modified only in 1988 when the concession of television networks became a decision to be taken not only by the president but also by the Brazilian congress.

[4] 99.84 percent of all the municipalities in the country are able to tune their television set to Globo. In: http://historiadatvbrasileira.e1.com.br/tvglobo.htm (accessed 20 January 2006).

[5] According to Mattelart and Mattelart (1990, 19), in 1970, 73 percent of the country's industries were situated in the southeastern region.

[6] Landay (1999, 27) makes a similar observation concerning the relationship between North American television and consumerism.

[7] See Brunsdon (1995) for a discussion on the role of soap opera in the development of feminist television scholarship.

[8] Aidar (1996) analyzes quantitative data gathered by the IBOPE (Brazilian Institute of Public Opinion and Statistics) on the number of telenovela viewers between August 1990 and January 1994. In Hamburger 1999, 282.

[9] Much like Brazilian telenovelas, Egyptian television serials provide explicit social and political commentaries on contemporary Egyptian life, something that American soap operas tend not to do (according to Abu-Lughod 1995, 196; and 2005).

[10] Since 2002, the Globo network has attempted to formally regulate its employees' participation in political campaigns. According to an internal communiqué, any employee wanting to participate publicly in a political campaign will not be able to participate in the network's programs during the period of the electoral campaign (in *Folha Online* 2002). More recently, a senator from the Brazilian congress suggested some modifications concerning the way electoral campaigns are conducted. Among this senator's suggestions is the prohibition of *showmícios* (i.e., the mixture of a show and a political campaign, a "showpaign"), a reduction in the campaign period, and the prohibition of the participation of television actors and actresses in the campaign (Wahrendorf Caldas 2005).

[11] Just as with telenovela writers, Brazilian actors and actresses are assumed to be progressive, politically engaged, and generally (though not always) left-wing sympathizers.

[12] I focus here on the case of Globo, since this network obtains the majority of all advertising revenues in Brazil (Mattelart and Mattelart 1990, 40).

[13] These magazines are published weekly or biweekly and are sold by subscription, in supermarket checkout racks, and at newsstands. *Contigo!*, for instance, has a circulation of almost 250,000 biweekly issues, and it cost R$3.90 in 1997.

[14] The end of dictatorship in Brazil in 1985 led to a gradual reduction in institutionalized censorship. Nowadays there is a federal authority that classifies the content of films and television programs and recommends appropriate hours for broadcasting to the networks. These recommendations are not directives. However, if the content of a telenovela (or any

other program) should come to be considered inappropriate (with, for instance, too much nudity, or with the depiction of sex scenes that are too explicit) for the time slot in which it is broadcast, then the Ministry of Public Affairs would have the authority to bring legal sanctions against the broadcasting network.

[15] See Ribeiro (2001) for a discussion about Brazilian television, politics, and the market, and Riegert, in this volume, for an analysis of North American television programs and their depictions of politics.

[16] See Pitanguy (2002) for an analysis of the relationship between feminism in Brazil and the struggle to bring women's rights into the public discourse.

[17] Political scientist Mala Htun (2002) points to a phenomenon that illustrates the divide between institutional politics and social issues, materialized under the form of a discrepancy between women's gains in Brazilian society and their under-representation in political office: Brazil has the lowest level of women's representation in national politics in Latin America, and yet, as Htun points out, it "has Latin-America's largest, most vibrant, and most diverse feminist movement, and has pioneered policy changes advancing women's rights" (Htun 2002, 733).

[18] The Afonso Arinos' law dates from 1951 and prohibits discrimination because of color, race, sex, or marital status of a person.

[19] In: http://revistaepoca.globo.com (accessed 17 January 2006).

[20] Having this discussion in mind, one could wonder why men enjoy telenovelas if they are so closely associated to the feminine. As I have discussed elsewhere (Machado-Borges 2003), men were generally reluctant to participate as informants in my research about telenovelas. It was important for many of them to assert that they were not emotionally engaged with the kinds of feminine matters that were discussed on these programs. On the other hand, male informants could openly show that they were engaged with telenovelas as potential *consumers* of the commodities displayed in it, for instance cars, computers, cellular phones, and erotic scenes with naked or half-naked actresses.

[21] Here in Scammel (2003, 126).

References

Abu-Lughod, Lila. 1995. "The Objects of Soap-Opera: Egyptian Television and the Cultural Politics of Modernity." In *Worlds Apart: Modernity Through the Prism of the Local*, edited by D. Miller. London: Routledge.

——. 1999. "Modern Subjects: Egyptian Melodrama and Postcolonial Difference." In *Questions of Modernity*, edited by T. Mitchell. Minneapolis: University of Minnesota Press.

——. 2005. *Dramas of Nationhood: The Politics of Television in Egypt*. Chicago: University of Chicago Press.

Aidar, Tirza. 1996. "Análise quantitativa dos Indices e do Perfil de Audiência de Telenovela por Segmento da População: Grande São Paulo e Rio de Janeiro, de 13/08/90 e 31/12/93." Internal Report. Campinas. NEPO:UNICAMP. Unpublished. In E. Hamburger (1999).

Alencar, Mauro. 2002. *A Hollywood Brasileira. Panorama da Telenovela no Brasil*. Rio de Janeiro: Editora Senac Rio.

Allen, Robert, ed. 1995. *To Be Continued—Soap-Operas Around the World*. London and New York: Routledge.

Alvarez, Sonia. 1990. *Engendering Democracy in Brazil*. Princeton: Princeton University Press.

BBC News. 2005. "Brazil's Lula 'Sorry' for Scandal," 12 August. http://www.bbc.co.uk (accessed 3 September 2005).

Brunsdon, Charlotte. 1995. "The Role of Soap Opera in the Development of Feminist Television Scholarship." In *To Be Continued—Soap-Operas Around the World*, edited by R. Allen. London and New York: Routledge.

Cohen, Lizabeth. 2001. "Citizen Consumers in the United States in the Century of Mass Consumption." In *The Politics of Consumption*, edited by M. Daunton and M. Hilton. Oxford: Berg.

Corner, John, and Pels, Dick, eds. 2003. *Media and the Restyling of Politics. Consumerism, Celebrity and Cynicism*. London: Sage.

Craske, Nikki. 1999. *Women and Politics in Latin America*. Cambridge: Polity Press.

DaMatta, Roberto. 1978. *Carnavais, Malandros e Heróis*. Rio de Janeiro: Zahar.

Faria, Vilmar, and Potter, Joseph. 1999. "Television, Telenovelas, and Fertility Change in Northeastern Brazil." In *Dynamics of Value in Fertility Change*, edited by Richard Leete, pp. 252–272. Oxford: Oxford University Press.

Folha OnLine. 2002. "Globo e Eleicões—Comunicado interno da Globo sobre participacão nas eleicões," 20 February. http://observatorio.ultimosegundo.ig.com.br /artigos/asp270220027.htm (accessed 17 January 2006).

——. 10 March 2004. "Outro canal: Globo bate recorde de merchandising social." http://www1.folha.uol.com.br/folha/ilustrada/ult90u42252.shtlml (accessed 26 August 2005).

——. 21 March 2004. "Globo faz operação para ter fama 'do bem.'" http://www1.folha.uol.com.br/folha/ilustrada/ult90u42602.shtml (accessed 26 August 2005).

Freyre, Gilberto. 1995 [1933]. *Casa Grande e Senzala: Formação da Família Brasileira sobre o Regime da Economia Patriarcal*. 22nd ed. Rio de Janeiro: Editora José Olympio.

Fry, Peter. 2000. "Politics, Nationality, and the Meanings of 'Race.'" *Daedalus* 129(2): 83–118.

Geertz, Clifford. 1973. *The Interpretation of Cultures*. New York: Basic Books.

Globo Online. 23 October 2005. "Referendo relevou descrença do povo no poder público." http://oglobo.globo.com (accessed 17 January 2006).

Hamburger, Esther. 1999. "Politics and Intimacy in Brazilian Telenovelas." Ph.D. dissertation, University of Chicago.

Holston, James. 1989. *The Modernist City. An Anthropological Critique of Brasília*. Chicago: University of Chicago Press.

http://historiadatvbrasileira.e1.com.br/tvglobo.htm (accessed 20 January 2006).

http://revistaepoca.globo.com (accessed 17 January 2006).

http://www.worldscreen.com/latinamerica.phg (accessed 20 January 2006).

Htun, Mala. 2002. "Puzzles of Women's Rights in Brazil." *Social Research* 69(3): 733–751.

IBGE (Instituto Brasileiro de Geografia e Estatística). 2003. Síntese de Indicadores Sociais 2002. *Estudos e Pesquisas—Informacão Demográfica e Socioeconômica*, 11. Rio de Janeiro: IBGE.

Kehl, Maria Rita. 1979. "Novelas, Novelinhas e Novelões: Mil e Uma Noites para as

Multidões." In *Anos 70: Televisão*, edited by E. Carvalho, M.R. Kehl, and S. Naves-Ribeiro. Rio de Janeiro: Editora Europa.

Landay, Lori. 1999. "Millions 'Love Lucy': Commodification and the Lucy Phenomenon." *NSWA Journal* 11(2): 25–47.

Lopez, Ana M. 1995. "Our Welcomed Guests–Telenovelas in Latin America." In *To Be Continued–Soap-Operas Around the World*, edited by R. Allen. London and New York: Routledge.

Machado-Borges, Thaïs. 2003. *Only for You! Brazilians and the Telenovela Flow*. SSAG. Stockholm: Almqvist & Wiksell International.

Mankekar, Purmina. 1999. *Screening Culture, Viewing Politics. An Ethnography of Television, Womanhood, and Nation in Postcolonial India*. Durham and London: Duke University Press.

Mattelart, Armand, and Mattelart, Michelle. 1990. *The Carnival of Images. Brazilian Television Fiction*. London and New York: Bergin and Harvey.

Mattos, Sérgio. 1990. *Um Perfil da TV Brasileira: 40 Anos de História, 1950–1990*. Salvador: A Tarde.

Mazziotti, Nora. 1993. "Acercamientos a las Telenovelas Latinoamericanas." In *Serial Fiction in TV–The Latin American Telenovelas*, edited by A.M. Fadul. São Paulo: ECA-USP.

Nogueira, Oracy. 1985. "Preconceito Racial de Marca e Preconceito Racial de Origem." In *Tanto Preto quanto Branco: Estudos de Relações Raciais*. São Paulo: T.A. Queiroz.

Ortiz, Renato; Ramos, José Mário; and Simões Borelli, Silvia H. 1991 [1989]. *Telenovela: História e Produção*. São Paulo: Brasiliense.

Pitanguy, Jacqueline. 2002. "Bridging the Local and the Global: Feminism in Brazil and the International Human Rights Agenda." *Social Research* 69(3): 805–820.

Reis, Elisa P. 2000. "Modernization, Citizenship, and Stratification: Historical Processes and Recent Changes in Brazil." *Daedalus* 129(2): 171–194.

Ribeiro, Renato Janine. 2001. "O Poder Público Ausente: a TV nas Mãos do Mercado." *Cadernos de Nosso Tempo* 5(2): 207–279. Rio de Janeiro: Edicões Fundo Nacional de Cultura (Ministério da Cultura).

Ribeiro, Santusa N., and Botelho, I. 1979. "A Televisão e a Política de Integração Nacional." In *Anos 70–Televisão*, edited by E. Carvalho, M.R. Kehl, and S.N. Ribeiro. São Paulo: Brasiliense.

Sansone, Lívio. 2003. *Blackness without Ethnicity. Constructing Race in Brazil*. New York: Palgrave Macmillan.

Scammel, Margaret. 2003. "Citizen Consumers: Towards a New Marketing of Politics?" In *Media and the Restyling of Politics*, edited by John Corner and Dick Pels. London: Sage.

Schelling, Vivian. 2004. "Popular Culture in Latin America." In *The Cambridge Companion to Modern Latin American Culture*, edited by John King. Cambridge: Cambridge University Press.

Schiavo, Márcio R. 1998. "Merchandising Social: Sexualidade e Saúde Reprodutiva nas Telenovelas." *Revista Brasileira de Sexualidade Humana* 9(2): 32–47.

Schneider, Ronald. 1996. *Brazil: Culture and Politics in a New Powerhouse*. Boulder, CO: Westview Press.

Simpson, Amelia. 1993. *Xuxa–The Mega-Marketing of Gender, Race, and Modernity*. Philadelphia:

Temple University Press.

Straubhaar, Joseph D. 1982. "The Development of the Telenovela as the Pre-eminent Form of Popular Culture in Brazil." *Studies in Latin-American Popular Culture* 1: 138–150.

——. 1984. "Brazilian Television: The Decline of American Influence." *Communication Research* 11(2): 221–240.

Tufte, Thomas. 1993. "Everyday Life, Women and Telenovela in Brazil." In *Serial Fiction in TV– The Latin American Telenovelas*, edited by A. Fadul. São Paulo: ECA-USP.

TV Folha, Folha de São Paulo. 3 December 1995. "Empresas Investem em Merchandising."

TV Programa, Jornal do Brasil. 14 July 1991. Interview with Gilberto Braga.

Veja. 28 February 1996. "Televisão: Os Reis da Tela."

Veja. 29 January 1997. "Ficção é Ignorar a Novela."

Veja. 12 February 1997. "Entre a Tela e a Vida Real."

Veja. 10 January 2001. "A Novela que Hipnotiza o País."

Vink, Niko. 1988. *The Telenovela and Emancipation–A Study on TV and Social Change in Brazil.* Amsterdam: Royal Tropical Institute.

Wahrendorf Caldas, Ricardo. 2005. "A Reforma Politica no Brasil Hoje." 23 August. http://www.unb.br/acs/artigos/at0805-06.htm (accessed 20 January 2006).

Waisbord, Silvio. 2002. "Grandes Gigantes: Media Concentration in Latin America." www.openDemocracy.net (accessed 24 January 2006).

World Bank. 2001. "World Development Indicators: Distribution of Income or Consumption." www.worldbank.org/data/wdi2001/pdfs/tab2_8.pdf (accessed 22 January 2003).

CHAPTER EIGHT

Traversing Authenticities: *The West Wing* President and the Activist Sheen

SUE COLLINS

The first time Martin Sheen put his politics on the line was in 1986 during a demonstration of civil disobedience over Reagan's Strategic Defense Initiative (Star Wars). Since this initial encounter with the law, Sheen has been arrested some seventy times as a result of his activism. Over the last twenty years, Sheen has involved himself in nonviolent and often quiet protests over such issues as nuclear weapons testing, military space technology development, U.S. foreign policy in Central America, and apartheid. He has advocated on behalf of the homeless, immigrants, gun control, and environmentalism. Most recently, Sheen, who is well known today for his role as U.S. President Josiah (Jed) Bartlet on the NBC political drama *The West Wing*, used his celebrity visibility to speak robustly against the war in Iraq despite the swelling criticism against celebrities publicly espousing an anti-war stance (McKenna 2003; St. John 2003; Whyte 2003). In a thirty-second spot airing on CNN in February 2003, Sheen as actor-activist on behalf of the organization United to Win Without War implored audiences in Washington, D.C., New York, and Los Angeles to oppose the Bush Administration's policy. This endorsement for the burgeoning anti-war movement, along with other public denunciations over the administration's war cries was not without controversy for Sheen, nor for NBC. When Sheen started getting harassed with hate mail and accusations of being a "traitor," and when "rightwingers" attacked the show in an effort to eradicate Sheen, NBC executives, according to Sheen, "let it be known they're very uncomfortable" with his anti-war activism (Sheen Faces Backlash Over War Protests 2003). The network counteracted the anti-war advertisement by distancing itself from Sheen's political views, proclaiming that his views were those of a private citizen and not the views of the network or its affiliates

(Sheen Faces Backlash Over War Protests 2003; Heaton 2003; Kenna 2003).[1]

Certainly NBC's riposte can be read as an attempt to protect one of its more popular shows from a ratings decline. *The West Wing*, after all, isn't just any program—it was a high ratings primetime series about contemporary politics, but one that traded on giving voice to non-dominant and liberal perspectives, as if to "speak truth to power," in ways that both edified and entertained its audiences. After its debut in the fall of 1999, *The West Wing* was acclaimed by popular critics and academics for its representation of the intricate and compromising business of U.S. government and White House political culture, and for its similarity to actual political issues and current events. The show was praised for engaging its audience with complex, ongoing, and overlapping narratives in a hallmark televisual aesthetic: steadicam long shots winding through and across the intricate set of White House corridors and staff offices creating a behind-the-scenes narrative framework of the building's internal processes; rapid-fire, walk-and-talk dialogue by erudite political operatives engrossed in private discourse on behalf of the public; and, of course, the insider's purview of the president revealed to us by Martin Sheen as noble-minded yet imperfect, confronted by the multiplicity and contradiction of his own identity as private man and public dignitary.

Only two seasons into the series, the intertexts of Sheen's star image both on camera as the world's most powerful political leader and off as socio-political actor-activist became yet more testimony to the much-noted, blurry boundaries between politics and entertainment. Bumper stickers appeared reading "Bartlet for President," and an Internet poll reported that Bartlet was receiving 8 percent of the presidential vote. After an appearance on *The Tonight Show* with Vice-President Al Gore, Sheen told press room reporters that the Green Party had asked him to run with Ralph Nader in the 2000 election for the real job in the White House (Seelye 2000). Of course, Sheen kept his day job, but his long-standing status as liberal activist raises a number of interesting questions about the relationship between socio-political change and popular culture and, particularly, about "celebrity activism." To start, how does Sheen manage his celebrity performance-as-commodity concomitantly with his sometimes highly visible support of marginalized and controversial viewpoints? In other words, how can Sheen be both a celebrity and an activist who actually dissents?

In this chapter I begin with the proposition that there is something contradictory about celebrity in the service of a progressive political and social critique of capitalism. Undeniably, Hollywood celebrities are cultural commodities dependent on capitalism's reproduction economically and ideologically, and in particular, on the commercial media system that produces and distributes celebrity by creating sustained audiences for its consumption, who in commercial print and broadcasting systems get sold to advertisers. In this way, celebrity can also be thought of as an audience-gathering mechanism critical to the project of commercial popular cultural production. Because of their dual relationship to cultural producers and audiences, it stands to reason that celebrities would want to minimize the possibilities of alienating audiences when they choose to represent and advocate for socio-political issues. For this reason, it may be easy to dismiss celebrity activism as culturally hegemonic. In using this term, I borrow from Jackson Lears (1983) to suggest that celebrities belong to a group of leaders, although less recognized as leaders in a formal sense, who are required to achieve "consent" on behalf of dominant structures of power, such as journalists, writers, teachers, and artists. Hollywood stars, whether implicated in the texts of capitalist cultural production or overtly as spokespersons, have sold most of what is quintessentially American, for better or for worse, from individualism and equality to extravagant consumption, democracy to imperialism, soap to war. It is the seemingly paradoxical nature of celebrity activism that makes the question both interesting and worth asking: what are the ways in which celebrities mobilize their politics for socio-political change and to what extent, given the constraints of their image as commodity and the uncertainty and high risk that characterize commercial cultural production? How might celebrity as a site for political meaning traverse the space between popular cultural representations of political realities and the "real" of socio-political action? And, as this book's introduction asks, how do our notions of what is "real" change when the "real" must also be entertaining; that is, when celebrity stands in for political participation and citizen activism?

This chapter grapples with these larger questions by exploring how celebrity manages the ostensible contradiction of celebrity activism. I begin by clarifying what I mean by activism, which is then held up to the behaviors of Hollywood "celebrity activists." Because the celebrity commodity form challenges autonomy when celebrities involve themselves with socio-political issues and movements, I argue that consonance in celebrity on- and off-screen meanings becomes an important measure in authenticating celebrity activism. Then I examine how meanings generated by *The West Wing* cross over to the real, and more narrowly, the intertexts between Jed Bartlet, the progressive television president, and Martin Sheen, the citizen-activist. In short, I argue that close articulation among discourses of authenticity in the texts of Sheen's on-screen characters, off-screen persona, and real person link his activism to his commodity form in such a way that both reproduces his celebrity status and enables his social function as a celebrity to be oppositional.

How Do We Know Activism When We See It?

To start, it is useful to consider what kinds of behavior constitute activism, and then what it is that celebrities are doing when they are referred to as activists. This is a question that does not go uncontested. What counts as activism, and for that matter, what counts as political in the contemporary media landscape, has become increasingly imprecise and difficult to pin down, particularly if one is using the classical Marxian sense of *praxis* as a yardstick. From a structuralist perspective there are behaviors that contest power in overt and direct ways; they are "out there" to be observed, evaluated, modified, and measured for their impacts. Commonly understood and traditionally theorized, these are activities that often coalesce at the grassroots level into social movements, but can also take form through non-governmental or transnational organizations. They are generally aimed at policy change and often framed in terms of social justice. They are organized around economic and social capital and orchestrated to gain visibility and to generate more oppositional practice. In short, activism has generally been understood as a form of agitation that acts as a "constraint on the power of political elites" (Clark 2000, 9). It is counter-hegemonic activity, a "rhetoric of agitation and control" (Bowers and Ochs 1971), which situates agency at the forefront of its possibilities for structural change. It might be argued that "activism" has become an over-worked term as less direct and more passive practices get classified under the rubric. New media certainly contribute to the broadening of activities that might fall into the spectrum of activist practice. Belonging to a political listserv, forwarding email for political purposes, or hyperlinking activist websites might be politically intended, but these kinds of measures have also been charged with the criticism of "armchair activism," which reminds us that there is something qualitatively different between signing an on-line petition and speaking up at a demonstration, or attending a sit-in. In other words, while consciousness and imagination are necessary conditions for activism, they are not sufficient. "Activism" denotes *action* or *praxis*, a putting of the body on the line, if you will.

In considering an undertaking as "activism," it is critical to retain a sense of resistance, struggle, or contestation against ideology, or as John Thompson defines ideology, "the ways in which meaning serves to establish and maintain relations of domination" (1990, 56). Here I am resuscitating Marx's treatment of ideology as critical; that is, as a concept whose usage is restricted to those ideas working to reproduce relations of domination by which social life is structured.[2] With this distinction, we have a basis by which to consider the salience of social practice that challenges these relations, and that is commonly identified in the contemporary sense as activism. If ideology is "that which protesters protest against" (Bouchier 1987, 28), then activism is practice that contests the projects and their meanings that work to maintain power and reproduce relations of domination. Social liberalism or progressivism is sometimes conflated with activism, but this is mistaken, for the former are socio-political orientations advocating reformist agendas of social and political change that are organized and instituted from within the prevailing mainstream frame of American political processes, while the latter concerns the methods used to contest power and is not limited to one socio-political orientation—the right may also challenge mainstream political policy through activist practice in order to actualize socio-political change. Activism moves beyond consciousness to intention and action, and it can assume a variety of forms, some of which exceed the constraints of legality. Although it is commonly accepted that a number of activities, both conventional and unconventional, constitute methods of activism, they are clearly not the same in degree (e.g., letter writing or boycotting versus physical protest such as sit-ins, or more dissenting methods involved in civil disobedience and guerrilla tactics). Another way to identify and analyze activism would be to consider how its practices might be classified qualitatively along a spectrum of "soft," "hard," or "radical," depending on the degree to which it is treated as agitation by political authorities.

"Celebrity Activism": What's at Stake?

If we are defining "activism" as counter-hegemonic activity, then celebrity activism is a problematic worthy of its own analysis, because celebrity is inextricably tied to its commodity form. This means that public opinion becomes just as much a determinant of activist practice, if not more so, than the response of political authorities. Yet there is little treatment of celebrity activism *qua activism*. There are an increasing number of scholarly analyses arguing for the study of celebrity as a dominant organizing principle in popular culture and media studies that can no longer be separated out of politics (Corner 2003; Jones 2005; Keller 1986; Pels 2003; Street 2002, 2003a; van Zoonen 2005). Some studies are interested in the way the celebrity frame is associated with or appropriated by politicians in terms of performance and aesthetics of style (Corner 2003; Keller 1986; Marshall 1997; Pels 2003; Street 2003b). Two studies that directly engage with celebrity activism equivocate on the term "activism" or fail to keep the critical distinction between activism (in the counter-hegemonic sense) and involvement in electoral politics separate in their analyses (Marks and Fischer 2002; West and Orman 2002). Running for public office or supporting politicians who do so are not particularly risky behaviors in American politics. But when celebrities become political in ways that overtly contest power, they take very real risks, some of which can and have cost careers.[3] As John Street (2002) argues, when celebrities become activists, their politics are both enabled and constrained by many factors such as the conventions of genre, their relationship to their audiences and corporate sponsors, the demands and methods of recruitment of the social movement eliciting their support, and how they imagine themselves as political beings. Notwithstanding these factors, celebrities must create a political persona that invokes their own credibility and authority, which then gets conferred onto the cause to which they are associated. Put another way, they must use these resources to demonstrate authenticity in order to get the attention and sympathy of the audiences they seek, and to protect themselves from retribution should they alienate audiences.

That said, much of what is termed "celebrity activism" in the popular press may seem intuitively more culturally hegemonic than meaningfully contestational. The term begs the question: how is it that entertainment celebrities can be both promoters and critics of capitalism at the same time? After all, as David Marshall (1997) notes, celebrities are much-watched public individuals who serve an important ideological function in their legitimation of capitalism. They are cultural commodities, organized around principles of capital accumulation, manufactured for the purposes of economic exchange, circulated by way of a fairly transparent process of publicity and hyperbole, and, by and large, dependent upon the logic of the cultural industries for their visibility and, therefore, for their reproduction in a commercial media system. Put another way, celebrity is a symbolic form whose transmission and reception within a commercial media system render it a cultural commodity (Thompson 1990). Celebrity is the democratization of fame, as Leo Braudy (1986) argues, but it is also the commodification of fame in which visibility is a function of its reproducibility vis-à-vis a commercial media system. Audiences derive meaning in their reception of celebrity, whether in terms of pleasure or distaste, and this influences "exchange" or economic value from a production standpoint. This means that celebrity value in relation to cultural production can be measured in terms of gathering audiences. It is in this sense that celebrity's success is located in its "circulation" (Hesmondhalgh 2002), and by this I mean the processes that work to distribute and promote celebrity for the purposes of creating sustained audiences for its consumption, whose attention ultimately deems the reproduction of celebrity status.

But celebrity complicates our understandings of cultural commodities, for it is both part of a cultural product—for example, a film or television program—

and a product itself whose value is unstable because its meanings are complex, fluid, relatively autonomous, and not wholly predictable. When celebrity moves within the field of entertainment, that is, across a variety of cultural texts, and when it ventures beyond entertainment, configurations of meanings accumulate and become intertextual. Celebrity meaning, then, is not contained by any one text, but rather becomes an intertextual amalgam of fluid meaning; celebrity is "a system of signs that includes chains of significations" (Marshall 1997, 58). This is not to say that there is always a positive relationship of symbolic meaning to economic value; for example, celebrity scandal produces more meaning apropos celebrity journalism but not necessarily more economic value for cultural producers whose interests are tied to other cultural commodities that house celebrity. Historically, this was evident by adoption of the studio contract system following the Fatty Arbuckle scandal, which worked to cap star salaries, but also to protect the studio's star capital through its morality clause by intimidating stars with the loss of their contract if they engaged in scandalous or potentially scandalous behavior. Celebrity transgressions today may reduce a celebrity's value and access to distribution, or worse, imperil the value of the larger text, such as actor Paul Reubens discovered when he lost his debut spot on the hit show *Everybody Loves Raymond* after being arrested on child pornography charges. Or, consider the problem of clutter. Stars have always resisted doing commercial endorsements for fear of damaging their star image (and, therefore, their value) with overexposure or trivial exposure. Today celebrity agents and managers attend to celebrity contracts in order to stabilize meanings by obliging celebrities to particular promotional activities, while also implicitly limiting or overseeing celebrity activity outside of entertainment that might risk celebrity value (Turner, Bonner, and Marshall 2000). Speaking more broadly, production strategies at various stages and across sectors of the cultural industries construct representations, then account for and monitor the dynamic of celebrity meaning through audience consumption. More accurately, perhaps, cultural producers attempt to reproduce and circulate celebrity by continually predicting the negotiation of meaning between the unstable celebrity sign and shifting audience tastes; in effect, they are guided as with other cultural products by the "nobody knows principle" (Caves 2000).

In thinking about celebrity as a system of meaning, Marshall (1997) argues that celebrity is produced differently across distinct industries, as well as within an industry, which allows the system to produce differentiated celebrity types for a range of audience consumption practices and popular taste. In the entertainment industry, the discursive construction of celebrity works to produce varying sensations of affect and identification in the subjectivities of audiences. The film celebrity, for example, is constructed around "the building and dissipation of the aura of personality," which works to establish distance from the audience, who then turns to extra-filmic texts (magazine interviews, television appearances, critics' commentary, etc.) in an effort to unveil the authentic self behind the celebrity hype (117). Television, on the other hand, works to reduce aura and collapse distance by employing modes of address that position the celebrity as a familiar personality, such as the talk-show host or news anchor and, to a lesser extent, the soap character, all of whom appear to audiences in the private domestic sphere, and whose real selves are more unified with their performances. The performance codes in the popular music industry position the celebrity closer to the audience through intimate displays of emotional sincerity and commitment manifest in the music itself and the venue of live performance, allowing claims of authenticity to resonate in ways distinct from television and film. The celebrity sign organizes the various meanings constructed and attributed to the celebrity both as performer and as the "real" person ostensibly underneath the construction, which taken together constitute the celebrity or star image, while it also functions to designate the individual as a commodity form. The celebrity image, then, is constructed in two sites of cultural production: the on-screen cultural products or texts that house the celebrity (i.e., film, television show, music video, etc.) plus all other sites of circulation involving promotion, publicity, criticism, and commentary, in short, all celebrity journalism.[4] For Marshall, celebrity in all its constitutive meaning is both a means of representing conceptions of individualism as a part of democratic capitalism, and a site to house the affective power of the crowd, which, when effectively achieved, acts in the service of consumer culture and capitalism, and thus serves an important ideological function.

Celebrities themselves manage their complex identities as image, labor, and property for cultural producers, and as personal assets (Dyer 1986).[5] Indeed, they strategize to accumulate and maintain their value, which should be seen as a kind of intertextually fluid capital, in order to reproduce and improve their celebrity status continuously. To do so, they must adopt, as Barry King (1986) puts it in his discussion of stardom as an occupation, a "strategy of performance" across all sites of intertextual circulation that is adaptive to pressures of the industry and the variable and changing tastes of audiences.[6] For Dyer, part of the "ideological effect" of stars is to "disguise the fact that they are just as much produced images, constructed personalities as 'characters' are" (1994, 22). This sense of constructed coherence between the star's on-screen performances and off-screen persona serves to invite audiences to locate the authentic as a pleasurable practice in the consumption of stars, that is, to continue to star watch and to look to celebrity journalism to find out who the star "really" is.[7]

While Dyer sees this working through of the consistencies and tensions between the characters, constructed public persona, and real person as the fundamental mechanism of the film-star image, Marshall argues that this "play" around identity and authenticity—that is, discovering the celebrity's authentic self—is consistent as a system in relation to celebrity. No matter where celebrity is positioned within the media industries, Marshall contends, it is the circulation of meaning around celebrity, "the connections between celebrities' 'real' lives and their working lives as actors, singers, or television news readers" that essentially "configure the celebrity status" (58). To be sure, audiences recognize that celebrity is discursively produced and multi-mediated in nature, and they attend to celebrity meaning as stratified; in other words, they acknowledge "stars" (high or rich in intertextual value) as of a different order than "B-" or "C-list" celebrities, or hyper-visible, short term "celetoids" (Rojek 2001), and they experience various forms and degrees of pleasure in "reading" the multitude of texts across the celebrity strata (Gamson 1994). While celebrity is a commodity produced and managed by the cultural industries, its meanings and its discursive power as a legitimate voice with access to media are evident only with respect to its audience. Celebrity is constructed by dominant culture, but its meanings are also constructed by audiences. As Marshall notes, conceptions of celebrity, whether descending from above or rising from below, are in constant transformation and negotiation, and they never cohere to form an essential celebrity identity. "This is an aspect of the working hegemony between different parts of a culture," Marshall argues, "including the most powerful and the least powerful groups, so that a loose fabrication of a commonality is in place to maintain a consensus among the population" (48). In this way, celebrity represents a "site for processes of hegemony" (49).

Much of what interests audiences in Hollywood and its stars, Dyer (1994) notes, involves the "process of contradiction and its 'management' and those moments when hegemony is not, or is only uneasily, secured" (3). Because the star image is constituted from various texts that come together to form a complex totality with a chronological dimension and a "structured polysemy" of multiple but finite meanings, in some cases elements of signification reinforce other elements, and in other cases elements are in opposition or contradiction (72). The star image, according to Dyer, is characterized by attempts to negotiate the differences between these significations. For example, in *Heavenly Bodies* (1986), Dyer shows how Marilyn Monroe, Paul Robeson, and Judy Garland's star images were concurrently held in tension around dominant discourses of the individual and of work in capitalist society, as well as seen to reveal their genuine selves through discourses consonant with their private or off-screen representations around sexuality, racial identity, and bodily health, respectively. In the case of Jane Fonda, Dyer (1994) notes that while her film roles became increasingly consonant with her politics in the 1960s and early 1970s, her off-screen radical associations were framed by the press not in terms of the political issues involved, but in relation to other aspects of her image (e.g., her father, her image as sex symbol, her acting), and, more significantly, with respect to the fact that *she* as a star was involved with the political issues. Similarly, Susan McLeland (2001) argues that Fonda's political involvement with the Vietnam War focused the attention of the American popular press on the appropriateness of her actions, reinterpreting her star persona in terms of "her disloyalty toward American values through a variety of radical, unfeminine behaviors" (232). Although she is still a subject of political contention for segments of the public, the press began to resolve her politics with her profession as an actress when her reconciliation with her father was made public in 1973, and when her later films featured roles that represented her antithesis, that is, characters who were "prowar or apolitical," but who achieved some kind of political "awakening" as a central theme of the film (248).

The issues of dissonance or contradiction in star images raise the question of what Marshall (1997) refers to as celebrity "transgressions," or the ways in which celebrities achieve independence from the meanings constructed to signify their image as consonant, which can be thought of as a kind of autonomy. Transgressions can involve the decomposition of the on-screen personality and the adoption of unconventional roles that produce dissonance in the celebrity persona, for instance, when a celebrity breaks his or her character type and experiments with new roles in character acting. Transgressions also arise from the way celebrities live their private lives, which is commonly framed in celebrity journalism as gossip and scandal, and which produces dissonance within the celebrity image. Marshall notes that transgressions "are also forms of risk in achieving autonomous status" because it is unknown the degree to which audiences will tolerate changes in the celebrity sign based on what celebrities do in their off-screen lives. As the symbolic value of celebrity changes with more meaning, so too does the audience's negotiation with those meanings, which may or may not change celebrity's economic value. Thus, it is the unstable nature of intertextuality that constrains celebrity autonomy when entertainment celebrities move outside of their field of expertise—in this case, show business—and into politics.

Celebrity Capital

One way to think about how celebrities are enabled and/or constrained when they trade on their celebrity status in politics is to employ Bourdieu's (1989; 1990; 1991; 1992) conceptions of capital, field, and habitus. For Bourdieu, all practice among people is subject to a basic opposition between economic and cultural power, and everything that people do, even when what they do seems disinterested or gratuitous, is motivated by the desire to maximize or accumulate material and/or symbolic profit. Bourdieu talks about profit more specifically in terms of different types of power that come from the particular configurations of capital (namely, economic, social, and cultural capital) that are required to inhabit the structured social spaces he calls fields (e.g., cultural production, economy, politics, religion, science, etc.), which operate by their own, yet similarly structured, laws of functioning, forms of authority, and systems for reward. Bourdieu's conception of capital extends understandings of power beyond the economic, for people engender resources such as social skills and networking, as well as education, know-how, and cultural aptitude and expertise. People are distributed across a field according to the volume and configuration of the capital they possess in relation to the political and cultural power that exists within the field, and they engage in a continuous struggle to improve or maintain their share of capital in order to stay in the field at the least, or better, to be at the top of the field. In short, a field is "a battlefield wherein bases of identity and hierarchy are endlessly disputed over" (Bourdieu 1992, 101).

People act within any given field according to conditionings associated with a particular class of existence which produce habitus, which Bourdieu defines as "systems of durable, transposable dispositions, structured structures predisposed to function as structuring structures" through which people perceive the world in particular ways and act in it (1990, 53). Although it is a unique set of dispositions in its purest sense, habitus is also a way of thinking about group membership that is shared by people with similar backgrounds and experiences. Habitus is both "structured" in that it is produced in part by patterns of social practice informed by past influences, and "structuring" because it generates and organizes practices without presupposing a conscious intention on the part of the agent. The habitus one acquires acts to constrain and motivate behavior depending on the position one occupies in society, which in turn is contingent upon one's endowment of economic, social, and cultural capital. The extent to which a person's capital is recognized or acknowledged by others constitutes one more form of capital, which Bourdieu calls symbolic capital—a diverse configuration of capital not reducible to economic capital—and it is this kind of capital that Bourdieu equates with prestige and fame (Johnson 1993). Bourdieu argues that symbolic power is conferred on those who possess symbolic capital (1989, 22), which means it can make people see and believe, confirm or transform the world through the equivalent of what might be obtained by force (1991, 170). This suggests that celebrities who act as spokespersons, even though they have little if any institutional power (Alberoni 1972)—they "occupy a dominated position in the dominant class" (Bourdieu 1993, 164)—contribute to the ideological work Bourdieu calls "symbolic violence" because they can legitimate perceptions of the world that serve to reproduce relations of domination.

Although Bourdieu does not theorize celebrity specifically, I have been arguing that celebrity is a product of large-scale production whose value for cultural producers is not based on its form as art *per se* or as inherently meaningful, but rather as reliably profitable. As such, celebrity is positioned closer to what Bourdieu calls the "heteronomous pole" of cultural production (as opposed to the "autonomous pole"), which is simply to say that it is constrained by the economic logic(s) of the media industries. This is not to suggest that celebrity has no autonomy, but rather, it is to highlight the complex dialectic of celebrity's stratification in terms of shifting intertextual value and producers' attempts to predict the appropriate matching of cultural products with audience tastes while managing the risks and uncertainty that characterize cultural production. *Celebrity capital*, I am arguing, is a particular configuration of symbolic capital that is required (among the other forms of capital) to inhabit and operate successfully as a cultural commodity within the field of entertainment. More precisely, celebrity capital signifies the varying and unstable ratio of symbolic to economic value that operates above some requisite level required to reproduce and circulate celebrity profitably. It is an amount or degree of recognizable intertextual meaning that sustains celebrity as an audience-gathering mechanism for cultural producers.

Authenticating Celebrity Activism

When celebrities move into the political field as activists, the idea is to mobilize their celebrity capital in order to call attention to issues and to generate resources. Of course, this is what social activist groups and movements are banking on when they recruit celebrities, who can bring visibility in terms of newsworthiness, as well as a snowball effect on resources— more money, status, participants, and supporters than a movement or campaign could procure independently (Lahusen 1996; Meyer and Gamson 1995; Prindle 1993; Simonson 2001), thus enabling a transfer of symbolic capital into very real economic power.[8] In effect, their visibility affords celebrities the symbolic power to act as spokespersons, but in the conversion of celebrity capital to symbolic capital that is expedient in the field of politics, they must also legitimize their claims to represent issues or, in other words, to achieve "standing" (Meyer and Gamson 1995). This assumes the engendering of some expertise related to the issue, but, more important, it challenges the extent to which they can disavow their economic interest—in other words, risk their celebrity status—while engaging in activist practice, that is, behavior that is counter-hegemonic to the project of capitalism. The choice of location within the political field in which they enter (i.e., issues or social movements associated with high vs. low controversy), the configuration of capital they construct, and the extent of their involvement must also minimize the possibilities for alienating audiences in order to keep their celebrity capital in the field of entertainment. Given the tension to avoid high controversy, it is easy to understand why celebrity involvement in social movements tends to gravitate the movements to more consensual issues, as well as shift the focus of attention from the issue to the celebrity (McLagan 2002; Meyer and Gamson 1995).

It is not unreasonable to assume that when celebrities get involved with activism, the extent or intensity of their engagement is constrained by public opinion. Indeed, I am arguing that this has something to do with how their celebrity capital positions them within the celebrity stratum and with the historical conjuncture at any given moment. Habitus may resolve, in part, what Prindle (1993) sees as a contradiction unique to Hollywood: the rich and famous coupled with liberal politics. The idea that stars, in particular, experience a similar habitus helps explain why the community has galvanized historically over a few core issues such as freedom of expression and other human rights. The liberalism that characterizes the entertainment industry is rooted in the political economy of Hollywood, distinguished by the paranoia and anxiety of uncertainty, rejection, exploitation, and abuse experienced by its denizens starting in the 1930s and culminating with the blacklist, and continuing with the threat of its revival. Celebrities also share common sentiments of guilt and reciprocity; they claim they want to "give back" to society in gratitude for their success, but this is also a form of reciprocity that functions in response to the degree in which audiences have paid and continue to pay attention to them. Although celebrities are no longer beholden to the tight rein of the studio system, the constraints on dissenting politics today are largely self-imposed, which is not to say that celebrities are precluded from activism, but it is to argue that they are predisposed to choose their associations within an increasingly commodified cultural climate.

This takes us back to the question of what it is that celebrities are doing when they become or get referred to as "activists." The April 2000 issue of the now-defunct *George* magazine features a tribute to ten celebrity activists "fighting for their causes," and it profiles one hundred "stars who do good offscreen." Few of these projects involve counter-hegemonic protest or demands for structural change, whereas the majority of celebrity causes are symbolic of consensual socio-political issues. Few would object to celebrities acting in the capacity of spokespersons to raise money to cure Alzheimer's, help the homeless, fund the Special Olympics, or fight for women's rights. Media events such as celebrity telethons, while enormously successful in terms of raising money, are safe forms of soft activism that function more like Band-Aids in lieu of attacking the disease. Jim McGuigan (1998), for example, argues that People's Aid and Comic Relief served as a substitute charity for official politics, taking the onerous responsibility off the British Government Aid program. Similarly, Liesbet van Zoonen points out that these celebrity events fail to resonate in the political field, so that success ends up being predominantly "along the lines of charity than of politics" (2005, 50). To be sure, celebrities need causes to enhance their circulation just as social activist groups and movements need celebrities to advance their agendas. In this way, there is a certain symbiosis between this soft activism and celebrity, which can be seen as "successful" for both the celebrity and the cause in some measure.[9] However, audience response to the intensification of celebrity politicization, particularly if seen as transgression, is itself increasingly unstable and unpredictable. Even though celebrities respond to their audiences when they choose their associations, as Street (2002) argues, it is unlikely that their audiences are self-politicized; more likely, robustly politicized audiences are "a result of marketing strategy of stars and their corporate sponsors—either that or politicized artists end up alienating their fans" (Street 2002, 435). While celebrity journalism might have us believe that celebrity's claims to activism are on the rise, few celebrities today actually engage in dissenting activism, that is, the kind of activism that might actually compromise their careers. In other words, what is commonly referred to as "celebrity activism" is more often a form of soft activism or philanthropy that performs a culturally hegemonic function.

This is not to say that the work of celebrity activists is inauthentic or purely reflective of their economic interests, although this may be the case with some. Most celebrities recognize, however, that their commodity form is also a form of visibility that can be harnessed on behalf of social good.[10] Stars, of course, can more easily manage the conversion of their celebrity capital into political capital than lesser-known entertainers because of their excess value to cultural producers. But what matters is that audiences recognize their activism as authentic. One measure of authenticity in light of celebrity, then, would be for audiences to detect the essential, "real," and ordinary person beneath the performance doing something political. Yet another measure of authenticity vis-à-vis activism as counter-hegemonic activity entails the degree to which celebrities are willing to risk their celebrity site as commodity in the constitution of political capital. In other words, when celebrities disavow their economic interests as Bourdieu suggests, they move closer to the autonomous pole within the field they inhabit. When celebrities put their careers at risk for their political autonomy, that is, when they act on their convictions despite the consequences, they construct new relationships with audiences—relationships based on the real, the authentic, of shared political sensibilities and alliances.

Martin Sheen, I am arguing, is one celebrity whose politics articulate to these measures of authenticity. This can be seen by looking at his longstanding activist history. But I am suggesting that what Sheen does on-screen matters, too, for his star image must be examined for the way his screen roles, as well as his managed off-screen appearances, publicity, and real, living person come together to form a complex whole. To "authenticate" the star image, according to Dyer (1994), is to look for the ways an actor "establishes a correspondence between the character as played and the social norms of the time—or the way he or she embodies a social type." Stars, Dyer argues, "collapse this distinction between the actor's authenticity and the authentication of the character he or she is playing" (23). It is this connect—that is, Sheen's really seeming to be what he appears to be—that secures his star charisma and authenticity. In looking at the ways in which Sheen's most prominent and recent television role reinforces his off-screen significations of activism and vice versa, I will show how discourses of authenticity work to reinforce a persona for Sheen that allows him to stabilize what some might call in the present climate his "radical" politics with his celebrity site as commodity. But first I will examine how *The West Wing* provides the frame by which to authenticate the political.

Traversing Discourses of Authenticity

As Kristina Riegert (in this volume) points out, *The West Wing* has been the focus of tremendous attention owing to its elision with "the real." The early popular discourse on the series tended to focus on analogies between the characters and the real politicians they are reputed to represent, as well as on the issues raised in narratives that link to or mimic reality, making the show "a referent for the real" (Pompper 2003, 23). Although Aaron Sorkin, creator, writer, and producer for the first four seasons of the show, claimed that he did not invent his characters to reflect the actual people in the White House, nor did he predominantly create his stories out of headlines (Waxman 2000), numerous interpretations argue to the contrary (Franklin 2000; Lewis 2001; Miller 2000; Podhoretz 2003). In any case, Sorkin did lend credence to the claims *The West Wing* makes about political realities by employing political experts as consultants, and Sorkin's scripts consistently tackled complex issues enmeshed in contemporary political events.[11]

In many ways, the observations and analyses on *The West Wing* intimate that there is something real or distinctly authentic about the show, while at the same time it is criticized for its exceeding idealism, and therefore its unreality (Unreality TV 2002; Auster 2001; Ezell 2003; Lehmann 2003; Leo 2002; Levine 2003). Notwithstanding these criticisms, Riegert rightly argues in this volume that *The West Wing* satisfies a "need for wish fulfillment in the political imagination of its public" (219). It is significant that Sorkin debuted *The West Wing* during the "moral disappointment of the Clinton presidency," providing the "perfect antidote for a nation weary of human frailty in its ultimate leader" (Ezell 2003, 160). To be sure, *The West Wing* has been acclaimed for representing the White House in terms of how it *should be*, how its staff *should conduct* themselves, and how the president, in particular, *should embody* virtuous and competent leadership in service of liberal democracy and the public good (Berger 2000; Franklin 2000; Lewis 2001). These modal verbs signify a sense of "the real" that moves beyond *The West Wing*'s narrative correspondence of specific, actual issues and events, and toward significations of authenticity that link to spaces for the political in the real world.

One way to operationalize this claim is to look at how constructions of authenticity traverse the Möbius strip of meanings that connect the politics of the show with realities of contemporary politics and, more specifically, President Bartlet's politics with the realism of Martin Sheen's activism. There are three principal ways in which I will discuss these links. First, the *mise en scène* of the show metaphorically invites a para-social relation between the show's physical signs and its audience.[12] Second, televisual aesthetics work to produce a feeling of authentic intimacy among the characters themselves, and between the characters and the show's viewers. And, more narrowly speaking, intertextual meanings articulate Jed Bartlet, the fictional president seen as his authentic self, to Martin Sheen, the living activist. I will discuss each of these in turn.

In the first instance, the show's set design physically constructs an insider's view of the White House and, more crucially, its west wing, where private political culture is meant to be free, or mostly free, of public-impression management. The televisual set of *The West Wing*, in Goffman's (1959, 195) terms, is the "back region" of electoral political performance, where audiences can "know" the authentic selves of Oval Office personnel as they confront the challenges of public service constrained by partisan politics.[13] Plotline and production values collaborate with the back-region setting to produce a feeling of inclusiveness and intimacy by inviting viewers to see what really goes on within the concealed spaces of political maneuvering and classified strategic planning. In this highly restricted zone, audiences are privy to the private experiences of the characters, to their principles and their passions, as well as to the preparation, frustration, conflict, compromise, camaraderie, triumph, and failure that go into governance and policy making. We see the White House staff strategizing over policy positions, but we generally don't see the outcome of policy, for example, legislative or public response, or the resolution of unfinished business. We witness the press secretary briefing the press, but we don't see the press's mediation of the briefings; we observe the president's senior aides briefing him for a debate or a speech, but we only get glimpses of the president performing for the public. Instead of seeing these political professionals as they might appear before the public, we see them personally, as fallible, righteous, vulnerable, in short, as ordinary people.[14]

In addition to the back-region exposure produced physically by the set and camerawork, intimacy-at-a-distance and extended drama are facilitated through the aspects of a television aesthetic that Horace Newcomb (1974) identifies as intimacy, continuity, and history. Intimacy, as Newcomb describes it, refers in part to the technical diffusion of televisual images into domestic space, which "brings people into the viewer's home," and to the phenomenological impact of the small screen, notable for its tendency to emphasize human relations, personalities, and emotions in domestic or intimate settings rather than vistas and action in expansive surroundings, which Newcomb implies are more appropriately saved for the film's big screen (245). Because series are regularly broadcast, television has the potential to extend plotlines, develop characters, and reinvigorate narratives and common cultural themes and thus intensify viewer involvement over time. Continuity in plotlines in *The West Wing* that nurture the re-emergence of policy debates, problem solving, wins, losses, and compromise, sometimes playfully but more often seriously offers viewers "sustained, extensive perspectives on complex, unfolding issues" (Pompper 2003). In theory, viewers become more personally involved with the program as they, in the informal setting of their homes, continually engage with the lives and actions of their favorite characters, whose behaviors are influenced by references to history, past memories, and behaviors, as well as contingencies of the present, most if not all of which are knowable by the audience. Newcomb argues that intimate knowledge possessed by viewers of the characters' intimacy among themselves is what makes social commentary in television successful (250). In their habitual partaking of television's aesthetics, audiences become, in effect, knowing fans in ways that are distinct from film. To be sure, the soap-opera frame makes *The West Wing* just as much, if not more, about people and relationships than about politics (van Zoonen 2005), and audiences become intimate with the characters of *The West Wing* not simply with respect to liking or loving to hate them, or in the sense of deeming them "media friends,"[15] but with respect to knowing fairly predictably what the characters' political standpoints are likely to be around an issue, and with whom they shall ally or battle. Knowingness, achieved through television's aesthetic combined with the show's trademark backstage set design and purview, renders a pleasurable viewing experience, but also evokes senses of authenticity around the show's larger philosophical claims made through its characters' beliefs, behaviors, and interactions concerning the nature of social justice, the democratic process, and civic duty as a noble calling.

Criticisms of the show's characters' idealism, optimism, and relational "un-reality" serve as a point of departure by which to locate another signifier of authenticity. What makes the show unreal for some is what inspires its enthusiasts to watch each week. These civil servants, when exposed by the viewers' backstage access to their authentic selves, represent incorruptible values[16] as they "serve at the pleasure of the president." Indeed, the senior aides, who stand in for the president and his agenda, must compromise for political expediency or give up the battles they are losing, but they do so without losing their larger vision of social justice and public welfare. In their devotion to the Bartlet Administration's politics and principles, they appear as extraordinary, as noble, sometimes even heroic, in sharp contrast to the public's perception of real politicians, Republicans or Democrats, writ large.[17] These people are Lippmann's expert class, no doubt able to earn a great deal more in the private sector: erudite elites, the social and intellectual superiors of most, the people many would like to see running the government, only we see their extraordinary selves tempered by the show's rhetorical use of space. They are not real, but they signify a normative sense of authenticity with respect to how public service and the political process should be, that is, doing politics out of a motivation to do good and to speak truth to power, as opposed to gaining power for power's sake. It can be argued that the public's impression of real politicians who obfuscate politics in their quest for power seem inauthentic by comparison, despite the employment of the celebrity frame to make politicians appear accessible, ordinary, down-to-earth, and therefore authentic (Pels 2003; Corner 2003; Street 2003b).

Much of the popular and scholarly discourse on *The West Wing* focuses on the way the show raises the standards of what governmental service and the presidency should look like. In fact, as Holbert et al. (2005; 2003) point out, interest in the show's potential influence is less about policy issues than about presentation of character. Nowhere is this focus more concentrated than with the role of Jed Bartlet, who has been referred to, among other favorable adjectives, as "smart," "funny," "charismatic," "omnicompetent," "heroic," "philosopher-king," and, of course, "too good to be true." Albert Auster (2001) argues that *The West Wing* may have achieved its popularity by "elevating the image of the Presidency to a position it probably hasn't held since the day Theodore Roosevelt left office, while at the same time demystifying the policy-making and political process," which, he notes, is the reverse of the "actual historical process" (39). In the first episode of the second season,[18] we learn that Bartlet was perceived early in his candidacy as "the real thing" by two of his soon-to-be-most-trusted and highly qualified senior aides, both of whom give up their lucrative jobs to get him elected. As with the characteristics of his closest aides, we come to know who Bartlet is as a man and leader of the "free world," not through his diplomatic and polished mediated performances, but from his interactions with insiders in the Oval Office, the Situation Room, at the poker table, or in a rare-book store, in his limousine, and in his private White House quarters. To the public he is the liberal, well-educated, Nobel laureate professor of economics and former Democratic governor of New Hampshire. But the audience sees him in private White House spaces where he is articulate without rehearsal, astute, serious and firm yet playful, devoutly Catholic, compassionate, loving, angry, anguished, and victimized by multiple sclerosis. We see him consult with his aides in his struggles to make the decisions "appropriate" for the office of the president while also endeavoring to live up to his personal liberal principles. We are witness to his self-discovery, reconciliation, and denial of his own contradictions. We know him not through mediated, spin-orchestrated political pundits and enemies—not as a celebrity politician—but through the perceptions of his most significant others, and in the spaces where he is vulnerable, insecure, fallible, and physically incapacitated by his disease.[19] In other words, we see him with his closest advisors and his family more in terms of his ordinary, authentic self.[20]

It is noteworthy that we do not see Bartlet exhibiting the characteristics of what John Street (2003a) calls the "celebrity *politician*": "an elected politician who uses the forms and associations of the celebrity to enhance their image and communicate their [sic] message" (3).[21] With the exception of the episode "20 Hours in L.A.," in which the Bartlet campaign courts Hollywood's vote for reelection, we do not see Bartlet employing the celebrity frame as a useful political tool. In fact, the notion of the politician "perceived as an actor performing a relevant 'persona,' a self as revealed to others" (van Zoonen, 72) is largely absent in the overarching *West Wing* narrative. This is not to suggest that Bartlet does not act out an observable political persona. On the contrary, much of what transpires on *The West Wing* occurs within the intersection between what John Corner (2003) identifies as the "sphere of political institutions and processes" and the "private sphere"—where Bartlet's private life interrelates with the institutions of government and the presidency. The behavior that is visible here is not strategically constructed for the public's consumption, such as it is in the "sphere of the public and the popular." Even when Bartlet's private life around his illness becomes public when he "goes personal" with his MS, the narrative around the disclosure is played out in between the private and institutional spheres. Similarly, Heather Hayton (2003) notes in her essay "The King's Two Bodies" that part of what makes *The West Wing* provocative is the elision of private and public boundaries evident by the use of physical space, and by content that makes it difficult for audiences, who in contemporary politics are accustomed to seeking out the real candidate under the packaged construction, to "divorce the character of Jed Bartlet from the Office of the Presidency" (67). Of course, Bartlet "performs" in Goffman's sense in the spaces of his everyday life, but in this space of interconnecting spheres of private life and back-region government processes, presentation of self moves away from the constructed political persona and closer to the authentic self. And it is here, of course, that we come to know Bartlet's political self as revealed to his aides, his priest, his psychiatrist, his family, and himself.

Textual analyses of *The West Wing* tend to highlight Bartlet's liberalism and, in some cases, critique the show for its left-wing bias, as well as note the similarities and the contradictions between Bartlet's and Sheen's politics. The fissures in Bartlet's liberalism and policy choices are evident early on in the series, such as his over-zealous willingness to bomb Arab countries and his authorization to assassinate an Arab state leader. These contradictions work to underscore Bartlet's essentially human and imperfect characteristics. Bartlet's liberalism is continuously tempered by bipartisan compromise, driven in large measure during the first three seasons by his ego and determination not to be a "one-term president." Although he tries to separate himself personally from the office, for example, when he tells his childhood priest that he prefers to be called "Mr. President" while anguishing over his decision not to stay an execution,[22] he is emblematic of the office in service to a larger institution. He may imagine himself as a "reformer" and the "most liberal president" in decades,[23] but the institutional structures within which he and his administration work for the most part dictate his policy choices and contain his political vision to mainstream processes with occasional left-of-center policy victories. Bartlet's authenticity is underpinned by the textual discrepancies between the man who endeavors to speak truth to power and the ideological formation that reproduces the presidency and constrains its use of power, for Bartlet cannot be an activist, nor is he Martin Sheen.[24]

The differences and similarities between the characters the actor plays and the actor him-or herself are constitutive of the actor's star image. The complex of meanings that emanate from Bartlet do not exist in discrete semiotic spaces independent of Martin Sheen. Rather, they are part of a structured polysemy in relation to the actor's on- and off-screen meanings and the audience's active interpretations of those meanings. The articulation of meanings around the political self for Bartlet and for Sheen are more in concert than they are contradictory. Sheen has commented that his character has "a liberal agenda" and that he is "in the right corner on all the issues, from the environment to women's rights to labor to the arms race" (Tucker 2000, 32). In an interview with The Guardian, Sheen suggested that The West Wing provides a platform to give visibility to social issues he considers critical, commenting that "If Bartlet had been a Republican, you wouldn't see me sitting here, I promise you" (Morrow 2001, 4). Long before his association with the series, Sheen professed that his activism was inextricably linked to his profession as an actor: "I don't stop being an actor when I attend a demonstration. I don't stop being an activist when I go to work as an actor." In keeping with this ideal, Sheen prefers roles that tend to reflect his political and religious convictions and refuses ones that are excessively violent or sexual, or that "tell non-truths" (Erlich 1990, 14). Although Sheen sees himself as politically distinct in certain ways from Jed Bartlet—for example, he is uncomfortable having to take militaristic actions in character that he is personally against, and he sees himself as unqualified to hold the position of president particularly owing to his pacifism—many aspects of Bartlet's character are modeled after Sheen's personal, authentic self: "I was told from the get-go the most important element was my character—me, Martin. How would I react? How would Martin react? They made him a Catholic because I'm a Catholic. They made him a Notre Dame graduate because I'm nuts about Notre Dame. All these personal things became part of the equation so we could flesh out a human being" (Currie 2004, W7). Sheen's devotion to Catholicism is reflected in Bartlet's deep faith and moral disposition. But, unlike Bartlet, Sheen claims that he "doesn't give a damn about politics"; rather, that he works for "peace and justice" (Whittaker 1993). In actuality, Sheen's politics are intimately connected to his religion; he refers to himself as a "radical Catholic," having been radicalized by his close relationship with activist Father Daniel Berrigan and spiritually inspired by Mother Teresa, both of whom he met during the shooting of two films in the early 1980s.

Interviews with Sheen in the popular press focusing on his politics call attention to his venerable history with activism coming out of spiritual awakenings early in his acting career and consonant with many of his screen roles. The popular discourse on Sheen reveals a persona that is consistent with the authentic activism practiced by Sheen. In other words, Sheen can be seen by audiences as an ordinary person with a history of doing something political and as a celebrity risking his celebrity site as commodity for his political autonomy. In the conversion of celebrity to political capital, Sheen achieves standing and thus authenticates his activism: he has "earned the right to talk" about political issues; he is "unafraid to take an unpopular stance" though it may hurt his celebrity status; he is "a fixture at protests" championing the causes of the Christian Left; he "puts himself on the line" for his beliefs; his "unswerving moral certainty" is difficult to argue with and harder to scorn; he cannot be accused of lip-service when he "has the guts to be thrown in jail" repeatedly; he is "sincere, modest, down to earth." Sheen's recent involvement in anti-war activism has prompted journalists to question him directly on whether his activism has hurt his profession. In numerous interviews Sheen acknowledges that it has cost him work, but that "anything of value has to cost you something" (Pattison 1999). At the same time, he believes he has secured work because of his activism, citing *The West Wing* as an example in a *Time Out* interview:

> I'm equally sure I've got things because of my commitment to social justice. That had a lot to do with them hiring me for *The West Wing*. I know it did, they've told me so. There are many actors who could have played the part better, but it gives the character a level of credibility that somebody who didn't take a stand on issues of social justice wouldn't have projected. (Braund 2002, 20)

Interestingly, Sheen acknowledges the relationship of his off-screen persona in authenticating his character role on *The West Wing*. Sheen is also aware that the show's progressive idealism comes into conflict with some of the "real" dealings of its network's owner, General Electric, a large provider for the military-industrial complex, so that "when we talk about matters of peace and social justice, we're talking to The Man that can alleviate a lot of pain and suffering, but makes a lot of profit off it" (Pattison 1999). Sheen's own impression of the show, on the one hand, is that it is "very much a part of the system," and a "kind of wishful thinking" that doesn't have "any power except of imagination" (Currie 2004, W07). On the other hand, he suggests that *The West Wing* can sometimes "ring a bell," perhaps a nonpartisan bell, by raising important issues that might spark debate: "We are not trying to get people to eat their vegetables; we are not trying to get people to become Democrats. We are basically trying to encourage people to get involved with public life so that politics isn't left to the wealthy and privileged" (Kupfer 2003, 39).

Shortly after Sheen's anti-war spot aired in February 2003, the *Los Angeles Times* published an op-ed piece entitled "A Celebrity, But First a Citizen," in which Sheen responds to his critics, defending his right and the right of others to exercise their citizen activism:

> [A]though my opinion is not any more valuable or relevant merely because I am an actor, that fact does not render it unimportant. Some have suggested otherwise, trying to denigrate the validity of this opinion and those of my colleagues solely due to our celebrity status. This is insulting not only to us but to other people of conscience who love their country enough to risk its wrath by going against the grain of powerful government policy.... Whether celebrity or diplomat, cabdriver or student, all deserve a turn at the podium. In speaking the truth as we know it, my friends and I have stood proxy for all those yet to join in this great public debate. (Sheen 2003, B11)

It has been suggested that Sheen wrote this op-ed to clarify his politics, in some measure, to appease NBC. However, in articulating his justification of dissenting politics for all Americans, he also contributes to the authentication of activism by his celebrity contemporaries who achieve consonance in their on- and off-screen political significations. In the case of *The West Wing*, it is no coincidence that the prominent commedian, "Air America" commentarist, and liberal activist Janeane Garofalo joined the series in its seventh season to play a role that tries to get the liberal Latino Democratic candidate elected, played by Latino advocate Jimmy Smits. There are steadfast Hollywood activists who convert their celebrity capital into political capital, in some cases despite the possibilities of backlash, and in other cases with relative ease. The Jane Fondas, Norman Lears, and Ed Asners of celebrity activism have in some measure paved the terrain for other outspoken celebrities, such as Susan Sarandon, whose anti-capital punishment activism inspired her starring in the 1995 film *Dead Man Walking*, or Michael Moore, whose filmmaking career has showcased his dissenting politics in popular culture. Celebrity transgression for one audience is authentic citizen activism for another.

Sheen and other celebrity progressives do their work and authenticate their activism, in part, by achieving identification with their audiences, which generates meaning in the real world. According to Dyer (1994), "audience identification" is accomplished in one of two ways: either when stars affirm alternative readings by audiences not recognized by dominant media and that speak to audience life situations, or when stars provide role models by which audiences can find alternative ways to inhabit or transform their life situations (183). But it is also significant, as Lynn Spigel (2004) points out, that the media environment in the twenty-first century has shifted to a "postnetwork system" that values audience fragmentation and narrowcasting and that weakens the patriotic narratives associated with the "cultural dominant" (256). In this mediascape, Sheen and other dissenting celebrities might be seen as hailing a niche for a new kind of celebrity politics that turns out to be "real" and entertaining.

Notes

[1] NBC's disclaimer also referred to a pro-war advertisement in response to Sheen's ad featuring former Republican senator and actor on *Law & Order*, Fred Thompson, permitting NBC to position itself squarely in the neutral zone in an attempt to inoculate itself and its shows from the controversy. Although the networks refused to run advocacy ads for or against the war, organizations backing the advocacy ads were able to secure ad spots from local cable companies.

[2] In *Marxism and Ideology*, Jorge Larrain (1983) argues that Marx intended ideology to be both *restrictive* in its usage—only standing for a particular set of ideas (i.e., the ruling-class ideas)—and *negative*—functioning to explain away contradictions. This is in sharp contrast to the neutralization of the concept that is evident in analyses underscoring "dominant ideology" as attributed to Marx, and demonstrated by Lenin, who repositioned ideology as "the battlefield but...no longer an instrument in the battle" (89). To neutralize ideology, Larrain argues, is to equate it with ideas serving any class or social group in general rather than with those ideas which inadequately represent material conditions, which Marx called the ideas of the ruling class. Equally significant, it is to eviscerate the mechanism (negation) by which contradiction, alienation, exploitation, and domination reproduce themselves. In other words, Marx's notion of contradiction, then, would no longer serve to reproduce its own conditions, which ideology functions to hide, distort, or explain away, and in the process, to reproduce itself. John Thompson (1990) maintains this line of argument by rightly suggesting that a negative and restrictive conception of ideology binds an analysis of ideology to critique so that ways of knowing can be critically differentiated.

[3] For example, see John Street (2002, 434).

[4] Dyer (1994) suggests that out of all the media texts that constitute the star image, publicity comes closest to revealing the authentic person because, at least ostensibly, it is not deliberate. Scandal is the exemplar of "genuine publicity" (69). However, Dyer does not sufficiently consider the question of authenticity in light of deliberate star engagement with off-screen political activism, despite the potential consequences of audience retribution.

[5] Paul McDonald (2000) distills Dyer's star composition into the elements of image, labor, and (economic) capital.

[6] Although King is concerned with film stars, his observations, as well as Dyer's, are also useful in understanding the larger celebrity construct. Moreover, King does not attend sufficiently to political activity as a site that must be managed as "performance."

[7] Historically, the star image was constructed by the studio through its control over fan magazines to coherently represent the actor as being essentially the same in real life as on screen; see Richard de Cordova (1990). Eventually audiences rejected studio manipulations and turned to sources outside of Hollywood's control for privileged access to the "truth" about stars (Dyer 1991).

[8] There are numerous recent examples in which celebrities were at the forefront of voluntary benefits and fundraisers. In the wake of 9/11, for example, "Tribute to Heroes" telethon and "Concert for New York," hosted by a profusion of actors, musicians, and sports stars, are estimated to have raised in a matter of hours close to $300 million combined, each

earning more money than any single celebrity charity event to date; see Boucher (2001) and McKinley (2001). Also noteworthy are Live Aid, Farm Aid, Comic Relief, Tsunami Aid, and various celebrity auctions to benefit victims of Hurricane Katrina.

[9] See, for example, Gubernick and La Franco (1994); Satchell (1997); Leff (1999); Shah (2002).

[10] Interestingly, as Andrew Tolson (2001) points out, a sense of authenticity can be claimed by the celebrity persona that achieves a moral justification for itself when it adopts humanitarian causes. This sense of authenticity concerns an "authentic *mediated* identity" that "claims the moral high ground, and gives a performance which is not seen as acting, because the animated script (of the interview, the press conference or TV presentation) coheres with the authored persona of the 'celebrity-being-ordinary'" (456–457).

[11] For example, in an interview Sorkin admitted that his frustration in watching Al Gore downplay his intelligence during the 2000 election prompted him to write the episodes involving the election between Bartlet and Senator Richey so that he could "rerun the last election and try a few different plays than the Gore campaign did" (Friend 2002, 31).

[12] Para-social interaction was first discussed by Horton and Wohl (1956), who defined it as a "simulacrum of conversation" between performers and spectators that occurs in a mass medium, for example, radio, film, or television, but is treated as if it is an interpersonal (face-to-face) medium. Horton and Wohl argue that the talk-show host, in combination with stage props and camera techniques, engages in informal conversation with audiences to "eradicate, or at least blur, the line which divides him and his show as a formal performance from the audience both in the studio and at home" (217), thereby establishing the illusion of a face-to-face relationship. John Thompson (1995) coins the term "mediated quasi-interaction" to describe the same phenomenon. I am adapting the conceptual framework to suggest that fictional contexts and televisual effects work metaphorically to promote "intimacy-at-a-distance."

[13] Goffman's (1959) dramaturgical framework makes the distinction between front and back regions where "performances" in formal and everyday life occur as a form of image management. The front region is the space where people expect to be observed, so they adjust their behaviors according to the norms appropriate for performance in that space. The back region is where people act less formally and more like their true selves. Although the front and back regions can be understood as physical space, they are also significant metaphorically as a kind of social space in which people subject to mediation act to manage their behaviors in order to control how they will be represented. In the case of a politician, for instance, the back region is where the preparation for front-region performances takes place. The capacity of electronic media to expose the back-region behavior of politicians and celebrities has been discussed by Meyrowitz (1985) and Thompson (1995; 2000). Alternatively, Dick Pels (2003), John Street (2003b), and John Corner (2003) note that politicians have adapted their front-region behavior to accommodate electronic media and thus appear in front-region contexts as if they are behaving as they would in the back region. For example, they try to act ordinary and thus reveal their authentic selves in formal or informal settings.

[14] An interesting break in the backstage frame in the seventh season produces yet another twist of authentic sensibilities when Congressman Matthew Santos (Jimmy Smits), running on the Democratic ticket, debates Senator Arnold Vinick (Alan Alda), a Republican, in a

"live" forum hosted by Forrest Sawyer, as himself, taped live for the entire episode, save the episode's ("The Debate") cold opening.

[15] Meyrowitz (1985) extends Horton and Wohl's model to a general "media friends" construct to suggest that para-social interaction can also characterize relations between actors playing fictional roles and fans.

[16] In another parallel moment with the "real," Al Franken, in July 2005, on his radio show on Air America, discussed the Karl Rove/Valerie Plame incident, comparing the Bush Administration with Bartlet's by commenting that no one in the west wing on *The West Wing* would knowingly "out" a CIA undercover agent.

[17] According to part 6 of a recent Pew survey, "Cynicism, Trust and Participation," "only about four-in-ten people (39%) believe that 'most elected officials care what people like me think'" (Pew Research Center for the People and the Press 2003).

[18] "In the Shadow of Two Gunmen, Part 1."

[19] An acute example of Bartlet's fragility in the face of his disease is presented in the sixth season when he begins to experience difficulty with his legs and is rendered temporarily paralyzed. He is forced to rely on the help of his burly assistant, Steward, to literally lift him from his chair ("Impact Winter"), and his wife, Abby, to assist him in putting on his pants ("Faith Based Initiative").

[20] Holbert et al.'s (2005) content analysis of *The West Wing* found that Bartlet displays different character traits in correspondence with the distinct roles of chief executive and private citizen, which provides "a unique vehicle by which an audience can establish a relationship with the American presidency" (512). In the former role, Bartlet displayed "principled" traits (honest, trustworthy, hard-working, responsible, and determined); in the latter, he displayed "engaging" traits (loving, warm, humorous, and compassionate).

[21] For example, these forms include the use of photo-ops linking themselves with stars; the appropriation of light entertainment or "non-traditional platforms of formats" to promote themselves; and the employment of promotional experts in the celebrity business.

[22] "Take This Sabbath Day."

[23] "The Stackhouse Filibuster."

[24] Interestingly, a fan chat comparing Bartlet and Sheen on the website Television without Pity discusses the ideal of having Jed Bartlet as the real president, and the unrealistic possibility of ever getting someone as liberal as Martin Sheen elected president.

References

Alberoni, Francesco. 1972. "The powerless elite: Theory and sociological research on the phenomenon of the stars." In *Sociology of mass communication*, edited by D. McQuail. Harmondsworth: Penguin Books. Original edition, 1962.

Auster, Albert. 2001. "The West Wing: To an Outsider it Celebrates the Importance of Public Service." *Television Quarterly* 32 (1):39-42.

Berger, Rose Marie. 2000. "Good Government?" *Sojourners*, May/June, 61-63.

Boucher, Geoff. 2001. "Celebrities Take to the Stage, Phone in Global Telethon." *Los Angeles Times*, 22 Sep 2001, A1.

Bouchier, David. 1987. *Radical Citizenship: The New American Activism.* New York: Schocken Books.

Bourdieu, Pierre. 1989. "Social space and symbolic power." *Sociological Theory* 7(1): 14- 25.

——. 1990. *The Logic of Practice.* Translated by R. Nice. Stanford: Stanford University Press.

——. 1991. *Language and symbolic power.* Translated by G. Raymond and M. Adamson. Edited by J. B. Thompson. Cambridge, Mass: Harvard University Press.

——. 1992. *An invitation to reflexive sociology.* Chicago: University of Chicago.

——. 1993. *The Field of Cultural Production: Essays on Art and Literature.* New York: Columbia University Press.

Bowers, John Waite, and Ochs, Donovan J. 1971. *The Rhetoric of Agitation and Control.* Reading, MA: Addison-Wesley Pub. Co.

Braudy, Leo. 1986. *The Frenzy of Renown: Fame and its History.* New York: Oxford University Press.

Braund, Simon. 2002. "President and Correct." *Time Out London*, 11 September, 20- 23.

Caves, Richard E. 2000. *Creative Industries: Contracts between Art and Commerce.* Cambridge, Mass.: Harvard University Press.

Clark, Wayne. 2000. *Activism in the Public Sphere: Exploring the Discourse of Political Participation:* Aldershot: Ashgate.

Corner, John. 2003. "Mediated Persona and Political Culture." In *Media and the Restyling of Politics*, edited by J. Corner and D. Pels. London: Sage Publications.

Currie, Tyler. 2004. "Martin Sheen - Actor, 'The West Wing'." *Washington Post*, Oct 17, 2004, W07.

deCordova, Richard. 1990. *Picture Personalities: The Emergence of the Star System in America.* Urbana: University of Illinois Press.

Dyer, Richard. 1986. *Heavenly Bodies: Film Stars and Society.* New York: St. Martin's Press.

——. 1991. "*A Star is Born* and the construction of authenticity." In *Stardom: Industry of desire*, edited by C. Gledhill. London: Routledge.

——. 1994. *Stars.* London: Educational Advisory Service British Film Institute. Original edition, 1979.

Erlich, Reese. 1990. "A Star's Activism, On Screen and Off." *Christian Science Monitor*, 28 December, 14.

Ezell, Pamela. 2003. "The Sincere Sorkin White House, or, The Importance of Seeming Earnest." In *The West Wing: The American Presidency as Television Drama*, edited by P. C. Rollins and J. E. O'Connor. Syracuse, N.Y.: Syracuse University Press.

Franklin, Nancy. 2000. "Corridors of Power." *The New Yorker*, 21 & 28 February, 290-294.

Friend, Tad. 2002. "West Wing Watch: Snookered by Bush." *The New Yorker*, 4 March, 30-31.

Gamson, Joshua. 1994. *Claims to Fame: Celebrity in Contemporary America.* Berkeley: University of California Press.

Goffman, Erving. 1959. *The Presentation of Self in Everyday Life.* Garden City, N.Y.: Doubleday.

Gubernick, Lisa, and Robert La Franco. 1994. "Charity as a Commodity." *Forbes*, September 26, 118-121.

Hayton, Heather R. 2003. "The King's Two Bodies: Identity and Office in Sorkin's *West Wing*."

In *The West Wing: The American Presidency and Television Drama*, edited by P. C. Rollins and J. E. O'Connor. Syracuse: Syracuse University Press.

Heaton, Michael. 2003. "Liberal, Conservative Characters Draw Line in TV Sand over Iraq." *Plain Dealer*, 7 March.

Hesmondhalgh, David. 2002. *The Cultural Industries*. London: Sage Publications.

Holbert, Lance R.;. Tschida, David A.; Dixon, Maria; Cherry, Kristin L.; Steuber, Keli, and Airne, David. 2005. "'The West Wing' and Depictions of the American Presidency: Expanding the Domains of Framing in Political Communication." *Communication Quarterly* 55 (4):505-522.

Holbert, R. Lance; Pillion, Owen; Tschida, David A.; Armfield, Greg G., Kinder, Kelly; Cherry, Kristin L; and Daulton, Amy R. 2003. "'The West Wing' as Endorsement of the U.S. Presidency: Expanding the Bounds of Priming in Political Communication." *Journal of Communication*:427-443.

Horton, Donald, and Wohl, R. Richard. 1956. "Mass communication and para-social interaction." *Psychiatry* 19:215-229.

Johnson, Randal. 1993. "Editor's Introduction." In *The field of cultural production*, edited by R. Johnson. New York: Columbia University Press.

Jones, Jeffrey P. 2005. *Entertaining Politics: New Political Television and Civic Culture*, *Communication, media, and politics*. Lanham: Rowman & Littlefield Publishers.

Keller, Suzanne. 1986. "Celebrities and Politics: A New Alliance." In *Research in political sociology*, edited by R. G. Braungart. Greenwich, CN: JAI Press, Inc.

Kenna, Kathleen. 2003. "Americans Pay Price for Speaking Out." *Toronto Star*, 9 August.

King, Barry. 1986. "Stardom as an occupation." In *The Hollywood film industry*, edited by P. Kerr. London: Routledge.

Kupfer, David. 2003. "Martin Sheen Interview." *The Progressive*, July.

Lahusen, Christian. 1996. *The Rhetoric of Moral Protest: Public Campaigns, Celebrity Endorsement, and Political Mobilization*. New York: Walter de Gruyter.

Larrain, Jorge. 1983. *Marxism and Ideology*. London: The Macmillan Press, Ltd.

Lears, T. J. Jackson. 1983. "From salvation to self-realization: Advertising & the therapeutic roots of the consumer culture 1880- 1930." In *The Culture of Consumption*, edited by R. W. Fox and T. J. J. Lears. New York: Pantheon.

Leff, Lisa. 1999. "Charities of the Gods." *Los Angeles Magazine*, May, 82+.

Lehmann, Chris. 2003. "The Feel-Good Presidency: The Pseudo-Politics of *The West Wing*." In *The West Wing: The American Presidency as Television Drama*, edited by P. C. Rollins and J. E. O'Connor. Syracuse, N.Y.: Syracuse University Press.

Leo, John. 2002. "Left Side Story." *U.S. News & World Report*, 7 October, 56.

Levine, Myron A. 2003. "The Transformed Presidency: People and Power in the Real *West Wing*. In *The West Wing: The American Presidency as Television Drama*, edited by P. C. Rollins and J. E. O'Connor. Syracuse, N.Y.: Syracuse University Press.

Lewis, Ann F. 2001. "The West Wing." *Television Quarterly* 32 (1): 36- 38.

Marks, Michael P, and Zachary M Fischer. 2002. "The King's New Bodies: Simulating Consent in the Age of Celebrity." *New Political Science* 24(3): 371- 394.

Marshall, David P. 1997. *Celebrity and Power: Fame in Contemporary Culture*. Minneapolis:

University of Minnesota Press.

McDonald, Paul. 2000. *The Star System: Hollywood's Production of Popular Identities*. London: Wallflower.

McGuigan, Jim. 1998. "What Price the Public Sphere?" In *Electronic Empires: Global Media and Local Resistance*, edited by D. K. Thussu. London: Arnold.

McKenna, Michael. 2003. "Hollywood Stages Its Own War."*Courier Mail*, 29 March.

McKinley, Jesse. 2001. "Media Heavyweights Chip in by Organizing an All-Star Benefit Concert." *New York Times*, 19 October.

McLagan, Meg. 2002. "Spectacles of Difference: Cultural Activism and the Mass Mediation of Tibet." In *Media Worlds: Anthropology on New Terrain*, edited by F. D. Ginsburg, L. Abu-Lughod and B. Larkin. Berkeley: University of California Press.

McLeland, Susan. 2001. "Barbarella Goes Radical: Hanoi Jane and the American Popular Press." In *Headline Hollywood: A Century of Scandal*, edited by A. McLean, and David A. Cook. New Brunswick, N.J.: Rutgers University Press.

Meyer, David S, and Joshua Gamson. 1995. "The Challenge of Cultural Elites: Celebrities and Social Movements." *Sociological Inquiry* 65: 181- 206.

Meyrowitz, Joshua. 1985. *No sense of place: The impact of electronic media on social behavior*. New York: Oxford University Press.

Miller, Matthew. 2000. "The Real White House." *Brill's Content* 3(2): 88- 96.

Morrow, Fiona. 2001. "Portrait: All the President's Manias." *The Guardian*, 16 January, 4.

Newcomb, Horace. 1974. *TV: The Most Popular Art*. Garden City, N.Y.: Anchor Press.

Pattison, Mark. 2006. Left of Center in 'The West Wing'. Horizon Magazine, 29 December 1999 [cited 2006]. Available from www.horizonmag.com/2/martin-sheen.asp.

Pels, Dick. 2003. "Aesthetic Representation and Political Style: Re-balancing Identity and Difference in Media Democracy." In *Media and the Restyling of Politics*, edited by D. Pels and J. Corner. London: SAGE Publications.

Pew Research Center for the People and the Press. 2005. *Evenly Divided and Increasingly Polarized: 2004 Political Landscape* 2003 [accessed 22 December 2005]. Available from http://people-press.org/reports/display.php3?PageID=755.

Podhoretz, Jon. 2003. "The Liberal Imagination." In *The West Wing: The American Presidency as Television Drama*, edited by P. C. Rollins and J. E. O'Connor. Syracuse, N.Y.: Syracuse University Press.

Pompper, Donnalyn. 2003. The West Wing: White House Narratives That Journalism Cannot Tell. In *The West Wing: The American Presidency as Television Drama*, edited by P. C. Rollins and J. E. O'Connor. Syracuse, N.Y.: Syracuse University Press.

Prindle, David F. 1993. *Risky Business: The Political Economy of Hollywood*. Boulder: Westview.

Rojek, Chris. 2001. *Celebrity*. London: Reaktion Books, Ltd.

Satchell, Michael. 1997. "Star-struck Charities Seek Famous Boosters." *U.S. News & World Report*, 22 September, 33.

Seelye, Katharine Q. 2000. "The 2000 Campaign: Campaign Briefing." *The New York Times*, 1 November.

Shah, Diane K. 2002. "Cause Celebs." *Los Angeles Magazine*, February, 54- 7, 125- 8.

"Sheen Faces Backlash Over War Protests." 2003. *The Seattle Times*, 5 March, F2.

Sheen, Martin. 2003. "A Celebrity, But First a Citizen; Being Famous Does Not Bar an American from Speaking Out Against an Unjust War." *Los Angeles Times*, 17 March, B11.

Simonson, Peter. 2001. "Social Noise and Segmented Rhythms: News, Entertainment, and Celebrity in the Crusade for Animal Rights." *The Communication Review*: 399- 420.

Spigel, Lynn. 2004. "Entertainment Wars: Television Culture after 9/11." *American Quarterly* 56(2): 235- 270.

St. John, Warren. 2003. "The Backlash Grows Against Celebrity Activists." *The New York Times*, 23 March.

Street, John. 2002. "Bob, Bono and Tony B: The Popular Artist as Politician." *Media, Culture & Society* 24(3): 433- 441.

——. 2003a. "Star Signs: Political Representatives as Popular Entertainers, Popular Entertainers as Political Representatives." Paper read at European Consortium for Political Research, at Edinburgh.

——. 2003b. "The Celebrity Politician: Political Style and Popular Culture." In *Media and the Restyling of Politics*, edited by J. Corner and D. Pels. London: Sage Publications.

Thompson, John B. 1990. *Ideology and Modern Culture: Critical Social Theory in the Era of Mass Communication*. Stanford, CA: Stanford University Press.

——. 1995. *The Media and Modernity: A Social Theory of the Media*. Stanford, CA: Stanford University Press.

——. 2000. *Political scandal: power and visibility in the media age*. Cambridge: Polity Press.

Tolson, Andrew. 2001."Being Yourself': The Pursuit of Authentic Celebrity." *Discourse Studies* 3(4): 443- 457.

Tucker, Ken. 2000. "Meet the Prez." *Entertainment Weekly*, 25 February.

Turner, Graeme, Frances Bonner, and P. David Marshall. 2000. *Fame Games: The Production of Celebrity in Australia*. Cambridge: Cambridge University Press.

"Unreality TV." 2002. *The Economist*, 6 July, 52.

Waxman, Sharon. 2000. "Inside the West Wing's New World." *George*, November, 54- 96.

West, Darrell M., and Orman, John M. 2002. *Celebrity Politics, Real politics in America*. Upper Saddle River, N.J.: Prentice Hall.

Whittaker, Paul. 1993. "An Actor in the War". *Sunday Herald Sun*, 17 October.

Whyte, Murray. 2003. "New Star Wars as Celebrities Face Backlash." *Toronto Star*, March 5, A01.

Zoonen, Liesbet van. 2005. *Entertaining the Citizen: When Politics and Popular Culture Converge, Critical media studies*. Lanham, MD: Rowman & Littlefield.

CHAPTER NINE

The Ideology of *The West Wing*: The Television Show That Wants to Be Real

KRISTINA RIEGERT

Despite the trepidations of television executives accustomed to viewing politics as "box-office poison," the political drama series *The West Wing* was extremely popular with audiences in its first season. Not only could it claim the coveted U.S. demographic of income earners over $100,000 per annum, it won critical acclaim in the form of multiple Emmy Awards and spawned a new generation of political drama series. The marketing of the program, the media discourse on it, and its fandom are all grounded in *The West Wing's* relationship to "real-life" events and how things "really are" or "should be" at the White House. This chapter contends that the televisual form and success of *The West Wing* must be situated within the context of an emotional need to reconnect, not simply with politics, but with "reality" as demonstrated by the popularity of reality-based programming. However, it is precisely in the attempt to reflect the "real" that the ideological discourse of *The West Wing* is insidious. A simple textual analysis reveals that progressive political ideals must be tempered by the "common sense" of compromise and, in its depiction of foreign policy, this realism translates into a defense of "universal" values, which at times justify U.S. exceptionalism, i.e., stances reminiscent of those currently taken under the Bush Administration. It is thus only in light of its attempt to reflect "the real" that the ideological power of *The West Wing* can be properly assessed.

The West Wing in the Context
of Reality Television Culture

The West Wing was first broadcast in the United States in 1999, at a time when a powerful force in the form of cheaply produced, spectacular, non-fiction programs that share the claim to "the real" started to change television culture (Magder 2004). The proliferation of hybrid reality television genres—docudramas, game docs, miniseries dramatizing historical figures and events—has rekindled debates about the impact of mass culture on the public sphere, the blurring of the boundaries between fact and fiction, and between politics and entertainment. What, for example, are the consequences of the dominance of popularized versions of history and real-life events? Do the cultural industries simply distort history to produce entertainment and spectacle, or do popular media representations make historical events more accessible to a greater number of people (cf. Baer 2001)? While these debates are worthy of consideration, it is held here that television as a medium of representation never can provide unfettered access to "reality." Therefore, much of the difference between drama and documentary, between mediated "fact" and "fiction," comes down to issues of modality (Fiske 1987, 308). In other words, the question is not how close this or that television program is to some *de facto* reality, but rather what are the codes and techniques that different media use to delineate "facts" or "fiction." Furthermore, we should not assume that audiences think reality-based programming is true to life, since the "aesthetics, editing, characterization, and dramatic structures" of reality-based television are part of the way such programs are discussed by fans, according to Holmes and Jermyn (2004, 10–11). So, instead of asking if audiences are fooled into believing that these programs are "real," they say, we should rather ask what is the powerful appeal of the "claim to the real."

Accounting for the appeal of the "real" cannot be adequately addressed in this chapter, but it is difficult to escape the irony that reality-based programming coincides with a point in our history when claims to truth of mediated imagery as "evidence" of what is depicted are more dubious than ever, thanks to digital technology. Arild Fetveit suggests that visual culture's dispersion of indexicality spurs a sense of a lost connection to the world and to reality. Reality television not only expresses this longing for a connection to reality; it also reclaims a relationship with "the evidential quality of photography said to be lost after digitalization" and "also seems obsessed with conveying a sense of connectedness, of contact with the world..." (1999, 800). This is nothing new, since authenticity and immediacy are qualities that have long been associated with television, especially its "liveness" and its ability to monitor events in real time, coupled with its pervasiveness in our everyday social and family lives (Bolter and Grusin 1999). This should not divert attention from the fact that live, unedited television is rare and that almost everything we see is packaged and produced.

According to media scholars, the explosion of reality-based formats and hybrid spin-offs makes it difficult to categorize them according to genre. What was once unscripted, fly-on-the-wall monitoring of average people's daily lives burgeoned into work-place dramas, only to morph into variations of celebrity exposés. Common to all these types of programs, however, is that they are marketed through "discursive, visual and technological claims to 'the real'" (Holmes and Jermyn 2004, 5). As Annette Hill expressed it, one of the appeals of these programs is the pleasure of voyeurism: "the moment of authenticity when real people are 'really' themselves in an unreal environment" (cited in Gillan 2004, 58). In this way, people gain insight into the lives of other people, and in the process, "...what results is an unstable text that encourages viewers to test out their own notions of the real, the ordinary, the intimate against the representation" (Murray and Ouellette 2004, 6).

In contrast to most reality-based formats, *The West Wing* has an expensively produced, highly scripted, all-star cast, created by *enfant terrible* Aaron Sorkin, whose elitist, fast-paced dialog makes no apology for itself but forces audiences to concentrate in order to follow it. Despite this, *The West Wing* provides a similar voyeuristic pleasure to that of the fly-on-the-wall logic of reality-based programming. Authenticity is gained through set designs that are as close to "real" as possible, creating the impression that audiences can look beyond the trappings of the most powerful center in the world and see not only politics in action, but the men and women behind the façade. Many of the characters have been given characteristics similar to the biographical factoids of the actors who play them: a storyline about the character Sam Seaborne seeing a call girl could be related to the real-life sex scandal actor Rob Lowe was involved in; Martin Sheen is a well-known leftist activist and a Roman Catholic (President Bartlet is a Catholic, progressive Democrat); Leo McGarry (John Spencer) was a sober alcoholic both in real life and in the series (Pompper 2003, 25). The cast of characters in the series also closely mirrors readily identifiable figures from the Clinton Administration (Podhoretz 2003, 222).

Another aspect of *The West Wing* that encourages audiences to associate it with the "real" is its sense of immediacy. Immediacy and urgency are gained through the tempo of the program, the fast-paced dialog, the famous "walking and talking" scenes shot with a steadycam, but also through the focus on real issues in the U.S. public debate, such as hostage-taking, natural catastrophes, or diplomatic crises. The temporal proximity of the current events chosen as topics continually forces audiences to ask, "Did this really happen?" Indeed, the speed with which the scripts were produced and the timing of their first run contributed to a number of coincidences with "real" political events, despite the claims of Aaron Sorkin and his associates that they avoid "current political issues." This claim does not appear credible in view of the numerous examples of real-world events dealt with in the show, like the spontaneously produced, heavily criticized, one-off episode "Isaac and Ishmael," which was specifically written after the attacks of September 11, 2001. Another example is when angry viewers complained that the NBC advertisement for the upcoming episode of "Night Five" in February 2002 made "unacceptable" connections to a real-life situation.

> Viewers pointed out the disturbing resemblance to the plight of Daniel Pearl, the *Wall Street Journal* correspondent who has been held captive, to this episode in which an American reporter is kidnapped. "It could seem distasteful," said John Miller, president of the network's in-house advertising firm. "We hadn't made the connection to Pearl until it aired last Wednesday and people called in and said, 'do you realize that what's on *The West Wing* is happening in real life.'" ("Night Five," Media Quotes. http://www.westwingepguide.com/S3/Episodes/58_NF.html)

An article search on the fan site Bartlet4America, using the term "reality," retrieves no less than sixty-six news articles and interviews with both former White House staff and program production staff, most from well-known news outlets.[1] The anecdotes of the ways *The West Wing* collides with "the real" range from a phone call from the Bush campaign asking whether George W. Bush could play a cameo role, to California Assemblyman Kevin Shelley's attempt to adjourn a Sacramento session with a short tribute to the memory of Mrs. Landingham, a character killed off at the end of the second season of the show (Shister 2001; Associated Press 2001; "Indecision 2000," 2001). This should serve to remind us that what has been called the "entertaining real" is not limited to the ecology of television: the personalities who appear in popular television programs are frequently the subject of press articles both in print and online. Media interest is sustained through the circulation of meaning about personalities and storylines as they move between fictional and non-fictional, and between mediated and non-mediated realms (see Collins and Machado-Borges in this volume).

According to Matthew Miller, former White House aides agree that *The West Wing*'s depiction of the process of politics, the gray areas of policy outcomes, as well as the dedication to public service, give audiences a better "feeling" of what it is like to work in the White House than "real-life" daily news coverage from the White House. This type of realism may, Miller contends (2000, 4), ultimately "renew interest in public life in ways that real politics brought to us by the real press corps can't." Pompper (2003) argues that *The West Wing* offers us "narratives journalism can't tell," meaning that the "how" and "why" of politics is what is often left out of news stories. This has to do with the fact that although journalism is charged with the responsibility of describing political "reality," it cannot convey the emotional depth, the motivations of public servants, or the context of political situations. Since, as Michael Wolff (2000) points out, "the face of politics has become ever more distant, practiced and phony," the success of *The West Wing* provokes some troubling questions: "Are we fantasizing about politics because we've lost all pretence of being interested in real politics? Will we compare what is happening in *The West Wing* to what is happening in the 'real world' and find our world lacking? Will we expect real world characters to have the same traits as those in *The West Wing?*" The answers are yes, yes, and yes.

The West Wing as Wish Fulfillment and Civics Lesson

According to a study by the Center for Media and Public Affairs, the dominant image of public servants in television entertainment up until the late 1990s has been that of corrupt, self-interested, or cynical individuals. *The West Wing*'s portrayals of more textured characters dedicated to public service have, according to the center, spawned more positive images of government in television content.

> Moreover, and perhaps most importantly, *West Wing* is already partly responsible for a change in television's thematic treatment of government. In the 1990's sample, three out of four themes (76%) criticized the political system by presenting politics as a dirty business, and political institutions as failing the citizens they are intended to serve. In the current sample, this figure was nearly reversed, with 62 percent positive and 38 percent negative instances. (Lichter et al. 2001, 11)

While the audience response has been unprecedented—*The West Wing* garnered between 13 and 17.1 million viewers until its fourth season, when it began a steady decline, hitting 11.3 million during its sixth season (Byrne 2005). The decline in the show's coveted 18-to-49-year-old demographic (which contributed to the departure of its originator, Aaron Sorkin) has been attributed to the way the show diverged from the "reality" of the Bush White House and the "mood of the country" (de Moraes 2003). Despite the decline, NBC retains the program, perhaps because of the type of audience attracted by it.

The West Wing, defined as an intelligently written show about intelligent people, appears to attract those individuals with higher educational attainment. Elder segments of society also watch this program more often. The West Wing depicts the daily workings of a liberal presidential administration and those individuals who lean to the left politically are more likely to view this program with greater frequency. Finally, those who turn to media for news also tend to watch with greater regularity this fictional presentation of American politics. (Holbert 2004, 17–18)

Interesting in this context is the last point, that there is a relationship between those who watch news and those who watch *The West Wing*, and this is especially true for males, independent voters, and non-voters. General interest in public affairs, even among non-voters, means greater engagement in *The West Wing*. This appears to be borne out by another study comparing regular viewers of television programs on government and civic themes with regular viewers of other types of entertainment programming; the former "are more likely to report that they are stimulated and engaged by their programs" than the latter. They also say more often that they "learn things from the shows they watch" (Princeton Survey Research 2004, section 5). This holds particularly true for those aged 18–24, where half (50 percent) of those who watched regularly said that "they learn a lot about government and politics from watching entertainment shows with government themes" (section 7). With regard to *The West Wing*, 57 percent of the regular viewers of the program said that they "have been moved to try to find out more about a political issue," 47 percent say they have "changed their thinking on an issue as a result of watching," 46 percent say that they have "changed their views of government and government employees" and, finally, "61 percent of the regular viewers of *The West Wing* say the character portrayals and the storylines are mostly or very accurate" (section 10).

This does not mean that viewership of entertainment shows with government and politics makes people more likely to engage in politics. These shows may rather, as van Zoonen (2005, 147) claims, entertain citizenship, i.e., "offer instruments to think about what citizenship should mean," or "invite a hospitable surrounding for the performance of citizenship." However, the Princeton Survey demonstrates that those with the right ethnicity, interest, and education to be engaged in politics are those who are watching these programs, not other segments of the population, let alone segments of other nations' populations.

In fact, much of the academic work on *The West Wing* has focused on possible or likely "real-life" comparisons and what effects this may have on U.S. politics. Pompper (2003, 19) contrasts *The West Wing* to political journalism, arguing that it exposes the relationship between politics and journalism (i.e., spin-doctoring, damage control, etc.), while "offer[ing] simple explanations for complex issues so that audiences may understand policies." A study by Stacey Beavers (2002) describes the "pedagogical potential" of *The West Wing* for putting a human face on political institutions and issues, and teaching otherwise apathetic students civic values. Holbert et al. (2003) found that viewers of *The West Wing* had a more positive view of the office of the presidency itself, insofar as subsequent to viewing they expressed more positive views of Presidents Bush and Clinton than before viewing.

The preoccupation of these studies with *The West Wing*'s perceived relationship to "real politics" could perhaps be seen in light of U.S. academic concern for the widespread problem of voter apathy and political cynicism, long considered two of the most complex problems of modern democracy. Ever since the 1970s, political scientists have recognized the alienation of growing groups of citizens from traditional political parties and declining voter participation, paralleled by the rise of the "post-materialist" movements around single issues, life-style interests, or personality-related political preferences based on trust and identification. Thompson (1995, 2000) traces this shift in the public sphere to the change from face-to-face interaction to mediated interaction and mediated "quasi-interaction," which increases the power accruing to visibility and promotes a new kind of intimacy blurring the boundaries between public and private life. Corner and Pels (2003, 7) argue that mediated democracy erects new structures of intimacy-at-a-distance, encouraging "new forms of visual and emotional literacy which allow audiences to 'read' political characters and 'taste' their style, enabling them to judge their claims of authenticity and competence in a more effective manner." Thus, personality, character, an individual's ideas, and authenticity become symbolic resources, and the marketing of image and identity is now an important part of politics.

This chapter cannot do justice to the extent of structural change in mediated democracies, but would rather argue that the individualization of political trust and the reliance on an emotional identification with the characters are some of the very qualities that have engendered the success of *The West Wing*. In this light, *The West Wing* appears to fill a vacuum, a need for wish fulfillment in the political imagination of its public.

Two studies of *The West Wing* focus on the notion of wish fulfillment or "the working through" of anxiety about political leadership and where American society is headed. Parry-Giles and Parry-Giles (2002, 210) suggest that *The West Wing* should be viewed as a romantic narrative reflecting the cultural anxieties accompanying "the postmodern condition in U.S. culture," representing both a hopeful and cathartic view of the presidency but also relying on the ideologies of "intellectualism, militarism, masculinity and whiteness." Loren Quiring (2003, 246) analyzes Aaron Sorkin's presidents in terms of rhetorical style and his equation of divinity and sanctity with oratory in what amounts to an attempt to "wrestle our television culture back into the great addresses in which a leader is once more, and always, a man of his word." It should, however, be noted that while *The West Wing* uses speeches, soliloquies, and angry arguments that make for great rhetoric, it also weaves practical politics and puny compromises into the mix. The wheeling and dealing is presented idealistically, as driven by real issues and sincere commitments (Lichter et al. 2001, 6).

Liesbet van Zoonen (2003, 2005) has argued persuasively for the need to understand "politics as soap," i.e., how personalization and dramatization may create spaces for popular political engagement. In particular, *The West Wing* is described as marrying notions of "rationality, progress and destiny," tradition- ally associated with politics, to a focus on relationships, emotions, fallibility, and sensation, associated with the soap opera. The soap opera norms in *The West Wing* can construct a

> ...hybrid understanding of politics in which the different logics of rational policy de- velopment, ideological struggle, personal convictions and preferences, public relations requirements, incompetence and bureaucracy unite into a coherent and persuasive picture of the "best possible" political practice. (2003, 112)

While not analyzing audience reaction to the program itself, van Zoonen speculates that this hybrid depiction of political life, with its mixture of public and private experience, is what allows audiences to identify and connect to politics as a phenomenon. It is in the vicarious identification with people in politics and the emotional resonance they evoke that the voyeuristic pleasures of reality programming are similar to those enjoyed by viewers of *The West Wing*.

Compromise: The Politics of Reality

The textual analysis on which the rest of this chapter is based demonstrates that the process of politics, so applauded for its approximation of real-life politics, ultimately works to undermine the progressive politics the characters represent. When all is said and done, the message to viewers is, more often than not, that the issues promoted by the Bartlet Administration are unrealistic. How does this happen? The aforementioned study by Parry-Giles and Parry-Giles (2002) focuses on the character of President Bartlet, describing his leadership style as dualistic: a typically "modernist" militaristic, heroic, and romantic leadership coalescing with a more "postmodern" one characterized by uncertainty, chaos, and collective decision-making. Although the present study focuses on the ideals and issues brought up in the show rather than on individual characters, the overarching conclusion is that another kind of duality is prominent: the struggle between *idealism* and *compromise*.

This duality goes beyond the obvious links that some have made to Democratic and Republican Party ideologies and stances (Lehmann 2001; Podhoretz 2003). In fact it lies in what can be seen as ideals declared as issue preferences by the characters, and the pragmatic solutions forced upon them by what is depicted as the necessity of image management, the strength of political opponents or practical difficulties. While not all issues raised result in policy decisions, when they do, it is inevitably the pragmatic compromises that prevail. Here it will be recalled that it is precisely TWW's "pragmaticism," its depictions of compromise solutions that are neither good nor bad, that former White House staff found so appealing in the program. Several authors in the Rollins and O'Connor anthology *The West Wing: The American Presidency as Television Drama* also point out the way the scripts present issues in terms of a debate without a conclusion, where there are two sides to an issue and the issue is left "fundamentally unresolved, giving audiences a sense of debates in progress" (cf. Pompper 2003, 29). This is also clearly the intention of creator Aaron Sorkin, who said:

> You know, one of the things I like about this world, or at least I like about the way we are presenting this world, is these issues are terribly complicated.... There, by and large, aren't good guys and bad guys. Your talking bout very learned people capable of arguing both sides of an issue, and it's that process that I enjoy dramatizing. (Levine 2003, 49)

While the need to compromise is clearly not simply an aspect of the "reality" of politics (but of all aspects of life), there is a systematic gap between the poetic hyperbole and Shakespeare-like oratory of ideals—not seldom spiced with statistics to demonstrate why these are valid political stances—on the one hand, and the chaotic politicking expressed as threats and promises made in order to block or pass legislation (or to silence those who would embarrass the president) on the other. Despite this gap, both aspects serve the same central dramaturgical purpose: to demonstrate how idealistic, hard-working, and committed the characters are to the best interests of the country.

One way of conceptualizing how this works in *The West Wing* is by appropriating what Fiske and Hartley (1978) once characterized as "claw back" in news coverage. "Claw back" refers to the way events potentially disruptive to commonly accepted versions of the truth are "mediated into the dominant value system without losing their authenticity" through an emphasis on certain aspects of an event or phenomenon rather than on another (Fiske 1987, 288–

300). Thus, a news correspondent in the field may describe the terror and suffering of the victims of a bombing, but the anchorperson could interpret these events as somehow logical in light of a broader context something that tends to mitigate the extent of the tragedy ostensibly by making it more understandable. In a similar way, although each WW episode builds on issues where the characters get to express their ideals and issue stances, these are "clawed back" to the political center by PR considerations, "practical" problems, and compromise solutions that are implied to be the stuff of "real life."

The supposition that there was a gap between political ideals and actual actions prompted a textual analysis of the content of the first four seasons of *The West Wing*.[2] The aim was simply to identify and compare the declared issue stances of members of the Bartlet Administration with the actions/decisions taken during the same or following episodes to resolve them. It has been suggested to me that *The West Wing's* dramaturgy is broadly based on three types of problems: the day-to-day politics of the political process; foreign policy or crisis "situations," where action is required and where audiences are brought into the consequences of these actions; or the working through of deeper constitutional issues through several episodes, sometimes a whole season (i.e., the revelation that President Bartlet had multiple sclerosis, the nomination of new Supreme Court justices, or Bartlet's invocation of the Twenty-fifth Amendment after his daughter's kidnapping). This is complicated by the fact that the script focuses on three or four subplots that are stitched together into one episode. Interviews with creator and writer Aaron Sorkin often point out that he likes compelling political arguments and uses "both sides of the issue" to build up a scene (Miller 2000). In any event, the first and third dramaturgical types (this section) are more about domestic policy and are process oriented, whereas the second is more foreign-policy oriented and depicts the "action" and its consequences (next section).

So how is "reality" conveyed through the script? The simple answer is through the rehearsal of idealistic issue stances with very few concrete outcomes. While there was no problem identifying the issue stances taken by members of the Bartlet Administration, it was much more difficult to detect the action taken or what decision was made in consequence. The political positions taken by the staff of *The West Wing* read like a vision of the good society, a Santa Claus wish list, if you will: they want educational reform, a patient's "bill of rights," the promotion of minorities to important positions in government, federal laws against hate crimes, continued funding for the National Endowment for the Arts, Public Service Broadcasting, and welfare reform. They favor stronger laws on gun control and limits on greenhouse gas emissions.[3] Sex education should be taught in the schools, but school prayer should remain outside of them. They are against the death penalty, and racial profiling, and they think that money should be reallocated from drug enforcement to drug treatment; they want to go after the big tobacco companies for misleading the public. They support women's rights (including abortion rights) and the rights of homosexuals (including same-sex marriages and the right to serve in the military). They are also in favor of campaign finance reform and against the use of "soft money" in campaign ads.

So what action or decisions does the Bartlet Administration take toward the realization of these ideals? Most efforts seem thwarted by the opposition or by public-relations considerations. In the premiere episode Deputy White House staffer Josh Lyman refers vaguely to a gun-control bill they passed that was so weak that "I'd say it's roughly the equivalent of fighting the war on Big Tobacco by banning certain color matchbook covers." The president's controversial nomination of Hispanic Roberto Mendoza to the Supreme Court ultimately succeeds, but not before Mendoza must accept the humiliation of spending time in jail, a victim of racial profiling that has to be kept in the dark because Toby "can't make a story of it" ("Celestial Navigation"). Another subplot related to racial profiling (in "The Drop-In") has to do with a famous comedian who, despite having been a fundraiser for Bartlet, is asked not to host a dinner in order to avoid drawing attention to a joke he made years ago on racial profiling that Bartlet laughed at.

In "Take This Sabbath Day," an appeal to stay an execution forces the president to decide whether to pardon the accused double-murderer or allow the execution. Despite his religious beliefs and those of his staff, Bartlet allows the execution because he is afraid of how "history" would view a stay, and because 70 percent of the American people are said to be in favor of the death penalty. Incidentally, the opinion of a large majority of Americans for a certain issue is apparently not always a sufficient reason to change one's stance on an issue. "Lame Duck Congress" centered on whether the administration should recall Congress in a final attempt to pass the Nuclear Test Ban Treaty. After having lost supporters of the treaty from his own party, the president decides to drop the issue. When Toby says that 82 percent of the people are for a "global arms treaty," Bartlet replies that people don't really understand the complexities and ramifications of international treaties; this is why they choose leaders who can decide for them. "The people" are thus considered better equipped to understand the death penalty and the American judicial system than the complexities of nuclear proliferation.

Campaign reform and soft money are two issues that form subplots across a number of episodes in *The West Wing*. While the Administration's move to appoint two reformers to the Federal Election Commission is tantamount to taking on "both party leaderships," Bartlet must backtrack when he runs for re-election. The issue of soft money is raised by his campaign manager Bruno Gianelli (in "Gone Quiet"), when he attempts to convince Sam and Toby that leaflets labeling the President as "Super Liberal" need to be countered by issue advertisements. Sam argues that this will look bad, since Bartlet is an outspoken supporter of campaign finance reform and against soft money. Gianelli says that is fine, but how can the president be expected to follow a law that doesn't exist? "But there is such a thing as leadership by example," says Sam. "Yes," says Bruno, "but they don't win elections." Sam thinks it is wrong to try "to get around the law," and Bruno doesn't want to lose the election by running under different rules than the opponent uses. Bruno's "reality" is that high ideals do not win elections, and Bruno gets his way: the issue ads are run.

When it comes to gay rights, the Bartlet Administration appears toothless. Same-sex marriages are made illegal by the "Marriage Recognition Act," and efforts by the president to "dangle his feet" by attempting to change the "Don't Ask, Don't Tell" rule about gays in the military are presented as not really serious. The issues pressed for by Amy Gardner, the head of a powerful woman's lobby, are often framed as "asking for too much" or "how much better will you do with the opposition?" Incidentally, van Zoonen (2003, 112) criticizes *The West Wing* for making women even less visible as power holders than in "real" politics. However, in later episodes, particularly in the sixth season, women become more visible with the promotion of Press Secretary C.J. Cregg to Chief of Staff and the presence of Deputy National Security Advisor Kate Harper.

Finally, despite frequent references to education as an administration priority, the occasional speech about too few teachers in the schools, an initiative on school vouchers, or a deal to put more computers in the classroom, little is mentioned regarding education during the four seasons under scrutiny. Regarding environmental policy, the fifth-season episode "Constituency of One" is in line with previous seasons. Here, C.J. finds out that Leo has censored an independent report by the Environmental Protection Agency on the negative effects of coal on the environment, despite the fact that "coal is the dirtiest energy on the planet." Leo justifies this by saying that there are no alternatives to coal, and he can't afford alienating the coal industry because the president's approval ratings are down.

These examples demonstrate that, despite *The West Wing* staff's commitment to a progressive agenda, issues such as more stringent laws on gun control and tobacco companies, reforming campaign finance, and a "patient's bill of rights" are demonstrated to be unattainable goals due to the necessity of compromise, the inability to "win," or the impossibility of changing "the system." In this way, *The West Wing* functions ideologically to "claw back" the utopian political ideals into the "realistic" realm of the political center. President Bartlet himself projects this combination of idealism and mainstream U.S. political values. His opposition to the death penalty, his stance on gays in the military and gun control are "clawed back" to mainstream political currents by his character's stout Catholicism, his neo-liberal globalization policy, and his habit of quoting Bible verses.

"Us" and "Them" in *The West Wing*

How does this struggle between compromise and idealism play out when it comes to the foreign policy of the Bartlet Administration? Like their news counterparts, the originators of *The West Wing* put less effort into providing a credible representation of U.S. foreign policy than they do of domestic-policy issues. During the first four seasons, the Secretary of State (if there is one) or State Department personnel are few and far between. Foreign policy in *The West Wing* is run mainly by Chief of Staff Leo McGarry, the Chairman of the Joint Chiefs of Staff, Admiral Fitzwallace, and a National Security Advisor, Nancy McNally.[4] Further, there appears to be a mixture of names of real countries who have been given fictional leaders—such as Indonesia, Haiti, and Russia—and fictional countries with fictional leaders. The viewer has no difficulty identifying two of the fictional countries: the Equatorial Republic of Kuhndu (Rwanda) and Qumar (a sort of Taliban-led Afghanistan placed in the Persian Gulf region). The only countries given fictitious names are those involving a genocide, which prompts a U.S. military intervention, and an erstwhile ally that has terrorists in its government.

Despite this, there is also a dualism when it comes to the way *The West Wing* depicts the United States in relation to other countries. When the United States must act externally, the ringing oratory for which the program is so widely admired is drafted into the realm of emotional and militaristic patriotism by President Bartlet himself. This more closely resembles the "real life" policies of the Bush Administration than the show's domestic-policy parallels with the policies of the Clinton Administration. So, instead of a dualism of progressive idealism and compromise, it is more appropriate to describe the foreign policy of *The West Wing* in terms of universalism and exceptionalism.

In this context, it is helpful to recall Billig's study *Banal Nationalism*, which describes the ideological consciousness of nationhood that comes to us through scholarship, the media, language habits, the rhetoric of politicians, etc. This consciousness is continually flagged through the syntax of the national "we" and in themes relating to our homeland, our national duty, and honor. One common vernacular distinguishes between "our patriotism" (good, necessary, and beneficial) and "their nationalism" (bad, primordial, and threatening), relegating the latter to right-wing ideologies, xenophobia, and primordial movements, although the two may take identical expression (1995, 55–59). More important for this analysis of the Bartlet Administration's foreign policy stances and actions are Billig's link between universalism and nationalism, and how a particular nation comes to symbolize what is now known as universal rights. It was, he says, during the French Revolution when the Enlightenment values of reason and the "rights of man" came to be embodied in the French nation as the values of "equality, fraternity and liberty." In other words, a particular state was made to coincide with or be synonymous with universal rights. The United States, as a superpower, currently embraces a discourse that claims both universality and exceptionalism.

> If nationalism involves imagining an international context, or international order, as well as imagining "ourselves" and "foreigners," then "we" can claim "ourselves" to be representing the interests of this international universal order: "we," in our great particularity, can be imagined to stand for "all of us," for a universal audience of humanity. Thus, the modern nation does not go to war merely for particular interest, but claims to be acting in the interests of "all nations" or the universal order of nations. (Billig 1995, 89)

Thus, U.S. leaders in the early 1990s invoked the concept of a "new world order" referencing a "we" that both recognizes the rights of others "while still reminding 'ourselves' that 'we,' the 'greatest nation in history,' are looking out for 'our' own interests" (ibid., 90). The themes of universality and exceptionalism, together with President Bartlet's aforementioned emotional patriotism and willingness to pursue military solutions, are key themes in the way foreign policy is portrayed during the first four seasons of *The West Wing*.

Many of these universalist and exceptionalist ideas are not particular to individual characters and are expressed as arguments by members of the Bartlet staff. In particular, Communications Director Toby Ziegler and Press Secretary C.J. Cregg are at times loudly critical of some countries and of U.S. policy, but these are seen to be personal positions. Since these characters are not supposed to "make foreign policy," they are allowed to air their opinions without having to consider the consequences. For example, the White House staff do not hide their morally superior tone when dealing with countries that are authoritarian or undemocratic (as in most cases). The Russians are chastised for their attempts to marginalize a tabloid journalist (implying censorship of free speech), for their inability to admit to nuclear accidents, and for helping the Iranians build a heavy-water plant. Toby writes a speech that avoids calling Indonesia "our friend," disciplining it for not being democratic, something he has reason to regret when he is told he humiliated the Indonesian president ("The State Dinner").

What Chief of Staff Leo McGarry and President Bartlet think and do matters more, and indeed both appear emotionally distressed every time an American citizen is killed abroad. (Indeed, one wonders whether the President *really does* call the parents of every U.S. citizen killed abroad.) In the episode "A Proportional Response," a plane carrying the president's doctor is shot down by Syria, and Bartlet demonstrates an "amateur" response by wanting to retaliate with a massive attack so that Americans, like the citizens of Ancient Rome, "shall walk the earth unharmed or the mighty power of the U.S. will be unleashed on them...." The joint chiefs and Leo finally get Bartlet to agree to a "proportional response" on a military target, because "that's what superpowers do." In a later episode, when a pilot from a stealth fighter is shot down over the no-fly zone in Iraq, Bartlet threatens to "invade Baghdad if I have to, to get him back" ("What Kind of Day It's Been"). President Bartlet's gung-ho militarism subsides a bit after the fourth season, although the eagerness to retaliate by bombing other countries when a few U.S. citizens lose their lives continues to be expressed by other characters, most notably Chief of Staff Leo McGarry.

Yet, the clear and present enemies are Islamic fundamentalism and terrorism. These are major themes that recur in different ways and contexts, and with increasing frequency, I might add, after the fourth season of *The West Wing*. As Billig (1995, 91) points out, "our" enemies are construed as standing *outside* the moral order: they do not simply oppose our values; they are outside of the boundaries of natural law and reason. This is the way Arab countries, not just fundamentalists, are often depicted in *The West Wing*: outside the boundaries of reasonable morals. On two occasions, the Press Secretary C.J. is critical of the administration's military cooperation with its Islamic allies (fictional) Qumar and Saudi Arabia, because of their treatment of women. Her monologue regarding Saudi Arabia is memorable, not simply because of its rhythm and pace, but because Saudi Arabia is depicted to be outside the boundaries of reason, rationality, and common sense:

> Outraged? I'm barely surprised. This is a country where women aren't allowed to drive a car. They're not allowed to be in the company of any man other than a close relative. They're required to adhere to a dress code that would make a Maryknoll nun look like Malibu Barbie. They beheaded 121 people last year for robbery, rape, and drug trafficking. They have no free press, no elected government, no political parties. And the Royal Family allows the Religious Police to travel in groups of six carrying nightsticks and they freely and publicly beat women. But "Brutus is an honorable

man." 17 schoolgirls were forced to burn alive because they weren't wearing the proper clothing. Am I outraged? No. That is Saudi Arabia, our partners in peace. ("Enemies Foreign and Domestic")

More telling about the tension between universalism and exceptionalism is the row between Toby and his ex-wife Andrea, a congresswoman, over a speech drafted for the United Nations General Assembly that sets out Bartlet's new, tougher foreign policy. Andrea and her colleagues on the committee are angry at Toby's speech:

ANDY: "America does not have a monopoly on what's right.... And even if we did, I think you are going to have a tough time convincing the Arab world.... The U.S. Constitution defends religious pluralism. It doesn't reduce all of the Arab world to fanaticism...."

TOBY: "Neither does this speech. It calls fanaticism fanaticism. So we are going to call it that. We respect all religions, all cultures.

ANDY: "To a point."

TOBY: "Yes, to a point. Grotesque oppression is not ok, just because it is institutionalized. If you ask me, I think we should have gotten into the game three-four decades ago. But they are coming for us now so it's time to saddle up.... We do know what's right."

ANDY: "...Toby, this is why they hate us."

TOBY: "There are a lot of reasons why they hate us. They'll like us when we win...."

Andrea asks him to put in some sentences that several members of the House Foreign Relations Committee have drafted.

TOBY: (reading) "Our goal is not to proclaim American values. We have deep respect for our Islamic brothers and sisters, and we have a great deal to learn from the values of tolerance and faith that are deeply held throughout the Islamic world.... Guess what? Our goal is to proclaim American values.... The reality is that the USA no longer sucks up to reactionaries, and our staunch allies will know what we mean."

ANDY: "We do not have any staunch allies in the Arab world, just reluctant ones. We have a coalition held together with duct tape. A coalition without which we cannot fight."

TOBY: "Nobody's blowing off the coalition. And that coalition will be plenty strong."

ANDY: "Oh, when we win? What is Egypt going to think? Or Pakistan?"

TOBY: "That freedom and democracy are coming soon to a theater near them, so get dressed."

ANDY: "You guys are on a thing right now.... But this one moment in time, you have to get off your horse, and simply put, be nice to the Arab world...."

TOBY: "Be nice? Well how about, when we instead of blowing Iraq back to the seventh century for harboring terrorists and trying to develop nuclear weapons, we just imposed economic sanctions and were reviled by the Arab world for not giving them a global charge card and a free trade treaty. How about when we pushed Israel for giving up land for peace? How about when we sent American soldiers to protect Saudi Arabia and we were told we were desecrating the Holy Land while ignoring the fact that we were invited...."

(This is played out in three separate scenes in "Night Five" and condensed here.)

This exchange appears to be a debate, but it actually only depicts one reasonable argument: Toby's argument. Toby argues for what seems to be the only rational and reasonable position: freedom of speech and freedom against repression. Andrea's argument is reduced to "can't you be nice?" and "think of our repressive allies." Toby's argument proclaims the moral high ground by saying that it is time to go after those who do not hold the universal values of freedom, i.e., the same values held by America. This idealistic unilateralism hides the "reality," brought up by Andrea, that America's support for repressive allies is the rule rather than the exception, and that dictating freedom to governments previously praised for their "stability" on the basis that they do not share U.S. values might seem bullying and hypocritical. Still, and maybe because he brings up what he perceives as injustices against the United States, Toby's idealistic unilateralism—*our way is better*—is the only one that makes intuitive common sense.[5] What is missing, both in this exchange and in C.J.'s monologue, are signs of an understanding of what types of values *are* held in the Arab world and why, exactly, they would be "our allies" if they don't "share our values."

This is also in line with Lynn Spigel's (2004, 244–245) argument that *The West Wing* episode of "Isaac and Ishmael" performs "some of the fundamental precepts of contemporary Orientalism." Here she is referring to Edward Said's (1978) critique of the way European and U.S. literary and knowledge production about the Arab world "others" Arabs as "the antithesis of Western humanity and progress" and ignores the cultural expression and multifaceted lived experiences of those in the region. Delineating the Arabic or Islamic "other" serves to maintain a sense of superiority through ignorance of the part played by "us" in the history of the current problems in the Middle East and also increases fear and the need for increased "national security."[6] Orientalism underlies much of the depiction of Islam and the Arab world in the first four seasons of *The West Wing*.

The idea that the United States is exceptional and does not need to play by the rules of the United Nations and the international community has been trumpeted by the George W. Bush Administration. This assumption is also at play in several different episodes of *The West Wing*. In the episode "War Crimes," where the proposed United Nations War Crimes Tribunal is at issue, Leo receives a visit from his old Vietnam War commander. The tribunal is described as "a thing of catastrophic proportions" where national sovereignty is at stake. Americans shouldn't be held accountable to anyone outside the United States, especially since the United Nations is not a democratic body. Leo says that while the president has not made up his mind, 130 countries have already signed, and doesn't this mean we are just "hedging our bets"? The officer tells Leo that he himself has committed what some would call a war crime when he unknowingly bombed a civilian target in Vietnam. The phrase "all wars are crimes" appears to settle the matter, as if to say there is nothing we can do.

The notion that the United States cannot always comply with international law, and indeed must take the law into its own hands, can be seen in the final episodes of the third season, where President Bartlet is confronted with evidence that the Defense Minister of Qumar, a supposed ally, really is the leader of a terrorist cell that ordered an attack on the Golden Gate Bridge. Since the evidence of his complicity was gained through torture (by the Russians of a Chechen), it would have been inadmissible as evidence in court. The president orders a covert assassination to remove this terrorist threat and does so, breaking his own executive order and that of international law, but not U.S. law. Although Bartlet suffers moral qualms after the assassination, the audience understands that rules have to be bent and that it was necessary for the United States to do this to counter a terrorist threat. While there are clear parallels with U.S. foreign and domestic policy here, the point is that, together with the other examples above, U.S. exceptionalism is shown to be driven by necessity, by "real" problems.

A noteworthy example of the tension between unilateralism and exceptionalism is "The Warfare of Genghis Khan."[7] The episode is interesting in that it appears to challenge U.S. foreign policy, but in the end accepts the premise on which it is based. An unannounced nuclear test explosion in the Indian Ocean prompts frantic efforts to figure out if North Korea or Iran is responsible. Convinced that it is the latter, because of the Iranian leadership's paraphrasing of passages allegedly from the Qur'an about killing infidels, the president orders B-2 bombers to be ready to unilaterally attack when they are sure it was Iran. Toby, playing a different role here, wonders whether it is not the United Nations that should deal with this problem, to which Leo replies:

The UN doesn't want this. They want to wring their hands and censure us after....
But they expect us to take care of things like this. And after they've exhausted themselves calling us warmongers and imperialists, they'll go home and quietly drink toasts
to their relief. (Television without Pity 2004, 10)

Leo confronts the Iranian representative, saying that the United States
believes that Iran is developing nuclear weapons. The representative denies it,
saying that it is against Islam and that "it is disconcerting to be dictated to by
the only transgressor in human history." It is the U.S. Vice-President who
suggests that the culprit could be Israel, since they would have to test their
nuclear weapons in order to put them on submarine-based missiles. President
Bartlet confronts the Israeli prime minister, saying that this test destabilizes
the region and makes the U.S. look like hypocrites on non-proliferation
policy. The Israeli prime minister responds that there is nothing hypocritical
in "looking after national interest. As Israel has a right to do." Bartlet argues
that proliferation breeds proliferation; bombs beget bombs. The Israeli prime
minister shoots back that the ideal number of nuclear states for the United
States is one. Deterrence for Israel is "not an option, but an imperative," and
they model their approach on the U.S. Cold War strategy of Mutually Assured
Destruction. They both tell each other: "Your argument boils down to asking
the world to trust you."

Here it is interesting to see that U.S. hypocrisy is demonstrated both
through the Iranian and Israeli arguments about U.S. exceptionalism. This
can also be discerned in Leo's regurgitation of the mainstream U.S. critique of
the United Nations, i.e., that it is not only ineffective and hypocritical, but it
secretly wants the United States to step in and act as the "world's police." The
ideological "claw back" happens when the problem simply "disappears," and it
is discovered to be Israel and not Iran that secretly tested a nuclear weapon.
The body language of President Bartlet and the Israeli prime minister as they
sit facing one another is provocative. It is as though the world's largest
superpower had the same problem as one of the world's smallest countries. Or
is it that the smaller country is simply an extension of the superpower? One
suspects the latter, since the world stands on the brink of a major crisis one
minute, and the next minute everything is back to "normal"—simply because
of trust. Furthermore, if the difference between Iran and Israel having a
nuclear weapon is simply a matter of "whether the world trusts them," then it
is not at all clear the "world" views the situation in the same way as the United
States. Yet the U.S. view is the same as "common sense"—that is, faced with an
"Islamic" threat, bomb first and ask questions later. Leo makes this clear when
he says why strikes are preferable "as opposed to sanctions, never-ending talks,
while a Hezbollah martyr leads a donkey cart packed with plutonium smack

into downtown Tel Aviv" (Television without Pity 2004, 14. Author's paren-
thesis).[8]

Conclusion

This chapter has argued that much of the audience appeal of *The West Wing* is
due to its relationship to authenticity and real-life events, as well as wish
fulfillment about how public servants "should be." Audiences get the pleasure
of being able to playfully test their knowledge of current events while enjoying
the personal relationships between characters that are human and fallible, but
do the best they can under difficult circumstances. In this way, *The West Wing*
appeals to its audiences in ways not dissimilar to reality television programs.

Scholarship on *The West Wing* tends to focus on two topics: the office of
the presidency and the possible "real" effects of the program on audience
views of government. I argue that another way of analyzing the program is to
problematize *The West Wing's* notion of the real: what is "realistic" about the
issues and outcomes in the script? If looked at in this way, it becomes clear
that there is a struggle between idealism and compromise whereby progressive
stances are "clawed back" to the political center, as if these were somehow
unrealistic. In foreign policy, there is a dualism between universalism (universal rights) and particularism (the United States lives by its own rules). President Bartlet and Leo display a militaristic and patriotic emotional bent easily
roused when Americans are killed overseas. Despite the fact that international
law is also based on universal rights, it is depicted as constraining to both U.S.
ideals and practice, and thus cannot always be followed. Those U.S. allies
(with the exception of Great Britain) mentioned on the show are often those
that must be lectured to.

The preoccupation with Islamic fundamentalism and the U.S. relationship to the Arab world clearly reflects the real-life agenda of the first years of
the twenty-first century, both in the frustrations of being "misunderstood" by
the Arab world and also in the depiction of "them" as incomprehensible,
beyond "our" value system and beyond "human feeling." The ideals of
freedom and democracy, and "our way is better," are used as rationalizations
to bomb first and ask questions later. The tension between ideals and practice,
so evident in the Bartlet Administration's domestic policy, is less so in foreign
policy. They are, however, both more "realistic" and therefore more typical of
the logic of *The West Wing*—the show that wants to be real.

Notes

[1] I am greatly indebted to three fan sites that have been very helpful in carrying out this research: www.bartlet4america.org/, Stephen Lee's www.newsaic.com/, and www.televisionwithoutpity.com.

[2] These eighty-plus episodes were those authored by the show's creator, Aaron Sorkin. The fifth and sixth seasons have also been perused and, generally speaking, appear to be consonant with the analysis of the first through fourth seasons.

[3] Although whether there is a specific environmental issue stance is elaborated very little. In one episode ("The Drop-In") where Deputy Communications Director Sam Seaborne describes the administration's policy as accepting greenhouse gases as the chief threat to the environment, and different "clean air acts" are given as examples of the administration pushing this agenda. In "Life on Mars," in the fourth season, responses to ads attacking the administration's position on regulations on automobiles not built for fuel efficiency were planned.

[4] This changes in later seasons. Particularly in the fifth and sixth seasons, foreign-policy issues become more and more important as plot devices.

[5] It should be noted that this episode aired in the United States for the first time on 6 February 2003—which was around the time it became clear, through televised debates taking place in the UN Security Council, that France, Germany, and Russia were unconvinced of the evidence used to justify a military intervention in Iraq.

[6] See also Said's later book, *Covering Islam* (1981), which further develops some of the arguments from *Orientalism*.

[7] This episode is from the fifth season, and while this season is not included in the textual analysis, it demonstrates that some of the same themes continue.

[8] Here Hezbollah is made to stand in for "any militant Islamic group," since the writers are oblivious to the fact that Hezbollah is a Lebanese group that claims to have freed Lebanese territory from 22 years of Israeli occupation. Since 2000, Hezbollah has transformed itself into a prominent Lebanese political party with roughly a third of the voting public. The United States still considers Hezbollah a terrorist group, but the European Union does not.

References

Associated Press. 2001. "Calif. Assembly Mourns TV Character." http://b4a.healthyinterest.net/news/000078.html. 10 May 2001 (accessed 20 April 2004).

Baer, Alejandro. 2001. "Consuming History and Memory through Mass Media Products." *European Journal of Cultural Studies* 4(4): 491–501.

Beavers, Staci. 2002. "The West Wing as a Pedagogical Tool." *The Teacher*, June. American Political Science Association: http://www.apsanet.org/PS/june02/beavers.cfm.

Billig, Michael. 1995. *Banal Nationalism*. London: Sage.

Bolter, Jay, and Grusin, Richard. 1999. *Remediation: Understanding New Media*. Cambridge, MA:

MIT Press.

Byrne, Bridget. 2005. "NBC Keeps 'Wing,' 'Joey,' 'Jordan.'" 17 March. *Eonline.* http://www.eonline.com/News/Items/0,1,16146,00.html (accessed 7 September 2005).

Corner, John, and Pels, Dick. 2003. "Introduction: The Re-Styling of Politics." In *Media and the Restyling of Politics: Consumerism, Celebrity and Cynicism,* edited by J. Corner and D. Pels. London: Sage.

de Moraes, Lisa. 2003. "'West Wing' Creator Aaron Sorkin Quits Ailing Series." *The Washington Post,* 2 May, p. C01. http://www.washingtonpost.com/ac2/wp-dyn?pagename =article&contentId=A3294-2003May1&notFound=true (accessed 13 September 2005).

Fetveit, Arild. 1999. "Reality TV in the Digital Era: A Paradox in Visual Culture?" *Media, Culture and Society* 21(6): 787–804.

Fiske, John. 1987. *Television Culture.* London: Routledge.

Fiske, John, and Hartley, John. 1978. *Reading Television.* London and New York: Methuen.

Gillan, Jennifer. 2004. "From Ozzie Nelson to Ozzy Osbourne." In *Understanding Reality Television,* edited by S. Holmes and D. Jermyn. London: Routledge.

Holbert, R.L. 2004. "Refining Predictions Concerning the Consumption of Entertainment-based Political Television: Moderator Variables and *The West Wing* Exposure." Paper to be presented at the annual meeting of the National Communication Association, Political Communication Division, Chicago.

Holbert, R.L. et al. 2003. "*The West Wing* as Endorsement of the U.S. Presidency: Expanding the Bounds of Priming in Political Communication." *Journal of Communication,* September, 53(3): 427-443.

Holmes, Sue, and Jermyn, Deborah. 2004. "Introduction." In *Understanding Reality Television,* edited by S. Holmes and D. Jermyn. London: Routledge.

"Indecision 2000: West Wing-style." Zap2it.com. 9 November 2001.

Lehmann, Chris. 2001. "The Feel-Good Presidency: The Pseudo-Politics of *The West Wing.*" *The Atlantic Monthly.* Posted 1 March. http://www.b4a.healthyinterest.net/news/000064.html.

Levine, Myron. 2003. "The West Wing (NBC) and The West Wing (D.C.): Myth and Reality in Television's Portrayal of the White House." In *The West Wing: The American Presidency as Television Drama,* edited by Peter Rollins and John O'Connor. Syracuse: Syracuse University Press.

Lichter, S.R.; Lichter, L.; and Amudson, D. 2001. "Is the Bumbling Bureaucrat Passé in Prime Time? Changing Images of Government on TV 1998–2001." Center for Media and Public Affairs, Washington, DC; The Council for Excellence in Government. http://www.excelgov.org/displayContent.asp?NewsItemID=3978&Keyword=ppStudies (accessed 19 May 2004).

Magder, Ted. 2004. "The End of TV 101: Reality Programs, Formats, and the New Business of Television." In *Reality TV: Remaking Television Culture,* edited by Susan B. Murray and Laurie Ouellette. New York: New York University Press.

Miller, Matthew. 2000. "The Real White House." *Brill's Content.* Posted on Bartlet4America News Archive, 1 March. http://b4a.healthyinterest.net/news/000004.html (accessed 19 May 2004).

Murray, Susan, and Ouellette, Laurie. 2004. "Introduction." In *Reality TV: Remaking Television*

Culture, edited by Susan B. Murray and Laurie Ouellette. New York: New York University Press.

"Night Five." Media Quotes. http://www.westwingepguide.com/S3/Episodes/58_NF.html (accessed 19 May 2004).

Parry-Giles, Trevor and Parry-Giles, Shawn. 2002. "*The West Wing's* Prime-Time Presidentiality: Mimesis and Catharsis in a Postmodern Romance" *Quarterly Journal of Speech.* 88 (2) May. 209-227.

Princeton Survey Research Associates. 2004. "Changing Channels: Entertainment Television, Civic Attitudes, and Actions" for The Media, Citizens & Democracy. A Project of the Counci for Excellence in Government and the USC Annenberg Norman Lear Center, September 2003, revised April 2004. http://www.excelgov.org/admin/FormManager/filesuploading/MCD.pdf.

Podhoretz, John. 2003. "The Liberal Imagination." In *The West Wing: The American Presidency as Television Drama*, edited by Peter Rollins and John O'Connor. Syracuse: Syracuse University Press.

Pompper, Donnalyn. 2003. "The West Wing: White House Narratives That Journalism Cannot Tell." In *The West Wing: The American Presidency as Television Drama*, edited by Peter Rollins and John O'Connor. Syracuse: Syracuse University Press.

Quiring, Loren. 2003. "A Man of His Word: Aaron Sorkin's American Presidents." In *Hollywood's White House: The American Presidency in Film and History*, edited by Peter Rollins and John O'Connor. Lexington: University Press of Kentucky.

Rollins, Peter, and O'Connor, John, eds. 2003. "Introduction." In *The West Wing: The American Presidency as Television Drama*, edited by Peter Rollins and John O'Connor. Syracuse: Syracuse University Press.

Said, Edward. 1978. *Orientalism.* New York: Pantheon Books.

——. 1981. *Covering Islam: How the Media and the Experts Determine How We See the Rest of the World.* New York: Pantheon Books.

Shister, Gail. 2001. "Bush in a Cameo Role? No Thanks 'West Wing' Producers Say." *Philadelphia Inquirer*, 12 January.

Spigel, Lynn. 2004. "Entertainment Wars: Television Culture after 9/11." *American Quarterly*, 56(2). 235-270.

Television without Pity. 2004. "The Warfare of Ghengis Khan." Season 5, Episode 13, Recap by Deborah. 1999-2005. http://www.televisionwithoutpity.com/story.cgi?show=4&story=6219&page=10&sort=.

Thompson, John. 1995. *The Media and Modernity: A Social Theory of the Media.* Cambridge: Polity Press.

——. 2000. *Political Scandal: Power and Visibility in the Media Age.* Cambridge: Polity Press.

Wolff, Michael. 2000. "Our Remote-Control President." *New York Magazine.* Posted on Bartlet4America News Archive, 4 December. http://b4a.helthyinterest.net/news/000033.html (accessed 19 May 2004).

Zoonen, Liesbet van 2003. "'After Dallas and Dynasty We Have...Democracy': Articulating Soap, Politics and Gender." In *Media and the Restyling of Politics: Consumerism, Celebrity and Cynicism*, edited by J. Corner and D. Pels. London: Sage.

——. 2005. *Entertaining the Citizen: When Politics and Popular Culture Converge*. Lanham, MD: Rowman & Littlefield.

CHAPTER TEN

The Reagans: Fiction, History, or Propaganda?

RUNE OTTOSEN

The relationship between film and politics occurs in two contexts. One takes place in the real world of politics where the film industry and its members run for office, support candidates, raise and contribute money to political campaigns, lobby governments for special favors, and work as political activists for a host of causes. The other relationship occurs on the big screen where film content serves as instruments for propaganda, as an agent for social change, and as a manipulator of public opinion. But sometimes these relationships intersect in an environment where fantasy and reality are so entangled that one cannot be separated from the other. (Giglio 2005, 2–3)*

Introduction

The television miniseries *The Reagans* was scheduled to be broadcast by CBS on 16 and 18 November 2003. But CBS changed its plans because of protests from, among others, Ronald Reagan's son Michael and Republican-led political groups, including the conservative think-tank Media Research Center, which urged major advertisers buying commercial time during the broadcast to review the script. The result was that the series ended up being broadcast in an edited version on the cable channel Showtime. Director Robert Allan Ackerman had already removed himself from the editing process after CBS decided to cut parts of the series, including some remarks made by Ronald Reagan about AIDS.

In a statement designed to justify the decision to pull the series from the schedule, CBS stated, "Although the mini-series features impressive production values and acting performances, and the producers have sources to verify each scene in the script, we believe it does not present a balanced portrayal of the Reagans for CBS and its audience" (*Fox News*, 4 November 2003).

Apparently it was not the quality of the series that provoked this response from CBS when *The Reagans* was finally aired on Showtime. The show received good reviews in *The New York Times* and the *Hollywood Reporter* (Garron 2003). It received seven Emmy Awards in 2004. Judy Davis and James Brolin, in the roles of Nancy and Ronald Reagan, were both nominated for Golden Globe Awards, although after CBS interfered with the script, they reportedly refused to do any publicity interviews for the miniseries.

To understand why it was so important for conservative lobbyists and the Republican Party to stop the series, we must think in terms of the image of Ronald Reagan as an icon of conservative values and strong leadership. He was voted number one on the list of "Greatest Americans" in the poll organized by the Discovery Channel, ahead of Abraham Lincoln (number two) and Martin Luther King (number three). The website www.Ronald.Reagan.com portrays Reagan as a national hero, with battleships and airports named after him. This fits poorly with the miniseries's image of Ronald Reagan as a shallow thinker, indecisive, partly lost in the past, and constantly manipulated by Nancy and his closest advisors—in many cases behind his back.

The controversy that surrounded the series raises important issues about the relationship between fact and fiction in historical portrayals such as this, issues linked to ethical aspects as well as to corporate influence on freedom of expression. In my analysis of *The Reagans* I will focus on its representation of foreign policy, the military-industrial complex, and social issues such as the framing of political opposition. Using as my basis the critical theory of thinkers such as Norman Fairclough, Noam Chomsky, Stuart Hall, Toby Miller, and Robert W. McChesney, I will argue that the framing of historical events and the portrayal of American foreign policy in the Reagan miniseries is deeply problematic. The series, however, does not entirely lack criticism on issues like Ronald Reagan's policy toward AIDS. In dealing with the framing of Reagan's alleged views on AIDS and homosexuality, I will raise the ethical issue of the presentation of real people in a series such as this.[1]

The Ethical Issues of Portraying Real People

In a letter to *Time* magazine at the time CBS decided to drop the series, Reagan's daughter Patti expresses concern about the way it frames the family story. She complains about numerous errors, including the claim that she was sent to a girls' college against her will, and Ronald Reagan's alleged homophobia:

I was about eight or nine years old when I learned that some people are gay—although the word "gay" wasn't used in those years.... My father and I were watching an old Rock Hudson and Doris Day movie. At the moment when Hudson and Doris Day kissed, I said to my father, "That looks weird." Curious, he asked me to identify exactly what was weird about a man and woman kissing, since I'd certainly seen such a thing before. All I knew was that something about this particular man and woman was, to me, strange. My father gently explained that Mr. Hudson didn't really have a lot of experience kissing women; in fact, he would much prefer to be kissing a man. This was said in the same tone that would be used if he had been telling me about people with different colored eyes, and I accepted without question that this whole kissing thing wasn't reserved just for men and women. (Quoted by Davis 2003)

As Patti Davis writes to the editors of *Time*, "You should know this because it's something the producers Craig Zadan and Neil Meron won't tell you" (ibid.). She also contests other parts of the presentation. "My mother is cast as a female Attila the Hun, and I and my siblings are unrecognizable to me" (ibid.). Davis raises the interesting ethical issue of the right to one's own story:

Many of the people depicted in the script are dead—Lew Wasserman, my sister Maureen, my grandparents, Don Reagan. They can say nothing about their portrayals. And my father, obviously, cannot correct the lies told about him [as he suffered from Alzheimer's disease]. (Ibid.)

Historians are debating the ethics of portraying dead people who can no longer defend themselves. In their literature they recommend interviews with the living or with relatives of the deceased in order to make adjustments or correct mistakes that might arise from written primary and secondary sources. Living relatives and other sources should, at the very least, be heard (Dahl 2004, 94-104). Patti Davis claims in her letter to *Time* that the authors or producers of *The Reagans* "never consulted any family member" (quoted in Davis 2003). Taking as an example a scene in which she steals pills from her mother to trade for amphetamines ("an addiction that ravaged me from the age of 15 well into my 20s"), she criticizes the way it was used to depict her mother as a heavy user of pills:

Many women in the 60s were prescribed tranquilizers, and my mother never noticed hers missing, so she couldn't have been using them too often. You won't get this context in the CBS movie; they just wanted you to know there were drugs on the premises. (Ibid.)

Patti Davis writes that she had several offers to tell her story after she published her first autobiography in 1992. She declined. "Foolishly, I believed I had control over my own material" (ibid.). The concerns expressed by Ronald Reagan's daughter should be taken seriously, since ethical issues are too often ignored in the entertainment industry. On the other hand, public figures like Ronald Reagan must expect to be portrayed in a critical manner both in journalism and fiction.

The Approach: Discourse Analysis and Framing

I will use a discourse-analytical approach to this analysis, treating the text of the film as part of an ongoing battle in which different segments of society try to influence public opinion (Fairclough 1995). The military-industrial complex, in alliance with conservative groups and including the ruling Republican Party, has an obvious interest in framing the U.S. battle for global hegemony in the most favorable light. But a fiction series must also balance the presentation of political issues in order to be convincing to the public. A variety of opinions—such as voices from the political opposition, dissidents, and peace groups—must to a certain degree be reflected if the treatment is to appear fair. How these discourses are balanced will be an important aspect of my analysis. Social and political issues tend to be reflected in the way we present facts—"language use conceived as social practice," as Norman Fairclough puts it (Fairclough 1995, 135).

I will also introduce frame analyses as a methodological approach, drawing upon the work of Gaye Tuchman. Her work was originally based on analyses of the journalistic process, illuminating the series of decisions where the choice to include some perspectives and to exclude others is essential (Tuchman 1978).

Drama as Writing of History

The Reagans should be categorized as a docudrama. According to Janet Staiger's definition, docudrama is "a fact-based representation of real events. It may represent contemporary social issues...or it may deal with older historical events" (Staiger). In most cases, a docudrama is produced in the manner of realist theatre or film. Events are usually portrayed by actors. Unlike mainstream drama, the docudrama claims to provide a fairly accurate interpretation of real events (ibid.).

For many members of the post-1960s population, television is the only means—apart from history classes in school—by which they are exposed to history. History as presented through television has always been controversial for historians, many of whom take the view that television history is tailored to serve the needs of the present rather than to portray the events accurately

(Bennett et al. 1981, 285). A series like *Roots*, based on Alex Haley's book of the same name, inspires debate over the essential question of fact versus fiction. That debate includes such issues as falsifying history (of which Haley has been accused), and how far one may go in using fictitious elements to dramatize what is presented basically as fact.

Social issues such as the history of the working class and the depiction of trade unions and class struggle, in particular, are seldom given fair and just treatment (Tribe 1981). There is a deep suspicion that with contemporary conflicts and wars such as the Vietnam War, the Gulf War of 1991, and the "war on terror" after September 11, the experiences of filmmakers and broadcasters themselves color their perception of history (Allan and Zelizer 2004). This could also be understood in the context of what Stuart Hall (1981) has called "hegemonic politics." In his work on cultural history, Hall draws attention to the need to "cut into" the actual historical process to understand how the dominant cultural understanding frames the portrayal of history. Actual class interest is hidden in the fog of "common understanding," dominated by narratives that purposely hide real social conflicts. Walter Benjamin has observed that "the adjustment of reality to the masses and of the masses to reality is a process of unlimited scope, as much for thinking as for perception" (qtd. in Grossberg 1996, 161).

For Hall (1984), hegemony is linked to the huge number of people exposed every day to media consumption and the professional codes defining the news and entertainment industries. The framework that structures media production, and the economic and political interest involved is not visible to the public. In light of the many aspects of *The Reagans* dealing with military and foreign policy issues, a closer look at the strategic cooperation between the Pentagon and Hollywood would seem to be warranted (Ottosen 2004).

The Political Economy of Film and TV Production

Toby Miller argues that the political economy of film and television production and textual analyses should be subjected to a common approach:

> Screen texts are commodities whose appeal lies in their meanings. Critical political economy is, therefore, a natural ally of textual analysis. But a certain tendency on both sides has maintained that they are mutually exclusive, on the grounds that one approach is concerned with structures of the economy, and the other with structures of meaning. This need not be the case. Historically, the best critical political economy and the best textual analysis, much of it undertaken within cultural studies, has

worked through the imbrication of power and signification along the continuum of culture, weighing production, meaning, circulation, interpretation, and context. (Miller 2003, 3)

As background, and as a point of departure for my textual analyses of the series, I will draw here upon an earlier work in which I analyzed the relationship between fact and fiction in war propaganda (Ottosen 2004; Nohrstedt and Ottosen 2005). The Pentagon-Hollywood relationship is one part of the new strategy in the battle for influencing public opinion on military affairs. In his book *Operation Hollywood: How The Pentagon Shapes and Censors the Movies*, David L. Robb revealed that the Pentagon has its own officers whose jobs are to be consultants on media scripts and to decide whether or not the Pentagon will take part in a production. Once the decision on cooperation is made, their roles are to be helpful to military personnel and to provide technical assistance in the form of equipment, aircraft, and ships (Robb 2004).

It is news to no one that the Pentagon has professionalized its information strategy since the Vietnam War, when the military temporarily lost its grip on public opinion (Ottosen 1994). The Pentagon-Hollywood relationship is one part of its new strategy.

The Pentagon receives about one hundred movie scripts every year and decides to cooperate in about a third of them. Negotiations and compromises are often necessary in order to satisfy the Pentagon. There is also competition in this field between the different branches of the military: an Air Force liaison officer works full-time "selling" the Air Force to Hollywood, and for the major movie *Air Force One*, the Air Force lent six F-158 aircraft free of charge (Gunn 1999).

Most interesting for me in this context are movies based on real wars. A good recent example is *Black Hawk Down*, based on the failed "Operation Restore Hope" in Somalia in 1992, in which eighteen American soldiers died (Ottosen 1997). In this case, the Pentagon liked the script because the heroic images of the soldiers dying in battle helped to rewrite a failed operation. So the film got Pentagon support, but at what price? "If you want to use the military's toys you've got to play by their rules," says military technical advisor John Lovett (AP 2001). The military historian Lawrence Suid (2002) explained in detail how this system works in the book *Guts and Glory*, calling it a "system for mutual exploitations."

Commercial television is of course the main link between the entertainment and news industries. The television series *The Agency*, produced by CBS, in which CIA agents save the world from Arab terrorists and villains, is produced in close cooperation with, and sponsored by, the CIA. The CIA has consultants working on the script, and the agency put its locations and manpower at the disposal of the series. According to *The New York Times*, the CIA explained its role by claiming that it was a part of the agency's strategy to get through to the public with "the truth about the CIA" and to persuade those who were worried about public opinion to increase the agency's funding to a total of $30 billion. Interestingly enough, the Norwegian commercial channel TV2 bought the rights to *The Agency* in Norway, according to the newspaper *Dagens Næringsliv*, without knowledge of the CIA's role in the making of the series.[2] These are but fragments of the politico-economical context into which market- and propaganda-driven forces embed the news media (Nohrstedt and Ottosen 2005).

Globalization and Cultural Imperialism

Series like *24 Hours*, with Jack Bauer as the ultimate hero, rescuing the homeland from evil Arab terrorists, are currently on air in many parts of the world. It is part of the competition in a global market. As Edward Herman and Robert McChesney showed in their book *The Global Media: The New Missionaries of Global Capitalism*, motion pictures and radio were among the first industries to compete in a global market. As early as 1914, 85 percent of the world's film audience was watching American movies (Herman and McChesney 1997, 13–14). One of the early players in this broadcasting market was CBS (mentioned above in connection with *The Agency*). CBS began its global career in radio and helped create the Voice of America as a propaganda tool for the U.S. government during the Second World War. The experience with film, broadcasting, and propaganda in general elevated the importance of communication in the minds of policymakers during the interwar years and has continued to do so today. As a result, American-based film companies still have commercial and political global hegemony. The global film industry is dominated by a few American companies such as Columbia, Twentieth Century-Fox, United Artists, MCA (Universal), Warner Brothers, Metro-Goldwyn-Mayer, and Paramount (Herman and McChesney 1997, 19). Historically, under U.S. broadcasting regulations, the networks NBC, CBS, and ABC have been restricted in what they are allowed to produce for domestic consumption. Thus, the major American program producers, and therefore the major global television production studios, were actually the film studios of Hollywood (Herman and McChesney 21). The present global market is dominated by Disney, Time Warner, Viacom, Universal, Sony Polygram, and The News Corporation.

And it appears that the world market for film and television is increasingly important for the American economy. In 1998, the biggest U.S. film studios increased their foreign rentals by one-fifth over 1997 rentals. Export figures virtually equaled the domestic figure of US$6.8 billion. The thirty-nine most popular films on the global market were produced in the United States (Miller et al. 2001, 4).

The introduction of global satellite television—with twenty-four-hour news and CNN as the first big player in this new market, and with the Gulf War in 1991 as its commercial breakthrough—changed the news industry forever. In an international comparative study, my Swedish colleague Stig Arne Nohrstedt and I have documented how television coverage of the Gulf War constituted the exportation of U.S. perspectives to a global audience (Nohrstedt and Ottosen 2001).

Time Warner bought CNN, and when Disney bought the television network ABC, it was clear that the merger of the entertainment and film industries with the news industry had begun. Rupert Murdoch had his breakthrough in the British media market (primarily newspapers) in the 1960s. With his major success in the U.S. market in the 1980s, his company The News Corporation purchased Twentieth Century-Fox, which led to creation of the Fox television network. I mention this as background to an understanding of how market conditions tended to restrict the independent, critical views expressed in series such as *The Reagans*.

Textual Analyses of *The Reagans*

Framing of the Genre: Fact or Fiction

In examining *The Reagans*, I have randomly selected elements fitting into my discourse-analytical approach that deal with social issues, U.S. foreign policy, and military affairs. I will look more closely at how the boundary between fact and fiction has been used to frame the series so that it advances the Republican strategy of serving a right-wing agenda. Since analyzing all the sequences here is impossible, I will start by presenting a short overview.

The Reagans is organized around the relationship between Ronald and Nancy from the time they met until the end of his presidency.[3] The first episode states: "This film is a dramatic interpretation of events based on public sources. Some scenes and characters are presented as composites." In this way viewers are told that this is a semidocumentary containing some fictitious elements, and it thus fits into the category of docudrama, as mentioned earlier.

The opening scene takes place in the White House in 1987. Reagan's advisor enters the room. The president is sitting in his chair watching an old movie. The advisor is talking to Nancy in a worried voice. "We all think he should hire a criminal defense attorney." The reason is that "they [the Senate] are talking about impeachment." Nancy is upset. "He is not a criminal." The president is also upset. "Ask that lying bastard. That lying son of a gun Oliver North who gave the money to the Contras." In this way we are introduced to one of the major events in the series, the Iran-Contra scandal in which weapons were sold to Iran as part of a plan to release American hostages in Beirut and raise money to undermine the Sandinista government in Nicaragua through support of the armed force, the Contras.[4]

The roles of Nancy and Ronald Reagan are defined in this opening scene. The president's wife is talking to advisors while the president is sitting passively in his chair, looking old and tired. It's implied here that the responsibility of the Iran-Contra scandal can be ascribed personally to Oliver North and thus separated from the actual policy of the United States at the time. I will return to the United States' actual foreign policy later, but here the point has to be made that the framing of Ronald Reagan as unwittingly manipulated by Oliver North is highly problematic. Even though conservative pressure groups claimed the CBS decision to stop the series should be celebrated as "a tremendous night," they had little to fear if one looks more closely at the way the series depicts important historical events. It could be argued that starting the miniseries with a scene raising the most controversial issue of Reagan's presidency, and letting him off the hook at the very beginning of the movie (Nancy's remark that he is not a criminal) by placing the responsibility on "the lying bastard" Oliver North, means that the most difficult issue in the Reagan legacy is dealt with right away. This interpretation is strengthened by Reagan's answer to his advisor's suggestion to get a criminal lawyer. "Why would I need an attorney?" he asks. "You wouldn't need one, you would *want* one," responds the advisor. Reagan's innocence is again implied. If he were guilty he would of course *need* a lawyer. By presenting this in what we could call a legal discourse, the problematic facts around the support for the Contras are relegated to the background.

The historical implication of a possible impeachment (as was the threat) is underlined by Reagan's remark that "they got Nixon" and "now they think they can get me." The scene ends with a close-up of Reagan's face and his remark, "All I wanted to was to save those people—that was all I wanted." That this "saving" included burning down farms, killing doctors and health workers, raping nurses and nuns on the border between Nicaragua and Honduras, and killing more than 3,000 innocent people (Burke 1988), actions authorized by the president himself, is not mentioned.[5] Also unstated is the fact that the policy of the U.S. government to undermine the legal and lawfully elected Sandinista regime in Nicaragua and, *inter alia*, to mine the harbors, was condemned by the International Court of Justice in The Hague as a violation of international law (Holleman and Love 1988). In his acceptance speech for the Nobel Prize for literature in 2005, Harold Pinter reminds us how Ronald Reagan's personal commitment to the Contras portrayed them. "The Contras are the moral equivalent of our Founding Fathers" (Pinter 2005).

Ronald Meets Nancy

After the opening sequence, the story quickly flashes back to 1949, when Ronald first meets the actress Nancy Davis. At the time Reagan is President of the Screen Actors Guild. Nancy is obviously attracted to Reagan from the very beginning, and, from this point, the series follows the Reagans as a couple—his start as a B-movie star; his career as a television host; his political career first as governor of California; and then on to the White House.

A concerned film studio boss had introduced Nancy to Ronald Reagan. She had been placed on a list of communists in the *Hollywood Reporter*, although she was very conservative and "republican." Here another theme is introduced, although never explicitly: Reagan's role in the anti-communist campaign organized by Senator Joe McCarthy. How a number of actors and other workers in the film industry lost their jobs and were blacklisted for suspected communist sympathies is well documented. Many were falsely accused, and many careers and lives were ruined (Doherty 2003). Ronald Reagan's role in this as President of the Screen Actors Guild is also well documented, including his testimony before the House Un-American Activities Committee in 1947.

It turned out that Nancy had the same name as another, more controversial, actor (although the only controversial thing she appears to have done was to sign a petition against blacklisting, itself seemingly a reason to be blacklisted). In the series, however, the issue of blacklists and the witch-hunt for dissidents is not framed as the problem. Nor is the fact that Nancy's case and many others demonstrate the lack of security and legality in the process. On the contrary, here we meet Ronald Reagan, who uses his position as head of the union and becomes the noble knight who saves Nancy from an embarrassing situation. But this, of course, is after Ronald has received a reassuring answer to his question of whether she *actually was* a communist sympathizer. In the process, Ronald asks Nancy out to dinner. He suggests that she change her name to avoid confusion. She assures him that she comes from a family with a father who "hates the reds." Reagan admits to being a Democrat but is frustrated because the party doesn't seem to "get it"—that is, the Democrats don't recognize that "Moscow is about to take over the world." In this context, the blacklisting and the witch-hunt for radicals and trade-union activists is not defined as a problem. The only problem seems to be: who is "soft" on the left? How the whole process of McCarthyism undermined American democracy and freedom of expression and created what Kovel has labeled "the dynamics of inquisition" (Kovel 1994, 123) has been clearly documented. But this atmosphere of fear and paranoia is not at all identified as a problem in the series. This passage in the film instead clears the ground for Reagan's switch from the Democrats to the Republicans later in the miniseries, since the Democrats are quite obviously too radical for a "patriot" like Ronald Reagan.

In his courtship of Nancy, Reagan is portrayed as closed and almost unable to talk about his feelings. Nancy threatens to move to New York but is persuaded by Ronald to stay. They share secrets eventually; Ronald admits his father was a drunk, and Nancy confesses that her father is not her real father—and that she's pregnant.

The film now takes a leap to 1953. Ronald and Nancy are married. Nancy is frustrated at being home with a crying and sobbing Patti, and Reagan's agent persuades him to go into television to avoid a new series of B-movies. It turns out that at first Reagan is skeptical about this new medium. Behind the scenes, Nancy arranges a weekend visit to her parents' home in Arizona so that Barry Goldwater, the presidential candidate for the Republican Party, and Ronald can meet. Goldwater is first seen delivering a hate-filled speech against trade unions. Anti-union rhetoric is one of the obvious features in *The Reagans*; even though, according to Goldwater, workers are supposedly living in a free country, "Hoffa can force [them] to join trade unions and pay dues in order to get a job." But Ronald Reagan replies that "big government" is worse than the union. As he so elegantly puts it, the United States is on the way to socialism, and the welfare state is "doing just as much harm to our way of life as the communists." Astonished, Goldwater replies, "Are you sure you're a Democrat?"

To put this anti-union rhetoric into perspective, we can draw upon the work of Chad Raphael who, in the essay "The Political Economics of Reali-TV," makes a distinction between what he calls "trash" television (including "crime time," "on-scene shows" such as *Who Wants To Be a Millionaire?*, and "tabloid television," with series such as *Survivor*) on the one hand, and made-for-television docudramas such as *The Reagans* on the other. The reason for the growth in the first category, trash television, is the huge rise in production costs in the 1990s of between 8 percent and 10 percent a year. Companies found themselves losing money on costly drama series and news production.

During this period CBS, for example, cut 30 percent of its administrative staff and 10 percent of its news division. In this way, the major broadcasters bypassed union labor and left most of the production to companies with cheap, unorganized labor.

In the 1980s and early 1990s, several strikes took place in the major trade unions in the film and television industry, including that of the American Federation of Television and Radio Artists (AFTRA). The industry responded by fighting back against the proposed demands, and many workers had to accept cutbacks in wages. Thereafter unions were increasingly bypassed, and contracts were given to smaller companies. This increase in labor unrest was, according to Raphael, both a response to and a motivating force in breaking the power of unions (Raphael 2004). To my mind, there could be a connection between the portrayal of trade-union issues in *The Reagans* and the way in which production companies today are involved in union-busting. Ronald Reagan's leadership of the Screen Actors Guild, as presented in the series, is a one-man show. We never see any results based on collective action by that union, nor any issue presented in what could be called a "labor discourse." All we meet is the "charming" Reagan dealing with his personal contacts in the industry on behalf of individually favored members.

Ready for the Republicans

After taking part in speaking tours promoting the "new medium" (television) at the beginning of the 1960s, Ronald is eventually picked up by the Republican Party. He is introduced to the financial elite of California. At a fancy dinner party, the women are seated at a table by themselves talking about how to ship off their kids to boarding school so that they can enjoy the good life. When they hear that Nancy is pregnant again, they offer her free designer maternity clothes—after all, she is Ronald Reagan's wife. Later, the Reagans are chatting at their kitchen table. Ronald is summing up the evening. "I liked those people tonight—they were really nice, don't you think, Nancy?" And rich.... "I have never seen so many rich people in one place.... Texaco, Shell, Mobil Oil—and they don't even look tired. They look like they spend all their time on vacation." The amazing thing about this sequence is that it's so forthright about the relationship between money and politics. The message to Nancy from the Republican Party officials in the dark corner at cocktail parties is clear: if you turn him into a Republican candidate, we will take care of you financially.

It turns out that the above-mentioned dinner party is meant to persuade Ronald to campaign for a seat in the U.S. Senate. Nancy is trying to talk him into it. Ronald reluctantly accepts after his agent is threatened with legal action for breaking antitrust legislation by mixing television commercials and entertainment programs, thus misusing his monopolistic position in the television market. Ronald admits that his personal preference would be to spend more time at the ranch because he is feeling "old and tired." But Nancy has other plans.

Political Career

The Reagans fast-forwards to the year 1963, with historical footage from President John F. Kennedy's funeral. Ronald's son Mike (from his first marriage) turns up after quitting school, and it's only at this stage that the other children learn they have a brother and sister from Ronald's previous marriage (openness is obviously not this family's strong suit). It upsets daughter Patti and contributes to the further souring of the mother-daughter relationship. A sub-theme in this conflict is Nancy's abuse of pills and Patti's stealing some of them for her own use. As mentioned above, this was one of the ethical problems dealt with by Patti in her letter to *Time* magazine.

During Barry Goldwater's 1964 presidential campaign, Ronald Reagan— with great fanfare—crosses over to the Republican Party. Backstage, party organizers are planning the race for governor of California and considering Reagan as a possible candidate. However, there is some doubt. "Can we run an actor for governor?" one of the advisors wonders. They all agree that Ronald is a "genius" at publicity, so why not go for it? The advisors in the Republican Party are the first to understand the potential power of the "television effect." Since voters have seen Ronald in their kitchens, living rooms, and bedrooms for years—through commercials—they will regard him as part of their lives. They will "know" him. This, in combination with his smooth rhetoric, will result in a political hit, advisors believe. The process of shaping Reagan into a top political figure begins.

One of the authentic clips in the film proves that Reagan also met resistance. Incumbent California Governor Pat Brown thinks he can use Reagan's background as an actor against him. After showing a film clip, Brown says, "One last thing. I am running against an actor. Remember who shot Abraham Lincoln." What Pat Brown didn't understand was that publicity was exactly the point of using the celebrity status of an actor to promote a campaign (Giglio 2005).

Other actors were to follow Reagan's example and capitalize politically on their fame, and in that respect, Reagan started a trend of which Arnold Schwarzenegger is merely the most recent example (Giglio 2005; Indiana

2005). In 2004, Schwarzenegger made the transition from the screen to public office in announcing his candidacy for the office of governor of California— the very place where Ronald Reagan started *his* political career. Or is it correct to call it a transition? Can we see a trend in which actors are successful in politics *because* acting and media performance are more important than politics itself (Corner and Pels 2003)? The list of show-business-celebrities- turned-politician is growing: Jerry Springer, the famous talk-show host, became mayor of Cincinnati in 1977; Clint Eastwood became mayor of Carmel, California, in 1986; Sonny Bono became mayor of Palm Springs and a California congressman, and television wrestler Jesse Ventura became gover- nor of Minnesota in 1998 (Ottosen 2004). It should be noted here that this actor-politician phenomenon is also quite common in India, where Bollywood has produced several politicians. It is a global, not just an American, phe- nomenon.

Framing Dissidence and Opposition

I have already made a point of the fact that the miniseries so openly promotes the views and lifestyle of the "rich and beautiful": to bring in Stuart Hall's hegemonic perspective, we could say that the discourse of the rich and beautiful is portrayed as a normal way of life. As Ernest Giglio reflects in his book *Here's Looking at You: Hollywood Film and Politics*, "What is truly alarming, however, is that Hollywood money gains the industry an unequal amount of access and an inordinate amount of influence while it blurs the line between public office and celebrity status" (Giglio 2005, 9). In striking contrast to this, there is no realistic and serious portrayal in *The Reagans* of dissident or progressive alternatives. We meet some hippie-like activists who try to interrupt a meeting during Reagan's campaign for governor, but we never hear any of their arguments or even understand what they are actually protesting against. What we do see is Reagan's tough response to the activists: "When I become your governor the first thing I'm going to do is to clean up the mess at our college campuses."

The next time we meet the opposition is during Reagan's time as gover- nor. The year is 1967, and authentic film clips from Vietnam leave no doubt about the background of the demonstration we are about to see. But again we hear no articulate arguments against the war—just a hippie mob screaming and shouting. The posters and slogans we see say "pig" and "fascist." There is no real representation of what we might call the "peace-movement discourse" or presentation of any arguments as they might have been advanced by the anti- war movement. We never learn why an increasing number of Americans at the time began to oppose the Vietnam War. (This was the beginning of 1968, when the war escalated and the United States prepared for the Tet Offensive. U.S. casualties increased, and protests against this illegal and undeclared war increased on a global scale (Page 1996, 22–23). But the footage in the miniseries contains nothing about the war itself. Instead we see a demonstration that is alleged to take place at the University of California, Berkeley. Governor Ronald Reagan is leaving a campus building with a look of resolve on his face. The mob is screaming and yelling without a clear message other than "fascist" claims against Reagan. He stops to give a message to the crowd: "I just gave the trustees at the university their notice. People are sick and tired of your walkouts." We hear a demonstrator shout, "Go back to Hollywood!," and this reduces the protest to a personal issue between the governor and the crowd. Reagan's response is tough: "The people put me here. I don't know what trust you are on, but you're gonna obey the rules or leave now."

Not a word about bombing, napalm, massacres, civilian casualties, or U.S. economic interests in Southeast Asia. As Anthony Easthope has noted, this way of dealing with the Vietnam War follows the pattern of many Hollywood movies:

> This inherited structure cannot cope with the Vietnam War. Doubt and uncertainty are encountered on every score—about napalming the enemy, trusting the leadership, unifying the command, the possibility or even value of victory. As the traditional genre falls into crisis, traditional Hollywood realism fails along with it. (Easthope 1988, 32)

This way of dealing with difficult historical events has a purpose, according to Easthope. "The Vietnam films are not mirrors but lamps. They do not passively reflect historical events; rather they are textual interventions, acts of signifying practice that *rework* on their own terms the ideologies they reproduce" (33). Easthope's point that the framing of the Vietnam War in many Hollywood productions avoids controversial issues certainly goes for *The Reagans* as well. The impact this war had on the American and global public is represented by an inarticulate mob incapable of producing any sympathy for its cause. Instead of entering into the peace movement discourse, we are presented with a vulgar representation of it.

The Dysfunctional Family

As Ronald Reagan takes up office as the governor of California, Nancy has her own problems. She's not at all satisfied with the governor's residence. (Nor will she be satisfied as First Lady with the White House.) She complains while showing her parents around, and her posh mother wrinkles her nose: "What happened to executive privilege?"

Drawing a parallel with how, as First Lady, Jacqueline Kennedy secured funding to redecorate the White House, Nancy approaches her rich friends to get them to sponsor a new home for the Reagans. The press picks up the story, and she is labeled "Fancy Nancy." And the trouble with the journalists doesn't stop there. Little Ron is rude to a reporter during an interview with Nancy and is ballet dancing in the living room—not at all living up to his father's expectation of a masculine son. Both Ron and his older sister Patti are growing up and distancing themselves from both their father's views and his political career. Patti is sent away to boarding school against her will and watches her parents bask in the limelight from a distance. She enters into a relationship with a rock musician and decides to "tie up her tubes" to avoid having children growing up as miserable as she is. After several failed relationships and a nervous breakdown, she comes home crying, and Nancy finally shows a human side, hugging her daughter and saying she can stay as long as she likes. Three days is enough, but this episode offers the rare portrayal of Nancy as a mother with empathy for her children. In contrast, Mike and Maureen, Ronald's two children from his first marriage, are kept at arm's length, although Mike is the most supportive of his father's politics. (Patti and Ron openly disapprove of their father's policies and the very idea of having a father as president.) Disappointed by the lack of support from his children, Ronald tells himself, "I can do a lot for America." Even as the First Family, after Ronald is finally elected president in 1980, the Reagans are constantly quarrelling. Even when Ronald survives the John Hinckley assassination attempt, they go on quarrelling, and Patti remarks: "What is it with this family? Not even a bullet can bring us together."

Ron, obviously Nancy's favorite, is pursuing a career as a ballet dancer. Ronald's homophobia is reflected throughout the series in the way in which the father-son relationship is presented. After Ron leaves a message on the telephone that he has moved in with a woman, Nancy is upset because she hadn't been informed, while Ronald sighs, "At least we now know he's not gay." After Ron's breakthrough as a ballet dancer, the first family goes backstage, and the president embarrasses his son by pointing out how "strong" he has always been—and good at (masculine) sports like football and basketball. He adds (almost speaking to himself), "Fred Astaire, Gene Kelly, nothing wrong with them either, strong...." Having read the film's epilogue (referred to at the end of this essay), I believe its portrayal of Ronald Reagan's homophobia must be seen in the light of his inability to take action to prevent the AIDS epidemic from exploding. It is, in fact, the only part in the series where Nancy gets any credit for coping with the problem. When it becomes clear that one of her advisors died from the disease, she urges the president to do something about it. "You're the president of the United States. If you don't talk about it, nobody will talk about it." Ronald chooses to close his eyes and turn around without responding. One wonders why more was not made of this, as it would have helped to make the series more balanced and convincing.

Ronald Reagan as a Loser—and Finally President

I now return to the series's depiction of Ronald Reagan's political career. Advisers in the Republican Party urge him to run against Richard Nixon in 1972. He loses the fight for the nomination and, when Nixon has to leave office after the Watergate scandal and Gerald Ford takes over and runs for office in 1976, Ronald is once again persuaded to fight for the nomination. This time, according to the miniseries, Nancy is strongly against it, as she doesn't want Ronald to seem a "loser." This is the one time her advice is ignored. A power struggle ensues between her and Reagan's consultants during the third attempt at nomination in the race against President Jimmy Carter in 1980. In this campaign an advisor, John Sears, sidetracks Reagan's closest friend and consultant of fifteen years, Mike Deaver. Sears tries to relegate Nancy to the sidelines and refuses to let her to go on the campaign tour with Ronald on the grounds that she distracts him. It ends with Ronald urging both Nancy and Mike Deaver to come back. Sears is kicked out. The moral is obvious: Ronald is a success when he has Nancy by his side.

The gender relationship in the marriage is worth a study in itself. Nancy is portrayed as the strong and manipulative one as evidenced, for example, by Patti's remark about the female version of Attila the Hun. In many ways she treats Ronald as a child, but she can also use tears and hysteria as weapons if everything else fails. "She even cries when the laundry is taken out," as Ronald sighs at one stage. And she gets her will most of the time. The construction of Nancy as the female counterpart to Ronald is an interesting case study of gender representation. Her interventions on his behalf ought, one would think, to feature her more sympathetically as a strong woman. But since she obviously breaks with the tradition of the silent housewife, she challenges the woman's role typical at that time and is portrayed basically as a "bitch." Television drama has never been the arena in which to put forward feminist ideas, so it is no surprise that she is constantly shown in the role of bitch; this also fits well into the stereotypes of other television dramas (Ruoho 1993).

Ronald Reagan and PR

Ronald Reagan was the first presidential candidate to systematically use PR agencies to ensure he got his message across to the public. Or, to be more specific, according to Noam Chomsky, "When we speak of the policies of the Reagan Administration, then, we are not referring to the figure set up to front for them by an administration whose major strength was in public relations" (Chomsky 1991, 74). If we regard the presentation of Reagan in the context of Chomsky's analysis of Reagan as a tool, the miniseries actually offers some insight, but mainly through the positive asides by his advisors regarding Reagan's communicative skills. We are offered little information about the systematic use of PR firms and commercial marketing in Ronald Reagan's campaign of 1980, which set new standards for PR in political campaigns and dramatically increased the commercialization of politics (Schiller 1992).

The miniseries offers small glimpses of Reagan's charm as he is playing around in the studio and acting out his "role" in front of the camera with a joke before a live broadcast to the nation. In Chomsky's analysis of Reagan's role as an actor in the White House, things are put into a more realistic context:

> Reagan's duty was to smile, to read from the teleprompter in a pleasant voice, tell a few jokes, and keep the audience properly bemused. His only qualification for the presidency was that he knew how to read the lines written for him by the rich folk, who pay well for the services. Reagan had been doing that for years. He seemed to perform to the satisfaction of the paymasters, and to enjoy the experience. By all accounts, he spent many pleasant days enjoying the pomp and trappings of power.... It is not really his business if the bosses left mounds of mutilated corpses in death squad dumping grounds in El Salvador or hundreds of thousands of homeless in the streets. One does not blame an actor for the content of the words that come from his mouth. (Chomsky 1991, 74)

Ronald Reagan as the "Winner" of the Cold War

President Dwight D. Eisenhower became famous for his speech on the "military-industrial complex" as he was leaving the White House at the end of his presidential term. His message was, in short, that an alliance between the arms industry, the armed forces, and influential segments of the political elite represented a threat to democracy that he was unable to control as president.[6]

This frank and open statement has been supported by analyses in the field of peace research and political science to verify the mechanisms at work in the arms race and military spending on a global scale (Gleditsch and Njølstad 1991). Several theories have been tested to explain the huge resources spent on development of new weapons systems. Part of this explanation is linked to mechanisms described by Eisenhower, but there is no doubt that rivalry with the Soviet Union was also an important component in the arms race during the Cold War. Thus the periods after the launch of Sputnik in 1957 and after the Soviet invasion of Afghanistan in 1979 represent periods of huge increases in U.S. military spending (Brauch 1990, 194–195). One can discuss the importance of such external and/or internal factors as mechanisms in the arms race, but the miniseries offers little insight into these issues.

Ronald Reagan himself became famous for his contribution to the arms race by the launching of his so-called Star Wars program. This is framed in the series as a "crazy idea" Ronald Reagan adopted after watching an old science-fiction movie in which warfare in outer space was an important component. Such a simplification and falsification of the mechanisms behind the Star Wars program is truly astonishing, and the portrayal of this important event during Ronald Reagan's presidency in the miniseries is remarkable in the light of existing literature in this field. In his famous "Star Wars" speech of 23 March 1983, President Ronald Reagan called for a renewed effort to develop a ground- and space-based missile system in the context of what was later called the Strategic Defense Initiative (SDI). The idea, in short, was to make all existing generations of nuclear weapons unusable and to develop a new generation of nuclear weaponry as a shield in outer space. In the peace research community this was regarded as a dramatic break with the existing regimen to control the arms race. In the literature it is generally accepted as representing a new offensive weapons system that would increase the danger of a nuclear war and make negotiations between the superpowers more difficult (Lindkvist 1989, 98–99).

The SDI program also had dramatic consequences for the whole "military-industrial complex," to use Eisenhower's words, since it changed the direction of research. The amount of resources that were made available to computer science and telecommunications involved budget cuts that hurt research in other academic fields (Mosco 1993). During the Reagan presidency, the U.S. government approved the largest-ever annual funding for a new weapons program by granting the SDI program US$4.15 billion and through it the construction of a major antiballistic missile system with a budget of US$60 billion. It provided enormous financial benefits to companies like General Motors, which owns Hughes Aerospace; major software firms; and General Electric, the parent of the television company NBC. No wonder there has been little critical journalism addressing these issues in U.S. broadcasting (Mosco 1993, 58).

The mechanism behind the militarization of the civil research community is a related theme, never touched upon in the miniseries. But, as Vincent Mosco points out, there are techniques for forcing a reluctant civil sector in the direction of militarization. As one Pentagon official put it when asked about IBM's unwillingness to carry out research in areas the Pentagon deemed important, "Either IBM will decide that it will be good to do research in this [SDI] field and to have a capability in it for defense in the 1990s or it will not. If it does not, there will be many others who will…. If IBM does not see that, then in my opinion their market share will decline" (quoted in Mosco 1993, 58).

The Star Wars program created during Ronald Reagan's presidency was essential to "the new world order" introduced by Reagan's successor, George H. Bush. After the war in the Persian Gulf in 1991, which used the Patriot missile and other "smart" weaponry, the United States revived the idea that SDI could become a reality. As President Bush told the workers at the high-tech Raytheon Company, which manufactured the Patriot, "For years we've heard that anti-missile defense won't work. The shooting down of a ballistic missile is impossible, like trying to hit a bullet with a bullet. Some people called it impossible; you called it your job" (Cockburn 1991; qtd. in Mosco 1993). Critics have noted that these kinds of remarks by the president built further on the illusion created by the Pentagon and reinforced by an uncritical media, despite the fact that the Patriot, as tried out by Israeli air defense in the Persian Gulf War, failed in most cases to hit Iraqi Scud missiles and did more damage than good to Israel's defense (Nohrstedt and Ottosen 2001). Later, the concept of high-tech warfare was absorbed by the entertainment industry into movies and computer games, reinforcing illusions about the wonders of military solutions in addressing human conflicts (Mosco 1993, 57–59).

As peace researcher Håkan Wiberg puts it, the overall negative consequences of the arms race can be summarized thus:

> War: armaments increase the risk of war, whether by making their possessors more belligerent, more reckless, or more likely to become the targets of pre-emptive wars, or by making "war by accident" more probable.
>
> Waste: military expenditures constitute waste by detracting from the societal or global resources available for constructive purpose. Armaments are therefore inimical to welfare and development.
>
> Threat: highly armed states can use their military power as leverage in forcing other states to make concessions that are detrimental to their sovereignty, security, and welfare.
>
> Militarization: heavily armed states also tend to get militarized in various other ways, from economy and political system to national culture. (Wiberg 1990, 352–353)

An alternative way of interpreting Reagan's presidency along the lines Wiberg suggests here could be to ask how Reagan's introduction of SDI caused a greater risk of world war and compromised domestic development by using even more of his country's resources on arms instead of on social welfare and education—not to speak of the brutalization of popular culture by a whole series of films, computer games, and cartoons glorifying wars and arms (Roach 1993). Popular culture would probably have glorified war even without Reagan's presidency, but I will argue that the miniseries fits well into a pattern in popular culture that avoids facing the problematic aspects of the militarization of society.

In *The Reagans* we are told that it was Ronald Reagan's triumph to open direct talks with Mikhail Gorbachev and discuss cuts in existing nuclear weapons. Reagan's plan of expanding the arms race into outer space is mentioned in a personal dialogue between the two presidents. Gorbachev urges him to stop the idea, but Reagan's response is, "Why don't you believe me when I say all I want is a shield?" Reagan refused to go into real talks about SDI in the top-level meeting with Gorbachev, starting the process that ended with the Intermediate Range Nuclear Forces Treaty (INF) agreement in 1987 and the Strategic Arms Reduction Treaty (START) agreement in 1991, reducing the number of traditional nuclear weapons. These agreements, and the fall of the Berlin Wall in 1989, are credited to Ronald Reagan in the miniseries—"You won the Cold War!," as one his consultants shouts. Ronald Reagan personally gets the credit for putting an end to the "Evil Empire" (as he called the Soviet Union on a number of occasions—an expression that Nancy in the series urges him to stop using because it sounds "silly"). Other explanations debated by historians for the breakup of the Soviet Union, such as the whole system rotting from within, are ignored.

One critical feature of the series is Ronald Reagan lying during discussions with Soviet delegates about having helped liberate Nazi concentration camps in Europe during the Second World War. We see the astonished consultants looking at each other, one mentioning the fact that Reagan had not left the United States during the war. Reagan is also famous for remarking that "facts are stupid things," which also puts his transition from acting to politics into perspective (Indiana 2005).

The Portrayal of the Bombing of Libya

Ronald Reagan's bombing of Libya in 1986 is introduced in the miniseries by real footage of the event. The dramatization is built around Ronald Reagan's televised speech starting with the remark, "Today Americans can stand tall."

This sequence, lasting only twenty-four seconds, also includes a passage showing four unidentified men standing in front of a television screen, one of them passing the remark, "You can't stop terrorism by killing 150 innocent civilians." My interpretation is that this short remark is meant to represent some kind of opposition (a human-rights group?) to this military action. But again we see potentially dissident people only as voices, their actual arguments unexplored. Despite the footage from Tripoli, the whole sequence makes no sense at all for those who are not familiar with the history of the event. We learn from Reagan's television speech that the act was a punishment for Libya's support for terrorism in Europe, but those are all the details we get.

The context of the bombing, as only an informed viewer would know, was the alleged Libyan connection to the 1988 bombing of Pan Am flight 103 over Scotland. One Libyan was later sentenced in connection with the bombing, and Muammar Gaddafi agreed to pay compensation to the victims. The problem for the Reagan Administration was not opposition to terrorism *per se*, but the fact that Gaddafi supported terrorists other than those supported by Reagan. Reagan's support for the terrorism of the Nicaraguan Contras, his support for UNITA in Angola and for Cuban exiles in Miami, are all examples of his tolerance of terrorist acts affecting innocent civilians (Blum 2001, 153). The only acts of terrorism supported both by Libya and the United States were those of the Moujahedeen in Afghanistan who, as we now know, included Osama bin Laden.

What the miniseries failed to inform the viewers was that the American bombing of Libya in April 1986 was a violation of international law and killed Gaddafi's own daughter and injured seven of his other children and his wife, all of whom were hospitalized. Later, 340 claimants who had been injured in the bombing or whose relatives had been hurt or killed filed suit against the White House and the Department of Defense under the Foreign Claims Act, although none of the claims got anywhere in the American judicial system (Blum 2001, 230).

Let's draw a parallel with the failed possible attack on the White House on September 11. What if it had killed or injured one or more of the president's family? Would that point have been missed in a later dramatization of the event?

The Missing Invasion of Grenada

Since the producers of this series had decided to spend a few moments on American military adventures during the Reagan presidency, it's remarkable that they did not mention the 1983 attacks in Lebanon by pro-Palestinian groups, which killed hundreds of U.S. soldiers, and the U.S. invasion of Grenada two days later. The invasion of Grenada was the first major military invasion by U.S. forces since the Vietnam War. In this small state in the Caribbean with only 110,000 inhabitants, the Pentagon took advantage of the unstable situation after the killing of Grenada's charismatic leader Maurice Bishop, who had taken power in a coup in 1979. Washington was driven by the fear of "another Cuba" in its backyard and saw the radical regime as an ally of the Soviet Union and Cuba. The Reagan Administration had been involved in several destabilization efforts before the obviously illegal invasion of 1983, which resulted in 135 U.S. soldiers being killed or wounded, while 400 Grenadians died. The invasion forces illegally confiscated documents from government offices in order to find "a smoking gun" regarding the alleged link between the Grenadian government and the Soviet and Cuban regimes, and evidence of alleged attempts by the Soviets to take over the island—as was stated in the Pentagon's propaganda and information campaign defending the occupation. No evidence for such plans was found, and CIA director William Casey later had to admit that there was no "real find" (quoted by Blum 2001, 212).

Though the miniseries' producers documented some of the military adventures of the Reagan era, it is remarkable that they picked the limited, though serious-enough, bombing of Libya, while the full-scale invasion of Grenada was completely ignored.

The Iran-Contra Affair Revisited

As has already been mentioned, *The Reagans* began with a scene from the Iran-Contra affair. The last part of the series is also devoted to this dramatic episode that partly ruined Reagan's reputation as president. Little light is shed on the actual consequences of Reagan's support for the Contras and the undermining of the legal Sandinista government in Nicaragua. The focus in the series is on the political consequences of the investigation by the Tower Commission (named after Senator John G. Tower). Pressured by the evidence that Reagan was indeed responsible for "ruining our foreign policy and making us a laughing stock in the Middle East," as Tower puts it in a personal confrontation with the president, Ronald Reagan is portrayed as confused and suffering memory loss—perhaps from Alzheimer's. Only after heavy pressure from Nancy and his advisors is he willing to speak to the nation on television, taking responsibility for the affair to avoid impeachment. And so the presidency of Ronald Reagan comes to an end with a sentimental farewell to White House staff.

In an epilogue to the film, some remarks are added. The most interesting is a link between the Iran-Contra affair and later developments in Iraq: "In 1984, during the Iran-Iraq war, the Reagan Administration removed Iraq from its list of terrorist nations and aided Saddam Hussein's military buildup." Also, Reagan's lack of commitment to the fight against AIDS is underscored with the words, "Today in the United States 890,000 people live with the AIDS virus. Over 500,000 have died from the disease, including 150,000 during the Reagan Administration."

This leads to the obvious question: Why were these simple facts and perspectives not incorporated more explicitly into the script and the movie itself? John Caughie argues that the format of television drama has obvious limitations in dealing with factual matters:

> Given this importance, the lack of rigorous attention to television drama itself and to the television play is surprising. At a formal level, there are questions of the mechanisms of the look and the subject of television drama which have barely begun to be asked, questions which are important not only for television itself, bringing to it work which has been done in film, but also for theory; television, in its different specificity, offers a resistance to universalized theories of representation, and to essentialisms of vision. (Caughie 1981, 328)

As the series comes to a close, Ronald and Nancy Reagan are leaving the White House. Reagan is suffering from Alzheimer's, and once again I will return to Patti's letter to *Time*, which describes a family now at peace with itself—a fact that is missing from the series. She admits that there were many problems in the past, but she criticizes the producers for not describing the family unity that emerged upon Ronald Reagan's death:

> We will continue to cherish the fact that we walked away from our old battlegrounds and discovered how much better peace feels. We will look at each other through the clear glass of the present, not the mud-spatter of the past. What a pity the producers missed out on that part of the story. (quoted by Davis 2003)

I will not argue with Patti's version of this newfound unity on Reagan's deathbed. It is clear that on the political side the miniseries reveals a still-existing split in the family, including Ron's public support for many progressive causes including opposition to President George W. Bush during the presidential campaign of 2004. On the other hand, the American public is regularly exposed to the ultra-right rhetoric of Michael in his role as talk-show host.

Conclusion

Returning to the discourse-analytical approach presented at the beginning of this chapter, I argue that global and military issues and the left wing, as well as Democrats, are seen in *The Reagans* in terms of the Republican discourse shared by the military-industrial complex. The miniseries raises great concern that drama series like this are writing history for new generations in a manner that reduces global conflict to fit into Ronald Reagan's own understanding of himself as—"winner of the Cold War"—a notion probably shared by most Americans. Alternative discourses such as that emanating from the peace movement and the left are almost invisible. In the few places where dissident voices are heard, they are framed as caricatures rather than serious alternatives, since their actual arguments are never presented.

After analyzing the series and following the public debate before and after the series, the biggest mystery to me is why right-wing circles in the United States were so concerned about its impact. Even the few examples of criticism, such as Reagan's inability to face the problems of AIDS and the strong influence Nancy had on his daily routines and politics, do not in any way damage the overall image of Ronald Reagan as the winner of the Cold War.

We now have copious documentation regarding how PR firms and the Pentagon have strategized to justify U.S. military interventions in Grenada, Panama, Iraq in 1991, Somalia in 1992, Yugoslavia in 1999, and Iraq in 2003 (Ottosen 1994; Nohrstedt and Ottosen 2001, 2004, 2005). The most disturbing thing about *The Reagans* as a miniseries is that it makes no attempt to deal with issues such as propaganda and PR in modern warfare. The series itself fits well into a propagandistic media strategy designed to glorify the American quest for global hegemony, rather than presenting historical facts dealing with the arms race, the Cold War, real wars, and global issues in a more comprehensive manner. The series is dominated by the discourse of the military-industrial complex, while alternative discourses are marginalized and relegated to the shadows.

To my mind, the series draws attention to the problems expressed by former President Eisenhower. The military-industrial complex is setting the agenda for public debate as well as public spending. The real problems created on the global scene with the sole remaining superpower—the United States—ignoring international bodies like the United Nations and the International Court of Justice in The Hague, are exemplified by the Iran-Contra scandal. To an even greater extent, this problem has become clear under the administration of George W. Bush with the invasion of Iraq and the implementation of the so-called Bush Doctrine.[7] The way in which many "real" wars are dealt with in fiction, movies, and other Hollywood productions represents a steady flow of propaganda that has little to do with the real history that should, in my view, be the subject of television documentary. I doubt it will be produced in Hollywood or broadcast by a major commercial television station.

Productions of drama series like *The Reagans* touches on ethical dilemmas dealing with real persons. CBS has never satisfactorily explained why it dropped the series. I can accept that ethical issues, linked to the objections from the family, must be taken seriously, but at the same time this must also be discussed within the framework of freedom of expression. Public figures and politicians have chosen the public arena and must expect to have some public discussion of their personal lives when it is relevant to their positions. Some of these dilemmas, dealt with by Patti Davis in her letter to *Time*, raise important issues for filmmakers and should be debated by them when films and series based on stories of real people are produced.

Notes

* Thanks to Gunn Bjørnsen, Elisabeth Eide, Berit von der Lippe, Stig Arne Nohrstedt, Toby Miller, and Kristina Riegert for useful comments on an earlier draft. Thanks also to Monica Seeber for language editing.

1 Reagan was still alive when the series was produced and broadcast.

2 *Dagens Næringsliv*, 13 September 2002.

3 The following subtitles are included in *The Reagans*: 1. Main Titles; 2. Meeting Nancy; 3. 77 Lives; 4. Reason to Stay; 5. Pregnancy and Proposal; 6. Turning Republican; 7. Family Ties; 8. Backroom Deals; 9. Running for Governor; 10. Leave to Deaver; 11. Not His Time; 12. The Offspring; 13. Playing Spoiler; 14. A New Campaign; 15. Mommy to the Rescue; 16. Projected Winner; 17. Under New Management; 18. A Couple of Ham Actors; 19. Assassination Attempt; 20. On Schedule; 21. Part of God's Plan; 22. Second Hand Clothes; 23. Confronting AIDS; 24. Re-election Time; 25. Damage Control; 26. Forgetfulness; 27. Arms for Hostages; 28. Iran-Contra Affair; 29. Ample Evidence; 30. Saying Good-Bye; 31. Epilogue/End Credits.

4 The operation was led by Lt. Col. Oliver North, who appears several times in the miniseries. For documentation of the role of Oliver North see Holleman and Love 1988.

5 On 9 March 1981, on the recommendation of CIA Director William Casey, President Ronald Reagan issued a formal presidential finding authorizing covert CIA activities against the Nicaraguan government (Holleman and Love 1988).

6 In the speech, Eisenhower said, *inter alia*, "...now we can no longer risk emergency improvisation of national defense; we have been compelled to create a permanent armaments industry of vast proportions. Added to this, three and a half million men and women are directly engaged in the defense establishment. We annually spend on military security more than the net income of all United States corporations. This conjunction of an immense military establishment and a large arms industry is new in the American experience. The total influence—economic, political, even spiritual—is felt in every city, every State house, every office of the Federal government. We recognize the imperative need for this development. Yet we must not fail to comprehend its grave implications. Our toil, resources and livelihood are all involved; so is the very structure of our society" (Eisenhower 1960).

7 The Bush Doctrine was announced in his State of the Union address of January 2003, with three main strands: the concept of "pre-emptive war"; regime change in hostile countries housing potential terrorists; and aggressive promotion of U.S.-style democracy.

References

Allan, Stuart, and Zelizer, Barbie, eds. 2004. *Reporting War. Journalism in Wartime.* London and New York: Routledge.

AP (Associated Press). 2001. "Pentagon Provides for Hollywood." (Unsigned news story published 29 May 2001.)

Bennett, Tony, et al., eds. 1981. *Popular Television and Film.* London: BFI Publishing/The Open

University.

Blum, William. 2001. *Rogue State. A Guide to the World's Only Superpower.* London: Zed Books.

Brauch, Hans Günther. 1990. "Weapons Innovation and U.S. Strategic Weapons Systems: Learning from Case Studies." In *Arms Race: Technological and Political Dynamics*, edited by Nils Petter Gleditsch and Olav Njølstad. London: Sage.

Burke, Al. 1988. *Misery in the Name of Freedom: The United States in Nicaragua 1909–1988.* Rolling Bay: Sea Otter Press.

Caughie, John. 1981. "Progressive Television and Documentary Drama." In *Popular Television and Film*, edited by Tony Bennett et al. London: BFI Publishing/The Open University.

Chomsky, Noam. 1991. *Deterring Democracy.* New York: Hill and Wang.

Cockburn, A. 1991. "Beat the Devil." *The Nation*, 8 July, pp. 42–43.

Corner, John, and Pels, Dick. 2003. *Media and the Restyling of Politics: Consumerism, Celebrity and Cynicism.* London: Sage.

Dahl, Hans Fredrik. 2004. *Mediehistorie. Historisk metode i mediefaget.* Oslo: N.W. Damm & Sønn.

Davis, Patti 2003. "The Reagans – from one of them." Letter posted to *Time*, Tuesday, 4 November. http://www.time.com/time/nation/article/0,8599,536971,00.html (accessed 21 July 2006).

Doherty, Thomas. 2003. *Cold War, Cool Medium: Television, MacCarthyism and American Culture.* New York: Columbia University Press.

Easthope, Antony. 1988. "Realism and Its Subversion: Hollywood and Vietnam." In *Tell Me Lies About Vietnam*, edited by Alf Louvre and Jeffrey Walsh. Milton Keynes: Open University Press.

Eisenhower, Dwight D. 1960. Military-Industrial Complex Speech. *Public Papers of the President.*

Fairclough, Norman. 1995. *Critical Discourse Analysis.* London: Longmans.

Garron, Barry. 2003. *"The Reagans." The Hollywood Reporter.*com, 1 December.

Giglio, Ernest. 2005. *Here's Looking at You: Hollywood, Film and Politics.* 2nd ed. New York: Peter Lang.

Gleditsch, Nils Petter, and Njølstad, Olav, eds. 1990. *Arms Race: Technological and Political Dynamics.* London: Sage.

Grossberg, Lawrence. 1996. "History, Politics and Postmodernism: Stuart Hall and Cultural Studies." In *Stuart Hall: Critical Dialogs in Cultural Studies*, edited by David Morley and Kuan-Hsing Chen. New York/London: Routledge.

Gunn, Benn. 1999. "Pentagon Runs Hollywood." Translation from Swedish newspaper *Hallandsposten.* http://www.illumanati-news.com/pentagon-hollywood.htm.

Hall, Stuart. 1981. "Notes on Deconstructing 'the Popular.'" In *People's History and Socialist Theory*, edited by R. Samuel. Boston: Routledge and Kegan Paul.

——. 1984. "The Cultural Gap." *Marxism Today* 28 (January): 18–23.

Herman, Edward S., and McChesney, Robert W. 1997. *The Global Media: The New Missionaries of Global Capitalism.* London: Cassell.

Holleman, Edith, and Love, Andre. 1988. *Inside the Shadow Government. Declaration of Plaintiffs. Counsel Filed by the Christic Institute U.S. District Court.* Miami, FL, 31 March.

Indiana, Gary. 2005. *Schwarzenegger Syndrome. Politics and Celebrity in the Age of Contempt.* New York/London: The New Press.

Kovel, Joel. 1994. *Red Hunting in the Promised Land. Anticommunism and the Making of America.* New York: Basic Books.

Lindkvist, Kent. 1989. "Det strategiske försvarsinitiativet som teknik, politik och strategi." In *Farväl til avsckräckningen,* edited by Håkan Wiberg. Lund: Lund University Press.

Miller, Toby. 2003. *Spyscreen: Espionage on Film and TV from the 1930s to the 1960s.* New York: Oxford University Press.

———; Govil, Nitin; McMurria, John; and Maxwell, Richard. 2001. *Global Hollywood.* London: British Film Institute.

Mosco, Vincent. 1993. "Communication and Information Technology for War and Peace." In *Communication and Culture in War and Peace,* edited by Collen Roach. London and New York: Sage.

Nohrstedt, Stig A., and Ottosen, Rune, eds. 2001. *Journalism and the New World Order: Gulf War and National News Discourses.* Gothenburg: Nordicom.

———, eds. 2004. *U.S. and the Others: Global Media Images on "The War on Terror."* Gothenburg: Nordicom.

———, eds. 2005. *Global War Local Views: Media Images of the War in Iraq.* Gothenburg: Nordicom.

Ottosen, Rune. 1994. *Mediestrategier og fiendebilder i internasjonale konflikter. Norske medier i skyggen av Pentagon.* Oslo: Universitetsforlaget.

———. 1997. "Rambo in Somalia? A Critical Look at Media Coverage of Operation Restore Hope." In *International News Monitoring,* edited by Kaarle Nordenstreng and Michael Griffin. Cresskill, NJ: Hampton Press.

———. 2004. "Fiction or News? A Quest for Multidisciplinary Research on the Entertainment Industry and Its Effects on Journalism." *Nordicom Information 2.*

Page, Caroline. 1996. *U.S. Official Propaganda During the Vietnam War, 1965–1973. The Limits of Persuasion.* London and New York: Leicester University Press.

Pinter, Harold. 2005. "The Nobel Lecture." *The Guardian,* 8 December.

Raphael, Chad. 2004. "The Political-Economic Origins of Reali-TV." In *Reality TV: The Remaking of Television Culture,* edited by S. Murray and L. Ouellette. New York: New York University Press.

Roach, Collen. 1993. *Communication and Culture in War and Peace.* London and New York: Sage.

Robb, David L. 2004. *Operation Hollywood: How the Pentagon Shapes and Censors the Movies.* New York: Prometheus Books.

Ruoho, Iris. 1993. "Gender on Television Screen and in Audience. Family Serial as a Technology of Gender." In *Nordisk forskning om kvinnor oc Medier,* edited by Ulla Carlsson. Gothenburg: Nordicom.

Schiller, Herbert. 1992. *The Ideology of International Communications.* New York: Institute for Media Analyses, Inc. Monograph Series 4.

Staiger, Janet (undated). *Docudrama.* The Museum of Broadcast Communications. http://www.museum.tv/archives/etv/D/htmlD/docudrama/docudrama.htm. (accessed 21 July 2006).

Suid, Lawrence 2002. *Guts and Glory: The Making of the American Military Image in Film.* Lexington: The University Press of Kentucky.

Tribe, Keith. 1981. "History and the Production of Memories." In *Popular Television and Film*, edited by Tony Bennett et al. London: BFI Publishing/The Open University.

Tuchman, Gaye. 1978. *Making News. A Study in the Construction of Reality.* London and New York: Free Press.

Wiberg, Håkan, ed. 1989. *Farväl til avsckräckningen.* Lund: Lund University Press.

——. 1990. "Arms Races—Why Worry?" In *Arms Race: Technological and Political Dynamics*, edited by Nils Petter Gleditsch and Olav Njølstad. London: Sage.

CHAPTER ELEVEN

Storytelling for a Nation: Spielberg, Memory, and the Narration of War

RIKKE SCHUBART

T his essay constitutes the first step in a larger study of history and memory in the postmodern American war movie. My first working hypothesis is this: Every film genre has *one* theme, *one* conflict, *one* essential question which, like a heart, pumps the blood through every vein and artery of the genre's body, something that pervades each and every film of the genre, precisely like the blood that runs through each and every part of our bodies. In the horror film this theme is man versus monster. In the western it is the conflict between wilderness and civilization. And in the war movie it is the relation between *history* and *nation*.

The hypothesis was born when I saw a pattern emerging from recent war movies. The pattern linked interviews with war veterans in Steven Spielberg's television series *Band of Brothers* (2001) to the use of archive footage in the war films *Courage Under Fire* (1996) and *Tears of the Sun* (2003), and to the use of factual information in the war films *Black Hawk Down* (2001) and *We Were Soldiers* (2002). Uniting these war narratives is the use of what I will call "historical pieces" below. I define "a historical piece" as an image, a scene, a text, or a non-diegetic sound-element that draws attention to itself as phenomenologically different from the fiction of which it is part and anchors the fiction to a historical reality presumably recognized as such by the audience. An example is Spielberg's film *Schindler's List* (1993), which ends with the text: "There are fewer than 4,000 Jews alive in Poland today. There are more than 6,000 descendants of the Schindler Jews." These words beg an audience to consider the film as a *historical* narrative—not necessarily an authentic and "true" narrative, but, still, a narrative with traces of the past. In this function the "historical piece" is related to "the trace," which Paul Ricoeur has discussed in *Time and Narrative* (1990). We shall return to the trace and Ricoeur.

The second working hypothesis is this: While the use of historical pieces in the war movie is not new, the extensive use of them and their central position in war narratives produced after 1991 is so striking as to constitute a new development within the genre.[1] For lack of a better term, I call the war films (and television series) produced after the fall of the Berlin Wall in 1989 and the dissolution of the Soviet Union and the Communist Party in 1991 "postmodern." My use of the term "postmodern" is not aesthetically motivated and does not draw on postmodernism as a distinct form or cultural movement. Rather, it relates to time (chronology) and ideology. The word may be misleading, but only partially so, as I also wish to acknowledge an ideological development, namely the fall of a distinct political and ideological Utopia (communism and the Soviet Union). A more precise term might thus have been "post-utopian" war narratives, since the period after 1989 is the fall of the Great Utopias of Eastern Europe. But then again, the war films work hard at re-inscribing a utopian aspect, which would also make "post-utopian" a misleading term. I shall, therefore, for lack of a better option, stick with "postmodern."

The return to history manifested in today's frequent use of historical pieces relates, I believe, to what Jean Baudrillard, speaking of the Gulf War, calls "a retreat of history" and a "collapse" (Baudrillard 1995, 70). I also believe the postmodern war movie can be seen as an attempt at repairing this collapse. We shall return to this at the end of this essay. For now, I wish to begin by going back to 1962 to John Ford's *The Man Who Shot Liberty Valance*.

Who Shot Liberty Valance?

Ford's film is a western, not a war film, but as I was writing this essay, *The Man Who Shot Liberty Valance* entered my mind and stubbornly refused to leave. I think this is because the film foregrounds three aspects that are important to my investigation: memory, storytelling, and Hollywood.

Two scenes especially commanded my attention. The first scene is toward the end of the film when Senator Ransom Stoddard (James Stewart) has finished telling his story about who shot the infamous gunman, Liberty Valance. Apart from the beginning and the end, the entire film consists of one long flashback, with Ransom remembering the past and telling it to the editor of the town's local newspaper, *The Shinbone Star*. Ransom did not shoot Liberty Valance, as the citizens of Shinbone have always believed, a belief that made them elect him as delegate to the Senate where he has had a political career. No, the shot was fired by a local cowboy, Tom Doniphon (John

Wayne), who refused to take sides in a conflict between the big ranchers and the small farmers, but felt obliged to help Ransom, whose unflinching belief in democracy made him face Liberty in a duel, but whose incapacity with a gun would surely have left him dead, had not Tom fired his rifle. Now, at the end of a lonely life, Tom lies dead in a simple wooden coffin, bereft of his boots, his gun, and his life-story. In fact, Ransom even walked away with Tom's girlfriend, Hallie (Vera Miles). The senator tells the coroner to return the missing boots and gun to the dead man, and the senator himself returns the missing life-story. When Ransom has finished, it is clear that the coffin contains not just a person or a cowboy, but *a metaphor* of the myth of how American democracy was born out of frontier violence and individual sacrifice.

At this point the editor of the newspaper tears up his notes. Will he print this story, these historical facts, in his newspaper? No. "This is the West, Sir. When legend becomes fact, print the legend." If "legend" stands for myth, then "fact" stands for historical facts. Ford's point is not, I think, that myth is better than fact but rather that it is in *the union of fact and myth* that we find the spirit of America: Gunman Liberty is the "frontier freedom" which must yield to civilization; Tom is the obsolete cowboy paving the way; and Ransom is the naive idealist guiding the nation toward democracy.

The second scene is from the middle of the film (before the duel with Liberty) when Ransom has settled down in Shinbone and is teaching the citizens of Shinbone to read, using Thomas Jefferson's *Declaration of Independence* from 1776 as text material. The small farmers are ignorant of their constitutional rights because they are illiterate and uneducated. In the classroom hang portraits of George Washington, America's first president, and Abraham Lincoln, who freed the slaves in 1863. The town's conflict with Liberty is thus narrated with Jefferson, Washington, and Lincoln watching from the sidelines. And the triangular conflict among attorney Ransom, gunman Liberty, and cowboy Tom is reflected in a national struggle for civilization and democracy. The local and individual story—that of the three men—reflects the national history of establishing the United States as a democracy.

Framing the plot of *The Man Who Shot Liberty Valance* is not one, but three frames: *memory*, *storytelling*, and *Hollywood*. First, the listeners—that is, the editor of *The Shinbone Star* and we, the watching audience—have our history corrected by the individual memory of an eyewitness. *Remembering* is central. Second, this individual memory is a story, which does not (yet) exist as a document or a monument. To borrow Ricoeur's terminology, it does not yet belong to "an archive." It needs telling in order to be recorded, to be fixed as a trace of history and become part of society's collective memory. This is what I mean by *storytelling*. Third, this recording, or fixation, of memory takes place via Hollywood. Fixation does not take place *in* the fiction; if Ransom remembers, the editor tears up his notes. Instead, director John Ford takes care of the storytelling, and Hollywood provides access to this recorded memory. We access history through the institution "Hollywood." In this widened sense—moving from the historical pieces of Jefferson, Washington, and Lincoln to the entire film—*The Man Who Shot Liberty Valance* has now become a "trace" of history, connecting past and present in a meaningful way. Indeed, the audience is wiser than the train conductor serving Ransom on the way back to Washington with the words: "Nothing is too good for the man who shot Liberty Valance."

The War Film

Recently, film theory has taken a cognitive approach to genre, where genre is considered to "mirror" and "match" our basic emotions rather than be social narratives with semiotic, semantic, and mythic qualities.[2] In the cognitive approach, an audience [thus] chooses genre films according to desired emotions and sensations: we see horror movies in order to be scared, action movies to feel excitement and "train" basic masculine qualities, etc. I disagree with this view of genre as simply an emotional cuing of our senses and want to return to mythic and semiotic genre theory, which entrusts genre with a function parallel to myth in primitive societies.[3] In this tradition, *texts* become recognizable *genres* when they tell stories that the members of society consider worth repeating again and again. The repeated viewing of genre films is a modern ritual where films function as myths anchoring the individuals of a society to its collective culture.

Some genres are well established and have been extensively analyzed. This is not the case with the war film. Academic studies use pragmatic definitions, as does Lawrence H. Suid in *Guts and Glory: The Making of the American Military Image in Film* (2002): "I am defining a war movie as one in which men appear in battle or in situations in which actual combat influences their actions" (Suid 2002, xii). Another example is Kathryn Kane writing about World War II films: "What is generally meant by that term, and what will be referred to here as the combat film, is those films that depict the activities of uniformed American military forces in combat with uniformed enemy forces during World War II" (Kane 1988, 86). Kane further adds two dichotomies to her description of the genre: the first is *victory* versus *defeat* (peace versus war, democracy versus tyranny, and so forth); the second is *individual* versus *group*: "the pulling together of the characters into a strongly united group" versus "the disintegration of the group through death in combat" (93). The first dichotomy is national, the second individual. Together the two themes are central to the war film.

To sum up: the war film (a) depicts uniformed men in battle with a uniformed enemy and (b) contains the two dichotomies of *victory* versus *defeat* and *individual* versus *group*. To these criteria I want to add two more: (c) the war film is about *actual* wars (thus ruling out science-fiction films like *Star Wars*), and (d) it is concerned with *contemporary* society (ruling out historical dramas like *The Last Samurai*). The fourth criterion is not about iconography (horses versus modern technology) but about different *uses of history*: where the historical drama sentimentally looks back to a national past for utopian solutions (such as Tom Cruise returning happily to live with the Japanese woman whose husband his character kills in *The Last Samurai* or Russell Crowe's character dying to defend the spirit of Rome in *Gladiator*), the war movie raises the question of the relationship between nation and history as *a contemporary debate of "us" versus "them."*[4] Every aspect of the war film revolves around this theme of nation and history—from ideological discussions of why the men fight to moral controversies over how the officers lead the men; from the director's aesthetic choices (such as having a 60 percent color saturation in most of *Saving Private Ryan*) to narrative choices (such as the unusual cutting from a wedding to combat in *Deer Hunter*). A film's use of historical pieces— extra-diegetic historical material in a fictional film—is just one expression of this relation between nation and history, and one aesthetic choice among many.

We now come to the historical piece that is used in war films in at least five different ways. First, if it can go unnoticed, it functions as *"just a scene."* An example is the archive footage in *Sands of Iwo Jima* (1949), where scenes with the actors climbing a mountain are mixed with archival footage of real airplanes dropping real bombs and real soldiers climbing real mountains. The intention is not to draw our attention to the archival footage as different from the fiction, but to create filmic realism. That is, the historical pieces are inserted to make the war scenes look *realistic* and not real. Second, another use is as *confirmation*; here the historical piece establishes an explicit link between the "real" history and the fiction. An example is *Courage Under Fire* (1996) which opens with a two-minute montage of news footage from the Gulf War in 1991. Third, we find *documentation*, which is stronger than confirmation. In *Black Hawk Down* (2001), texts with information about a failed American mission in Mogadishu, Somalia, in 1993, document that the plot is not just based on facts, but the story also *took place as narrated by the fiction*. The historical pieces demand status as documentation. The fourth use is *repair*. An example is *Tears of the Sun* (2003), which opens with journalistic coverage of civil war in an unnamed African country.[5] This opening begs for somebody to *do* something, to *intervene*, to *repair* what is broken. This use of historical pieces is often followed by a character who doesn't belong in the war movie—the hero—and points to a utopian solution. (In *Tears of the Sun* Special Forces Lieutenant Waters, played by Bruce Willis, saves the day.) *Repair* is often used by the *critical war film*, which is situated between the (pro-) war film and the anti-war film. If the first sees war as a valid response to a problem, the second sees war as an invalid response, and the critical war film is conflicted in its attitude to war; a problematic situation is bad, war is worse, and to choose between the two is a moral dilemma.[6]

The fifth and final use of the historical piece is *recollection* or *memory*. In this use, the historical piece points back to the past and inserts a memory of past events into the present fiction, often with the use of eyewitnesses. It is with this type of historical piece that we shall be concerned in the remainder of this essay.

Spielberg and the Memory of War

Memory is linked to notions of *truth* and *justice*. This is why eyewitnesses play a central part in our judicial system. To have been an eyewitness to an incident means you become a link to the truth about this incident. How did it happen? When? Who did what? Thus, genres like crime fiction, psychological thrillers, and courtroom dramas are obsessed with eyewitnesses; these persons are individuals who can testify to what happened in the past and who can give a crime a culprit. Through its link to the past, memory is related to *truth* and *justice*. To put a memory to proper use is to do justice, to make it serve a mission of truth.

Now, three things will concern us: the overlapping of the past with the present; the overlapping of individual memory with collective memory (that is, history); and the overlapping of narrative with memory and truth. In *Memory, History, Forgetting* (2004), Ricoeur writes of the central position of memory in regard to history; memory requires narration to become part of our history:

> ...it is through the narrative function that memory is incorporated into the formation of identity.... The circumscription of the narrative is thus placed in the service of the circumscription of the identity defining the community. A history taught, a history learned, but also a history celebrated. To this forced memorization are added the customary commemorations. A formidable pact is concluded in this way between remembrance, memorization and commemoration. (Ricoeur 2004, 84, 85)

Through memory, the past is linked to the present. The eyewitness is a bridge between then and now, enabling us to move in time. In an earlier work, *Time and Narrative* (1990), Ricoeur writes that "the frontier that separates the historical past from individual memory is porous, as can be seen in the history of the recent past...which blends together the testimony of surviving witnesses and documentary traces detached from their authors." He continues: "[A] bridge is constructed between the historical past and memory by the ancestral narrative that serves as a relay station for memory directed to the historical past" (Ricoeur 1990, 114).

In *Time and Narrative*, Ricoeur distinguishes among three categories of time. There is *lived time* or *psychic time*, which is our private experience of living, growing older, acquiring our own history—the "time of the soul." Then there is *universal time* or *cosmic time*, which is "the time of the world." Between these two is placed *historical time* or *chronicle time*, which is "ordinary time." This is the time of calendars and of history, an accountable time, where events and things are narrated—or, rather, remembered and narrated—and turned into what Ricoeur calls "documents" and "monuments," which are recorded in "archives" of knowledge. Events, texts, memories, and objects are "traces" of the past, which we use to locate ourselves in time and history (for instance, before and after Christ). Our notion of history is constructed through the concepts of the calendar, the idea of the succession of generations, "and above all, in its recourse to archives, documents, and traces. These reflective instruments are noteworthy in that they play the role of connectors between lived time and universal time" (Ricoeur 1990, 104). We will keep in mind that memories as well as entire texts—such as films—are "traces" of history. Such traces can function as "connectors" between different categories of time, passing knowledge from one to the other.

If "historical pieces" are not a new phenomenon in the war movie, they acquire their present central status with the films of Steven Spielberg. Starting with *Schindler's List* (1993), a war drama about the real Oskar Schindler who, during World War II, saved the Jews working in his factory, Spielberg went on to direct *Saving Private Ryan* (1998), about the American invasion on D-Day. According to Spielberg, this was the most accurate war film ever made, and accusations of historical inaccuracy prompted Spielberg and actor Tom Hanks to produce the ten-part television series *Band of Brothers* (2001), at the time the most expensive television series ever made.

Memory

Of the three texts—*Schindler's List*, *Saving Private Ryan*, and *Band of Brothers*—I shall focus on *Band of Brothers*. However, all three are narrated with a memory of the past as the structuring principle.

We see this in the very first scene of *Schindler's List*, where a candle is lit in a present-day kitchen. The scene is in color, and the camera zooms in on the candle. As it burns out, the image changes to black and white, then fades to Poland and to the registration of Jews in 1939. Registration. Documentation. The link among memory, history, registration, and documentation starts here, a link that will continue through *Saving Private Ryan* and *Band of Brothers*. The film ends with Schindler's Jews walking down a hill hand in hand, the music rich, full, melancholic as the image morphs from the actors to the real Schindler Jews today, from black and white, in which the story is narrated, back to full color. What we see are the real survivors, the eyewitnesses, as well as their descendants, children, and grandchildren. (During the filming Spielberg conceived the idea of a media archive of visual testimonies, realized a year later with the establishment of the Shoah Foundation and containing 52,000 visual testimonies of survivors of the Holocaust.)[7]

The narrative strategy is repeated in *Saving Private Ryan* (1998), which opens with the American cemetery in Normandy, where an old man is visiting a grave accompanied by his wife, his son, daughter-in-law, and four grandchildren behind him. He falls to his knees, and the camera zooms in on his crying blue eyes, then cuts to the invasion of Normandy and the text: "June 6, 1944." We now get the story of Captain Miller (Tom Hanks), who leads a rescue team with the mission of finding one soldier, Private Ryan, who is somewhere behind enemy lines. After Ryan (Matt Damon) is found and saved, the camera zooms in on Miller (Tom Hanks), who is dying from his wounds. On the soundtrack General George C. Marshall reads a letter of condolence to Ryan's mother (whose three other sons have fallen in combat in the war). Marshall quotes a letter written by Abraham Lincoln to yet another mother of a fallen soldier, this during the American Civil War: "And I quote: 'I pray that our heavenly father may assuage the anguish of your bereavement and leave you only the cherished memory of the loved and lost and the solemn pride that must be yours to have laid so costly a sacrifice upon the altar of freedom.'" This is a link from the memory of the survivors of World War II to another war with other "loved and lost" soldiers, a link from within the fiction from the present (Marshall) to the past (Lincoln). Then the image of the young Ryan watching the dead Miller morphs into that of the old man visiting Miller's grave in the cemetery—a link from World War II to today's peacetime.

The technique of structuring the narrative around memory is repeated a third time in *Band of Brothers* (2001), this time with real war veterans whose names we get at the end of the tenth and final episode. Episode one opens with two minutes of interviews with war veterans narrating:

WAR VETERAN: We were in a store and a guy in that store told us to put our uniforms on. "What the hell are you talking about?" He says: "The USA is in a war with Japan." We couldn't believe that.

SECOND WAR VETERAN: Our country was attacked. It's a different.... It wasn't like Korea or Vietnam. We was attacked. And, you know, it was a feeling of.... Maybe we're just dumb country people where I come from, but, a lot of us volunteered.

THIRD WAR VETERAN: I did things, I didn't do them for medals and I didn't do them for accolades, I did them because...it's just what had to be done.

Even if the audience has not been informed about the status of these voices from the past (actors or real people?) we immediately recognize them as eyewitnesses to what we are about to see, the story of Easy Company during World War II from their initial training in 1942 to the invasion of Normandy on 6 June 1944, and until the war ended in August 1945. The voices of the men link the past to the present; they have privileged access to history. They represent, or rather, they *are* individual memories, traces of the past about to become our collective memory. They are "the point where the living memory of survivors confronts the distantiated, critical gaze of the historian," Ricoeur writes in *Memory, History, Forgetting* (2004, 87).

Of what use is someone's individual memory to us? What is the duty of memory? "[I]t is justice that turns memory into a project; and it is this same project of justice that gives the form of the future and of the imperative to the duty of memory.... The duty of memory is the duty to do justice, through memories, to an other than the self." Memories urge us to remember, to put the past to use in the present and to put memory into the service of justice. The authentic memories of the war veterans are executive producer Spielberg and screenwriter Tom Hanks's way of responding to the critique raised against *Saving Private Ryan* for being historically incorrect and thus not "true."[8] *Saving Private Ryan* was loosely based on the real soldier Sergeant Frederick Niland, one of four brothers who served during World War II. Of the four two died, one was captured and later returned, and Frederick made it back himself after being dropped too far inland. *Band of Brothers* responds to the critique by employing the most trustworthy of all proofs: the living eyewitness. The series is based on historian Stephen E. Ambrose's *Band of Brothers: E-Company, 506th Regiment, 101st Airborne from Normandy to Hitler's Eagle's Nest* (2001, first published in 1992), an account of Easy Company during World War II based on interviews with the war veterans from Easy Company.

Life-story

In the war movie the survivor, the victim, and the eyewitness are one and the same character—namely the soldier—who is almost always a private. This foot soldier, whose view of things is restricted by his lack of information, is our access point to the combat zone, which is the field of action and narration.

In *Band of Brothers*, Lieutenant Winters (Damian Lewis) is the primary witness, and it is his voice-over we hear during the unfolding of the story over the ten episodes. Episode two is "Day of Days," the day of the invasion where soldiers parachute over Normandy, France. When he lands, Winters meets the soldier Hall (Andrew Scott) from Able Company. "Coach? Sir, it's Hall, Sir. I was on the basketball team." Hall is "lost," as he puts it, but Winters reassures him: "We're not lost, Private. We're in Normandy." (As if Normandy was a familiar place near home and not an enemy war zone.) As Winters and Hall move toward the meeting point through enemy country, they team up with soldiers from Easy Company. Initially the soldiers won't accept Hall into their group and derogatively call him "cowboy." This causes confusion as to where he is from. "And this is Hall, Able Company." "Known as Cowboy." "You from Texas?" "Manhattan." Hall fights to be accepted by the group, and he volunteers to join a mission to eliminate a four-gun German battery at Brécourt Manor firing on Utah Beach. During the mission Hall is finally accepted by Guarnere (Frank John Hughes), the soldier who coined his nickname. "Hiya, Cowboy," Guarnere yells during heavy gunfire. "Shut your fucking guinea trap, Gonorrhea," Hall yells back. "He's all right that kid," Guarnere laughs. In the next scene Hall is shot in the German trenches. The camera, having jumped up and down to illustrate the hectic chaos of the assault, rests for the first time. It rests on Hall's face, which has a bloody gun wound at the temple. Winters stops and looks at him, kneels at his side, shocked and sad. In the trenches Winters finds some papers, which turn out to be maps.

On the night of the "Day of Days," the soldiers are back at the meeting point after a successful mission, the destruction of the German battery firing on the American invasion forces. Winters wanders alone in the streets as his friend Nixon catches up with him.

NIXON: Hey, you know that map you found? It had every Kraut gun in Normandy.

WINTERS: I lost a man today.

NIXON: Oh.

WINTERS: Hall. A John Hall. New Yorker. Got killed today at Brécourt.

NIXON: I never knew him.

WINTERS: Yeah, you did. Radio op. 506th basketball team, Able Company. He was a good man. Man. Not even old enough to buy a beer.

NIXON: Hey, Dick. I sent that map up to Division. I think it's gonna do some good.

The successful mission is mirrored through the loss of Hall, who is not a soldier, but a person, Hall. Nixon doesn't remember him, but Winters does. He was on the basketball team, and he recognized Winters as his coach, not as an officer. Soldiers are individuals, not numbers, and the loss of one life is the price for saving many.

Hall, however, is not an entirely honest historical piece. The soldiers from Easy Company are recognized in the closing text: "For destroying the German guns at Brécourt Manor the following medals were awarded." Then follows a list of names awarded Bronze Stars, Silver Stars and one name—Lieutenant Richard Winters—awarded The Distinguished Service Cross. While Guarnere, Malarkey, Lipton, and more of the soldiers in the television series are on the list, Hall isn't. Is he fictitious? No, there is indeed a Private Hall, who barely receives two lines in Stephen E. Ambrose's book *Band of Brothers*: "Pvt. John D. Hall of A Company joined the group. Winters ordered a charge on the third gun. Hall led the way, and got killed, but the gun was taken" (Ambrose 2001, 82). Nothing further is said about Hall. He might as well have been fictitious, since the story given him in episode two is invented by the script-writers. Hall is intended (and invented) to serve as a human "sacrifice." He is the individual through whom the larger and more abstract notion of "sacrifice" and "victory" is illustrated. The meaning of his death is rendered through the eyewitness Winters, who "sees" him as an individual, acknowledges his bravery (Hall volunteered for the mission to destroy the battery), and connects his death to his individual act of bravery. Nixon, on the other hand, merely sees Hall as a loss. But then, Nixon wasn't in the assault. Later, Nixon will also "see" soldiers as individuals.

Meaning

"Day of Days" ends with yet another historical piece, this text: "Easy Company's capture of the German Battery became a textbook case of an assault on a fixed position, and is still demonstrated at the United States Military Academy at West Point, today."

The loss of Hall is weighed against the lesson learned from the elimination of the German battery. The television series links the two incidents: on one side, the loss of one individual, a soldier; on the other side, an important military victory. According to the German philosopher Wilhelm Dilthey, we create meaning in our lives by creating a thread we weave through things, a life-story, which is not based on "the mere relation between causes and effects" but is founded in "values, purposes, meaning, significance" (Dilthey 2002, 89). Meaning is created by memory; it arises when we who are situated in the present look back into the past and arrange the valorized events, incidents, and moments of the past in a "category-of-meaning." Our "life-story" arises from such reconfiguration of the past. To make our life meaningful, we create meaning by accentuating some of our memories—those we deem important to us—and erasing others. "Every life has its own significance. This is found in the construction of meaning; any moment which can be remembered is valuable in itself, but it is at the same time in the entirety of recollection that it becomes meaningful" (90). Recollection is not any memory. It is *those memories* that fit our values, our purpose, the significance we give our life, the meaning we invest it with. Value is not *in* a life. It is *given to* a life, like a melody is born from a pattern of tones. Life can be compared to "the chaos of harmonies and disharmonies. Each of these is a tone-image in the present; however, they have no musical relation to each other" (92). Only a "category-of-meaning" over-comes the random "next-to-each-other-ness," which otherwise is the condition of life.

In other words, to make life meaningful we find a meaning and invest life with it. We do this as individuals, and we do this collectively when we narrate our historical time, our chronicle time. This is what *Band of Brothers* does by linking Hall's death to the successful destruction of the German battery firing at American soldiers on Utah Beach. One death against many losses. It is interesting that Spielberg three years earlier in *Saving Private Ryan* had brought the American losses on Omaha beach back to life, followed by Miller's mission to save Private Ryan. Here, there were two sets of losses being weighed against each other: the American losses in the invasion vs. the loss of the war, and the mission with eight men vs. the loss of one man's life. The result was a public philosophical debate at the time of the premiere in Denmark as to whether it is morally possible to weigh one number of lives against a larger number of lives. Is this valid reasoning? How big a sacrifice is democracy worth? Can we "count" lives, and does it make a difference what race or nationality or religion the life has—American, German, Russian, Jew? (Significantly, we often hear the number of losses during World War II given as six million Jews killed, and more rarely as the approximately six million dead Germans or almost twenty-nine million Russians, of which twenty million were civilians).[9]

Such a difficult and complex question is made simple in episode two of *Band of Brothers*: Losses are metaphorized and condensed into one life—Hall's:

one American life to prevent the loss of many American lives. (The maps Winters found guarantee that fewer American soldiers will be killed in the battle with the Germans.)

Debt

When the Vietnam War ended in 1974, Hollywood developed a critical attitude toward wars outside the United States. Michael Cimino's *Deer Hunter* (1978), Francis Ford Coppola's *Apocalypse Now* (1979), Stanley Kubrick's *Full Metal Jacket* (1987), and Oliver Stone's *Platoon* (1986) all portrayed the Vietnam War as futile or, at best, meaningless. John Wayne's *The Green Berets* (1968) attempted to transfer the simple heroism of "good" versus "evil," which could be employed when dealing with World War II, to the war in Vietnam. But after 1968 such a simple dichotomy was contested with skeptical and critical narratives.

I think it is highly significant that almost *none* of the spectacular, high-profile, ambitious, and often expensive war films produced about the Vietnam War employ historical pieces—not even simple text pieces such as, for instance, the inserted factual texts in *Black Hawk Down*. These films, produced in a culture influenced by postmodernism and the "fall" of great narratives, are themselves great narratives and very un-postmodern. They are traumatized by the fall of an American idea of innocence. In fact they are haunted by a sense of "loss" of innocence, "loss" of purpose, of meaning, of value. America is not portrayed as a shining example of Civilization and Democracy (the founding values in *The Man Who Shot Liberty Valance*). Perhaps because they have lost the sense of purpose, they do not refer directly to a historical past but to a traumatic *memory* of the past. (Oliver Stone's *Platoon* was fiction inspired by his own experience as a soldier in Vietnam, thus drawing on an individual's memory of the past, but not qualifying this memory as historical.)

After Vietnam the war film is haunted by the past and loses Dilthey's "category-of-meaning." The genre wants to heal the trauma but must first find, re-open, and cleanse the infected wound. It wants to find a cure but must first name the disease. Between 1968 and 1992, the trauma swells within the American war movie. The only attempts at repair are the utopian war films of Sylvester Stallone and Chuck Norris, action stars who turn the war film into action films with war settings and a hero providing a utopian solution. *Rambo: First Blood Part II* (1985) and *Rambo III* (1988), as well as *Missing in Action* (1984) and *Missing in Action 2: The Beginning* (1985), should be read as mythic replies to a wounded historical memory.[10]

Things change with the postmodern war movie. Here, the historical pieces are used to differentiate between "meaningful" and "meaningless" wars (thus World War II in *Saving Private Ryan* is "meaningful," while the civil wars in *Black Hawk Down, Tears of the Sun* [2003], and *Savior* [1998] are "meaningless"), between "good" and "bad" actions, between significance and lack of significance. Comparing national memory to individual memory, Ricoeur speaks about the traumatized memory haunted by incidents in the past. Taking inspiration from Freud's notion of compulsive repetition, mourning, and melancholia in the essays "Remembering, Repeating, and Working-Through" (1914) and "Mourning and Melancholia" (1917), Ricoeur discusses strategies for resolving such trauma. One strategy is recollection and mourning. "Memory does not only bear on time: it also requires time—a time of mourning" (Ricoeur 2004, 74).

Memory must pay its debt to the victims. Here, a separation from the *active* memory of mourning to the *passive* memory of melancholia is important. Melancholia cannot forgive. Mourning forgives and, ultimately, forgets, so that the individual can move on into his or her future. This is how I read the end of *Schindler's List*, where each Jew places a stone on Schindler's grave, while their names appear at the bottom of the image. First are the children Janek and Danka, whom Schindler personally snatches from the hands of the German soldiers in a concentration camp. They are—like Ryan in *Saving Private Ryan*—now old and accompanied by grandchildren. Then comes the housemaid Helen Hirsch, aged and in a wheelchair, but half a century ago so beautiful that Amon Göeth had to beat her every night to keep temptation away. Schindler won her from Göeth in a poker game. And so forth. The characters from the fiction appear in the flesh. A historical piece informs the audience: "There are fewer than 4,000 Jews left alive in Poland today. There are more than 6,000 descendants of the Schindler Jews." The last historical piece is the text: "In memory of the more than six million Jews murdered."

"In memory of": Such a formulation insists that we must not forget the past but must remember and "extract from traumatic memories the exemplary value that can become pertinent only when memory has been turned into a project. If the trauma refers to the past, the exemplary value is directed towards the future" (Ricoeur 2004, 86). In this light we must understand Captain Miller's last words whispered into Ryan's ears in *Saving Private Ryan*: "James. *Earn this. Earn it.*" The then-young Ryan morphs into the old Ryan in the cemetery and turns to his wife: "Tell me I led a good life? Tell me I am a good man?" Has he paid his debt to Captain Miller and the soldiers who sacrificed their lives "at the altar of freedom"? Were the losses—their lives—worth it?

Storytelling

To tell a story we need what Dilthey calls a "category of meaning." Without a thread guiding us through the chaotic "next-to-each-other-ness" of the events in the past, no meaning will arise. This is because meaning, significance, and sense are not *in* the events themselves. These things are, as previously noted, *given to* events by us, the storytellers. To make sense of the past we need a "category-of-meaning"—a storyline guiding us through the labyrinth of time, such as the life-story of Hall explaining to us the meaning of war as it's reflected in one soldier's death.

At the end of the tenth and final episode of *Band of Brothers*, "Points," the audience finally gets names to match the faces of the war veterans. In the last scene, Winters—now no longer a lieutenant but a major—tells the soldiers of Easy Company that the war is over. They will finally be sent home. While the men play baseball on a sunny green field, Winters narrates in voice-over what later happened to the men—the real soldiers—in their lives. From Dick Winters, played by actor Damian Lewis, saying, "there is not a day that goes by when I do not think of the men that I served with who never got to enjoy the world without war," the picture fades to black, then cuts to the war veteran Dick Winters and six other men from Easy Company:

> DICK WINTERS: It's a very unusual feeling. It's a very unusual happening and a very unusual bonding.

> CARWOOD LIPTON: We knew that we could depend on each other. And so we were a close-knit group.

> DONALD MALARKEY: Just brave, so brave it's unbelievable. I don't know anybody that I admire more than Bill Guarnere and Joe Toye. And they were very special.

> BILL GUARNERE: I'm just one part of the big war. That's all. One little part. And I'm proud to be a part of it. Sometimes it makes me cry.

Of special interest are the last two interviews of *Band of Brothers*, with Lipton and Winters, closing the television series:

> CARWOOD LIPTON: Henry V was talking to his men. He said, "From this day to the ending of the world, we in it shall be remembered. We lucky few, we band of brothers. For he who today sheds his blood with me shall be my brother."

> DICK WINTERS: Do you remember the letter that Mike Ranney wrote me? You do? Do you remember how he ended it? [Winters quotes:] "I cherish the memories of a question my grandson asked me the other day, when he said, 'Grandpa, were you a hero in the war?' Grandpa said, 'No. But I served in a company of heroes.'"

The veterans weave the thread of their life-stories back and forth through history: Carwood Lipton quotes an English king, Henry V. In fact, he doesn't quote the king, but Shakespeare's play, *Henry V*. Dick Winters quotes a letter from another soldier from Easy Company, Mike Ranney. The ending thus links the personal histories of the eyewitnesses to two different relay stations of knowledge: that of culture and history through the Shakespeare quote, and that of the passing of generations through the Ranney quote. The first is our collective memory, a product of the past that lives as traces in the present through documents. The second is our biological and individual memory, passed on from generation to generation. Here we find the overlapping of an older generation (the veterans) and a younger generation (the television audience), of story and history, memory and fiction.

Band of Brothers is collective storytelling to a nation. It is a wound being healed—the wound of Vietnam. And it is a debt being paid—not to the veterans from World War II who were honored, but to the veterans of the Vietnam War who became engulfed in the disillusion of a lost war, wounded national pride, and traumatized historical memory.

History: Memory, Story, Fiction

In today's stream of docudramas and reality shows, media researchers see "a return to the real," which, as far as I have understood, is a longing for the personal and the individual, for authentic and "real" sensations, for stepping into reality.[11] Similarly, I think in the postmodern war movie's use of historical pieces we find a *return to history*, which I understand as a longing for a *meaningful* life-story, which can provide us with a *collective* history based on shared values, purposes, meanings, and significances. "Collective memory," says Ricoeur, "constitutes the soil in which historiography is rooted" (2004, 69).

My historical pieces are but small parts of a larger project, namely the *re-writing of history*. During the Gulf War in 1991, Jean Baudrillard wrote three articles, the last (written after the war had ended) entitled "The Gulf War Did Not Take Place." This should not be seen as a sign of humor or of denial, but as a sign of postmodern disillusion. His point was that this was not a war, but an act of terrorism. And the non-war was not a historical event, but a sign of the collapse of history:

> ...in the case of the Gulf War as in the case of the events in Eastern Europe, we are no longer dealing with "historical events" but with places of collapse. Eastern Europe saw the collapse of communism, the construction of which had indeed been an historic

event, borne by a vision of the world and a utopia. By contrast, its collapse is borne by
nothing and bears nothing, but only opens onto a confused desert left vacant by the
retreat of history and immediately invaded by its refuse. (Baudrillard 1995, 70)

Baudrillard's "collapse" is similar to the American disillusion after Vietnam. How to explain events that disturb the pattern made by the thread with
which we weave history together? The only response is to change the pattern.
Or, better yet, to rewrite history. To find a new thread, to invent historiography anew. This is what Spielberg aims at in the interweaving of fact and
fiction, memory and history. This is what the postmodern American war film
does when it incorporates historical pieces into fiction. Where the war movie
in the 1980s responded naively and mythically to a sense of crisis, lamenting
the status quo and a lost innocence or lost national honor, the 1990s saw the
development of a self-conscious war film working at documentation, recollection, and reparation. It is still too early to say, but it looks like a movement
that can be compared with Ricoeur's evolution from cultural melancholia into
cultural mourning.

The collapse of history is answered by a return to the eyewitness, to historical facts, "traces" of the past as well as "traces" of the real. The response to
a "lack" or "collapse" of history is answered by the full presence of "history."
Meaningless events—wars—are made meaningful. This must not, however, be
interpreted as a move from myth to fact, from lies to truth. We remain in
Hollywood. The only difference is that this territory has engulfed areas until
now regarded as protected. Recently I was asked about the relation between
fact and fiction, and between history and story in the context of American
film and European culture. First I was asked by colleagues in the humanities at
a public seminar, and afterwards on the national Danish television news. Is it
not a problem, the first group felt, if American films are "untrue" when
narrating historical events? Are historical films not *especially* indebted to
historical "truth" and ethically obliged to serve "justice"? Is, asked the news
journalist, our understanding of the "real" not disturbed when borders
separating fact and fiction are blurred?

In a time of globalization and modern visual media technology, news trav-
els fast. Good stories travel faster. Reality, however, *does not travel at all*. It is
only the stories told about it that travel. Here I join the skepticism of Baudrillard, who insists that "the image and information are subject to no principle
of truth or reality" (Baudrillard 1995, 12).[12] To link *any* image or information
to truth or reality would be naive, whether we're talking about news or fiction.
Even if the postmodern war film invokes history, reality, and memory, it
would be just as naive for us to relate the historical pieces to "truth" or
"reality" as to believe that Senator Ransom Stoddard told us, the audience, a

"true" story. John Ford knew this in 1962. Whether Spielberg and the directors of postmodern war movies know this is less obvious. Judging by the memorialization taking place outside the fictional world (in the form of foundations, museums, or historical bonus-material on the DVDs), the intention is indeed to cross from (past) history to (present) fiction and move into a new history (the future).

History does not stand in the same relation to fiction as truth does to lie or black to white. History is, like fiction, a story told from a selection of traces, documents, and monuments. Thus, two quotes open Stephen Ambrose's historical book *Band of Brothers* from 1992: Lipton quoting *Henry V* and Winters quoting a letter from a fellow soldier. Did Spielberg ask the veterans to repeat the lines from Ambrose's book when he conducted the interviews in 2000? Is this reality or a reconstruction of reality? In the American cemetery in Normandy where *Saving Private Ryan* opens and closes, the white crosses of stone rise proudly above the ground. If you drive a few miles farther you come to the German cemetery for the German soldiers who died in Normandy. Here, the stones are black and square, placed flat on the ground. One monument to be noticed, another to be overlooked.

To construct historical time is to select among the traces of the time of the soul (personal memory) and cosmic time (events in time). To construct fiction is to select the elements that will tell our collective life-story. Neither should be thought of as "true." When it comes to historiography, the writing of history can be false. Fiction, however, is neither true nor false. The historical pieces invite, or rather *implore*, us to link the fiction to history, memory, and truth. We must acknowledge this return to history as a significant historical development today. However, we—the audience—must resist the temptation to mistake fiction for truth. A new history is being written for a new world order and for future generations. The postmodern war film is part of this process.

Filmography

Sands of Iwo Jima	1949	Allan Dwan
Man Who Shot Liberty Valance, The	1962	John Ford
Deer Hunter, The	1978	Michael Cimino
Apocalypse Now	1979	Francis Ford Coppola
Missing in Action	1984	Joseph Zito
Missing in Action 2: The Beginning	1985	Lance Hool
Platoon	1986	Oliver Stone
Full Metal Jacket	1987	Stanley Kubrick
Schindler's List	1993	Steven Spielberg
Courage Under Fire	1996	Edward Zwick
Saving Private Ryan	1998	Steven Spielberg
Savior	1998	Predrag Antonijevic
Gladiator	2000	Ridley Scott
Band of Brothers	2001	television series
Black Hawk Down	2001	Ridley Scott
We Were Soldiers	2002	Randall Wallace
Hart's War	2003	Gregory Hoblit
Last Samurai, The	2003	Edward Zwick
Tears of the Sun	2003	Antoine Fuqua

Notes

[1] Historical pieces are often used in relation to war, for instance in *The Siege* (1998, Edward Zwick), *Courage Under Fire* (1996, Edward Zwick), *The Substitute 3: Winner Takes All* (1999, Robert Radler), and *Tears of the Sun* (2003, Antoine Fuqua).

[2] For examples of cognitive film genre theory see Murray Smith, *Engaging Characters: Fiction, Emotion, and the Cinema* (Oxford: Clarendon Press, 1995) and Torben Grodal, *Moving Pictures: A New Theory of Film, Genres, Feelings, and Cognition* (Oxford: Oxford University Press, 1997).

[3] I discuss genre, film, and myth in my Ph.D. dissertation published as *Med vold og magt: Actionfilm fra Dirty Harry til The Matrix* (*Mission Complete: The Action Movie from Dirty Harry to The Matrix*) (Copenhagen: Rosinante, 2002). Two central references to mythic genre criticism are Thomas Schatz, *Hollywood Genres: Formulas, Film-Making and the Studio System* (New York: McGraw Hill, 1981) and Will Wright, *Sixguns and Society: A Structural Study of the Western* (Berkeley: University of California Press, 1975). This subject ought to receive further attention.

[4] The themes of *nation* and *history* are central to many genres, and it would take a separate essay to discuss the use of nation and history in different genres. In the western it seems to me that the two themes are played out as the *establishment* of American values through the confrontation of the wilderness and the defense of civilization, and in the war film the themes are played out in a debate over how such values are *employed* in the contemporary international political arena (with America as "civilization" and Vietnam, or any other enemy country, as "wilderness").

[5] The historical piece in the opening of *Tears of the Sun* (2003) is television news coverage of a military coup in Nigeria with journalistic speak. The scenes appear to be real news coverage. There is, however, no "president Samuel Azuka," and research reveals that the speak is fiction. Whether the images are fictitious too is unclear (they appear real). This use of historical pieces is interesting, as it not only mixes fact and fiction, but also manipulates fiction to appear to be fact inserted into fiction.

[6] With a hero in a war film the focus shifts from the theme of integration versus disintegration of a group of soldiers to the theme of victory versus defeat—examples of the heroic war film are *Missing in Action* (1984, Joseph Zito), *Missing in Action 2: The Beginning* (1985, Lance Hool), *Rambo: First Blood Part II* (George P. Cosmatos, 1985), *Rambo III* (Peter MacDonald, 1988), and *Tears of the Sun* (Antoine Fuqua, 2003). In terms of genre these films place themselves between the war film and the action film.

[7] The Shoah Foundation's website is http://www.vhf.org/.

[8] The critique against Spielberg is discussed in Suid, *Guts & Glory*, 634–636.

[9] For an estimate of casualties during World War II by nationality, see, for instance, Wikipedia, http://en.wikipedia.org/wiki/World_War_II_casualties#Casualties_by_country.   Most sources estimate Russian casualties at between twenty-six and twenty-nine million.

[10] *Missing in Action 2: The Beginning* (1985) has a historical piece at the start of the film: Ronald Reagan visits Arlington Cemetery and promises that "we write no last chapters. We close no books, we put away no final memories. An end to America's involvement in Vietnam cannot come before we have achieved the fullest possible accounting of those missing in

action." After this, Colonel Braddock (Chuck Norris) escapes with his men from a prison camp in Vietnam. This use of the historical piece is an example of *repair*, with the historical piece documenting the need for action and the hero responding to this need.

[11] See Hal Foster, *The Return of the Real: Art and Theory at the End of the Century* (Cambridge: MIT Press, 1996) and Anne Jerslev, ed., *Realism and "Reality" in Film and Media*, Northern Lights. Film and Media Studies Yearbook 2002 (Copenhagen: Museum Tusculanum, 2002).

[12] Quoted from Paul Patton's "Introduction" to *The Gulf War*. The quote is from another text of Jean Baudrillard, "Les charniers de Timisoara," in *L'Illusion de la fin ou la grève des événements* (Paris: Editions Galilée, 1993).

References

Ambrose, Stephen E. 2001. *Band of Brothers: E-Company, 506th Regiment, 101st Airborne from Normandy to Hitler's Eagle's Nest*. Reading: Pocket Books.

Baudrillard, Jean. 1995. *The Gulf War Did Not Take Place*. Bloomington: Indiana University Press.

Dilthey, Wilhelm. 2002. "Udkast til en kritik af den historiske fornuft." In *Hermeneutik: En antologi om forståelse*, edited by Jesper Gulddal and Martin Møller, pp. 81–111. Copenhagen: Gyldendal.

Kane, Kathryn. 1988. "The World War II Combat Film." In Handbook of American Film Genres, edited by Wes D. Gehring. Westport, CT: Greenwood.

Ricoeur, Paul. 1990. *Time and Narrative*, vol. 3. Chicago: University of Chicago Press.

——. 2004. *Memory, History, Forgetting*. Chicago: University of Chicago Press.

Suid, Lawrence H. 2002. *Guts & Glory: The Making of the American Military Image in Film*. Lexington: University Press of Kentucky.

Contributors

Mark Andrejevic is Assistant Professor for the Department of Communication Studies at the University of Iowa. He is the author of *Reality TV: The Work of Being Watched* (Rowman & Littlefield, 2004). He is currently working on a book about new media and cybernetic control called *The Limits of Interactivity: Democracy, Surveillance, and the Network Society*, which is scheduled to be published in 2007.

Göran Bolin is Professor in Media & Communication Studies at Södertörn University College. He is also Research Director at the Centre for Baltic and East European Studies. Bolin has worked in or headed research projects on violence in the media, youth and cultural production, entertainment television and the relation between production practices and textual expressions, media consumption and the production of value in cultural industries, media structure and use in the Baltic Sea region, mobile phone use, etc. Among his international publications he has written for *Young Nordic Journal of Youth Research*; *Nordicom Review*; *Screen*; *AV/Montage*; *Media, Culture & Society*; *Javnost/The Public*; *Social Semiotics*; *MedieKultur*; *International Journal of Cultural Studies*. He has edited eight books, most recently the volume *The Challenge of the Baltic Sea Region. Culture, Ecosystems, Democracy*.

Thaïs Machado-Borges is an anthropologist and research fellow at the Institute of Latin American Studies, Stockholm University, Sweden. She is the author of *Only for You! Brazilians and the Telenovela Flow* (Almqvist & Wiksell International, 2003) and is currently researching on the theme of social inequality, bodies and physical interventions among lower-income and middle-class women in Brazil.

Valentina Cardo is a PhD student in politics at the University of East Anglia. Her thesis focuses on the politics of reality TV and deals with issues of political representation, participation and community.

Sue Collins is a PhD student in the Department of Culture & Communication, New York University. Her dissertation research is on the U.S. domestic propaganda campaign of WWI and its recruitment of stardom as a source of political authority and mechanism of governance in the constitution of cultural citizenship.

John Hartley is a Federation Fellow (Australian Research Council) and Research Director of the ARC Centre of Excellence for Creative Industries and Innovation at Queensland University of Technology in Australia. He is a Distinguished Professor of QUT and Adjunct Professor of the Australian National University. He was foundation dean of the Creative Industries Faculty (QUT) and previously head of the School of Journalism, Media and Cultural Studies at Cardiff University in Wales. He is the author of 15 books, translated into a dozen languages, including *Creative Industries* (ed., Blackwell, 2005), *A Short History of Cultural Studies* (Sage, 2003), *Communication, Cultural and Media Studies: The Key Concepts* (Routledge, 2002), *The Indigenous Public Sphere* (w. A. McKee, Oxford, 2000), *Uses of Television* (Routledge, 1999) and *Popular Reality* (Arnold, 1996). He is Editor of the *International Journal of Cultural Studies* (Sage) and a Fellow of the Australian Academy of the Humanities.

Jeffrey P. Jones is Assistant Professor in the Department of Communication and Theatre Arts at Old Dominion University. He is the author of *Entertaining Politics: New Political Television and Civic Culture* and co-editor of *The Essential HBO Reader*, as well as numerous book chapters and articles on the intersection of entertainment and politics.

Rune Ottosen is Professor in Journalism at Oslo University College. He has published numerous books and articles in the field of journalism, cultural history, environmental issues and international conflict. He is co-editor with Professor Stig-Arne Nohrstedt of the volumes *Journalism and the New World Order* (Nordicom, 2001), *U.S. and the Others. Global Media Images on "The War on Terror"* (Nordicom, 2004) and *Global War - Local Views. Media Images of the Iraq War* (Nordicom, 2005) Rune Ottosen is Deputy Director of the Norwegian Association of Press and Media History.

Kristina Riegert is Associate Professor in Media and Communication at Södertörn University College and the Swedish National Defence College. She is the editor of *News of the Other* (2004) and author of *The Image War* (2003) and *'Nationalising' Foreign Conflict* (1998). Her research interests are globalization, comparative television news, war coverage and propaganda, television's role in national identity and political content in entertainment programming.

Rikke Schubart is Associate Professor at the University of Southern Denmark where she teaches film studies. She is the author of *Super Bitches and Action Babes: The Female Hero in Popular Cinema, 1970-2006* (forthcoming spring 2007, McFarland) and co-editor of *Femme Fatalities: Representations of Strong Women in the Media* with Anne Gjelsvik. She has written several books in Danish on the horror film and the action cinema and co-edited anthologies. She is chief editor of the Danish scientific media journal *MedieKultur*. She is currently working on a book on the American war movie from 1991 to the present.

John Street is Professor of Politics at the University of East Anglia. Among his publications are the books, *Mass Media, Politics and Democracy* and *Politics and Popular Culture*.

Index